A Step-by-Step Guide to REAL ESTATE PRINCIPLES in California

*Everything You Need to Know
to Pass the California
Real Estate Examination*

David E. Calhoun

California
Academy of
Real
Estate

"WE CARE"

Northridge, California

THIRD EDITION

"Listing" and "Deposit Receipt" contracts reprinted with permission of California Association of Realtors. Endorsement not implied.

SUMMARY: Covers beginning real estate principles with special emphasis on California Real Estate Law. Simple language and clear examples to assist the consumer, student and educator with their real estate ventures.

The author and publisher have researched all sources to ensure the accuracy and completeness of the information contained in this book. We assume no responsibility for errors, inaccuracies, omissions or any other inconsistency herein. Readers should consult an attorney or accountant for specific applications to their individual real estate ventures.

TABLE OF CONTENTS

Introduction

INTRODUCTION

Terminology is very important when learning any new subject. Real Estate has its own special vocabulary. The following **"OR"-"EE"** rule will assist your comprehension of the various subjects in this text.

As a general rule, words ending in **"OR"** indicate the **"GIVER"** or the owner, words ending in **"EE"** indicate the **"RECEIVER"**.

> The parties to a will are the DEVISOR and the DEVISEE.
> The parties to a deed are the GRANTOR and the GRANTEE.
> The parties to a lease are the LESSOR and the LESSEE.
> The parties to a mortgage are the MORTGAGOR and the MORTGAGEE.
> The parties to an option are the OPTIONOR and the OPTIONEE.
> The parties to an offer are the OFFEROR and the OFFEREE.
> The parties to a business opportunity are the TRANSFEROR and the TRANSFEREE.
> The parties to a trust deed are the TRUSTOR and the TRUSTEE.
> The parties to a land contract are the VENDOR and the VENDEE.
> VENDOR and VENDEE also identify the parties to a Bill of Sale.

Additional vocabulary words and their definitions are found in the GLOSSARY at the end of this textbook.

PROPERTY

All property may be classified as either personal property or real property. The difference between personal property and real property is distinguished by mobility.

A. PERSONAL PROPERTY - Personal property is any property that is movable. A chattel is another term for personal property. Personal property may be alienated, assessed, hypothecated or become real property. Personal property is usually located at the domicile of its owner and is under the regulations and jurisdiction of the law of the owner's domicile. Personal property may be transferred by a bill of sale but it is not always required. Personal property is considered transferred when the possession of the item is delivered. A title search of personal property is not very accurate as compared to a title search of real property in the public records.

B. REAL PROPERTY - Real property is any property that is immovable. Real property may be alienated, transferred by will or deed, or become personal property. Real property may be classified as land, appurtenances, buildings and fixtures.

1. LAND

a. The "legal theory" or "legal concept" of land is that land ownership is not limited by surface boundaries, but extends from the center of the earth to the heavens above.

b. The ownership of land includes the right of lateral and subjacent support by the adjoining land. This means that if an individual excavates his property and his neighbor's property caves-in or falls onto his property, he would be liable for damages to his neighbor's property.

c. Land may be divided either horizontally or vertically.

2. APPURTENANCES

a. Anything that belongs to real property is in itself real property.

b. Anything that "runs with the land".

c. Anything used with land for the benefit of the land.

d. Examples of appurtenances include: buildings, covenants which benefit the land, easements, fences, a watercourse, water rights, restrictions, and stock in a mutual water company.

3. FIXTURES

    a. Definition - Personal property that is attached to a building or to the land so that it changes its character and becomes real property.

    b. There are five tests to determine if the property is a fixture:

        1. Method of attachment (Manner of annexation) - What method was used to attach the item?

        2. Adaptability of the property - How adaptable is the item to the property (venetian blinds)?

        3. Relationship of the parties - In a sale it would be the buyer and seller. In a lease, it would be the landlord and tenant.

        4. Intention of the parties - What was the intention of the parties when attaching the item? *Intention is the most important test.*

        5. Agreement between the parties - Any item may be removed if there is an agreement between both parties written into the purchase contract or lease.

    c. Trade Fixtures - Items of personal property attached to real property, but which are necessary to the carrying-on of a business or trade. These are considered personal property and may be removed by the tenant or owner. Trade fixtures are not appurtenant to the land or building. Property is personal if it is a trade fixture.

    Prior to the expiration of a business lease the tenant may remove both fixtures used for manufacturing purposes, and items affixed for domestic use. The tenant must completely repair all damage that resulted from the removal of these items.

4. GROUND ITEMS

    a. Fructus Industriales - Certain items produced by the annual labor (industry) of man. A planted crop such as: corn, wheat, lettuce, etc.

    b. Fructus Naturales - Certain items produced by nature. Examples include: minerals in the ground, trees, shrubs, and vines which do not require cultivation.

    c. Growing crops are considered to be real property because they are attached to the land. Until a crop is harvested, sold or mortgaged it is real property.

    d. The tenant has the right to the growing crops on the land that is leased.

    e. A buyer is entitled to the growing crops when the disposition of such crops is not discussed when negotiating a real estate transaction.

    f. Undrilled crude oil is considered to be real property and the owner has the right to extract it.

C. PROPERTY REVIEW

REAL PROPERTY

All that is not personal property.

EXAMPLES:

Untapped underground mineral, oil
  & gas deposits - The right to these.
Rooted "Fructus Naturales".
An incident to the land.
Stock in a mutual water company.
Planted shrubbery & trees.
An installed water heater (Fixture).
Airspace over the property.
Easements (Appurtenant or In Gross).
Uncut timber sold with the land.
Uncultivated grove of trees.
Backyard fence.
Built-in appliances.
Realty.
Land and buildings.
Fixtures (Wall bed, venetian blinds).
Pump & Well (Considered an improvement).
The right to remove iron ore or undrilled
  crude oil from the ground.

PERSONAL PROPERTY
(Chattel)

All that is not real property.

EXAMPLES:

A load of gravel.
Minerals that have been mined.
Lumber stacked on the ground.
Shares in a real estate syndicate
  owning real property.
Stock in a real estate corporation.
Deeds, Deed of Trust, Mortgages.
A Promissory Note.
Trade Fixtures.
Growing crops sold under a contract
  but not yet severed.
Cabinets in a mobile home.
Leasehold interest in real property.
Cultivated annual crops.
Growing crops on leased land.
Appliances installed by a tenant in
  an apartment.
Extracted minerals.
Chose in action (intangible).
Chose in possession (tangible).

Notes: 1. Tenements - All rights connected with the land which pass with the transfer of the land.

2. Deciduous - Trees which shed their leaves at the end of the season.

3. Emblements - The right of a tenant farmer to harvest his crops.

4. Property is real if not personal.

5. Property is personal if other than real.

6. Airspace is not real property when related with appurtenances, realty, trees and posts.

7. Mineral, Oil & Gas rights are automatically transferred when a property is sold.

8. The most distinguishing characteristic of personal property is its mobility.

9. Mortgages and liens on real property are considered to be personal property exclusively.

10. A search of the county records is more accurate in reference to the title of real property than to the title of personal property.

11. Distinguishing characteristics of real estate include: it is very costly, it is a long term investment, and it is likely to increase in value. Immobility is not considered to be a distinguishing characteristic of real estate.

12. Property may be considered as the rights or interests a person has in a thing owned.

13. A trade fixture is not an appurtenant.

14. Vegatation is considered to be real property. Vegatation includes trees, bushes, and grass.

REVIEW QUIZ

SECTION I - Matching - Select the letter below which best describes, defines, or relates to the following numbered terms.

1. Personal property
2. Emblements
3. Liens
4. Fructus Industriales
5. Real property
6. Deciduous
7. Fructus Naturales
8. Appurtenances
9. Fixtures
10. Tenements

a. An example of personal property.
b. An example of real property.
c. All rights connected with the land which pass with the transfer of the land.
d. Certain items produced by nature.
e. The right of a tenant farmer to harvest his crops.
f. The most distinguishing characteristic is its mobility.
g. Anything that runs with the land.
h. May be classified as land, buildings, fixtures, and appurtenances.
i. Certain items produced by the annual labor of man.
j. Trees which shed their leaves at the end of the season.

SECTION II - True/False - Select either true or false in response to the following statements.

1. The "legal theory" of land is that land is not limited to surface boundaries, but extends from the center of the earth to the heavens above.
2. The ownership of land does not include the right of lateral and subjacent support by the adjoining land.
3. The cost of an item is a test to determine whether property is a fixture.
4. Growing crops are considered to be personal property because they are attached to the land.
5. Stock in a mutual water company is an example of real property.
6. The right to extract undrilled crude oil is considered to be personal property.
7. Trade fixtures are considered personal property.
8. Mineral, oil, and gas rights are automatically transferred when a property is sold.
9. The time of annexation is a test to determine whether property is a fixture.
10. Fructus industriales are items produced by nature.

SECTION III - Multiple Choice - Select the letter which best completes the statement or answers the question.

1. In reference to the title of personal property, which of the following statements is incorrect?

   A. Title to personal property is considered transferred when possession of the property is delivered.
   B. A search for the title of personal property may be made with as much accuracy as a real property title search of public records.
   C. A written instrument may be used to convey title but is not generally considered necessary.
   D. Personal property is generally located at the domicile of its owner and is under the regulations and jurisdiction of the law of the owner's domicile.

2. Which of the following is not considered to be real property?

   A. Leaseholds in real property.
   B. Easement appurtenant.
   C. Uncut timber.
   D. The right to extract undrilled crude oil.

3. Personal property attached to a building or land in such a way that it becomes real property is referred to as:

   A. An appurtenance.
   B. A fixture.
   C. An attachment.
   D. An inclusion.

4. All property is:

   A. Real if a life estate.
   B. Personal if a fixture.
   C. Personal if not real.
   D. Any of the above.

5. Which of the following is not appurtenant to the land?

   A. Fences.
   B. Watercourse.
   C. Dwelling.
   D. Trade fixture.

6. An item of personal property may be referred to as:

   A. A freehold.
   B. A fee.
   C. A tenure.
   D. A chattel.

7. Which of the following is an example of personal property?

   A. Mineral rights.
   B. Growing trees.
   C. An existing mortgage.
   D. An easement.

8. Personal property may be:

   A. Alienated.
   B. Assessed.
   C. Hypothecated.
   D. All of the above.

9. Real property would not include:

   A. An appurtenant easement.
   B. Airspace.
   C. Realty.
   D. A leasehold held by the tenant of the building.

10. Prior to the expiration of a business lease, which of the following could be properly removed?

    A. Fixtures used for manufacturing purposes.
    B. Trade fixtures.
    C. Affixed items of domestic use.
    D. All of the above.

11. An owner of land has:

    A. The right of lateral support.
    B. The right of subjacent support.
    C. Both A and B.
    D. None of the above.

12. Real property is considered to be:

    A. Land only.
    B. Land, buildings, and chattels.
    C. Land and building only.
    D. Land, fixtures, and appurtenances.

13. Which of the following least determines whether or not an item is personal property?

    A. Manner of annexation.
    B. Intention of the parties.
    C. Time of annexation.
    D. Relationship between the parties.

14. When referring to some types of real estate leases, the term emblements refers to:

   A. Invalid work.
   B. The right of a tenant to harvest his crops.
   C. Permanent attached fixtures.
   D. Farm equipment and machinery.

15. The legal concept of land is that it:

   A. Is subject to transfer by escheat.
   B. May be passed by purchase or inheritance.
   C. Is not limited to surface boundaries, but extends upward to the sky and downward to the center of the earth.
   D. None of the above.

Answers may be found in Appendix C (Back of text)

ESTATES

Estates means the same as ownership. Estates may be classified as: Those Estates You Own and How You Own Estates.

Those Estates You Own:

1. Freehold Estate.

   A. Fee Simple Estate.
   B. Fee Simple Defeasible.
   C. Life Estate

2. Less-Than-Freehold Estate.

   A. Estate For Years.
   B. Periodic Tenancy.
   C. Estate At Sufferance.
   D. Estate At Will.

How You Own Estates:

1. Severalty Estate.
2. Joint Tenancy Estate.
3. Tenancy-In-Common Estate.
4. Community Property.
5. Syndications.
6. Corporations.
7. Partnerships
8. Real Estate Investment Trusts

A. THOSE ESTATES YOU OWN.

1. **FREEHOLD ESTATE** - Any individual who owns property has a freehold estate. This includes a Fee Simple Estate, Fee Simple Defeasible Estate and a Life Estate.

   a. **Fee Simple Estate** (Fee, Fee Simple Absolute, Perpetual Estate, Estate of Inheritance) - The best way to own property. There are no limitations, and you may do with the property as you so desire. It is the greatest interest a person may have in real property. The ownership is:

      1. For an Indefinite Duration (You may keep it for as long as you want);

      2. Freely Transferable (You may sell it, lease it, give it away or borrow money on it).

      3. Freely Inheritable (When you die you may will it to whomever you choose) - A fee simple estate may be transferred by will or without a will (intestate succession) and said transfer can be made with or without consideration.

b. **Fee Simple Defeasible Estate** (Fee Simple Qualified Estate) - The ownership is based on conditions or limitations as to the use of the property.

Example #1: I will sell you the property for $1.00 as long as you use the property for a book store. This limitation of use could have been placed on the property either by a covenant (promise) or a condition. If the owner uses the property for something else, then he violates the use limitation. Violation of a covenant results in monetary damages. Violation of a condition (condition subsequent) results in forfeiture of the right of ownership (the property reverts to the previous owner).

Example #2: A grant deed includes a condition to state, "Alcoholic beverages cannot be used on the property;" the buyer (grantee) would have a fee simple defeasible estate.

c. **Life Estate** - Ownership is limited in duration to the life of the individual who holds it. A person who retains the property for the remainder of his life, has a life estate.

1. The holder of a life estate may do anything with a life estate except WILL IT. He may sell it, lease it, rent it, give it away or borrow money against it. An individual who purchases the property from the holder of the life estate may remain in possession until the death of the holder of the life estate. When a person who has a life estate leases the property for five years, and then dies one year later, the lease is void because death terminates a lease on a life estate. Death also terminates a loan on a life estate. If you ever loan money to a person with a life estate, always be sure to take out life insurance to cover the amount of coverage embodied in the loan in case of death.

2. **Estate in Reversion** - Upon the death of a life tenant the property reverts (goes back) to the person who gave it to him.

3. **Estate in Remainder** - Upon the death of a life tenant the ownership goes to a designated third party, rather than the original owner.

4. **Variation Life Estate** - A life estate may extend beyond the life of the life tenant. This usually occurs when an individual has a life estate designated in another individual's life. **Example:** Mr. "A" gives his property to Mr. "B" for the life of Mr. "C". Mr. "B" may keep the property for the duration of Mr. "C's" life. If Mr. "B" dies first, his heirs may keep the property as long as Mr. "C" is alive. When Mr. "C" dies, the property reverts to Mr. "A". In this example, Mr. "B" has a life estate and Mr. "A" has an estate in reversion.

Notes: 1. An estate in fee is a Freehold Estate.
2. Sale of mineral, oil and gas rights, giving a right-of-way, and leasing property does not affect a Freehold Estate.
3. Fee Simple Estates and Life Estates are Freehold Estates.
4. Ownership interests, possessory interests and security interests may be held in real property.

5. Ownership rights include: usage, transference, disposal, possession and enjoyment.
6. A Fee Simple Estate is the highest form of ownership.
7. Fee simple most nearly means an estate in property.
8. The term "of indefinite duration" is usually associated with an estate of inheritance, not a leasehold estate.
9. A Fee Simple Estate is freely transferable with or without consideration.
10. A Fee Simple Estate is freely inheritable by will or intestate.
11. A Fee Simple Estate is not free of all encumbrances, it may exist with an encumbrance recorded against the title. The Fee Simple Estate is usually encumbered with loans, easements, restrictions, etc. These encumbrances do not affect the Fee Simple Estate.
12. An easement is not an estate in real property.
13. A Life Estate is a Freehold Estate, it is not a Less-Than-Freehold Estate.
14. The life tenant has an estate in real property.
15. A Life Estate may be created by deed or will.
16. A Life Estate may exist with another estate on the same property at the same time.
17. More than one estate may exist on the same property at the same time.

2. **LESS-THAN-FREEHOLD ESTATE** (Leasehold Estate) - A less-than-freehold estate is an estate that is owned by the tenant. The tenant is an individual who hires real property from the owner for his exclusive possession. The owner of the property releases possession while retaining ownership of the property.

   a. **Parties to a Lease**

      1. **Lessor** - The landlord is referred to as the lessor. When real property is leased or rented, the landlord has a freehold estate.

      2. **Lessee** - The tenant is referred to as the lessee. The leasehold interest lies within the lessee. The tenant has a less-than-freehold estate which is also called a **Chattel Real.** The lessee has the exclusive right of use and possession of the property. Temporary possession is not the ownership of the property. The lessee has an interest in the real property; however, that interest is personal property, and is governed by the laws applicable to personal property. The lessee also has the right of "Quiet Enjoyment" which is possession without disturbance. In every lease there is an implied or expressed covenant by the lessor to the lessee of quiet enjoyment.

   b. **Classification of Leasehold Estates** - Leases may be classified as Definite or Indefinite in duration. Leasehold Estates are divided into the following:

      1. **Periodic Tenancy** (Period-to-Period) - An estate in which the lessee is in possession of the property from period-to-period (either day-to-day, week-to-week, month-to-month or year-to-year) as designated by both lessee and lessor in their agreement. Renting property on a quarterly basis is called periodic tenancy. When a lease expires, but the lessee remains on the premises and continues to make payments on the lease, the tenancy is considered to be renewed by the parties. The property is leased for the

same duration of time; however, the time cannot exceed one month when the rent is payable monthly, and can never exceed one year (A three year lease with quarterly payments cannot exceed one year if the tenant remains on the premises).

2. Estate for Years - An estate in which the lessee is in possession of the property for a definite and specific duration. **Examples:** It may be for 45 days; from June 1st to August 10; March 1983 to April 1984; or a tenant renting for a period of six months. An advance notice is not required to cancel the lease because the termination date is fixed in advance.

3. Estate at Sufferance - An estate in which the lessee, who has rightfully come into possession of the property, retains possession after the expiration of the term without the consent of the lessor. An estate at sufferance may be terminated without notice.

4. Estate at Will - An estate in which the lessee is in possession of the property for an indefinite duration and the tenancy may be terminated without notice of the lessor or lessee. An estate at will may be created by expressed agreement or by operation of law. California law requires that notice must be given; therefore, it is not used in our state.

c. Requirements of a Valid Lease - No special language is necessary to create a lease; however, the intention to rent the property must exist. The lease language must include:

1. Name of the parties.
2. Description of the property.
3. Amount of rent (Method of payment).
4. Term of the lease.

d. Miscellaneous Requirements of a Valid Lease

1. Capacity of the parties.
2. Execution, delivery and acceptance of the lease.
3. Leases for longer than one year must be in writing.
4. When in writing, the lease must be signed by the lessor.
5. Paying rent and entering into possession (**PART PERFORMANCE**) of the property is an implied acceptance on the part of the lessee. This makes the lease binding between both parties without containing the signature of the lessee.
6. To record a lease, it must be acknowledged by the lessor. Recording is not required to make a lease valid.
7. The creation of a lease for longer than one year must: be in writing, provide for a definite duration, and state the amount of rent, as well as the time and manner of payment. It does not have to be signed by both the lessor and lessee.
8. Rental payments are not required to be paid in advance to create a valid and enforceable lease.

e. Types of Lease Agreements

1. Combination Lease - A lease which incorporates two or more different types of leases into one lease agreement. The owner of a commercial property in a rapidly growing community would probably receive the highest profit from a lease if he incorporated a percentage lease with a triple net lease. This would result in the rental fee being based on the percentage of the gross receipts with a minimum guarantee. In addition, the lessee pays the maintenance, insurance and taxes (Gross receipts should increase with the growth of the community).

2. **Graduated Lease** (Step-Up Lease) - Lessee pays rent that may increase or decrease depending upon factors to be determined in the future.

3. **Gross Lease** - Lessee pays rent at a fixed rate. Lessor pays the insurance, taxes and utilities.

4. **Ground Lease** - Lessee rents the land only.

5. **Net Lease** - Lessee pays a fixed rent plus some of the expenses for the property leased, such as insurance, maintenance and taxes. A net lease provides net income to the lessor. When the lessee pays all taxes, insurance and maintenance, it is called a **Triple Net Lease.** The lessor does not have to pay the maintenance and the operating expenses in a triple net lease.

6. **Percentage Lease** - Lessee pays rent based on a percentage of the gross income, usually with a minimum guarantee. A parking lot or an auto storage garage would have the highest percentage lease. A chain grocery store would have the lowest percentage lease.

7. **Sandwich Lease** - A leasehold estate that lies between the primary lease and the operating lease. **Example:** Mr. "A" leases his property to Mr. "B" for five years. Two years later Mr. "B" sublets the property to Mr. "C" for one year. Mr. "B" is in the middle; therefore, he has a "sandwich lease".

8. **Straight Lease** (Flat Lease) - Lessee pays the same amount of periodic rent for the entire term of the lease.

f. **Transfer of Lease by Lessee** - A lessee may assign or sublease all or part of the leased property, unless the original lease prohibits any transfer.

1. **Assignment** - The original lessee (assignor) transfers the entire lease to a new lessee (assignee). The assignee has primary liability as the tenant. The assignor has secondary liability. When the lessee assigns all his interest in a lease, the receiver becomes the tenant.

2. **Subletting** - The original lessee transfers a portion of the lease to a new lessee (sublessee). The original lessee remains primarily liable on the original lease. A sublease creates ownership with possessory rights without having title to the real property. When real property is subleased, the interest of the original lessee is a sandwich lease.

g. **Tenant Cancellation Rights** - A tenant may cancel a lease if:

1. Any unreasonable physical characteristics of the property are made.
2. Property is destroyed or condemned by eminent domain.
3. Quiet enjoyment or possessory rights are violated.

4. Evicted by the landlord.

5. A condition of the lease is broken. A condition would be: "The landlord is required to make certain that repairs are made to the property." If the landlord fails to repair, the tenant may cancel the lease, or make the repairs in an amount not to exceed one month's rent and then deduct the repair costs from the next month's rent. This remedy is not allowable more than twice in twelve months.

h. Landlord Cancellation Rights - A landlord may cancel a lease if:

1. Tenant commits waste (destroys the property).

2. Property is used for illegal purposes.

3. A condition of the lease is broken.

4. Tenant does not pay the rent. Landlord has three options:

    a. Lease could be considered still in effect and landlord may sue the tenant for the rent as it becomes due;

    b. Cancel the lease and take possession of the property and lease to a new tenant (if new rent is not equal to the amount of the cancelled lease, sue original tenant for the difference);

    c. Evict the tenant. To evict a tenant, it will take three (3) steps.

Step One: A three day notice to quit or pay rent must be personally served on the tenant.

Step Two: Institute judicial proceedings (**Unlawful Detainer Action** is used by the offended lessor). In court, the landlord will receive a Writ of Possession (court proclaims in writing that landlord may have immediate possession of the property).

Step Three: Sheriff evicts the tenant.

Notes: 1. A lease is an estate in real property.

    2. The leasehold estate is owned by the lessee.

    3. An estate for years is a less-than-freehold estate. The owner of a business lease has a less-than-freehold estate.

    4. Reversion describes the right of the lessor in a leasehold estate.

    5. "Tenure of Lease" means Definite or Indefinite. Indefinite tenancy is described in periodic tenancy, estate at sufferance and estate at will.

    6. A covenant of "quiet enjoyment" relates to possession.

    7. A lease for one year or less may be oral.

    8. The terms "combination", "flat", and "triple net" refer to leases.

    9. Death does not cancel the lease. Sale of the property does not cancel the lease. The lease is binding on the new owner when the property is sold.

10. Constructive Eviction - Constructive eviction is an act of the landlord which interferes with the tenant, but is not actual eviction. This constitutes a breach of a covenant or warranty of quiet enjoyment. An example would be the inability of the tenant to obtain possession because of a significant defect in title or a condition which makes occupancy dangerous. A tenant may abandon a rental property without giving the required notice if there is constructive eviction by the landlord. Constructive eviction may be: threat of expulsion by the landlord; an eviction notice is given by the landlord; unwarranted or excessive changes or alterations in the property are made by the landlord; unwarranted delays by the landlord after notice to make repairs of damages which make the property unfit for occupancy; and condemnation of the entire property by the power of eminent domain (the tenant can never abandon a lease if the excessive wear and tear was created by the tenant himself).

11. Duration - Agricultural or Horticultural leases have a maximum length of **51 years**. City and Urban leases have a maximum length of **99 years.**

12. Extending - the same parties extend the existing lease.

13. Exculpatory Clause - relieves the landlord of liability for personal injury to a tenant as well as property damage.

14. Let - the temporary use of the property to be rented.

15. License - A personal, non-assignable and revocable permission to enter the property of another person for a specific reason (parking garage, motel room, theatre, etc.).

16. Renewing - the same parties renew the existing lease.

17. Rent - Consideration for the possession and use of the property for a certain length of time. **Contract Rent** - The actual amount of the bargained rent paid between the landlord and the tenant. **Economic Rent** - The expected rent a property may yield if it was available for rental at the time of the appraisal. Rent available to comparable properties in the open market.

18. Sale-Leaseback - The owner of the property sells the property, but retains possession and use, by leasing it from the buyer. The owner's fee simple estate then becomes a less-than-freehold estate. The grantor becomes the lessee and the grantee becomes the lessor. A net lease is usually used in a sale-lease-back, this creates a long-term and carefree income for the lessor.

19. Security Deposits: On Unfurnished Residential Property it may not be more than two (2) months rent. On Furnished Residential Property it may not be more than three (3) months rent. Landlord must return the security deposit within three (3) weeks after the tenant leaves the premises. The landlord must advise the tenant as to the disposition of any deposit held within three (3) weeks after termination of a rental (Three weeks or twenty-one days). Any prepaid rent received by the landlord is taxable in the year received.

20. Surrender - To cancel a lease by mutual consent of the parties prior to the expiration date. Surrender relates to a lease contract.

21. Consider that a landlord received the first month's rent in advance on January 1st and the other terms of the lease were not stated. If the tenant takes possession on February 20th, this would be considered the first month of the tenancy. The rent for the second month will not be due until March 20th.

22. In a lease, the law implies an unexpressed warranty on the part of the lessor to quiet enjoyment of the property by the lessee, regardless of the paramount claim of title. Paramount claim of title is the position of the original lessor in a sandwich lease. The sublessee is usually unaware of this claim because the claim does not place any restriction on the warranty of quiet enjoyment.

23. The three day notice is not used to evict the delinquent tenant. The actual eviction of the tenant requires judicial procedure.

24. In reference to the Fair Housing Laws, a landlord cannot require a single tenant to have a co-signer.

B. HOW YOU OWN ESTATES - Tenancy means a mode of holding title (ownership). If a buyer does not understand how to take title to the property, tell him to seek the advice of an attorney and a certified public accountant.

1. **Severalty Estate** - The ownership of property by one individual. An individual who takes title in severalty takes title as the sole owner of the property.

   a. A city holds the title to parks, public buildings and recreation areas in severalty.

   b. A corporation holds title to real property in severalty.

2. **Joint Tenancy Estate** - The ownership of property by two or more persons. To create a joint tenancy estate there must be four unities. The four unities are **Time, Title, Interest and Possession.**

   a. Four Unities

      1. **TIME** - All joint tenants must enter tenancy at the same time. A joint tenant cannot be added at a later date.

      2. **TITLE** - All joint tenants are named in one document (May be created by deed or will).

      3. **INTEREST** - All joint tenants must have an equal undivided interest. If two people own together, it must be 1/2, 1/2; three people must be 1/3, 1/3, 1/3; four people must be 1/4, 1/4, 1/4, 1/4; etc. **Undivided interest** means that an individual cannot distinguish any specific portion as his part of the property.

      4. **POSSESSION** - All joint tenants have equal undivided rights of possession. One tenant cannot charge rent to another joint tenant for use and possession of the property.

16

b. Right of Survivorship - The most important element of a joint tenancy estate is the Right of Survivorship. Right of Survivorship means that a joint tenant can never will his interest. Upon the death of a joint tenant, his interest is automatically terminated. Therefore, the delay always incident to the probate of a will would be avoided. This means that upon the death of a joint tenant, his property will not be distributed by the probate court, but pass automatically to the surviving joint tenant(s).

c. A joint tenancy estate can be created by: Joint tenants deeding their interests to themselves and others as joint tenants; a husband deeding his separate property to himself and wife as joint tenants; tenants in common deeding to themselves as joint tenants; husband and wife deeding their community property interests to themselves and others as joint tenants; or executors of an estate or trust deeding interests as joint tenants.

Notes: 1. A corporation can never be a joint tenant.
2. Joint tenancy is a single estate. If any of the four unities are not present or destroyed, a joint tenancy cannot exist.
3. A person may hold both personal property and real property as a joint tenant.
4. Joint tenancy can never be presumed. If people want to hold title as joint tenants, it must be stated on the deed or bill of sale. On a deed, it is written after the names of the grantees. On a bill of sale, it is written after the names of the vendees. There are not any specific words to be used as long as it implies joint tenancy or a joint tenancy estate.
5. A joint tenant may sell the property, give the property away, lease the property, or borrow money against the property.
6. A lender will not usually make a loan to an individual joint tenant borrower. If he did, the lender would be placed in a precarious position upon the death of the individual joint tenant borrower. This would, in turn, cause lengthy delays when trying to collect on the loan from the surviving joint tenants.
7. Joint tenancy is an undivided interest with the right of survivorship. Survivorship relates to time, title, interest and possession.
8. Upon the death of a joint tenant, his creditors cannot receive satisfaction from surviving joint tenants. A surviving joint tenant is not liable for unsecured debts of the deceased joint tenant.
9. A lien does not sever joint tenancy; however, a foreclosure will sever the interests of the joint tenancy.

3. Tenancy in Common - The ownership of property by two or more persons. To create a tenancy in common estate there must be one unity, the unity of **Possession.**

a. All tenants in common have an undivided right of possession. One tenant in common cannot charge rent to another tenant in common.

b. Tenancy in common is an example of a fee simple estate. Each owner may do anything with his interest. The most important factor to remember about tenancy in common is that **YOU MAY WILL YOUR INTEREST IN THE PROPERTY.**

c. Property owned with an unequal interest with the right of survivorship is considered a tenancy in common estate. Remember that joint tenancy requires an equal interest.

17

d. When two individuals do not indicate the method of taking title, the courts presume tenancy in common. If heirs to a will receive an undivided interest in real property, it is also presumed to be tenancy in common.

Notes: 1. A type of ownership which provides for an undivided interest and can be passed on to an individual's heirs, is tenancy in common. An advantage of tenancy in common is that each owner may will his interest. When a tenant in common dies intestate, the interest does not pass to the survivors, it goes to the rightful heirs.
2. The tenant in common may transfer his interest separately without the consent of the other tenants.
3. When two or more individuals own property as tenants in common, each tenant has a separate title to his undivided interest.
4. A tenant in common may have an unequal interest in the property.
5. A tenant in common cannot be charged rent for use of the property.
6. A husband and wife could take title as tenants in common if they wished to will an interest to their children from a previous marriage.
7. A brother and sister may take title to real property as a fee simple estate, as joint tenants, or as tenants in common.

SITUATIONS:

1. Two or more individuals should take title as joint tenants when they want the lone survivor to have title to the entire property.

2. "A" and "B" own as joint tenants, if either dies, the other owns in severalty.

3. "A" and "B" own as joint tenants, If "B" sells to "C", "A" and "C" own as tenants in common. Joint tenancy becomes tenancy in common when one tenant deeds his interest to a third party. Two unities are destroyed (Time and Title).

4. "A" and "B" own as joint tenants, if "B" sells 1/2 of his interest to "C", then "A", "B" and "C" are all tenants in common. "A" has 1/2 interest, "B" has 1/4 interest and "C" has 1/4 interest. Joint tenancy becomes tenancy in common when one joint tenant deeds a portion of his interest to a third party. Three unities are destroyed (Time, Title and Interest).

5. Husband and wife own as joint tenants. If the husband dies and wills his interest to his child from a previous marriage, the child receives nothing. The wife owns in severalty because a joint tenant can never will his interest. If a joint tenant dies, his interest is cancelled.

6. A woman and her brother own as joint tenants. If the woman deeds her interest to herself and her husband, the joint tenancy is broken. The brother has 1/2 interest, the woman has 1/4 interest and her husband has 1/4 interest. Two unities are destroyed (Time and Interest).

7. "A", "B" and "C" own as joint tenants. If "B" sells his interest to "W", then "A" and "C" remain joint tenants (1/3 interest each) and "W" is a tenant in common with 1/3 interest. Two unities are destroyed (Time and Title). If "A" recently died and willed his interest to "X", "X" would receive nothing because a joint tenant can never will his interest. "A's" interest automatically transfers to the surviving joint tenant ("C"); therefore, "C" has a 2/3 interest and "W" has a 1/3 interest as tenants in common.

4. **Community Property** - Community property includes all property acquired by husband and/or wife during marriage when not acquired as their separate property. Separate property of the husband and/or wife includes: all property owned by either spouse prior to marriage; any profits from such separate property; damages collected from court action; profits from a separate business; and, all property acquired by gift or inheritance during marriage.

    a. Community property laws originated from Spanish Law through the Treaty of Guadalupe Hidalgo, between Mexico and the United States.

    b. Real estate transactions which require signatures of both husband and wife include: selling, encumbering (borrowing money), and leasing for more than one year.

    c. Real estate transactions which require only one signature of either husband or wife include: buying, listing, and leasing for one year or less. When the husband and wife purchase a property and the deed indicates the name of one spouse, it is assumed that one spouse holds the title for the community.

    d. Either spouse may arrange to will their one-half interest of community property to anyone of their choosing. A surviving spouse is entitled to one-half of the community property.

    e. Should either spouse die without a will (intestate succession), then:

        1. All of the community property goes to the survivor.

        2. Their separate property is divided between the surviving spouse and the children.

            a. When there is only one child, the separate property will be divided one-half to the spouse and one-half to the child.

            b. When there is more than one child, the separate property will be divided one-third to the spouse and two-thirds to the children.

Notes: 1. Community property is similar to joint tenancy because of equal interests.

    2. A deed stated, "John Smith and his wife Barbara". The title is presumed to be vested as community property.

    3. If either husband or wife sells real property or buys encumbered real property without written consent of the other, the other spouse has one year to void the transaction.

    4. If either husband or wife signs a listing to sell community real property and the broker procures a ready, willing and able buyer, and the other spouse refuses to sell, then the broker could sue the community property for his commission.

    5. Each spouse may sell community personal property without the other's written consent. Personal necessities, such as clothing or house furnishings, are an exception.

6. Neither spouse may give away community personal property without the other's written consent.

7. The Latin phrase *Et ux* means "and wife". *Et al* means "and others".

8. Any property owned individually prior to marriage remains so even after marriage.

5. **Real Estate Syndication** - Real estate syndication includes a variety of entities under which people join together to invest in real estate which otherwise would be beyond their individual financial resources.

   a. Real estate syndicates give an individual the ability to use greater leverage and are one of the best methods to overcome liquidity problems created by most real estate investments.

   b. The method of syndication depends on practical, legal and tax implications. Joint venture syndication groups may be created through: an unincorporated group holding title as tenants in common, corporations, general partnerships, limited partnerships, or real estate investment trusts. Most real estate syndications in California are created as limited partnerships.

      1. **Corporation** - A corporation is a legal person or artificial person created by law that has the rights and powers which were given to it by the charter and by-laws under which it was formed. A corporation uses a practical, centralized management system while giving stockholders limited liability. The personal assets of officers and stockholders of a corporation are immune from paying a legitimate debt incurred by a corporation. A corporation is rarely used in real estate syndications because of the possibility of double taxation.

         a. A corporation would not be able to qualify as a joint tenant because it has a perpetual existence (A legal person can never die).

         b. A corporation can qualify as a tenant in common.

         c. A corporate seal is a legal impression authorizing the authenticity of a corporation when executing (signing) a document. A corporate seal on a deed indicates that the person signing the deed is properly representing the corporation.

         d. A corporate seal affixed to a deed is usually sufficient to transfer marketable title if the transaction is within the ordinary scope of business for the corporation.

         e. When a corporate officer, who is licensed as a real estate broker, wishes to obtain a salesperson's license, he may, if the chief executive officer, who is responsible for management and operations, has a real estate broker's license and is the broker for the corporation.

         f. The easiest and quickest procedure for a corporation to raise additional funds is to sell more common stock.

2. **General Partnership** - A general partnership is created when two or more individuals joint venture for a specific business purpose. Each partner has the unconditional use of the assets of the other partner.

   a. A general partnership does not have to be in writing.

   b. A general partnership does not avoid the double taxation element of a corporation.

   c. A general partnership does create unlimited liability. It binds all partners to pay all of the debts of the controlling partnership. When general partners obtain a loan, they will be held liable jointly and severally. This means that a creditor may look to the personal assets of any of the partners in a general partnership.

   d. Upon the death of one partner, the surviving partner becomes the exclusive holder of the partnership until completion of the partnership business. The holding manager is then accountable to the estate of the deceased partner.

3. **Limited Partnership** - A limited partnership is created when one or more general partners and one or more limited partners jointly venture for a specific business purpose. This provides the limited partner with limited liability (the limited partner is only liable for his investment capital written into the partnership agreement).

   a. A limited partnership must be in writing.

   b. A limited partner cannot make decisions affecting management policies.

   c. A limited partnership is taxed as a partnership and avoids the double taxation element of a corporation.

   d. A limited partnership usually reflects an increased deduction for individual tax purposes as well as limited liability.

4. **Real Estate Investment Trust (REIT's)** - A REIT may be created under federal law when at least **100** or more individuals joint venture as a corporation or as an unincorporated group to invest exclusively in real estate and real estate financing. Management of a REIT is performed by one or more directors (trustees).

   a. REIT's may be classified as equity trusts, mortgage trusts or combination trusts. An equity trust owns all types of real property and its primary source of earnings is from rental income. A mortgage trust loans money on a short or long term basis, using the real property as security for the loan. Its sources of earnings are from the interest charged, or from commissions and discounts earned, on loan transactions. A combination trust may develop, own or lease real estate and provide real estate financing as its source of earnings.

b. Miscellaneous requirements of the REIT include: A REIT may not hold real estate primarily for resale to the public as a normal business practice; Fifty percent of the REIT may not be owned by five or fewer investors; Each investor must receive transferable shares as evidence of his investment, and each of these shares must have an equivalent vote in determining the policies and procedures of the trust; Investments must provide for a minimum of ninety-five percent of the REIT's gross income (Seventy-five percent must be provided from real estate investments); Less than thirty percent of the REIT's gross receipts may come from short term profits that result from the sales of stocks or securities held for less than six months, including sales of real property held for less than four years (This does not include any involuntary transactions).

Notes: 1. Real estate syndications are usually formed as a partnership, the most common being the limited partnership.

2. To create a syndication with the least amount of income tax liability, an investment group will most likely form a limited partnership.

3. A real estate broker who is also an investor in a syndication which purchases a property that the broker had listed, must disclose his ownership interest or else the seller is not liable to pay him a commission.

4. The Real Estate Commissioner is least concerned about a syndicate formed as a corporation.

5. Limited liability can be accomplished by forming either a limited partnership, a corporation or a real estate investment trust.

6. A limited partner cannot assist in the management of the partnership.

7. Creditors may seek the personal assets of any individual owner of a general partnership.

8. The best places to check to see who has the authority to sign a document for an unincorporated group are the charter and the by-laws.

9. Failure to disclose the condition of title and all encumbrances in a real estate syndication could result in a $10,000 fine, 10 years in the state prison, or one year in the county jail, or both fine and imprisonment.

10. Leverage is the significant factor to an investor in a real estate syndicate.

11. A real estate broker engaged in securities transactions is exempt from licensing by the Department of Corporations if the transaction is owned by 100 or less investors and it is in a form of a joint venture, which is a limited or general partnership.

12. A real estate broker must be licensed by the Department of Corporations if he engages in the sale of securities transactions which involve a corporation, REIT or a syndication that sells, leases or finances Mineral, Oil and Gas interests.

REVIEW QUIZ

SECTION I - Matching - Select the letter below which best describes, defines, or relates to the following numbered terms.

1. Estate for Years
2. Economic Rent
3. Surrender
4. Contract Rent
5. Limited Partnership
6. Severalty Estate
7. Community Property
8. Periodic Tenancy
9. General Partnership
10. Fee Simple Defeasible

a. Is not required to be in writing.
b. Similar to joint tenancy because of equal interests.
c. The ownership of property by one person.
d. Renting property on a quarterly basis.
e. Ownership based on conditions or limitations as to the use of the property.
f. The actual amount of bargained rent paid between the landlord and tenant.
g. The expected rent a property may yield if available for rental at the time of appraisal.
h. Lessee is in possession of the property for a definite and specific duration.
i. To cancel a lease by mutual consent of the parties prior to the expiration date.
j. The most common type of real estate syndicate.

SECTION II - True/False - Select either true or false in response to the following statements.

1. Any individual who owns property has a life estate.
2. A fee simple estate is the highest form of ownership.
3. An advance notice is not required to cancel an estate for years because the termination date is fixed in advance.
4. The lessor does not have to pay the maintenance and the operating expenses in a triple net lease.
5. A lease is an estate in real property.
6. Security deposits for unfurnished residential properties may not be more than three months rent.
7. The most important element of a joint tenancy estate is an equal undivided interest in the property.
8. The creation of a lease for longer than one year does not have to be in writing.
9. Either spouse may arrange to will their one-half interest of community property to anyone of their choosing.
10. The most common type of a real estate syndicate formed in California is usually a corporation.

SECTION III - Multiple Choice - Select the letter which best completes the statement or answers the question.

1. An estate in which a tenant who rightfully came into possession of the property, and who retains possession after the expiration of the term, without the consent of the landlord, is referred to as:

    A. An estate at will.
    B. An estate at sufferance.
    C. A life estate.
    D. A periodic tenancy.

2. Which of the following is not considered a less than freehold estate?

    A. Month-to-month tenancy.
    B. Estate at sufferance.
    C. A life estate.
    D. Estate for years.

3. Which of the following expresses most accurately the greatest ownership in real property?

    A. Fee simple estate, life estate and estate at will.
    B. Ownership, security interests and right of possession.
    C. Freehold, leasehold and estate at will.
    D. Less than freehold, freehold and leasehold.

4. In the event of a business failure the creditors would look to the personal assets of any of the principals of:

    A. A limited partnership.
    B. Partnership.
    C. Corporation.
    D. None of the above.

5. A family rents a condominium at the beach from June 1st to August 1st, this is referred to as:

    A. A tenancy at will.
    B. A periodic tenancy.
    C. A tenancy at sufferance.
    D. An estate for years.

6. When four individuals own property as tenants in common:

    A. There is only one title that represents the undivided interest of the co-tenants.
    B. A surviving tenant holds title in severalty.
    C. Each tenant has a separate title to his undivided interest in the property.
    D. A tenant's interests terminates upon his death.

7. Which of the following is required to create a joint tenancy estate?

   A. Equal interest by each party.
   B. Husband and wife relationship.
   C. The words "taken as joint tenants" next to the names of the joint tenants.
   D. All of the above.

8. In a business partnership, if one of the partners should die, the surviving partner:

   A. Operates the business by himself until the heirs of the estate are able to assume the responsibility.
   B. Cannot transact any of the partnership business because death cancels the partnership.
   C. Becomes exclusive manager of the partnership property until completion of the partnership business.
   D. Becomes a partner with the heirs.

9. Which of the following would create a tenancy in common estate?

   A. A joint tenant gives his interest to a third party.
   B. One of three joint tenants dies.
   C. A joint tenant wills property to a third party.
   D. None of the above.

10. Able and Baker own property as joint tenants. If Able obtains a loan from a lender:

   A. Baker is placed in a less desirable position because Able has created a security interest on Baker's ownership.
   B. The lender is placed in a precarious position and he may encounter lengthy delays in collection upon the death of Able.
   C. The joint tenancy is terminated.
   D. The deed of trust is invalid unless executed by Baker.

11. Which of the following statements is always considered to be incorrect?

   A. A surviving spouse is entitled to one-half of the community property, the balance may be willed to other heirs of the deceased.
   B. The husband may sell community personal property for value without the consent of the wife.
   C. The wife alone cannot sell community real property unless the spouse gives written consent.
   D. Separate property of either spouse becomes community property of the survivor upon death.

12. A corporation can never take title as:

   A. Tenancy in common.
   B. Partnership.
   C. Joint tenancy.
   D. Any of the above.

13. The title to parks, playgrounds and public buildings owned by the city is held in:

   A. Tenancy in common.
   B. Joint tenancy.
   C. Community property.
   D. Severalty.

14. When an instrument is signed by a corporation it also attaches a seal that does which of the following?

   A. It indicates that it may be recorded.
   B. It implies the authority of the person signing.
   C. It shows that consideration has been given.
   D. All of the above.

15. A brother and sister own property as a joint tenancy estate. All of the brother's affairs were separate. The brother died penniless, leaving many unsecured debts.The creditors could:

   A. Place a lien against the sister's property.
   B. Not receive satisfaction because the property is owned by the sister.
   C. Appeal to the probate court which would be able to pay creditors out of the sale of the sister's property.
   D. Attach the property that was owned as a joint tenancy estate.

Answers may be found in Appendix C (Back of text)

TITLE

Title is the right of ownership. A right is something you cannot see or feel, it is without body or substance. Title is the imaginary, intangible right of ownership which is vested in an individual to the exclusion of all others. This exclusive right is usually referred to as a **Condition of Ownership** or an owner's **Bundle of Rights**, and it may be in personal or real property. The owner may do whatever he desires with the property. He may possess it, use it, sell it, lease it, rent it, give it away, borrow money against it, or even do nothing at all with it. Property is best described by "Bundle of Rights".

A. ACQUISITION OR TRANSFER OF TITLE - Title to property may be transferred by accession, deed, or involuntary alienation.

1. **Accession** - The right of an owner to add to his property by artificial or natural means.

   a. Artificial - An improvement. A fence built on a property against the owners' wishes would be acquired by accession.

   b. Natural - Water rights.

   1. **Accretion** - The gradual build-up of land as the result of the action of water. The adjoining property owner would gain title to the land by accretion. (Accretion is synonymous with Accession.)

   2. **Reliction** - Addition of land by the permanent withdrawal of a river or sea.

   3. **Alluvium** - The deposits of dirt added to the land as a watercourse flows through the property.

   4. **Erosion** - The gradual wearing away of land through natural processes. Loss of title to land may result from erosion. Erosion is the opposite of accretion.

   5. **Avulsion** - The sudden or violent flow of water that may tear land away from the property. Avulsion may also be considered the opposite of accretion.

   6. **Riparian Rights** - The right to a reasonable use of water adjacent to a person's property. These rights could never be found in a deed, a policy of title insurance or examination of the county records. These rights relate to land that borders a watercourse, not a lake, ocean or seashore.

      a. Riparian rights refer to the flowing water of rivers, streams and watercourses.
      b. An owner may sell any portion of the property not adjacent to the watercourse without transferring riparian rights.

c. Ordinarily an owner of riparian property (land) may transfer any portion of the land to a non-riparian owner.

d. Sale of land not adjoining a river does not transfer riparian rights unless transferred by expressed agreement.

e. Riparian rights may be severed by condemnation or prescription.

f. Riparian owner usually owns the land to the middle of a river or stream. Owner will only own the land to the river's edge if the river is navigable.

7. **Littoral Rights** - The right to a reasonable use of lake or ocean water adjacent to a person's property.

8. **Percolating Water** - Underground water that is not confined to any specific or well defined channel. It may be used by adjacent property owners.

9. **Water Table** - Indicates the depth at which natural water may be found below the surface of the ground. (A **DEPTH TABLE** has nothing to do with water; it is used in appraising.)

10. **Appropriation** - The state gives permission to a non-riparian owner to divert water from a nearby watercourse.

11. Every property owner has the right to protect his property against overflowing surface water. The owner may dig a ditch or place sandbags to protect his property.

12. The owner must consult with the local flood control district to build a dam to hold water for a specific property.

13. Property may be deeded to the high tide line in tidal areas.

2. **Deed** - A deed is a written document which transfers title to real property from one individual to another. The primary function of a deed is to provide evidence of a change of title or transfer of an interest in real property.

a. **Parties to a Deed**

1. **Grantor** - The person or entity giving the deed is referred to as the grantor.

2. **Grantee** - The person or entity receiving the deed is referred to as the grantee.

b. **Requirements of a Valid Deed**

1. A valid deed must be **IN WRITING**.

2. A valid deed must include the **NAME OF THE GRANTEE**.

a. The grantee must have the capacity to receive title as a legal or natural person.

b. The name of the actual grantee may be fictitious (fictitious business name or D.B.A.); however, a deed to a purely fictitious grantee would make a deed void.

c. The grantee may be any age or may be legally or mentally incompetent (Grantor may deed property to a minor).

3. A valid deed must include an adequate **DESCRIPTION** of the property.

    a. A legal description is not required. A street address would be sufficient to create and record a deed; however, the deed would not be insurable by a title insurance company.

    b. The description of appurtenances, improvements and easements is not required.

    c. An ambiguous legal description is considered to be a **Patent**, which may be curable by the parties involved with or without judicial proceedings. (Do not confuse this with the other form of **Patent**, which is a conveyance of title or sovereign grant by the government.)

4. A valid deed must include a **GRANTING CLAUSE**. This is an action phrase stating words of conveyance, such as: I give, I grant, I transfer, I convey, etc.

5. A valid deed must include the **SIGNATURE OF THE GRANTOR.**

    a. The grantor must be legally competent. The law requires that the grantor must be eighteen years of age or older and mentally competent. Legal incompetence or incapacity of the grantor causes the deed to be void.

    b. A deed is considered executed when it is signed by the grantor.

    c. A deed may be signed with an "X" or a "mark". This requires the presence of two witnesses.

    d. A deed would be considered void if the signature was discovered to be a forgery.

Notes:
1. The seller of the property is usually the grantor. The buyer of the property becomes the grantee. It is common practice for the grantee to receive a deed on property that is encumbered.
2. A deed does not have to be acknowledged or dated to be valid.
3. Consideration is not required to create a valid deed.
4. An **Exception** in a deed withholds part of the property from the grant.
5. A **Reservation** in a deed gives the grantor an implied warranty to enter and use the property for a specific purpose (usually extracting mineral, oil or gas from the land).
6. A deed does not have to be recorded to transfer title.
7. There must be an agreement by both the grantor and grantee to alter a deed in escrow. The deed is considered void from inception if both parties do not agree to change the deed, and the recordation of the deed does not have any effect on the validity of the deed having been modified without consent from both parties.
8. A deed is most like accession, when compared to adverse possession, eminent domain and succession.
9. Alienation means that property is transferred from one person to another person. Alienation is a contract of conveyance. Alienation is the opposite of acquisition.
10. Recording the deed protects certain rights of the grantee.

11. Oral instructions "not to record a deed until the death of the grantor" do not affect the validity of the deed.

12. A deed may be used only one time; it may never be assigned or endorsed. If a person desires to return title to the individual from whom he received title, it is necessary to execute a new deed.

c. **Requirements of an Effective Deed** - A deed must be delivered and accepted to be effective. Title passes when a deed is delivered.

   1. Delivery may be manual, conditional or by recording.

   2. The recordation of a deed raises the presumption of delivery.

   3. A deed given to a buyer which was not acknowledged or recorded is considered a valid delivery. A deed given to the grantee is the best evidence that title has been transferred, even if the grantee did not record the deed because it was not acknowledged by the grantor.

   4. The effective delivery of a deed depends upon the immediate intention of the grantor to pass title. **Example:** Mr. "A" goes to Europe. Before leaving on his vacation he gives a deed to a friend, Tom Jackson, with these instructions, "If I die, you can have the property". Jackson agreed not to record the deed until Mr. "A" died. Upon his return, even though, Mr. Jackson's son with the same name (Tom Jackson, Junior), had recorded the deed; based on Mr. "A's" intention, Mr. "A" still owns the property.

   5. Delivery of a deed is difficult to prove if a person executed a deed to one of his children and gives it to an escrow to hold until after his death. Transfer of a property with a deed conditioned upon death is ineffective.

d. **Classification of Deeds**

   1. **Grant Deed**

      a. The most common method to transfer title to real property in California.
      b. Must include the word **GRANT**.
      c. Carries two implied warranties by the grantor:
         1. That he has not previously conveyed the property (he owns the property).
         2. That the property being transferred is free of any encumbrances not disclosed by the grantor.
      d. There is a conveyance of after-acquired title. A grant deed transfers any present or future interest in the property.
      e. A grant deed is presumed to convey a fee simple estate unless otherwise specifically stated.

   2. **Quitclaim Deed**

      a. Usually gives the least protection or guarantee, compared to other deeds.
      b. Contains no implied or expressed covenants or warranties of title, and guarantees nothing.

c. There is not a conveyance of after-acquired title. A quitclaim deed transfers the present, but not future interest in the property.
d. Commonly used to remove defects on title, such as a "Cloud on Title".
e. A quitclaim deed is used to release present claims, rights and title of the grantor. A quitclaim deed to "quiet" a title would be provided by the grantor.
f. A quitclaim deed that has been executed and delivered, but is not recorded, is valid as between the parties and invalid as to subsequent recorded interests without notice.
g. The holder of an unrecorded quitclaim deed who does not occupy the property is in a very weak position against loss of his property due to a claim against the title by another individual.

3. Gift Deed

a. Commonly used to transfer title for love and affection (good consideration).
b. Does not imply similar warranties as a grant deed.
c. When property is transferred by a gift deed, the deed may be challenged by the grantors' creditors if they feel that the individual is giving away the property to avoid paying a debt.

4. Warranty Deed

a. The warranties are expressed (in writing) rather than implied.

b. Rarely used in California because it has been replaced by a grant deed with its implied warranties, and by the use of title insurance which provides more protection than the warranty deed.

5. Miscellaneous Deeds include: TRUST DEED, RECONVEYANCE DEED, SHERIFF'S DEED and TAX DEED.

3. Involuntary Alienation - Title to real property may be acquired or transferred by operation of law or court order. There are many situations in which the courts may establish or transfer the title to real property contrary to the expressed wishes of the owner. Examples of involuntary alienation include: Adverse Possession, Eminent Domain, Execution Sale, Foreclosure, Partition Action, Quiet Title Action and a Tax Sale.

a. Adverse Possession - The legal right to acquire title to property due to actual physical possession of the property. Specifically, this means to take property away from another individual without paying for it.

1. Requirements

a. Open and notorious possession and use of the property.
b. Possession must be continuous for five years.
c. Some evidence of color of title or claim of right. This claim of title may be based upon nothing more than physical possession of the property.
d. Possession must be hostile to the owner (against his wishes).
e. Claimant must pay all property taxes for the five year period.

2 . Miscellaneous

a . Possession and use does not mean that you have to reside or live on the property.

b . The claim of right does not have to be in writing.

c . You do not have to pay the property taxes before they become delinquent.

d . Quiet title action or a quitclaim deed may be used to perfect the title. The court order or deed must be recorded to perfect a marketable title.

e . Adverse possession cannot be used to acquire property dedicated for public use, including property that is owned by the government.

f . An individual who has permission for temporary use of any portion of his neighbor's property and has continuous use of said property for any number of years, cannot acquire the property by adverse possession (lacking the requirement of being HOSTILE to the owner).

g . Adverse possession is not created when possession is given through a defective document conveying title.

h . A confrontation with the owner is not required for adverse possession.

b . Eminent Domain - The right of the government to take away private property for public use. Compensation is paid to the owner at the **FAIR MARKET VALUE** of the property.

1 . Condemnation is the "act of taking" or "taking of" property when using the power of eminent domain. **Inverse Condemnation** occurs when an individual party forces the government to purchase his property. The reason may be noise created by a nearby airport or freeway. The statute of limitations for inverse condemnation is three years.

2 . The power of eminent domain may be used by federal, state and local governments, improvement districts, public education institutions, public utilities companies, and similar public or semi-public groups.

3 . Acquiring property for a railroad, the extension of an airport, or for the widening of streets are examples of "to take for public use".

4 . Severance Damages - When a portion of a lot is taken by eminent domain and the remaining portion of the lot loses its value because of the property division, the property owner may be able to sue for such losses.

5 . Eminent domain does not apply to changes in the zoning ordinances.

6 . Expropriation - To take by public authority through the power of eminent domain.

7 . Condemnation, expropriation and eminent domain apply to taking property for public use. They can never be used to place regulations on the use of the property.

8 . When the city, county or state want to take private property for public use and they are unable to negotiate an agreement with the property owner, they can proceed with the acquisition of the property by eminent domain.

9. Practical use is not an important consideration in the exercise of eminent domain.

10. **Involuntary Conversion** - Involuntary conversion is the destruction, theft, seizure, requisition, or condemnation (through eminent domain) of property. When an owner receives money for a property that has been destroyed or condemned, this is involuntary conversion.

c. **Execution Sale** - Property is seized and sold by the court to satisfy a judgment.

d. **Foreclosure** - The right to sell property at public auction to satisfy a delinquent real estate loan.

e. **Partition Action** - Court proceedings by which co-owners seek to sever their joint ownership of property.

f. **Quiet Title Action** - Court proceedings to remove a Cloud on Title. It may be used to clear title (perfect title) on tax sales, forfeited title on a land contract, or ownership based on adverse possession.

g. **Tax Sale** - The right of the government to sell the property to satisfy any unpaid taxes. The usual method used to sell the property is by auction.

B. TRANSFER OF TITLE UPON DEATH

1. **Probate** - Judicial proceedings to provide for the disposition of a decedent's estate.

   a. Probate takes place in **SUPERIOR COURT** within the county where the property is located. The laws of the state where the property is located will prevail even if the deceased had lived in another state.

   b. Requirements to sell property in probate include:

      1. All procedures of probate require the approval of the court. Any offer accepted by the executor must be approved by the court.

      2. An exclusive right to sell listing may be given to a broker for a period not to exceed 90 days.

      3. The broker's commission is established by court order.

      4. Any offer to purchase must be for a price which is not less than 90% of the appraised value of the property.

      5. When an offer has been received, the court will then hold an auction.

      6. At the auction, the opening bid must be equal to the initial bid, plus 10% of the first $10,000 bid, plus 5% of any balance amount over $10,000 in the initial bid.

Example 1: An $80,000 bid was received by probate, what is the minimum opening bid? **Answer: $84,500**

Solution:

Initial Bid	$80,000	
10% of first $10,000	$10,000	= 1,000
5% of balance	($70,000)	= 3,500
	Subtotal	= 4,500
	Initial Bid	= 80,000
Minimum Opening Bid		= 84,500

Optional Solution: Take 5% of the initial bid, plus $500, and add it to the initial bid.

Initial Bid: $80,000
  X .05 (5%)
  4,000 + 500 = 4,500 (Subtotal)
              80,000 (Initial Bid)
              84,500

Example 2: A $50,000 bid was received by probate, what is the minimum opening bid? **Answer: $53,000**

Solution:

Initial Bid	$50,000	
10% of first $10,000	$10,000	= 1,000
5% of balance	($40,000)	= 2,000
	Subtotal	= 3,000
	Initial Bid	= 50,000
Minimum Opening Bid		= 53,000

Optional Solution: Take 5% of the initial bid, plus $500, and add it to the initial bid.

Initial Bid: $50,000
  X .05 (5%)
  2,500 + 500 = 3,000 (Subtotal)
              50,000 (Initial Bid)
              53,000

2. **Will** - A will is a written document which is used to provide for the disposition of a decedent's estate. Another name for a will is a **TESTAMENT**.

  a. **Decedent's Representative** - The individual named in the will to dispose of the decedent's estate is called the **EXECUTOR** (**EXECUTRIX** is used to identify a female executor).

  b. **Miscellaneous Terminology**

   1. **Abstract of Judgment** - A summary of court proceedings in probate.

   2. **Ambulatory** - Describes a will in which the terms and conditions may be changed.

34

3. **Bequeath** - To give by will. Bequeath is the opposite of intestate.

4. **Bequest** - A gift of personal property by will.

5. **Codicil** - An addition, deletion or supplement which changes the will.

6. **Decedent** - A deceased individual.

7. **Demise** - Transferring the title of property by will (also by lease).

8. **Devise** - A gift of real estate by will (land passed in a will). Bequest is to personal property as devise is to real property.

9. **Devisee** - The individual who receives real property by will.

10. **Devisor** - The individual who gives or disposes of real property by will.

11. **Lineal** - Refers to the line of ancestry.

12. **Testate** - To leave a will upon death. The individual leaving his will is called the **TESTATOR** (**TESTATRIX** is used to identify a female testator).

c. **Classification of Wills** - There are three types of wills allowed in California. They are: a holographic will, a nuncupative will and a witnessed will.

1. **Holographic Will** - A will which is entirely written, dated and signed in the testator's own handwriting.

2. **Nuncupative Will** - A will which is not required to be in writing. It is a verbal statement in expectation of immediate death for the disposition of personal property.

3. **Witnessed Will** - A will which is signed by the testator in the presence of two or more witnesses.

3. **Intestate Succession** - A legal method to provide for the disposition of a decedent's estate if a person dies without leaving a will. Title to real property may be passed by succession. Division of a decedent's estate is enforced by statutory provisions provided by a court of proper jurisdiction.

a. **Decedent's Representative** - The individual appointed by the probate court to dispose of a decedent's estate is called the **ADMINISTRATOR** (**ADMINISTRATRIX** is used to identify a female administrator).

b. **Miscellaneous**

1. To die **INTESTATE** is to die without leaving a will.

2. An administrator is not part of a will.

3. Intestate succession is the acquisition of title through court order.

4. If an individual dies intestate, his heirs would receive the estate by probate court action.

5. Intestate is most completely the opposite of bequeath or bequest.

4. **Escheat** - The legal process by which title to property reverts to the State when an individual dies without heirs and without leaving a will.

   a. Any proper heir has five years in which to make a claim to the property.

   b. A fifth cousin is too far removed to be considered a qualified heir.

   c. The Attorney General's initiation of judicial proceedings will permit the property to be sold two years after death.

   d. The usual method used by the State to sell property is an auction.

   e. Transfer of title is by a State Controller's Deed.

   f. An individual can never take title to real property by escheat.

   g. Property would escheat to the State if probate determines a will to be invalid and the deceased does not have any heirs, even if the will stated an individual was to receive the property. Property may be subject to an existing lease.

C. **PROTECTION OF TITLE** - When property is transferred, it is necessary to establish a marketable title or to perfect the title. This does not imply that the title is perfect, but that the title is free from any legitimate objections. Reasonable assurance as to the marketable title has evolved through the years by the use of an abstract of title, a certificate of title, a guarantee of title, and presently title insurance.

1. **Abstract of Title** - A SUMMARY of all pertinent documents relating to conveyances and encumbrances affecting the property. To determine the history of title on a specific property, a title insurance company will compile an abstract of title by making an examination of the county records. An abstract of title gives the least protection to a new owner. Initially, an abstract of title was replaced by a Certificate of Title; however, it was ultimately replaced by Title Insurance.

2. **Certificate of Title** - An abstract company examines the conveyances and encumbrances affecting the property, then it issues an OPINION as to the present owner and the status of any existing encumbrances on the property. A certificate of title states the opinion of the abstract of title.

3. **Guarantee of Title** - An abstract company would do more than examine the conveyances and encumbrances affecting the property. As the name implies, it would guarantee the title as it appears in the public records. However, the records may be incomplete or erroneous, and they do not always reveal any unlawful conveyances.

4. Title Insurance - An insurance policy which protects the insured against specified risks based on the type of policy purchased. A policy of title insurance is usually demanded by the purchaser to assure the marketable title. Title insurance may be classified as a standard policy, extended policy, or an A.L.T.A. policy.

a. Standard Policy of Title Insurance (California Land Title Association - C.L.T.A.) This policy is most frequently used when purchasing a home in California. This policy does not require a survey of the boundary lines or any physical on-site inspection of the property. It does not insure against zoning restrictions imposed by government limitations, patent exceptions, mining claims, boundary lines, encroachments, unrecorded easements, unrecorded liens, or the rights of individuals in possession of the property. It does insure against:

1. Risks of record.
2. Forgery (a forged deed in the chain of title).
3. Lack of capacity (a deed signed by a mentally incompetent individual).
4. Lack of authority (a deed signed by an agent whose authority has expired).
5. Defective delivery of instruments of title (a stolen deed).

b. Extended Policy of Title Insurance - This policy requires a survey of the boundary lines and a physical on-site inspection of the property. This policy does not insure against actions of civil authorities in the area or zoning restrictions imposed by government limitations. This policy insures the buyer (borrower) and is paid for by the buyer (borrower). This policy insures against ten items - the previous five items covered in the standard policy, plus an additional five items. The total coverage includes:

1. Risks of record.
2. Forgery.
3. Lack of capacity.
4. Lack of authority.
5. Defective delivery of instruments of title.
6. Unrecorded encumbrances (easements and liens).
7. Encroachments.
8. Parties in possession.
9. Incorrect boundary lines.
10. Any claims which a physical inspection would show (mining claims, patent exceptions, and water and mineral rights).

c. A.L.T.A. Policy of Title Insurance - The American Land Title Association policy insures the same ten items covered in the above extended policy. This policy insures the lenders, but is paid for by the borrower.

Notes:
1. Chain of Title (History of Title, Chain of Ownership) - A history of conveyances and encumbrances affecting the title. It lists everyone who owned the property.

2. A history of title is usually searched by attorneys or title insurance employees.

3. Title companies search the county clerk's office, county recorder's office and the federal land office to conduct a title search.

4. A title search usually takes place in a title plant, which contains the records of all the recorded documents concerning real property in that county.

5. A legal description of the property is required to obtain a policy of title insurance. The policy does not require a description of the improvements (buildings) on the property.

6. When purchasing title insurance, the buyer will pay only one initial premium at the time of issuance.

7. A title insurance policy will not cover every claim made against the title, such as zoning or government restrictions. Undisclosed defects known to the buyer and seller are also excluded from a title insurance policy.

8. A title insurance policy will cover the condition of title as to the date of purchase of the policy and any expenses insured when defending the title of the property.

9. A key set of books maintained by a title insurance company is referred to as the Book of Abstracts.

10. According to federal law, a specific title insurance company cannot be a contingency of the sale when using an FHA insured loan.

11. A preliminary title report will disclose ownership interests and encumbrances on the property. It is only a report, not an insurance policy. The seller will always appear as the trustor in a preliminary title report.

12. All title insurance companies are regulated by the insurance commissioner. However, each company may establish individual costs for title insurance premiums.

13. Traditionally, title insurance is paid for by the seller in Southern California and the buyer in Northern California. Terms as to whom will purchase the title insurance are negotiable.

14. Title insurance cannot be assigned or endorsed over to a new buyer. A new policy is required upon transfer of title to the property.

15. A standard policy is best distinguished from an extended policy by encroachments.

16. The warranty in a grant deed "that there are not any undisclosed encumbrances" is not covered in a standard policy of title insurance.

17. The standard policy insures against a recorded deed in the chain of title that was not properly delivered.

18. A standard policy of title insurance provides protection for the owner against the incapacity of a previous grantor.

19. Title insurance is most frequently used by the grantee to assure his title to the real property.

20. In the event a second trust deed lender insists on title insurance at the time the loan is being made, the party who will most likely pay for it is the trustor (borrower).

21. The additional risks covered under the extended coverage policy are those that the insured could discover by physical survey and inspection of the property (protection against capital improvements being on your neighbor's property).

22. Processing a policy of title insurance follows this procedure: examination of the chain of title; determination of the amount of insurance required; and protection of the insured against the loss of title.

23. Title insurance companies will insure: the validity of a lease, free of liens and encumbrances; the validity of an easement; or, losses from undesirable restrictions in a grant deed which are known or believed to be enforceable.

D. EVIDENCE OF TITLE - The right of ownership in real property may be demonstrated by either constructive or actual notice.

1. Constructive Notice - Constructive notice may be created by either recording of an instrument (document) at the county recorders office, or by taking possession of the property.

a. Recording - Recording an instrument of title is to give constructive notice to the entire world of the existence and content of the instrument. Recording a deed gives sequential notice of a new interest in the property and protects the interest of the grantee.

1. County records are public records and may be used by any individual without the presence of a county employee.

2. If a property is located in more than one county, the instrument must be recorded in each county in which the property is located to give constructive notice in the respective counties.

3. All documents in the county recorder's office are indexed in alphabetical order according to the names of the parties of the instrument. Deeds are indexed by the names of the grantor and grantee.

4. The priority of recordation will usually determine the rights of the individuals (**FIRST TO RECORD, IS FIRST IN RIGHT**). Exceptions to this rule include a subordination clause, mechanics liens, and tax liens.

5. The requirements to record a deed include the following: the deed must be acknowledged by the grantor; it must contain the name and address of the individual to whom the tax bill is to be mailed; documentary transfer tax must be paid; and the stamps received from the tax payment must be affixed onto the deed.

6. An acknowledgment is a written declaration executed in the presence of an authorized individual (usually a notary public) stating that the signature was a voluntary and true act.

7. An instrument must be acknowledged by the individual from whom it was given. A deed is acknowledged by the **GRANTOR**, a lease is acknowledged by the **LESSOR**, and a land contract is acknowledged by the **VENDOR**.

8. An acknowledgement of a deed may be witnessed by an out of state notary public.

9. An acknowledgement of a deed executed by a corporation may be witnessed (notarized) by an employee of the corporation, if the employee does not have a personal interest in the transaction.

10. Title must be transferred in the same name as it was vested when recorded. Any subsequent name change in the chain of title would create a defect which could Cloud the Title. **EXAMPLE:** A single woman purchased property as Mary Brown, she later married Jim Smith and then sold the property as Mary Smith. "Mary Brown" is still on title which creates a cloud on title. A cloud on title may be eliminated by quitclaim deed or quiet title action.

SITUATION: An individual purchased a property for $120,000. The property is encumbered with a $70,000 first trust deed and a $20,000 second trust deed. The buyer gives a $50,000 cash down payment and agrees to assume the existing first trust deed. In this transaction, the reconveyance of the second trust deed would be recorded first, followed by the grant deed.

b. **Possession** - Notice resulting from possession has the same effect as the notice given by recording.

1. The possession by any individual other than the recorded owner will require an inquiry as to that person's interest in the property.

2. Examples of constructive notice include: a stranger in possession of the property with an unrecorded deed, and, telephone lines across the property.

3. The knowledge of a stranger holding an unrecorded deed is not constructive notice.

4. A holder of an unrecorded deed, who does not occupy the property, has not given constructive notice. This can place him in a very weak position if another person challenges his ownership of the property.

2. **Actual Notice** - An individual may be conscious of the circumstances in which the owner received title to the property, and at the same time is aware that the owner has not recorded the deed nor is he in possession of the property. Therefore, there is no constructive notice, only actual notice, as to the owner of the property.

REVIEW QUIZ

SECTION I - Matching - Select the letter below which best describes, defines, or relates to the following numbered terms.

1. Accretion
2. Avulsion
3. Administrator
4. Bequest
5. Bequeath
6. Grant Deed
7. Devise
8. Executor
9. Testator
10. Quitclaim Deed

a. An individual leaving a will upon death.
b. A gift of real estate by will.
c. The person named in the will to dispose of the decedent's estate.
d. To give by will.
e. Contains no implied covenants nor guarantees anything.
f. The gradual build-up of land as a result of the action of water.
g. A gift of personal property by will.
h. The violent tearing away of land by water.
i. Conveys after-acquired title.
j. The person appointed by the probate court to dispose of the decedent's property.

SECTION II - True/False - Select either true or false in response to the following statements.

1. Title is best described by the term "Bundle of Rights".
2. If an individual dies intestate, his heirs will receive the estate by will.
3. Bequest is to personal property as devise is to real property.
4. Riparian rights are covered in a policy of title insurance.
5. Avulsion is the opposite of accretion.
6. A deed may be signed with an "X" or a "mark".
7. A deed to a fictitious grantee would make the deed void.
8. A deed does not have to be acknowledged to be valid.
9. A quitclaim deed is used to release present claims and title of the grantee.
10. For a valid deed to effectively convey title, the deed must be intentionally delivered and accepted.

SECTION III - Multiple Choice - Select the letter which best completes the statement or answers the question.

1. A patent is considered to be:

   A. A security device.
   B. A grant by a sovereign.
   C. A deed.
   D. None of the above.

2. The term most nearly associated with title by accession is:

   A. Adverse possession.
   B. Dedication.
   C. Accretion.
   D. Prescription.

3. Which of the following are implied warranties of a quitclaim deed?

   A. That the grantor is giving up his interest in the property.
   B. That the grantor has not previously conveyed the title.
   C. That the title is free from all encumbrances not disclosed to the grantee.
   D. None of the above.

4. All of the following items are essential to a valid deed, except:

   A. It must be acknowledged.
   B. There must be a granting clause.
   C. It must be in writing.
   D. The parties must be competent to convey and capable of receiving the grant of the property.

5. Mr. Jones died while living in Arizona. He owned real property in Los Angeles, California. His heirs became involved in a dispute in reference to his property. Which of the following is true?

   A. Federal laws prevail.
   B. County laws prevail.
   C. The laws of the state where the property is located prevail.
   D. The laws of the state where Jones died prevail.

6. A deed is void from inception if:

   A. The grantee is incompetent.
   B. The grantee is a minor.
   C. The grantee takes title in an assumed name.
   D. None of the above.

7. Bequeath is most nearly the opposite of:

   A. Testate.
   B. Intestate.
   C. Bequest.
   D. Beneficiary.

8. The effective delivery of a deed is dependent upon:

   A. Acknowledgement by the grantor.
   B. Intention of the grantor.
   C. Grantee having knowledge of its existence.
   D. Recordation of the deed.

9. Which of the following is an important consideration in the exercise of the power of eminent domain?

   A. The proposed use must be practical, and just compensation must be paid.
   B. The proposed use must be public, and just compensation must be paid.
   C. The proposed use must be both practical and public.
   D. The owner's inconvenience must not be greater than the government's convenience.

10. A property on which there is a title policy issued is least likely to be personally inspected by an employee of a title company under:

    A. An extended coverage policy on rural property.
    B. An A.L.T.A. policy.
    C. A standard coverage.
    D. An extended coverage policy.

11. The right to use, possess, enjoy, transfer and dispose of a thing to the exclusion of all others best describes:

    A. Equity.
    B. Estate.
    C. Real Estate.
    D. Ownership.

12. In California, a warranty deed was ultimately replaced by a:

    A. Grant deed with its implied warranties.
    B. Policy of title insurance.
    C. Reconveyance deed.
    D. Quitclaim deed.

13. In reference to ownership of property with riparian rights, all of the following statements are true, except:

    A. An owner of riparian land may ordinarily convey any part of the land to a non-riparian owner.
    B. Sale of land not adjoining a river does not transfer riparian rights unless transferred by expressed agreement.
    C. Riparian rights cannot be severed by prescription or condemnation.
    D. An owner may sell any part of the land not adjacent to the river without transferring the riparian rights.

14. A history of conveyances and encumbrances affecting the title to real property is referred to as a:

    A. Title Search.
    B. Chain of Title.
    C. Cloud on Title.
    D. Color of Title.

15. Which of the following is a benefit of an extended coverage policy of title insurance over a standard coverage policy of title insurance?

    A. Protection against capital improvements on your neighbor's property.
    B. Protection against lack of capacity.
    C. Protection against forged deeds.
    D. Protection against recorded instruments.

Answers may be found in Appendix C (Back of text)

VOLUNTARY LIENS

An **ENCUMBRANCE** is anything which loads, burdens, limits, or affects the fee simple title or the physical use of the property. Property may be affected by money or non-money encumbrances. A money encumbrance is referred to as a **LIEN**. A lien is used to make property security for a **VOLUNTARY** debt or other **INVOLUNTARY** financial obligations. A lien may be classified as either a **SPECIFIC** or **GENERAL** lien. A specific lien may affect a definite property. A general lien may affect any and all properties within the State of California. All liens are encumbrances, but all encumbrances are not liens because non-money encumbrances affect the physical condition or use of the property. Encumbrances may be classified as voluntary liens, involuntary liens, and non-money encumbrances. **Voluntary liens** include notes secured by a mortgage or trust deed and a land contract.

A. **MORTGAGE** - A mortgage is used to borrow money. A mortgage is an interest, not an estate in real property. A mortgage is a contract of pledge. This means that the borrower promises or pledges to give his title to the lender if he defaults on his promise to make payments.

1. **Parties to a Mortgage**

   a. **Mortgagor** - The borrower is referred to as the mortgagor. The mortgagor gives an interest in real property as security for a loan, but does not alienate (transfer) the title. The mortgagor has an equitable interest (use and possession) in the property.

   b. **Mortgagee** - The lender is referred to as the mortgagee. The mortgagee receives an interest in real property as security for a loan. The mortgagee does not have an estate in real property.

2. **Instruments of a Mortgage**

   a. **Mortgage Note** - The mortgage note is the evidence of the debt. The mortgagor is the party who signs the note.

   b. **Mortgage Contract** - The mortgage contract is given as security for the promissory note. It creates a lien on the property and states that the mortgagee may foreclose on the property to satisfy the debt if the mortgagor defaults on the loan. The lien of the mortgage is a mere incident of the debt. Execution of a mortgage contract does not transfer title.

3. **Satisfaction of Debt** - Satisfaction is a contract of conveyance. This means that the loan is discharged from the records upon payment of the debt. When a note secured by a mortgage has been paid in full, the mortgagee must issue and record an instrument referred to as a **SATISFACTION OF MORTGAGE** (Certificate of Discharge).

4. **Default** - Grounds for default on a mortgage usually include, illegal use or improper maintenance and care of the property, using the property for other than the intended purpose, and non-payment of the mortgage installments or property taxes. A lender must pursue his legal rights within four (4) years of any delinquency or forfeit such rights (A mortgage note and contract will outlaw in four (4) years).

5. **Foreclosure**

    a. **Judicial Action** - Foreclosure of a mortgage usually takes place in Superior Court where the following will occur:

    1. A complaint is filed with the court.
    2. The court will hold a trial.
    3. The court will issue a decree of foreclosure (The mortgagor may reinstate the loan at any time before the decree is issued).
    4. The court will order the property to be sold to satisfy the debt.

    b. **Court Auction** (Sheriff's Auction) - The property is sold to the highest bidder. On the day of the auction the highest bidder (buyer) does not receive possession of the property. An instrument referred to as a **CERTIFICATE OF SALE** is given to the buyer at the auction. The certificate of sale is good for one year, or three months, depending upon the amount of the highest bid.

        1. **Insufficient funds** - When the proceeds from the highest bid are inadequate to satisfy the entire debt, the redemption period will be one year.

        2. **Sufficient funds** - When the proceeds from the highest bid are adequate to satisfy the entire debt, the redemption period will be only three months.

    c. **Equity of Redemption** - The mortgagor may retain possession of the property during the one year or three month time period. He may buy back the property by paying off the entire mortgage, plus foreclosure costs, accrued interest, late fees, penalties, etc. (The equity of redemption in a mortgage benefits the mortgagor). The maximum time for the mortgagor to legally stay in possession of the property is one (1) year.

    d. **Transfer of Title** - When the mortgagor cannot raise the funds to save the property during the redemption period, then the highest bidder (buyer) will take the certificate of sale back into court at the end of the redemption period and exchange it for a **SHERIFF'S DEED.**

e. Disbursement of Funds

1. Insufficient funds - When the highest bid is inadequate to repay the entire mortgage, the court will grant the mortgagee a **DEFICIENCY JUDGMENT** for the unpaid balance.

2. Sufficient funds - When the highest bid is adequate to repay the entire mortgage, the funds will be paid as follows:

1st - Foreclosure costs and expenses.
2nd - Tax and assessment liens.
3rd - Mortgagee receives mortgage balance.
4th - Any excess is given to the mortgagor.

f. Power of Sale
It is possible to conduct a foreclosure at a public sale if the mortgage contains a "Power of Sale" (Similar to a Trustee's Sale). A deficiency judgment can never be obtained at a public sale.

Notes:
1. In the event of foreclosure on a deed which has been given as security for a loan, the deed is valid as a mortgage and must be treated similarly to a mortgage by being foreclosed by judicial action.
2. In case of default, the mortgagee may take possession of the property (without foreclosure or sale) and rent the property, applying the rental income to the mortgage obligation (Mortgagee in Possession).
3. A mortgage is usually released by a Satisfaction of Mortgage.
4. Without any agreement to the contrary, priority is usually given to the first recorded mortgage.
5. A mortgage must be acknowledged by the mortgagor to be recorded.
6. The mortgage is not a negotiable instrument.
7. In case of "hard times" and default, a mortgage would usually provide more protection than a trust deed or land contract.
8. The mortgagor has an equitable interest in the property.
9. A mortgage is an interest in property, it is not an estate in property.

B. TRUST DEED (Deed of Trust)
A trust deed is a security device used to borrow money in which the borrower transfers his naked legal title and gives the power of sale to a neutral third party. A trust deed is an interest, not an estate in real property.

1. Parties to a Trust Deed

a. Trustor - The borrower is referred to as the trustor. The trustor gives his naked legal title as security for a loan. The trustor holds equitable title (use and possession) in the property. An owner who borrows money and executes a trust deed is the trustor.

b. Beneficiary - The lender is referred to as the beneficiary. The beneficiary advances money to the trustor. The beneficiary does not have an estate in real property.

c. Trustee - The neutral third party is referred to as the trustee. The trustee is the holder of the "naked legal title".

2. Instruments of a Trust Deed

   a. Trust Note - The trust note is the evidence of the debt. The trustor signs the note as the maker. The note is not recorded.

   b. Trust Deed - The trust deed is given as security for the promissory note. It is signed by the trustor. The trustor gives the "naked legal title" to the trustee to act as security for the loan. The trust deed creates a security interest in the title for the beneficiary by the action of the trustor. The trust deed creates a fiduciary relationship (relationship of trust) between the trustee and the beneficiary. In relation to the promissory note, the lien created by the recorded trust deed is merely incidental to the debt. When there is a discrepancy in the terms of the trust deed and the note, the terms and provisions of the note will prevail.

3. Recordation of a Trust Deed
- A trust deed does not have to be recorded to be legally effective; however, recording a trust deed gives constructive notice that there is a lien on the property. In the absence of an escrow, the broker must record a new trust deed within one week after the transfer of title; however, if the lender instructs the broker not to record a trust deed, the broker does not have to record it.

4. Satisfaction of Debt
- When a note secured by a trust deed has been paid in full, the beneficiary must notify the trustee. The trustee must then issue and record an instrument referred to as a **RECONVEYANCE DEED**. The reconveyance deed must be executed and recorded within a reasonable period of time after the loan is paid in full. A valid reconveyance deed must be signed by the trustee. The trustee will deliver a reconveyance deed to the trustor. The reconveyance deed transfers title from the trustee to the trustor. A reconveyance deed is not used to transfer title when an individual pays all cash for the property. The reconveyance deed is given to the borrower paying off the loan, then he can give a grant deed to the new buyer. Reconveyance after final payment must be as soon as possible. The lien of a recorded trust deed is removed from the county records when the reconveyance deed is recorded.

5. Default
- Grounds for default in a trust deed usually include, illegal use or improper maintenance and care of the property, using the property for other than the intended purpose, and non-payment of the trust deed installments or property taxes. The beneficiary can never consider default for detrimental zoning. A valid and enforceable trust deed does not require the trustor to have fire insurance, to pay property taxes prior to becoming delinquent, or to comply with health laws and police regulations; however, there are clauses in most trust deeds which give the lender the right to foreclose based on these reasons. The power of sale in a trust deed will never outlaw. The trust note will outlaw in four (4) years; therefore, the beneficiary must foreclose within four years of default, or forfeit this right.

6. Deed in Lieu of Foreclosure
- The beneficiary may agree to accept a deed in lieu of foreclosure. This eliminates the additional costs and expenses of a foreclosure on the property. A deed in lieu of foreclosure is not usually used when there are junior liens on the property because the junior liens will remain in effect against the property. The trustor will usually sign a quitclaim deed when giving a deed in lieu of foreclosure to the beneficiary.

7. Foreclosure
- A trust deed may be foreclosed by a Trustee's Sale or Judicial Action.

a. Trustee's Sale - When a trustor defaults on a loan and does not reinstate the trust deed, the beneficiary would initiate a Trustee's Sale. A Trustee's Sale is authorized by the trustor giving the "power of sale" to the trustee when signing the trust deed.

1. **Notification of Default** - A "Notice of Default" must be recorded to initiate the Trustee's Sale. The trustee sends a copy of the "Notice of Default" to the trustor, to any subsequent lien holders, and to any individual who recorded a "Request for Notification of Default". When a "Notice of Default" is received by the borrower, his best course of action is to exercise his right of reinstatement.

   Request for Notification of Default - An instrument which may be recorded by a junior lien holder to insure that he is informed of any foreclosure proceedings on the property. Upon foreclosure, a trustee must notify a junior lien holder within ten days if there is a recorded "Request for Notification of Default". A trustee must notify a junior lien holder within thirty days even if the instrument is not recorded. A recorded "Request for Notification of Default" usually protects the holder of a junior trust deed.

2. **Reinstatement Period** - The trustee with a "power of sale" in a trust deed must wait three (3) months prior to advertising a Notice of Sale. During the initial three (3) months, the trustor may stop the Trustee's Sale by making the loan current. This means that the trustor must pay all delinquent payments, accrued interest, penalties, foreclosure costs, etc., to stop the sale of the property. The reinstatement period begins with the recordation of the Notice of Default. The trustor may actually reinstate the loan up to five (5) business days prior to the date of the Trustee's Sale.

3. **Publication Period** - The trustee will execute and record a "Notice of Sale". At least twenty (20) days prior to the sale, the Notice of Sale must be:

   a. Mailed by registered or certified mail to the trustor or any person requesting notice of default.
   b. Posted on the property.
   c. Posted in at least one (1) public location.
   d. Published once a week in a newspaper of general circulation in the city, county, or judicial district where the property is located.

At least fourteen (14) days prior to the sale, the Notice of Sale must be recorded at the county recorder's office. During the publication period the trustor's reinstatement rights will continue until five (5) business days prior to the date of the Trustee's Sale. During the last five (5) days prior to the actual Trustee's Sale, the trustor has the right of redemption. This means that the trustor may stop the Trustee's Sale by paying off the entire loan plus all the delinquent payments, accrued interest, penalties, foreclosure costs, etc. The property will be sold to satisfy the debt when the trustor is unable to pay off the entire loan prior to the actual Trustee's Sale.

4. Public Auction - At the Trustee's Sale, the trustee will sell the property to the highest bidder. The trustee will execute an instrument referred to as a "Trustee's Deed". The Trustee's Deed transfers title from the trustee to the new buyer (highest bidder). A valid Trustee's Deed must be signed by the trustee. All rights of the trustor (borrower) always expire with the Trustee's Sale.

5. Disbursement of Funds

    a. Insufficient funds - If the highest bid is inadequate to repay the entire trust deed, the beneficiary suffers a loss. A deficiency judgment can never be obtained at a Trustee's Sale. After the sale of the property, the beneficiary cannot initiate court action to obtain a deficiency judgment. Therefore, the defaulting trustor cannot be held liable for any loss at a Trustee's Sale.

    b. Sufficient funds - When the highest bid is adequate to repay the entire trust deed, the funds will be paid as follows:

        1st - Foreclosure costs and expenses.
        2nd - Tax and assessment liens.
        3rd - Beneficiary receives trust deed balance.
        4th - Any excess is given to the trustor.

b. Judicial Action- A trust deed may be foreclosed in court when the beneficiary wishes to obtain a deficiency judgment. This court action is exactly the same procedure as the court auction in a mortgage and provides the trustor with the opportunity to redeem the property as in a mortgage. After the court foreclosure, the trustor may retain possession of the property for one (1) year.

Notes: 1. A trust deed is an interest in property, it is not an estate in property. A trust deed is an encumbrance as well as a lien on real property.
        2. The note is not recorded. The trust deed is recorded.
        3. The security for the note and the trust deed is the value of the encumbered property.
        4. A reconveyance deed is used with a trust deed; it is never used in a Trustee's Sale.
        5. A trust deed may be assigned.
        6. The "power of sale" in a trust deed is given by the trustor to the trustee.
        7. When the trustor does not reinstate the loan, the beneficiary will institute a foreclosure sale.
        8. The Code of Civil Procedure regulates the actions of the trustee. The trustee does not have any real authority. The actual activity of the trustee must be at the request of the beneficiary.
        9. The period of time to conduct a Trustee's Sale is approximately four months.
     10. The Trustee's Sale requires a posted notice of sale, notice of default, and an advertised notice of sale.
     11. The redemption period of a trust deed is significantly different than a mortgage (5 days vs. 1 year).
     12. After paying all lien holders and the cost of the Trustee's Sale, the remaining funds go to the trustor.
     13. The trustee's signature is required on the reconveyance deed and the trustee's deed.

14. A Trustee's Sale does not eliminate mechanic's liens or real estate tax liens.
15. A Trustee's Sale does not eliminate any federal tax liens when the federal government is not properly notified of the sale.
16. The Notice of Sale must include the street address of the property or the name and address of the beneficiary who will give directions to locate the property.
17. A period of slow economic inflation benefits the trustor.
18. The priority of trust deeds is usually established by the date and time of recordation at the County Recorder's Office.
19. Any change in boundary lines, restriction agreements, consolidation agreements, or the priority of the trust deed can only be made with the consent of the beneficiary.
20. The relationship of the trustor to the beneficiary is comparable to the relationship of the mortgagor to the mortgagee.

C. MISCELLANEOUS MORTGAGES AND TRUST DEEDS

1. **First Trust Deed** - The primary financing on a property is referred to as a first trust deed or the superior lien.

2. **Junior Trust Deed** - It is usually necessary to obtain secondary financing in a transaction where the purchaser's cash down payment, plus funds from the first trust deed, do not add up to the total purchase price. This secondary financing is referred to as a junior trust deed. A junior trust deed may be 2nd, 3rd, 4th, etc. (any trust deed which is not a first trust deed). Junior trust deeds are usually for lesser amounts of money and for a shorter period of time than the first trust deed. Private lenders and sellers are the best source of funds for a junior trust deed. The lender making secondary financing on a property is best protected by the equity of the borrower. When there is a foreclosure on a superior lien, the holder of a junior lien will probably reinstate the superior lien, and then foreclose on his junior trust deed. When payments are not received on a second trust deed, the beneficiary may foreclose, even though the payment is current on the note secured by the first trust deed. At the foreclosure sale of a junior trust deed, the funds will be paid as follows:

1st	-	Foreclosure costs and expenses.
2nd	-	Tax and assessment liens.
3rd	-	Beneficiary of first trust deed.
4th	-	Beneficiaries of junior trust deeds in order of priority (2nd, 3rd, etc.).
5th	-	Any excess is given to the trustor.

3. **Purchase Money Encumbrance** - A purchase money mortgage or trust deed may be given for a portion or all of the purchase price when financing real property. When purchasing property with a down payment, and the balance of the purchase price is borrowed from anyone (lending institution, friend, or the seller), this is a purchase money trust deed. **NOTE: "FOR THE PURPOSE OF PURCHASING".** The indebtedness of the borrower may be a soft money loan or a hard money loan.

   a. **Soft Money Loan** - There is not any actual borrowing of money, it is an extension of credit device where the seller receives a note secured by a trust deed or mortgage on the property for a portion or all of the purchase price. The note is signed by the trustor or the mortgagor (the buyer).

b. **Hard Money Loan** - There is actual cash received or cash placed on account for the borrower when purchasing the property. The actual loaning of money is either from a private individual or a financial institution. Proceeds from a hard money loan may be used to purchase real property or personal property, such as an automobile. A hard money loan can be:

1. A cash loan.
2. A note secured by a first trust deed from an institutional lender.
3. A purchase money loan from a Savings and Loan.
4. Secondary financing from a mortgage company.

Notes: 1. The lender may have the opportunity to secure a deficiency judgment on a hard money loan; however, a deficiency judgment can never be obtained when the hard money loan is for the purchase of an owner-occupied dwelling of four (4) units or less.

2. A deficiency judgment can never be obtained at a Trustee's Sale when foreclosing on a purchase money encumbrance which is merely an extension of credit type loan. This prevents any court action for money damages by the seller against the buyer.

3. A purchase money encumbrance given as a portion, or all of the purchase price takes priority over all liens against the buyer (borrower) which exist at the time of purchase.

4. In a purchase money mortgage, the mortgagor is the individual who signs the note.

5. A loan may be considered a purchase money trust deed if: the loan was made by an institutional lender, the seller extended credit to the buyer, a hard money loan was made, or a loan was made to purchase a three-unit apartment building.

6. A seller carryback mortgage creates a specific voluntary lien.

4. **Blanket Mortgage or Trust Deed** - A single mortgage or trust deed which covers more than one property. It is usually used when one property is not sufficient collateral for a loan. **EXAMPLE:** An individual wants to borrow $90,000 using a free and clear property as security for the loan. The property is appraised at $70,000. The individual also owns other unencumbered property which he can use as security for the loan. The lender will probably require him to sign a blanket trust deed using both properties as security for the loan.

a. A blanket encumbrance is usually used with construction loans to builders and developers of tract homes built for speculation.

b. A blanket encumbrance usually contains a **RELEASE CLAUSE,** which provides that upon the payment of a specific portion of the debt, a certain property will be released from the blanket encumbrance. The beneficiary will give a **PARTIAL RECONVEYANCE** from the blanket encumbrance. When a property is sold under a blanket encumbrance which does not contain a release clause, any money received must be placed into a trust account for the benefit of the purchaser.

c. The amounts paid off to release a property are usually proportionately larger for the first properties sold. This is because the best property is usually sold first. This increases the security on the remaining properties and protects the investment as individual properties are sold.

d. Trust deeds, mortgages, and mechanic's liens may be a blanket encumbrance. Real property tax can never be a blanket encumbrance because it is on one property.

e. The term "partial reconveyance" is associated with a blanket encumbrance.

f. A partial release clause in a blanket encumbrance will benefit the borrower.

g. A partial reconveyance deed is the instrument which will be requested by the beneficiary under a blanket encumbrance.

h. In a new subdivision, if the blanket encumbrance does not contain a conditional release clause, the real estate commissioner may require the purchaser's deposit to be placed into an impound account. This is for the the benefit of the purchaser.

5. Chattel Mortgage - A mortgage used when personal property is the security for the debt.

6. Fictitious Mortgage or Trust Deed - A previously recorded mortgage or trust deed which is referred to in subsequent documents to avoid the repetition of common details.

7. Open-End Mortgage - A mortgage which allows the mortgagor to borrow additional money after the loan has been reduced, without rewriting the original mortgage. An open-end mortgage benefits the borrower.

8. Package Mortgage - A mortgage which uses real property and personal property as security for the debt.

9. Wrap-Around Mortgage (All-Inclusive Trust Deed (AITD), Overriding Trust Deed, Hold Harmless Trust Deed) - A mortgage or trust deed which is subordinate to, but also includes the encumbrance to which it is subordinated.

a. A lender assumes payments on the existing loan of the borrower and takes from the borrower a junior loan with a face value equal to the amount outstanding on the old loan, plus any additional amount of money borrowed. **EXAMPLE:** There is an existing $60,000 trust deed on your property. A lender could loan you $20,000 by assuming responsibility of the existing $60,000 trust deed and having you execute an $80,000 note secured by an All-Inclusive Trust Deed on the property. The $60,000 loan is included in the $80,000 AITD. You make one payment to the new lender on the $80,000 AITD. The new lender continues to make the payments on the existing and underlying $60,000 trust deed.

b. The seller continues to pay on the existing loan and takes back from the buyer a junior loan with a face value equal to the amount outstanding on the old loan, plus any additional amount of money owed to the seller from the buyer (borrower). **EXAMPLE:** There is an existing $60,000 trust deed on your property. You may sell the property and continue to pay on the existing $60,000 loan and have the buyer execute a $70,000 note secured by an All-Inclusive Trust Deed on the property. You continue to be responsible for the existing, underlying $60,000 trust deed, while receiving payments on the $70,000 AITD.

Notes: 1. Mortgages and trust deeds are both security devices.
2. A purchase money trust deed is a specific lien.
3. A hard money loan is a cash loan.
4. Mortgages and trust deeds are different in reference to the parties, title, and statute of limitations.
5. Mortgages and trust deeds are similar in reference to the redemption period following a judicial sale.
6. A revolving line of credit is similar to an open end mortgage.
7. After-acquired title - The parties of a trust deed may agree to create a lien on a property not yet acquired. Title acquired by the trustor following the execution of the trust deed is an advantage to the beneficiary because it is also security for the debt in a similar manner as if it were acquired prior to the execution of the trust deed. **EXAMPLES:** Personal property becomes affixed to the real property; additions to or improvements to the property by the trustor; or, additional property is purchased by the trustor.

D. **PROMISSORY NOTES** - A promissory note is the primary evidence of a debt.

1. **Negotiable Instrument** - To create a negotiable promissory note there are seven (7) requirements. A negotiable promissory note must be:

a. A written promise.
b. To pay money.
c. At a fixed or future time.
d. Signed by the maker.
e. Payable to order or to bearer.
f. An unconditional promise.
g. Made by one individual to another.

2. **Parties to a Note**

a. **Maker** - The individual who signs the note and promises to make the payments on the note.

b. **Payee** - The individual to whom the note is given and to whom the promise is made.

c. **Holder in Due Course** - An individual to whom the negotiable note is given through an assignment or endorsement. The innocent third party then takes the note:

1. In good faith and for value.
2. Before it is overdue.
3. Without knowledge of any defects.

3. **Negotiation of the Note** - The transfer of the negotiable instrument to a third party may be completed with one of the following types of endorsements:

a. **In Blank** - The holder simply signs his name.

b. **Restricted** - The holder restricts any future negotiation of the instrument by writing, "pay to the order of ABC Bank, for deposit only", and then signs his name.

c. **Special** (Selected) - The holder selects an individual to whom the instrument is to be negotiated to by writing "pay to the order of (name of transferee)", and then signs his name.

d. **Without Recourse** (Qualified) - The holder makes no guarantee, nor warranty, when giving the instrument to a third party by writing, "without recourse", and then signing his name. The qualified endorsement is used when the holder of the note does not want to be liable for any payments. This protects the endorser from liability if the note goes into default.

4. **Defending the Note** - When the note is in default and the holder in due course brings an action to collect on the note, the maker can use a real defense against the holder in due course. The maker can use a personal defense against the original payee but not against the holder in due course.

   a. **Real Defenses**

      1. An incompetent maker (minor child or insane maker).
      2. An illegal document (a usurious interest).
      3. Forgery of the note (the maker did not sign it).
      4. A material alteration of the note (holder changes the obligations).

   b. **Personal Defenses**

      1. Fraud (false statements of the payee).
      2. Lack or failure of consideration (payee never received what was promised for the note). Lack of consideration to the maker of the note is not a valid defense against the holder in due course.
      3. Prior payment or cancellation of the note (failure of maker to pick up the note after it was paid in full).
      4. A set-off (a reverse obligation where the payee owes the maker a similar amount owed by the maker of the note).

   c. **Examples**

      1. The holder in due course would be prevented from making a claim if the note: did not have a signature of the maker; if the note was altered; or, if the note was due and payable prior to being negotiated to the holder in due course.
      2. The failure of the payee to give promised consideration to the original maker does not prevent the endorsee from making a claim as a holder in due course.

5. **Classification of Notes**

   a. **Fully Amortized** - Consists of level payments including principal and interest, at an interest rate which will be completely paid off at maturity.

   b. **Partially Amortized** - Consists of level payments including principal and interest, but requires a balloon payment because the maturity date is prior to the time allowed for total amortization.

c. Straight - Consists of interest payments only over the duration of the loan and requires all of the principal to be paid at maturity with a balloon payment. A straight note accrues more interest than an installment note when the interest rate and the duration of the loans are identical.

d. Negative Amortization - Consists of payments that are less than interest only. This means that the principal balance on the loan will increase with each payment.

Notes:
1. Promissory notes include installment notes, personal checks, and drafts. A mortgage is not a negotiable note.
2. A note is never given as security for a loan.
3. A note secured by a purchase money trust deed is a legally enforceable evidence of a debt.
4. A note is usually not recorded.
5. When the terms "jointly" and "severally" are written in the note, all of the borrowers are responsible for repayment of the debt.
6. Discounting a note is to sell the note for an amount less than the balance due at the time of the sale. To receive the greatest amount on a discount note that is in default, the holder forecloses by a Trustee's Sale. Upon the foreclosure of a trust deed, which secures a discounted note, the demand for payment will be based on the face value of the note, even though it was purchased at a discount (The holder of a $25,000 note which was purchased for $22,000, would foreclose for the entire $25,000).
7. The holder in due course is usually an innocent person who purchases a negotiable instrument without knowledge of any defect. The holder in due course is not identified in the note.
8. The buyer of a note is most interested in whether or not the note is seasoned, meaning, has the note had a good payment record over a certain period of time.
9. The role of the holder in due course is of interest in reference to negotiable instruments.
10. A note will outlaw four (4) years from the maturity date, or four (4) years from the date of default.
11. The terms "blank", "special", "restrictive", and "qualified" are associated with endorsements.
12. A note is valid if it contains a clause which requires either prior written notice to assume it, or approval by the beneficiary prior to its assumption.
13. The trustor signs the note for the amount borrowed.
14. Interest charged on a real estate loan is usually simple interest.
15. The calculation of interest charged on the principal plus the accrued interest is referred to as compound interest.
16. Loan costs are usually lower on an amortized loan.
17. A reduction in foreclosures, and the lender's risks are usually the result of amortization.
18. An acceleration clause in a note enhances the value of the note, but does not affect the negotiability of the note.
19. **Offset Statement** - A statement by the owner of the property when the existing note secured by a trust deed is purchased or assigned to an investor. It provides information as to the status of a lien against the property. This includes the principal balance, amount of payments, interest rate, duration of the note, etc.
20. **Beneficiary Statement** - A statement by the lender as to the status of a lien against the property. A beneficiary statement provides information as to the amount of principal due on the loan.

E. CLAUSES

1. **Acceleration Clause** - Gives the lender the power to declare all sums owed immediately due and payable upon the happening of a certain event, such as default. When a loan is "called" by a lender, this means that the lender accelerates all money which is due. A loan which must be paid in full, in the event the property was sold due to default, would include an acceleration clause. A real estate licensee would have to read the note to determine the presence of an acceleration clause. An acceleration clause does not affect the negotiability of the instrument. An acceleration clause benefits the lender.

2. **Add-on Clause** - Gives the borrower the right to borrow more money.

3. **Alienation Clause** (Due on Sale Clause) - Alienation means to transfer. Thus, an alienation clause gives the lender the right to call all sums owed to be immediately due and payable upon the transfer of title. This is a specific type of acceleration clause. It is based on the resale of the property, which makes it different from the typical acceleration clause. A loan containing an alienation clause can never be assumed without the approval of the lender. An alienation clause benefits the lender. Alienation is the opposite of acquisition. The borrower does not require the consent of the beneficiary to transfer title to real property. Transfer of title takes place when the grantor signs the deed. Permission to transfer title is only required when an alienation clause is present in the note and trust deed. The loan can be assumed at the existing interest rate if an alienation clause is not present in the note and trust deed. A clause in a mortgage is valid when it requires written permission from the mortgagee before someone can assume the existing mortgage.

4. **Assignment of Rents Clause** - Gives the lender the right to take possession of the property upon the default of the borrower, and to collect rents which may be applied to the loan balance and to any costs incurred by the lender. The assignment of rents clause benefits the beneficiary.

5. **Defeasance Clause** - Gives the mortgagor the right to redeem the property after the foreclosure sale upon payment of the mortgage debt. The defeasance clause benefits the mortgagor.

6. **Escalator Clause** - Provides for an increase or decrease of certain items to cover specified contingencies which are usually tied to an index or a certain event. It is usually found in a lease agreement to provide for rent adjustments based on a cost of living index.

7. **Lock-in Clause** - The borrower is prohibited from paying the loan off in advance. A lock-in clause is not allowed on owner occupied residential property consisting of four (4) units or less.

8. **Or More Clause** - The borrower may pay off the existing loan in advance without penalty. An "or more" clause permits the borrower to make accelerated payments and avoid any prepayment penalty. The "or more" clause benefits the borrower.

9. Prepayment Penalty Clause - The right of the lender to charge the borrower with an additional payment if the principal balance of the loan is paid in full prior to maturity of the loan. A prepayment penalty clause benefits the beneficiary. A prepayment penalty cannot be charged after a loan is five years old on owner occupied residential property consisting of four units or less. A prepayment penalty is sometimes required of a trustor who makes advance payments on his loan. The beneficiary is most likely to waive a prepayment penalty when a new loan can be made on the property at a higher interest rate.

10. Release Clause - Provides for the partial reconveyance of a specified property from the blanket encumbrance upon the payment of a specific portion of the debt.

11. Recording Clause - Prohibits the document from being recorded. A recording clause is unenforceable and does not affect the negotiability of the note.

12. Subordination Clause - An agreement by the holder of an encumbrance to relinquish priority and take an inferior, or lower position, to other encumbrances or future liens on the property. A subordination clause is most likely found in a trust deed used to acquire land on which the buyer intends to place a short term construction loan. Subordination is the opposite of superior. A subordination clause benefits the trustor.

   a. A subordination clause in a second trust deed allows the first trust deed to be refinanced without affecting the priority of the first trust deed.

   b. A subordination clause is most beneficial to a developer who wants to finance land and, later, secure financing for the improvements.

   c. The absence of a subordination clause may cause a problem when financing a parcel of land on which the owner plans to borrow money for construction of a house.

   d. A subordination clause allows for both a construction loan to take priority, and for a first trust deed to be refinanced or extended without losing priority; and it is more of a risk to the seller and may cause increased cost in the land and more stringent release clauses.

   e. A subordination clause may assist the borrower (buyer) by placing the lender of a larger amount of money in a more favorable position.

13. Transfer Clauses - Provides for a buyer to take over an existing loan on the property being purchased.

   a. "Subject To" a Trust Deed - The buyer takes over the existing loan without being liable for the loan. The seller remains primarily liable for the loan. The "subject to" clause benefits the buyer because he cannot be held personally liable for a deficiency judgment. A lender may obtain a deficiency judgment against an individual selling his property "subject to" the existing loan. The seller is totally liable.

   b. "To Assume" a Trust Deed - The buyer takes over the existing loan and becomes primarily liable for the loan. The seller is secondarily liable for the loan. The "to assume" clause benefits the seller. A seller may be liable for a deficiency judgment if the existing loan is transferred to the buyer. When a seller wants to be sure he will be released of all liability from an existing loan, he should have the buyer pay cash for the property and pay off the loan.

  c. **Substitution of Liability Clause** - Provides an agreement in which the lender relieves the seller from liability on the existing loan.

  d. **Assumption Fee Clause** - Provides the lender with the right to charge an assumption fee when the loan is being transferred.

Notes: 1. **Hypothecate** - To use an item as security for a debt without giving up possession of the item. When real property is used as security for a loan it is hypothecated. A trust deed hypothecates real property. Hypothecate is the opposite of a pledge agreement.

    2. **Pledge Agreement** - To use an item of personal property as security for a debt. Real property can never be pledged. A pledge agreement is the opposite of hypothecate. **EXAMPLES:**
      a. Borrowing money on an existing trust deed. When an individual wants to borrow money on a trust deed that he owns, he is asked to sign a pledge agreement.
      b. Using a $50,000 note as security to borrow $20,000. The $50,000 note is considered a pledge agreement.
      c. Mr. Jones needs $3,000 for a vacation cruise. He holds a note secured by a trust deed on a property. Mr. Smith offers to loan Mr. Jones the $3,000 if he can hold the note secured by the trust deed as his security. The note secured by the trust deed is considered a pledge agreement.

    3. A trust deed usually contains provisions requiring the trustor to keep the property in good condition and repair, to pay taxes and assessments before they become delinquent, and to keep the property insured against fire and other hazards. These clauses are not required to create a valid trust deed.

    4. When buying property in a new subdivision, a clause in the sale contract stated, "A purchaser cannot erect a 'for sale' sign until all the parcels are sold by the subdivider". This clause is illegal and unenforceable; therefore, an individual owner may place a sign of reasonable dimensions on his own property if he so desires.

SITUATIONS:

1. A property is encumbered with an $80,000 first trust deed and a $20,000 second trust deed. The highest bid at a Trustee's Sale is $70,000. The holder of the second trust deed would not receive any funds from this sale.

2. A property is encumbered with a $40,000 first trust deed, a $15,000 second trust deed and a $5,000 third trust deed. The highest bid at the Trustee's Sale is $54,000. The holder of the first trust deed is paid in full; the holder of the second trust deed is paid $14,000; and the holder of the third trust deed would not receive any funds from this sale.

3. Mr. James sold his property to Mr. Slokim for $120,000. The property is encumbered with a $70,000 first trust deed and a $50,000 second trust deed. Mr. Slokim made a $50,000 down payment and assumed the existing first trust deed. The reconveyance of the second trust deed will be recorded prior to the recordation of the grant deed.

4. A property is encumbered with a $43,000 first trust deed and a $23,000 second trust deed. The highest bid at the Trustee's Sale is $69,000. The holders of the first and second trust deeds are paid in full. The $3,000 cash surplus is given to the trustor.

5. A property is encumbered by a first trust deed and second trust deed. The trustor makes his payments on the second, but does not pay the first. The trustee in the first trust deed records a "Notice of Default". The beneficiary of the second trust deed reinstates the first trust deed, and then, forecloses on his second trust deed.

6. Consider the following:

   1/15/80: Grant deed - Grantor is Able; Grantee is Baker.
   2/1/81: Trust deed - Trustor is Baker; Beneficiary is Fong.
   3/1/81: Lease - Lessor is Baker; Lessee is Davis.

   Due to a recent foreclosure, Fong now has title to the property. Fong may increase or decrease the rent, because after a Trustee's Sale, when the beneficiary or highest bidder takes title to the property, his title has priority all the way back to the date in which the trust deed was executed and recorded. Any leases or liens (except tax liens) created on the property after that date are automatically cancelled.

F. **LAND CONTRACT** (Real Property Sales Contract) - A land contract is a security device used to sell real property on credit terms with the seller retaining the legal title to the property and the buyer receiving an equitable title in the property. This is a common method for the seller to extend credit to the buyer in the purchase of real property. Do not let the term "land" confuse you. A land contract can be used to finance any type of property, including land, houses, apartment buildings, commercial and industrial properties.

   1. **Parties to a Land Contract**

      a. **Vendor** - The seller in a land contract is referred to as the vendor. The vendor retains legal title to the property.

      b. **Vendee** - The buyer in a land contract is referred to as the vendee. The vendee acquires equitable title to the property. The buyer under a land sales contract has the right to do anything with his property as long as he makes the payments. The buyer has the right to use and possession of the property. The buyer's equitable interest in the property is freely transferable and freely inheritable.

   2. **Requirements for a Valid Land Contract**

      a. Competent parties.
      b. Mutual consent (offer and acceptance).
      c. Lawful object.
      d. Consideration.
      e. In writing.

3. Miscellaneous Requirements for a Valid Land Contract

   a. Terms of the contract (method of payment, duration, etc.).
   b. A land contract used in conjunction with new subdivisions must include both a legal description of the property and the underlying encumbrances on the property.
   c. Tax estimate (When given, it must state the basis for the estimate).

4. Recordation of a Land Contract

   a. A land contract must be signed and acknowledged by the seller (vendor) to be recorded.
   b. A clause prohibiting the recordation of a land contract is unenforceable. The vendor can never prohibit the vendee from recording the contract, even when the contract contains a clause prohibiting such recordation.

5. Encumbrances

   a. When the land contract is still in effect, the buyer can never borrow more money because he only has equitable title.
   b. The seller has legal title to the property; therefore, he can borrow more money on the property. The seller may only borrow up to the amount owed on the land contract. In order to borrow additional money above the amount owed on the land contract, the seller must receive written permission from the buyer.
   c. Funds received by the vendor under a land contract must be used toward the payment of an existing trust deed on the property.

6. Transfer of a Land Contract

   a. The land contract may be assigned by the vendor; however, the vendor must also transfer title to the assignee.
   b. The land contract may be assigned by the vendee; however, the vendee will remain primarily liable unless he is released from liability by the vendor. Assignment by the vendee is only permitted when the land contract does not contain an alienation clause and does not have any restrictions which prohibit an assignment or resale.

7. Foreclosure on the Land Contract

   a. When the vendee abandons the property, a recorded land contract creates a "cloud" on the title.
   b. Upon default, the name of the vendee must be removed from the county's record in order to resell the property. This may be accomplished by obtaining a quitclaim deed from the original vendee. When the vendee will not execute a quitclaim deed, the legal remedy used by the vendor is a "quiet title action".
   c. The vendor may usually retain any of the vendee's cash investment up to the time of default; however, he can never obtain a deficiency judgment against the vendee. The presumed advantage of a land contract is that the vendor may easily eliminate any interest of the vendee, in the event of default, by initiating a suit for specific performance. However, this presumption has been considerably weakened since the courts have often concluded that the foreclosure may

be unreasonable. When the vendee defaults, the vendor will most likely have to proceed with further court action to clear the title and regain possession of the property. This process is usually slower than foreclosure proceedings in a trust deed.

Notes: 1. A land contract may be referred to as: "installment sales contract", "agreement to convey", "agreement for purchase and sale", "land sales contract", or "land contract of sale".

2. A land contract may be referred to as a security device.

3. A land contract is used as a substitute for a note secured by a trust deed.

4. In a land contract, the financial relationship of the seller to the buyer is comparable to the relationship between the beneficiary and the trustor.

5. A land contract is different from a grant deed, in reference to title, interest conveyed, and signatures of the parties.

6. A land contract is used to transfer equitable title to a buyer.

7. The buyer purchasing property under a land contract acquires a possessory interest in the property.

8. Under a land contract between two individuals, the seller must maintain a separate trust fund account for the prorated taxes and insurance monies. The vendor must hold these impound payments in trust; however, he can use them for other purposes if he has written permission from the vendee.

9. A mortgage, trust deed, or land contract may be used as a security device to encumber real property.

10. When a home being purchased under a land contract is destroyed by an earthquake, fire, or other disaster, the buyer in possession is required to make future payments. When legal title or possession is not transferred, the risk of loss is on the seller. When legal title or possession is transferred, the risk of loss is on the buyer (**Uniform Vendor and Purchaser Risk Act**).

11. An individual with insufficient funds to purchase a property, may have someone else purchase a property for cash, then, immediately resell to him at any price and terms agreed to between the parties of a land contract.

REVIEW QUIZ

SECTION I - Matching - Select the letter below which best describes, defines, or relates to the following numbered terms.

1. Acceleration Clause
2. Or More Clause
3. Hard Money Loan
4. Subordination Clause
5. Discounting
6. Soft Money Loan
7. Fictitious Mortgage
8. Land Contract
9. Alienation Clause
10. Package Mortgage

a. To sell a note for an amount less than the balance due at the time of sale.

b. Real property is sold on credit terms with the seller retaining the legal title to the property.

c. A mortgage which uses both real and personal property as security for the loan.

d. Gives the lender the right to call all sums owed to be immediately due and payable upon the transfer of title.

e. Allows the borrower to make an accelerated payment and avoid any prepayment penalty.

f. A previously recorded mortgage which is referred to in subsequent documents to avoid the repetition of common details.

g. A device that extends credit between the buyer and seller where there is not any actual borrowing of money.

h. Gives the lender the power to declare all sums owed to be immediately due and payable upon the happening of a certain event.

i. An agreement by the holder of an encumbrance to relinquish priority and accept a lower position to other encumbrances or future liens.

j. There is actual cash received or placed on account for the borrower when purchasing the property.

SECTION II - True/False - Select either true or false in response to the following statements.

1. The mortgagee has an estate in real property.
2. The trustor signs the note as the maker.
3. The "power of sale" is given by the beneficiary to the trustee.
4. The trustor under a trust deed holds equitable title in the property.
5. A purchase money trust deed between the borrower and the lender is a general lien.
6. Property tax can never be a blanket encumbrance.
7. An endorsement containing the words "without recourse" is a qualified endorsement.
8. A trust deed must be recorded to be legally effective.
9. Any excess funds at a Trustee's Sale are given to the beneficiary.

10. A promissory note is the instrument which is used as the primary security for the debt.

SECTION III - **Multiple Choice** - Select the letter which best completes the statement or answers the question.

1. Which of the following is true in reference to a trust deed?

   A. A trust deed is security for the note.
   B. A note is security for the trust deed.
   C. When the note is destroyed, the trust deed is of no value.
   D. When the trust deed is destroyed, the note is of no value.

2. An owner of a property defaults on the first trust deed and the beneficiary forecloses through court action. After the foreclosure sale, the owner may retain possession for:

   A. 30 days.
   B. Approximately four months.
   C. One year.
   D. Ten years.

3. Security for a note and trust deed can be:

   A. Stability of the money market.
   B. Credit of the borrower.
   C. Value of the encumbered property.
   D. All of the above.

4. Who would benefit most from a subordination clause in a trust deed?

   A. The beneficiary.
   B. The trustor.
   C. The trustee.
   D. None of the above.

5. A purchase money trust deed may be defined as a trust deed:

   A. Which provides for additional advances to the trustor without writing a new trust deed.
   B. Which includes chattels such as household appliances as additional collateral.
   C. Taken on several parcels.
   D. Taken on all or part of the purchase price.

6. A developer wants to purchase land and later secure financing for improvements. What clause would be most beneficial to the developer in the original trust deed used to purchase the land?

   A. Subordination clause.
   B. Exculpatory clause.
   C. Acceleration clause.
   D. Alienation clause.

7. Trust deeds and mortgages are:

   A. Real property.
   B. Interests in land.
   C. Chattel reals.
   D. None of the above.

8. Which of the following is an advantage to the seller of real property in using a land contract in the sale of the property instead of giving a grant deed and taking back a large first trust deed?

   A. A deficiency judgment can be obtained in the event of default.
   B. The seller can prohibit the vendee from recording the contract when the contract includes a clause prohibiting such recordation.
   C. Foreclosure proceedings are faster, thereby permitting the vendor to recover possession quickly from the vendee.
   D. None of the above.

9. An endorsement in a negotiable instrument included the words "without recourse," this is what type of endorsement?

   A. Restricted.
   B. Qualified.
   C. In blank.
   D. Special.

10. Which of the following words placed in a promissory note would commit all borrowers for repayment?

    A. Jointly.
    B. Individually.
    C. Individually and severally.
    D. Jointly and severally.

11. An acceleration clause was made part of a negotiable note. The inclusion of the acceleration clause will:

    A. Not have any effect on its negotiability nor would it be of any benefit.
    B. Cause it to lose its negotiability.
    C. Not have any effect on its negotiability.
    D. Make it less negotiable.

12. In a judicial foreclosure where the mortgagor fails to exercise his right to redeem, possession of the property during the period of redemption is held by:

    A. Mortgagee.
    B. Mortgagor.
    C. Bailiff.
    D. Beneficiary.

13. A reconveyance deed is used in connection with:

   A. Trust deed.
   B. Mortgage.
   C. Foreclosure.
   D. Land contract.

14. A trust deed and mortgage are different in all of the following ways, except:

   A. Statute of Limitations.
   B. Parties.
   C. Title.
   D. Redemption period following a judicial sale.

15. The party who holds the title in a land contract is the:

   A. Vendor.
   B. Vendee.
   C. Trustee.
   D. Beneficiary.

Answers may be found in Appendix C (Back of text)

INVOLUNTARY LIENS

A. Mechanic's Lien - A mechanic's lien may be filed when an individual contractor is not compensated for labor or materials for the improvement of real property.

1. Parties to a Mechanic's Lien

    a. General Contractor - The general contractor is the individual hired by the property owner.

    b. Subcontractor - The subcontractor is hired by the general contractor. Subcontractors include anyone who supplies materials for construction and laborers who do the framing, flooring, cabinets, landscaping, etc.

2. Preliminary Notice - A preliminary notice must be given to the property owner, general contractor, and construction lender prior to filing a mechanic's lien. Preliminary notice must be given within twenty days of the furnishing of labor and materials. This gives notice that if the bills are not paid, the property will be subject to a mechanic's lien.

3. Starting Time - Mechanic's lien rights start on the date of commencement of construction. This means that in the event of default and foreclosure, the mechanic's liens will take priority over mortgage and trust deed liens recorded on the property after the beginning of work, because the priority of a mechanic's lien dates back to the first day of construction.

4. Completion Time - The mechanic's lien filing period is limited based on the completion of work. Completion of work may be determined by any of the following:

    a. Occupation or use of the property by the owner or the owner's agent accompanied by cessation of work.
    b. Acceptance by the owner or the owner's agent of the work of improvement.
    c. A cessation of work on the property for a continuous period of sixty days.
    d. A cessation of work on the property for a continuous period of thirty days or more when the owner files for record a "notice of cessation".

5. Notice of Nonresponsibility - An owner or any individual who may have an interest in the property may protect his interest against a mechanic's lien created by parties in possession by using a notice of nonresponsibility. After obtaining knowledge of work on the property, the owner has **TEN (10) DAYS** to give notice that he will not be responsible for the work by posting a notice of nonresponsibility on the property and recording a verified copy of the notice with the county recorder. **EXAMPLE:** When an individual who sold his home on a land contract drives by the premises and notices that a new roof is being installed, he should post and record a notice of nonresponsibility within ten days after discovery of the work. This would protect him in the event the roofing contractor is not paid and files a mechanic's lien against the property.

6. Notice of Completion - A notice of completion should be recorded within the county where the property is located within ten (10) days after completion of the work of improvement. The notice of completion benefits the owner because it shortens the filing period for mechanic's liens.

There is a limited amount of time to file or record a mechanic's lien. This will vary based on whether the notice of completion has been recorded.

a. Not Recorded - When the notice of completion is not recorded, all contractors have **90 DAYS** after the completion of the work in which to file a mechanic's lien on the property.

b. Recorded

1. General Contractor - When the notice of completion is recorded, then the general contractor will only have **60 DAYS** after the completion of the work in which to file a mechanic's lien on the property.

2. Subcontractors - When the notice of completion is recorded, then the subcontractors will only have **30 DAYS** after completion of the work in which to file a mechanic's lien on the property.

Notes: 1. A mechanic's lien is a specific lien filed against the property which benefited from material or labor.

2. A mechanic's lien must be verified and recorded to be effective.

3. A mechanic's lien which is recorded today will undoubtedly take priority over an unrecorded trust deed and a trust deed that was recorded yesterday.

4. The lender will usually release the final payment on a construction loan after the lien period has expired.

5. A notice of nonresponsibility, notice of completion, and notice of cessation will all have an influence on the recordation of a mechanic's lien. A notice to quit refers to a lease and does not have any influence on a mechanic's lien.

6. All subcontractors and the general contractor may file mechanic's liens on a new subdivision.

7. A mechanic's lien may be a blanket encumbrance.

SITUATIONS:

1. An individual remodeling his own home and doing all the work himself has creditors for both an unpaid lumber bill and an unpaid hardware store bill. These creditors could take action to collect by filing mechanic's liens against the property.

2. When a construction loan is recorded after any building materials are delivered, all mechanic's liens will take priority over the loan.

EXAMPLE: May 1st - $1,000 worth of lumber is delivered.
May 2nd - $30,000 construction loan is obtained.
June 3rd - Additional lumber is delivered valued at $1,000.
July 1st - $4,000 for painting.
August 1st - Owner takes possession.
August 20th - Mechanic's liens are filed by the painter for $4,000 and the lumber company for $2,000.

On August 20th a foreclosure sale nets $30,000. Disbursement of funds from the foreclosure sale are as follows:

Net sales price	$30,000
Painter receives	4,000
Lumber company receives	2,000
Lender receives balance	24,000

3. When the general contractor is paid in full and he does not pay a subcontractor, the subcontractor may file a mechanic's lien against the property.

B. ATTACHMENT - An attachment lien is the seizure of property by court order. An attachment lien is obtained prior to court action. Property is seized and retained by the court as security for the satisfaction of a potential judgment in a lawsuit. An attachment lien will freeze the title to the property and assure the availability of the defendant's property if a judgment is awarded to an individual plaintiff.

1. An attachment is a lien.

2. An attachment lien is good for three (3) years. An extension may be given upon the approval of the court.

C. JUDGMENT - A judgment is the final court decision as to the rights of an individual in a lawsuit. A judgment is obtained after court action.

1. **Abstract of Judgment** - An abstract of judgment is an instrument given by the court which may be recorded in any county to create a judgment lien. This will usually precede the writ of execution.

2. **Writ of Execution** - A writ of execution is a court order authorizing the sale of real property to satisfy a judgment. A writ of execution is dependent upon the issuance of a judgment.

Notes: 1. A judgment is always an involuntary lien.
2. A judgment must be recorded to be effective.
3. A judgment is considered to be a general lien. A judgment recorded against the owner of a single property is a general lien.
4. A recorded judgment lien is good for ten (10) years.
5. A writ of execution is considered to be a lien.
6. When comparing a judgment to a mechanic's lien, a judgment is effective when recorded; however, a mechanic's lien may be effective prior to its recording date because the mechanic's lien rights start on the date of commencement of construction.

D. DEFICIENCY JUDGMENT - In the event of default and foreclosure, a lender may have the opportunity to secure a deficiency judgment on a trust deed.

   1. A deficiency judgment may be obtained on the following:

      a. A note secured by a trust deed executed in favor of a private lender to secure a loan in which the funds were used to purchase an automobile.

      b. A purchase money trust deed where the rights of the federal government are affected (F.H.A and V.A insured or guaranteed loans by the federal government).

   2. A deficiency judgment cannot be obtained when:

      a. The loan is a purchase money trust deed.

      b. The remedy of "power of sale" is used to foreclose by a Trustee's Sale.

      c. The fair market value of the property exceeds the total encumbrances on the property.

      d. A note is secured by a first trust deed, executed in favor of a conventional lender, with the proceeds used to purchase a single family residence.

      e. A note is secured by a second trust deed executed by the buyer in favor of the seller of the property.

      f. A note that is secured by a first trust deed is taken back by a subdivider as part of the purchase price on an improved lot.

E. LIS PENDENS - A lis pendens is an instrument filed with the county recorder to give constructive notice to the public that the title or right to the possession of a specific property is in litigation. A lis pendens is not a lien; however, it is similar to an attachment lien because it is used to freeze the assets of an individual prior to a judgment being awarded by the court. A lis pendens will go into effect when recorded prior to court action. It will remain in effect throughout the court proceedings and continue in effect until the final judgment is rendered by the court.

F. PROTECTION AGAINST A JUDGMENT - The owner of real property which is used as a principal residential dwelling may protect his home against unsecured judgment creditors by filing at the County Recorder's Office an instrument referred to as a **DECLARATION OF HOMESTEAD.**

   1. Qualified Property - In order for a property to qualify for the homestead exemption, it must be the place where the individual resides and may include, but is not limited to, the following:

      a. A single family residence.
      b. A mobile home.
      c. A houseboat.
      d. A condominium.
      e. A stock cooperative.

f. A community apartment project.

g. An apartment building in which the owner occupies one unit as his residence.

h. A single family residence with adjoining vacant land on which the owner is planning to construct an additional rental unit.

2. Unqualified Property

a. Vacant land.

b. A personal residence that is presently under construction.

3. Requirements for a Valid Homestead

a. A homestead must contain:

1. The name of the declared homestead owner (name of the spouse, if married).
2. Description of the property.
3. A statement that the claimant is a resident on the property at the time the homestead is recorded.

b. The homestead must be recorded to be valid.

c. The homestead must include a statement that the facts stated in the homestead declaration are known to be true as the personal knowledge of the individual executing the homestead.

4. Amount of Homestead Exemption

a. A **$50,000** exemption is allowed for a single person (any member of a household who is not head of a family unit).

b. A **$75,000** exemption is allowed for married individuals and for an individual who is head or member of a family unit.

c. A **$100,000** exemption is allowed for any individual who is at least 65 years of age or when declarant is physically or mentally disabled.

5. Termination of the Homestead

a. Recordation of a **DECLARATION OF ABANDONMENT** will terminate the homestead (Voluntary abandonment).

b. Sale of the property automatically terminates the homestead. An individual selling his property by grant deed does not have to record a declaration of abandonment to create a valid homestead on his new property (Involuntary abandonment).

c. A homestead may be invalidated by the recordation of a second homestead which, by its terms and conditions, abandons the previously recorded homestead (the new homestead must declare that it supersedes the prior homestead).

d. Moving from the property does not terminate the homestead.

e . Renting the property does not terminate the homestead.

f . A homestead may be invalidated by a homestead recorded on another property.

6 . **Legal Effect of the Homestead** - When the equity in the property exceeds the amount of the homestead exemption, the property could be sold to satisfy the judgment creditors. In the event the property value exceeds the amount of the homestead exemption and the liens, a judgment holder can have the property sold and he will receive the amount due him above the exemption and liens.

EXAMPLE 1: One spouse executed and recorded a homestead on a personal residence which is valued at $63,000 and encumbered with a $29,000 first trust deed. This property could not be sold because there is insufficient equity to satisfy a creditor ($63,000 minus $29,000 equals $34,000 equity. The exemption for a married individual is $75,000. The $34,000 equity does not exceed the $75,000 exemption; therefore, the property cannot be sold).

EXAMPLE 2: An individual who is the head of a household filed a homestead on his residence, which is worth $126,000. There is a $58,000 first trust deed recorded against the property. When a creditor recorded a $14,000 judgment lien against the property, what is the legal effect of the homestead?

Value	$126,000
First trust deed	-58,000
Equity balance	68,000
Exemption	75,000

Conclusion: The equity does not exceed the exemption; therefore, the creditor cannot force the sale of the property.

EXAMPLE 3: A $25,000 judgment is obtained by a creditor against Mr. & Mrs. Slick. The homestead was recorded prior to the judgment. The property is sold for $138,000 and the balance of the first trust deed is $50,000. The judgment creditor could force the sale of the property because the equity exceeds the exemption.

Value	$138,000
First trust deed	-50,000
Equity balance	88,000
Exemption	75,000

Conclusion: The equity exceeds the exemption by $13,000; therefore, the property can be sold to partially satisfy the judgment. The creditor will receive $13,000 cash and a $12,000 deficiency judgment against Mr. & Mrs. Slick ($25,000 Judgment - $13,000 Received = $12,000 Deficiency Judgment).

7. **Reinvestment of Exemption** - When a property is sold to satisfy a judgment, the individual owner receives a homestead exemption. The amount of the homestead exemption must be reinvested into another personal residence within **SIX (6) MONTHS** after the sale. When the amount of the exemption is not reinvested within six months, then a creditor with a deficiency judgment can collect on his judgment. In other words, the money is not exempt when it is not reinvested within the six month time period.

Notes:
1. A homestead must be recorded to be effective.

2. A homestead is not a lien on real property.

3. A homestead is only valid on one (1) property at a time (a personal residence).

4. A husband or wife may declare a homestead without the consent of the other spouse.

5. A statement that the claimant is married is not a requirement for a valid declaration of homestead.

6. A judgment has prior claim to a declaration of homestead when either the judgment is recorded prior to the homestead, when the homestead is invalid, or when the homestead has been abandoned or relinquished.

7. A homestead does not protect against secured liens such as taxes, mortgages, trust deeds, or mechanic's liens.

G. LIEN REVIEW

1. Assessment liens and tax liens will be discussed in another chapter.

2. Taxes and public improvement assessments have priority over trust deeds and mechanic's liens contrary to the date created. **EXAMPLE:** A public improvement assessment created on April 15, 1985 has priority over a trust deed executed on March 27, 1985 and recorded on March 29, 1985, a trust deed executed and recorded on March 28, 1985, and a mechanic's lien resulting from work started on March 27, 1985.

3. A lien is an encumbrance.

4. A lien is a creditor's right in the property of the debtor that may be used to satisfy the debt.

5. Voluntary liens include mortgages, trust deeds, and land contracts.

6. Involuntary liens include mechanic's liens, attachments, judgments, taxes, and assessments.

7. A specific lien is on a specific property or properties. Examples include a mortgage, trust deed, land contract, assessment, attachment, property taxes, mechanic's lien, and homeowner's association fees.

8. A general lien is on any property of the debtor. Examples include judgment, income tax liens, inheritance tax, corporation and franchise taxes, and the decedent's debts.

9. Deed restrictions, leases, and easements are not liens. They are contractual limitations of ownership.

10. A mortgage is both a lien and a contractual limitation of ownership.

11. Government liens always take priority over all other liens. Multiple government liens will usually have parity with one another.

REVIEW QUIZ

SECTION I - Matching - Select the letter below which best describes, defines, or relates to the following numbered terms.

1. Mechanic's lien
2. Attachment
3. Writ of execution
4. Abstract of judgment
5. Lis pendens
6. Homestead
7. Notice of completion
8. Notice of nonresponsibility
9. Declaration of abandonment
10. Judgment

a. A court order authorizing the sale of real property to satisfy a judgment.
b. Protects the home from a forced sale by judgment creditors.
c. A legal notice indicating a pending lawsuit.
d. Protects the owner against liens created by parties in possession of the property.
e. Shortens the filing period for mechanic's liens.
f. A specific lien filed against a property which benefited from material or labor.
g. Is always a general lien.
h. An instrument given by the court which may be recorded in any county to create a judgment lien.
i. Terminates the homestead when recorded.
j. The actual seizure of property for payment of money prior to obtaining a judgment.

SECTION II - True/False - Select either true or false in response to the following statements.

1. Mechanic's lien rights start on the date of commencement of construction.
2. A mechanic's lien is a general lien.
3. A mechanic's lien must be recorded to be effective.
4. A mechanic's lien that is recorded today will undoubtedly take priority over both an unrecorded trust deed and a trust deed that was recorded yesterday.
5. An attachment lien is good for five years.
6. A judgment recorded against the owner of a single property is a general lien.
7. A deficiency judgment may be obtained if the loan is a purchase money trust deed.
8. A homestead is a specific lien.
9. Sale of the property automatically terminates the homestead.
10. Public improvement assessments have priority over trust deeds and mechanic's liens contrary to the date recorded.

SECTION III - Multiple Choice - Select the letter which best completes the statement or answers the question.

1. A money judgment when recorded is always:

   A. A voluntary lien.
   B. An involuntary lien.
   C. A superior lien.
   D. An equitable lien.

2. A creditor's right in the property of the debtor that may be used to satisfy the debt is, in its broadest sense, referred to as:

   A. An attachment.
   B. A judgment.
   C. A lien.
   D. A pledge.

3. Lis pendens is in effect:

   A. Until legal action begins.
   B. During court proceedings.
   C. Until final judgment.
   D. All of the above.

4. Who can file a mechanic's lien on a new subdivision?

   A. Architect.
   B. Contractor and subcontractor.
   C. Grade operators.
   D. All of the above.

5. Robert Smith purchased a home from Henry Jones who took back a trust deed for part of the purchase price. This encumbrance is:

   A. A specific lien.
   B. A general lien.
   C. An individual lien.
   D. None of the above.

6. A recorded judgment lien is valid for:

   A. 1 year.
   B. 3 years.
   C. 5 years.
   D. 10 years.

7. A search of the county records in the county recorder's office will, in all cases, reveal a valid and existing:

   A. Easement.
   B. Homestead.
   C. Land contract of sale.
   D. Security agreement.

8. From the date of levy, if no extension is given by the courts, an attachment lien outlaws:

   A. In 1 year.
   B. In 3 years.
   C. In 5 years.
   D. Never.

9. Who would be least likely held liable for a deficiency judgment in the event of foreclosure?

   A. Grantee who assumes a loan from the grantor.
   B. Grantor whose loan was taken over by the grantee on a "subject to" basis.
   C. Grantor whose loan was assumed by the grantee.
   D. Trustor who defaulted on a loan and lost the property through the Trustee's Sale.

10. An action that is dependent upon the issuance of a judgment is:

    A. A writ of attachment.
    B. Unlawful detainer.
    C. A desist and refrain order.
    D. A writ of execution.

11. In the State of California, an individual cannot receive a deficiency judgment if:

    A. The loan is a purchase money trust deed.
    B. Remedy of power of sale is used.
    C. Fair market value of the property exceeds the sum of the encumbrances.
    D. Any of the above.

12. Mr. Jones is using Mr. Smith's swimming pool and suffered an injury. If Jones instituted court action and obtained a judgment against Smith for $2,500, it would be:

    A. A voluntary lien.
    B. A general lien.
    C. A specific lien.
    D. An abstract lien.

13. A judgment when recorded against the owner of a single property is:

    A. A general lien.
    B. A specific lien.
    C. A voluntary lien.
    D. Not a lien until the writ of execution is given.

14. A member of a household who is not head of the household may file a homestead declaration for an exemption of:

    A. $30,000.
    B. $45,000.
    C. $50,000.
    D. $75,000.

15. A mechanic's lien filed today undoubtedly takes priority over:

   A. A trust deed recorded yesterday.
   B. A tax lien.
   C. An unrecorded trust deed executed last week.
   D. Both A and C.

Answers may be found in Appendix C (Back of text)

NON-MONEY ENCUMBRANCES

A. EASEMENT - An easement is a nonpossessory interest to use the land of another individual for the purpose of ingress and egress. This means that an individual has the right to enter and leave his property by crossing property which is owned by another individual. An easement is not an estate, it is the right to the use and enjoyment of another's property short of an estate.

1. Parties to an Easement

　　a. Dominant Tenement - The property which benefits from the easement.

　　　　1. The dominant tenement does not have to join the servient tenement at the boundary line.

　　　　2. The dominant tenement can never retain any rights to an easement with the transfer of title to the property (the grantor cannot keep the easement).

　　b. Servient Tenement - The property which is burdened by the easement.

　　　　1. The property in which the easement crosses over is the servient tenement.

　　　　2. The servient tenement furnishes the easement for the dominant tenement.

2. Appurtenant Easement - An appurtenant easement requires two parcels of land owned by two different individuals. An appurtenant easement belongs to the dominant tenement and **RUNS WITH THE LAND.** This means that the easement is capable of being transferred when the property is sold by the owner of the dominant tenement. The new buyer automatically receives the existing easement and will have the same rights to it as the previous owner.

3. Easement in Gross - An easement in gross is an easement which is not appurtenant to any specific land. It is a personal right that is not attached to the land; therefore, a dominant tenement does not exist. An encumbrance is created on the land and, in effect, constitutes an interest in the land.

　　a. The right of a utility company to erect poles and string wires across the land is an easement in gross.

　　b. An easement in gross is the most common type of easement on residential property.

4. **Creation of an Easement** - An easement is usually created for the benefit of the owner of adjacent property. An easement may be created by:

   a. **Dedication** - Land that is given for public use.

   b. **Deed** - An easement may be created by conveyance.

   c. **Implication of Law** (Necessity) - An easement is created by necessity so a property is never landlocked. An easement is created when there is continuous and obvious use over a long duration.

   d. **Condemnation** - A government agency may take land for an easement under the power of eminent domain.

   e. **Prescription** - An easement is created by securing the use of the land by adverse possession. The legal right to acquire the easement is based on actual physical use of the property. This means to use the property against the wishes of the owner. The requirements for obtaining a prescriptive easement are generally the same requirements as obtaining title to property by adverse possession. A prescriptive easement must meet all the same requirements of adverse possession, except payment of the property taxes. The prescriptive easement does not convey title, it is only a right to use the land which is owned by another individual. Requirements include:

      1. Open and notorious use of the property.
      2. Possession must be continuously and uninterrupted for five (5) years.
      3. Some evidence of claim of right (this claim of use may be based on nothing more than the physical use of the property).
      4. Possession must be hostile to the owner (against his wishes).

5. **Termination of an Easement** - An easement may be terminated by the following:

   a. **Destruction of the Servient Tenement** (the improvement is destroyed).

   b. **Agreement Between the Parties**

      1. Abandonment.
      2. Quiet Title Action.
      3. Written release by the dominant tenement (quitclaim deed).

   c. **Merger** - Merger of the dominant tenement with the servient tenement.

   d. **Non-use for Five (5) Years** - A prescriptive easement is the only easement that can be terminated by non-use.

Notes: 1. An easement is real property.
2. An easement is an encumbrance on real property. Land subject to an easement is said to be encumbered.
3. An easement is not a lien.
4. An easement does not have to be mentioned in a deed.
5. A deed to an unlocated easement is valid.
6. When an individual is not a property owner, but has an easement across a property, he has an easement in gross.

7. An easement in gross encumbers the servient tenement.
8. An easement in gross does not benefit the adjacent land.
9. The terms dominant and servient refer to an easement.
10. A lessee may create an easement across the leased property for the benefit of a third party for the duration of the lease.
11. Permissive use of a road through another individual's property would prevent the creation of an easement by prescription.
12. An easement may be created by prescription when the property is used openly for a period of five (5) years.
13. An easement can never be terminated by prescription, at will by the owner of the property, or revocation by the servient tenement.
14. An easement is an interest which may be protected against interference by any outside third party.
15. Termination due to non-use refers to a prescriptive easement.
16. An easement may be terminated by filing a quitclaim deed.
17. When a subdivider gives a ten (10) foot easement for utility purposes across the rear of all the properties, this is referred to as an easement in gross.
18. Similar to adverse possession; a confrontation with the owner is not required to create a prescriptive easement.

B. LICENSE - A license is a personal, nonassignable, and revocable permission to enter the property of another individual for a specific reason without possessing any interest therein.

1. Examples include meter reader and invited business or social guests.

2. A license is different than an easement because a license may be revoked.

C. NUISANCE - An interference or obstruction to the use and enjoyment of the property (overhanging trees, noise, pollution, odors, etc.).

D. ENCROACHMENT - The extension of a building or other structure on one property onto an adjoining property.

1. An encroachment is an encumbrance.

2. A neighbor has three (3) years to pursue his legal rights to have an encroachment removed from his property.

E. RESTRICTION - A restriction is a limitation as to the use of real property. Restrictions on real property are created by government regulations and private restrictions (agreement between the parties or by deed).

1. Government Regulations (POLICE POWER) - The federal, state, and local governments have the authority to regulate the use of property in order to protect and preserve the health, safety, morals, and general welfare of the public. Prior to the use of government restrictions, the use of property was usually determined by the highest and best use based on economic considerations.

a. Planning Commission - Every city and county within the State of California must have a planning commission.

1. **Master Plan** - The primary function of the planning commission is to develop and execute a master plan for the community. The master plan will include both a general and specific plan for the community. A general plan would normally include:

   a. Residential, industrial, and commercial areas.
   b. Streets and highways to include arterial highways.
   c. Existing patterns of public streets.
   d. Flow of traffic on freeways.
   e. Seismic safety.
   f. An economic base with shopping centers and trade facilities.
   g. Adequacy of air and surface transportation (airline terminal, bus and train depot).

   After the general plan has been adopted, the planning commission can create a specific plan to specify the type of development which is best suited for the environment.

2. **Environmental Impact Report** - An environmental impact report may be required by the local planning commission prior to the approval of any new subdivision. The reason for this report is to spell out the major impact of the proposed project on the environment, to show ways to mitigate or relieve the impact of the project on the environment, and to offer alternative solutions to the project.

3. **Zoning** - The planning commission has the authority to create zoning laws which specify the use of a property in a certain location. This is probably the best tool used to create a master plan. The primary reason for zoning laws is to promote the general health, safety, and welfare of the community. Zoning laws promote orderly growth and control urban expansion, prevent an encroachment on agricultural land, and prohibit the undesirable use of land rather than compelling specific use of land. Zoning laws do not control street design or construction. When a city or county establishes land use restrictions on a property with respect to building use, building height, and set-backs, this is an example of zoning. Zoning by a municipality is the best example of police power. Zoning symbols are inconsistent throughout the state; however, here are some basic symbols:

   A - Agricultural
   C - Commercial
   M - Manufacturing or Industrial
   P - Parking
   R - Residential

4. **Rezoning** - In most situations, zoning ordinances cannot be created to be retroactive. However, in eliminating nonconforming uses from an area, rezoning ordinances may be created to allow for a reasonable period of time within which any such abuses can be eliminated from the environment, or to prohibit rebuilding and expansion. The highest and best use of the property is not always the same as the zoning restriction; therefore, zoning restrictions could cause a property to be more unmarketable than private deed restrictions because zoning restrictions legally impose restrictions on the use of the property. Changes in the zoning ordinances could alter the

use of the property and affect the value of the property. When a petition for rezoning is denied, it may be appealed to the City Council or the County Board of Supervisors. Any unreasonable decision in reference to rezoning may be further appealed by taking judicial action.

5. **Variance** - A variance is a petition for a one time minor change which will permit a property to be used for a purpose other than indicated by the present zoning. This exception of use requested in the variance cannot be offensive to the neighbors. An individual owner who suffers a hardship because of a change in zoning can receive an exception variance to the new zoning which will be a benefit to him. When a petition for a variance is denied, it may be appealed to the City Council or the County Board of Supervisors. Any unreasonable decision in reference to a variance may be further appealed by taking judicial action.

b. **Housing and Construction** - The housing and construction industries in California are governed and controlled by the State Housing Law, the Local Building Code, the Contractors License Law and the Health and Safety Code.

1. **State Housing Law** - The State Housing Law sets the minimum building requirements throughout the entire State of California. It applies even when a county has a Local Building Code. The State Housing Law is enforced by the **LOCAL BUILDING INSPECTOR**.

2. **Local Building Code** - The Local Building Code sets the minimum building requirements for the local community. This includes protection of the health and safety of the community. The Local Building Code is enforced by the **LOCAL BUILDING INSPECTOR**.

   a. **Building Permit** - Prior to construction, a building permit must be obtained from the Department of Building and Safety. This allows for the enforcement of the building code and protects the property values in the neighborhood.

   b. **Exception** - An individual builder wishes to specifically replace materials which have not been approved in accordance with the Local Building Code. The local building inspector could approve the "exception" if it would not constitute a safety hazard.

   c. When comparing the Local Building Code to the State or Federal Building Codes, the code which has the highest standard for health and safety will prevail (**THE MOST STRINGENT WILL PREVAIL**).

   d. The Local Building Code does not establish the cost or type of material to be used, nor does it include the size, height, or architectural design for buildings.

3. **Contractors License Law** - Any individual who works as a contractor to improve real property must be licensed by the Contractors State License Board. This protects the general public against fraud by contractors and subcontractors. The Contractors License Law is enforced by State Officials.

83

4. **Health and Safety Code** - The Health and Safety Code sets the minimum health requirements within the State of California. The Health and Safety Code is concerned with subdivision sanitation. Approval and control of sanitary facilities is enforced by the **LOCAL HEALTH OFFICE.**

2. **Private Restrictions** (Deed Restrictions) - Private restrictions may be referred to as covenants, conditions, and restrictions (**CC&R's**). They may be created by deed, a written agreement, or by the general plan of the subdivision restrictions. Deed restrictions are usually created by the developer of the new subdivision. The most common procedure to establish deed restrictions in a new subdivision is to record the **DECLARATION OF RESTRICTIONS** in the County Recorder's Office; then, in the deed to each buyer, make reference to the recorded restrictions. Deed restrictions, as a general rule, are created for the protection of property owners. Deed restrictions are considered to be reasonable limitations on ownership which protect the value of property. Private restrictions in a deed do not usually affect the marketability of real property; rather, they enhance the property by protection of the condition of the property.

a. **Covenant** - A covenant is an agreement written into a deed or other instrument to do or not to do a certain activity. A covenant may insist upon certain uses or non-uses of the property. The penalty for violation of a covenant is judicial action for **MONETARY DAMAGES** or an **INJUNCTION.**

b. **Condition** - A condition is a qualification of ownership which can only be created by a **DEED.** The penalty for violation of a condition may result in the **FORFEITURE OF TITLE.** A condition may be classified as a Condition Precedent or Condition Subsequent.

1. **Condition Precedent -** A qualification of a contract or transfer of property providing that unless and until a given event occurs, the full effect of a contract or transfer will not take place. This means that the condition must be met prior to the transfer of title.

2. **Condition Subsequent** - A condition attached to an already vested estate or to a contract whereby the estate is defeated or the contract is extinguished through the failure or nonperformance of the condition. This means that if the condition is not met, there may be a loss in the ownership of the property.

Notes: 1. The California State Legislature authorizes the city or county to create zoning ordinances (State enabling acts allow for the creation of zoning laws and restrictions).

2. Restrictions affect the physical aspects of the property. Restrictions have nothing to do with the debts or liens against the property.

3. The use of land is enforced by the owner of the land, the owner's agreement as to how the land is to be used, and by the government.

4. The primary function of deed restrictions and zoning ordinances is to protect and stabilize property values. The availability of public transportation is also required to stabilize property values in a residential neighborhood. Newness of a single family residence does not usually stabilize value.

5. Declaration of Restrictions - A Declaration of Restrictions is a written instrument which is used to create restrictions on a new subdivision.

6. Deed restrictions are created by the grantor to restrict the use of the property for any legitimate purpose.

7. Deed restrictions are encumbrances on real property which benefit the grantee.

8. The most common procedure to enforce private restrictions on real property is an injunction.

9. An individual property owner should consult the zoning laws and deed restrictions prior to building a fence on his property.

10. Condemnation is not considered to be Police Power.

11. When the local zoning laws contain a provision "for residential purposes only", they do not limit the size of the buildings. Instead, they allow the builder to construct a single family dwelling, a duplex, a triplex, a fourplex, or a large apartment complex.

12. A condition is different from a covenant because a condition can only be created by deed. A covenant may be created at a later time.

13. The penalty for violation of a condition is more stringent than the penalty for violation of a covenant.

14. Restrictions on a new subdivision usually include limitation on the size of each property, limitation on the square footage of the improvements and the number of stories or height of the improvements.

15. A deed restriction which prohibits the placement of a " for sale sign" on the property in a new subdivision is unenforceable because it infringes upon the owner's right to sell his property.

16. A restriction that sets the minimum amount of money allowed for improvements on the property is unenforceable.

17. The most stringent restriction usually prevails. **EXAMPLE:** A subdivider required a 15,000 square foot minimum lot size; subsequently, the local authorities changed the zoning laws to require a 10,000 square foot minimum lot size. In this example, the original deed restrictions take precedence.

18. There is no compensation for Police Power.

19. Land use planning and zoning ordinances are examples of Police Power. A deed restriction is not an example of Police Power.

20. A zoning regulation permits a specific use of the property. When a deed restriction limits the zoning regulation, the deed restriction will prevail.

21. Certificate of Occupancy - An instrument issued by the building inspector to certify that the building is ready for occupancy.

22. Changes in zoning (public restrictions) may be initiated by a subdivider, developer, individual property owner, or the government.

23. **Injunction** - A court order preventing a person from acting or restraining a person from doing a specific act.

24. **Down zoning** means to change from high density use to a lower density use. Examples include down zoning from C-1 to R-1 or from R-3 to R-1.

25. Eminent domain is not considered to be a portion of police power or zoning.

26. Local building codes usually set the highest building requirements.

REVIEW QUIZ

SECTION I - **Matching** - Select the letter below which best describes, defines, or relates to the following numbered terms.

1. License
2. Servient Tenement
3. Encroachment
4. Variance
5. Easement
6. Covenant
7. Dominant Tenement
8. Exception
9. Police Power
10. Condition

a. The right to the use and enjoyment of another's property short of an estate.
b. A one time minor change which will permit a property to be used for a purpose other than current zoning.
c. A builder's request to substitute material not approved by the building code.
d. The property which is burdened by the easement.
e. A qualification of an estate which is created in a deed.
f. The authority of the federal, state, and local governments to regulate land use.
g. A promise to do or not to do a certain act.
h. The property which benefits from an easement.
i. To build an improvement across the property line onto an adjoining property.
j. A personal, nonassignable, and revocable permission to enter a property for a specific reason.

SECTION II - **True/False** - Select either true or false in response to the following statements.

1. The dominant tenement must join the servient tenement at the boundary line.
2. A dominant tenement cannot retain any rights to an easement with the transfer of title to the property.
3. A prescriptive easement can be obtained by open and notorious use over a long period of time.
4. An easement is a nonpossessory interest in real estate.
5. An easement is considered to be personal property.
6. An appurtenant easement is the most common type of easement on residential property.
7. A neighbor has three years in which to pursue his legal rights to have an encroachment removed from his property.
8. A deed restriction is an example of Police Power.
9. Zoning ordinances control street design and construction.
10. When the local building code is in effect, a builder must comply with the least stringent of the local building codes and the state housing laws.

SECTION III - Multiple Choice - Select the letter which best completes the statement or answers the question.

1. The authority which allows government bodies to create restrictions and zoning ordinances was made legally possible by:

   A. The planning commission.
   B. The master plan of each county.
   C. State enabling acts.
   D. City and county ordinances.

2. Land subject to an easement is said to be:

   A. Encumbered.
   B. Restrained.
   C. Rescinded.
   D. Appurtenant thereto.

3. All of the following are correct in reference to an appurtenant easement, except:

   A. The dominant tenement would benefit and the servient tenement would be burdened.
   B. The easement would run with the land.
   C. There must be two tracts of land under separate ownership.
   D. The dominant tenement must join the servient tenement at the border.

4. An easement may be terminated by all of the following procedures, except:

   A. Abandonment.
   B. Merger of the dominant tenement with the servient tenement.
   C. Prescription by the owner of the servient tenement.
   D. Release by the owner of the dominant tenement.

5. An easement on real property may be terminated by filing:

   A. A reconveyance deed.
   B. A quitclaim deed.
   C. A defeasance clause.
   D. A statement of nonresponsibility.

6. A subdivider granted a seven foot easement across the rear of all his lots for utility purposes. This is referred to as:

   A. A prescriptive easement.
   B. An easement in gross.
   C. An appurtenant easement.
   D. A dedicated easement.

7. Zoning regulations established by a municipality will have all of the following effects, except:

   A. Control building construction and street designs.
   B. Prohibit undesirable use of land rather than compelling specific ones.
   C. Prevent encroachment on agricultural land.
   D. Promote orderly growth and control urban expansion.

8. A deed to an unlocated easement is:

   A. Valid.
   B. Void.
   C. Unenforceable.
   D. Voidable.

9. An appurtenant easement is:

   A. An interest in land capable of transfer.
   B. Personal to the holder and incapable of transfer.
   C. An interest in land incapable of transfer.
   D. A possessory interest in the land of another person.

10. In order to protect the property values and enforce building codes, a building permit should be obtained prior to the commencement of construction from:

   A. The planning commission.
   B. The county building inspector.
   C. The county health office.
   D. The board of supervisors.

11. The parcel of land referred to as the servient tenement:

   A. Loses its status upon transfer of title.
   B. Is the portion burdened by the easement.
   C. Has an easement appurtenant attached thereto.
   D. Is the portion benefited by the easement.

12. The requirements for taking an easement by prescription are basically the same as those for taking title to property by:

   A. Adverse possession.
   B. Eminent domain.
   C. Neither A nor B.
   D. Both A and B.

13. Kent purchased real property from Jackson which included an appurtenant easement for use of a road. The deed to the buyer had an adequate description of the land but did not make any reference to the easement. The buyer:

   A. Received a clouded title.
   B. Releases the easement to the servient tenement.
   C. Took title to landlocked property without a right of entry.
   D. Has the same rights as Jackson had to the easement.

14. A man purchased a property and discovered after the close of escrow that a neighbor's fence was four feet over the property boundary line on his side. The broker was unaware of this fact. The two neighbors were unable to reach an amicable settlement. In this situation:

A. The neighbor had acquired title by adverse possession.
B. The buyer could hold the broker responsible.
C. The buyer could sue the neighbor for encroachment based on trespass.
D. The buyer could sue the title insurance company under a standard policy of title insurance.

15. All of the following are liens on real property, except:

A. Unpaid recorded judgment against unsecured debts.
B. Unpaid real property taxes.
C. Recorded restrictions.
D. Installment payment on bond assessment not yet due.

Answers may be found in Appendix C (Back of text)

DEPARTMENT OF REAL ESTATE

Most laws in California originated from English Common Law; however, Community Property laws originated from Spanish Law through the Treaty of Guadalupe Hidalgo between Mexico and the United States. The actual real estate laws are created by the **State Legislature** and are contained in the **Business and Professions Code**.

A. **REAL ESTATE COMMISSIONER** - The Real Estate Commissioner is the chief executive officer of the Department of Real Estate. The Commissioner is appointed by the governor. His primary responsibility is to determine administrative policy and enforce the provisions of the real estate law. Regulations of the Real Estate Commissioner have the force and effect of law.

1. To qualify for an appointment as the Real Estate Commissioner, an individual must have been actively engaged in the real estate business as a broker for five years or possess related experience associated with the real estate industry.

2. The Commissioner has the power to hold formal hearings to determine issues which involve a licensee. The Commissioner must exercise his rights against a licensee within three (3) years after the violation of the real estate law. This time period may be extended to ten (10) years when the violation was fraud.

3. When the Commissioner requires legal advice, he will consult with the State Attorney General.

4. Duties of the Commissioner do not replace court action. Violations of the real estate law will be prosecuted by the District Attorney in the county where the alleged violation took place.

B. **REAL ESTATE ADVISORY COMMISSION** - The Real Estate Advisory Commission will meet at least four (4) times per year to consult and discuss with the Commissioner the policies and procedures of the Department of Real Estate which best serve the public and those licensed by the department. The members of the real estate advisory commission are appointed by the Commissioner.

1. The real estate advisory commission consists of ten (10) members. To qualify for an appointment to the real estate advisory commission:

   a. Six (6) members must have been actively engaged as real estate brokers.

   b. Four (4) members may be selected from the general public who possess related experience associated with the real estate industry.

2. Members of the real estate advisory commission serve without any compensation; however, actual expenses may be refunded when performing duties in connection with the real estate advisory commission.

C. REAL ESTATE FUND - The real estate fund is divided into two accounts.

1 . **Education and Research Account** - Eight (8%) percent of all license fees collected are placed into the education and research account. These funds are used for education and research programs to monitor the many changes in the real estate industry in order to protect the general welfare of the public.

2 . **Recovery Account** (Recovery Fund) - Twelve (12%) percent of all license fees collected are placed into the recovery account. The recovery fund was created to protect the general public. It provides funds for an individual who has received a judgment against a real estate broker for misrepresentation, or any other illegal action. When the broker does not have any means to pay the judgment, or has filed bankruptcy, the judgment creditor may seek reimbursement for damages from the recovery fund.

   a . **$20,000 Maximum** - Each claimant or each transaction may receive a maximum of $20,000 from the recovery fund.

   EXAMPLE 1: An individual who obtained a $22,000 judgment against an insolvent broker would receive a maximum of $20,000 from the recovery fund.

   EXAMPLE 2: Three owners have a 1/5th, 1/5th, and 3/5ths undivided ownership interest in a property that the broker misrepresented to them. They obtain a $25,000 judgment against an insolvent broker. The individual with the 3/5ths interest would receive a maximum of $12,000 from the recovery fund. ($20,000 multiplied by 3/5th equals $12,000).

   b . **$100,000 Maximum for Multiple Transactions** - The maximum amount which may be received from the real estate fund against a single broker is $100,000.

   c . The real estate license will be suspended until repayment is made to the fund.

REGULATIONS OF THE REAL ESTATE COMMISSIONER

Ethics and Professional Conduct Code

CODE OF ETHICS AND PROFESSIONAL CONDUCT

2785. Professional Conduct. In order to enhance the professionalism of the California real estate industry, and maximize protection for members of the public dealing with real estate licensees, whatever their area of practice, the following standards of professional conduct and business practices are adopted.

(a) Unlawful Conduct in Sale, Lease and Exchange Transactions. Licensees when performing acts within the meaning of Section 10131 (a) of the Business and Professions Code shall not engage in conduct which would subject the licensee to adverse action, penalty or discipline under Sections 10176 and 10177 of the Business and Professions Code including, but not limited to, the following acts and omissions:

(1) Knowingly making a substantial misrepresentation of the likely value of real property to:

(A) Its owner either for the purpose of securing a listing or for the purpose of acquiring an interest in the property for the licensee's own account.

(B) A prospective buyer for the purpose of inducing the buyer to make an offer to purchase the real property.

(2) Representing to an owner of real property when seeking a listing that the licensee has obtained a bona fide written offer to purchase the property, unless at the time of the representation the licensee has possession of a bona fide written offer to purchase.

(3) Stating or implying to an owner of real property during listing negotiations that the licensee is precluded by law, by regulation, or by the rules of any organization, other than the broker firm seeking the listing, from charging less than the commission or fee quoted to the owner by the licensee.

(4) Knowingly making substantial misrepresentations regarding the licensee's relationship with an individual broker, corporate broker, or franchised brokerage company or that entity's/person's responsibility for the licensee's activities.

(5) Knowingly underestimating the probable closing costs in a communication to the prospective buyer or seller of real property in order to induce that person to make or to accept an offer to purchase the property.

(6) Knowingly making a false or misleading representation to the seller of real property as to the form, amount and/or treatment of a deposit toward the purchase of the property made by an offeror.

(7) Knowingly making a false or misleading representation to a seller of real property, who has agreed to finance all or part of a purchase price by carrying back a loan, about a buyer's ability to repay the loan in accordance with its terms and conditions.

(8) Making an addition to or modification of the terms of an instrument previously signed or initialed by a party to a transaction without the knowledge and consent of the party.

(9) A representation made as a principal or agent to a prospective purchaser of a promissory note secured by real property about the market value of the securing property without a reasonable basis for believing the truth and accuracy of the representation.

(10) Knowingly making a false or misleading representation or representing, without a reasonable basis for believing its truth, the nature and/or condition of the interior or exterior features of a property when soliciting an offer.

(11) Knowingly making a false or misleading representation or representing, without a reasonable basis for believing its truth, the size of a parcel, square footage of improvements or the location of the boundary lines of real property being offered for sale, lease or exchange.

(12) Knowingly making a false or misleading representation or representing to a prospective buyer or lessee of real property, without a reasonable basis to believe its truth, that the property can be used for certain purposes with the intent of inducing the prospective buyer or lessee to acquire an interest in the real property.

(13) When acting in the capacity of an agent in a transaction for the sale, lease or exchange of real property, failing to disclose to a prospective purchaser or lessee facts known to the licensee materially affecting the value or desirability of the property, when the licensee has reason to believe that such facts are not known to nor readily observable by a prospective purchaser or lessee.

(14) Willfully failing, when acting as a listing agent, to present or cause to be presented to the owner of the property any written offer to purchase received prior to the closing of a sale, unless expressly instructed by the owner not to present such an offer, or unless the offer is patently frivolous.

(15) When acting as the listing agent, presenting competing written offers to purchase real property to the owner in such a manner as to induce the owner to accept the offer which will provide the greatest compensation to the listing broker without regard to the benefits, advantages and/or disadvantages to the owner.

(16) Failing to explain to the parties or prospective parties to a real estate transaction for whom the licensee is acting as an agent the meaning and probable significance of a contingency in an offer or contract that the licensee knows or reasonably believes may affect the closing date of the transaction, or the timing of the vacating of the property by the seller or its occupancy by the buyer.

(17) Failing to disclose to the seller of real property in a transaction in which the licensee is an agent for the seller the nature and extent of any direct or indirect interest that the licensee expects to acquire as a result of the sale. The prospective purchase of the property by a person related to the licensee by blood or marriage, purchase by an entity in which the licensee has an ownership interest, or purchase by any other person with whom the licensee occupies a special relationship where there is a reasonable probability that the licensee could be indirectly acquiring an interest in the property shall be disclosed to the seller.

(18) Failing to disclose to the buyer of real property in a transaction in which the licensee is an agent for the buyer the nature and extent of a licensee's direct or indirect ownership interest in such real property. The direct or indirect ownership interest in the property by a person related to the licensee by blood or marriage, by an entity in which the licensee has

an ownership interest, or by any other person with whom the licensee occupies a special relationship shall be disclosed to the buyer.

(19) Failing to disclose to a principal for whom the licensee is acting as an agent any significant interest the licensee has in a particular entity when the licensee recommends the use of the services or products of such entity.

(b) Unlawful Conduct When Soliciting, Negotiating or Arranging a Loan Secured by Real Property or the Sale of a Promissory Note Secured by Real Property. Licensees when performing acts within the meaning of subdivision (d) or (e) of Section 10131 of the Business and Professions Code shall not violate any of the applicable provisions of subdivision (a), or act in a manner which would subject the licensee to adverse action, penalty or discipline under Sections 10176 and 10177 of the Business and Professions Code including, but not limited to, the following acts and omissions:

(1) Knowingly misrepresenting to a prospective borrower of a loan to be secured by real property or to an assignor/endorser of a promissory note secured by real property that there is an existing lender willing to make the loan or that there is a purchaser for the note, for the purpose of inducing the borrower or assignor/endorser to utilize the services of the licensee.

(2) (A) Knowingly making a false or misleading representation to a prospective lender or purchaser of a loan secured directly or collaterally by real property about a borrower's ability to repay the loan in accordance with its terms and conditions;

(B) Failing to disclose to a prospective lender or note purchaser information about the prospective borrower's identity, occupation, employment, income and credit data as represented to the broker by the prospective borrower;

(C) Failing to disclose information known to the broker relative to the ability of the borrower to meet his or her potential or existing contractual obligations under the note or contract including information known about the borrower's payment history on an existing note, whether the note is in default or the borrower in bankruptcy.

(3) Knowingly underestimating the probable closing costs in a communication to a prospective borrower or lender of a loan to be secured by a lien on real property for the purpose of inducing the borrower or lender to enter into the loan transaction.

(4) When soliciting a prospective lender to make a loan to be secured by real property, falsely representing or representing without a reasonable basis to believe its truth, the priority of the security, as a lien against the real property securing the loan, i.e., a first, second or third deed of trust.

(5) Knowingly misrepresenting in any transaction that a specific service is free when the licensee knows or has a reasonable basis to know that it is covered by a fee to be charged as part of the transaction.

(6) Knowingly making a false or misleading representation to a lender or assignee/endorsee of a lender of a loan secured directly or collaterally by a lien on real property about the amount and treatment of loan payments, including loan payoffs, and the failure to account to the lender or assignee/endorsee of a lender as to the disposition of such payments.

(7) When acting as a licensee in a transaction for the purpose of obtaining a loan, and in receipt of an "advance fee" from the borrower for this purpose, the failure to account to the borrower for the disposition of the "advance fee".

(8) Knowingly making false or misleading representation about the terms and conditions of a loan to be secured by a lien on real property when soliciting a borrower or negotiating the loan.

(9) Knowingly making a false or misleading representation or representing, without a reasonable basis for believing its truth, when soliciting a lender or negotiating a loan to be secured by a lien on real property about the market value of the securing real property, the nature and/or condition of the interior or exterior features of the securing real property, its size or the square footage of any improvements on the securing real property.

REVIEW QUIZ

SECTION I - Matching - Select the letter below which best describes, defines, or relates to the following numbered terms.

1. Real Estate Commissioner
2. Community Property
3. State Legislature
4. English Common Law
5. Real Estate Advisory Commission
6. Code of Ethics and Professional Conduct
7. Business & Professions Code
8. Attorney General
9. District Attorney
10. Governor

a. Most California Laws originated from here.
b. Rules & regulations created by the Real Estate Commissioner.
c. Appointed by the Real Estate Commissioner.
d. Gives legal advice to the Real Estate Commissioner.
e. Originated from Spanish Law.
f. Contains the Real Estate Law.
g. Prosecutes violations of the Real Estate Law.
h. Appoints the Real Estate Commissioner.
i. Creates the laws for the state.
j. Primary responsibility is to determine administrative policy and enforce the provisions of the Real Estate Law.

SECTION II - True/False - Select either true or false in response to the following statements.

1. The Real Estate Law is contained in the Civil Code.
2. The actual laws in California are created by acts of the State Legislature.
3. Most laws in California originated from Spanish Law.
4. Regulations of the Real Estate Commissioner have the force and effect of law.
5. The Real Estate Commissioner must exercise his rights against a licensee within five years.
6. The Code of Ethics and Professional Conduct is a set of rules and regulations created by the Real Estate Commissioner.
7. The Code of Ethics encourages a real estate broker to be honest and truthful with all parties of a transaction.
8. The Code of Ethics encourages a real estate broker to maintain adequate, accurate, and complete records of all transactions.
9. The maximum amount which may be received from the Real Estate Fund against one broker is $250,000.
10. An individual who obtains a judgment against an insolvent broker will receive a maximum of $20,000 from the Recovery Fund.

SECTION III - **Multiple Choice** - Select the letter which best completes the statement or answers the question.

1. Other than Community Property Laws, most laws in California:

   A. Have no effect on California property held by a resident of Arizona.
   B. Come down from Mexican and Spanish Law.
   C. Are found in the U. S. Constitution.
   D. Were derived from English Common Law.

2. Real Estate Law is derived from:

   A. Department of Real Estate.
   B. Acts of the legislature.
   C. Regulations of the Commissioner pursuant to the Real Estate Law.
   D. The State Constitution.

3. A real estate broker sold a property to three people jointly with the property conveyed to them under one grant deed - "1/5th to the first person, 1/5th to the second person, and 3/5ths to the third person". These owners recently filed a lawsuit against the broker for damages based on the broker's misrepresentation of the property . The court awarded a $25,000 judgment against the broker, but when they tried to collect, they found out that the broker was bankrupt. If they were to apply to the Department of Real Estate for an award from the recovery account, the amount that the holder of the 3/5ths interest could receive from the recovery account would be:

   A. $12,000.
   B. $15,000.
   C. $20,000.
   D. $25,000.

4. Regulations of the Real Estate Commissioner:

   A. Originate with the State Legislature.
   B. Are contained in the Civil Code.
   C. Have the force and effect of law.
   D. Regulate only the employees of the Department of Real Estate.

5. A broker misrepresents a property to a buyer. This is realized only after the transaction is completed and causes a financial loss to the buyer. The buyer sues the broker and obtains a judgment, but when he tries to collect, he discovers that the broker does not have any assets. The buyer should:

   A. Obtain a writ of execution against future earnings of the broker.
   B. Appeal to the local board of realtors.
   C. Try to receive a reimbursement from the real estate fund.
   D. Consider it just bad luck and give up trying to collect.

6. The Real Estate Law is contained in the:

    A. Business and Professions Code.
    B. Civil Code.
    C. Legislative Code.
    D. Uniform Commercial Code.

7. The maximum which may be recovered from the recovery account against one broker is:

    A. $20,000.
    B. $40,000.
    C. $100,000.
    D. $250,000.

8. Assume that a licensed real estate broker commits an act that is a violation of the Real Estate Law. The Commissioner loses his rights to exercise his jurisdiction over that broker:

    A. Never.
    B. When the broker moves to another state.
    C. When the broker's license expires.
    D. Three years after committing the act.

9. A broker handled a real estate transaction for Mr. Clark, who lost a substantial sum of money. Clark subsequently sued the broker and was awarded a $22,000 judgment. After exhausting all means of collecting from the broker, Clark appealed to the real estate recovery account. The maximum he may receive is:

    A. $10,000.
    B. $11,000.
    C. $20,000.
    D. $22,000.

10. A broker acted as an agent in selling three separate properties to three separate buyers. During the negotiations the broker misrepresented all three properties and the buyers brought suit for damages against the broker. One buyer was awarded a $10,000 judgment, another a $15,000 judgment, and the third a $25,000 judgment. The broker was insolvent and bankrupt, so all three buyers appealed to the recovery fund for restitution. The buyer with the $25,000 judgment could recover a maximum of:

    A. $10,000.
    B. $12,500.
    C. $20,000.
    D. $25,000.

11. The recovery fund was established for which of the following reasons?

    A. To provide funds for education and research in the real estate industry.
    B. To protect the real estate broker from personal liability in a real estate transaction.
    C. To insure that the general public has access to funds when they cannot recover from a real estate broker after court action or other means.
    D. All of the above.

12. The Code of Ethics and Professional Conduct is:

    A. Only for brokers.
    B. A set of regulations by the Real Estate Commissioner.
    C. A model for operating a real estate business.
    D. Optional, but preferred behavior for all real estate licensees.

13. Members of the Real Estate Advisory Commission are:

    A. Elected.
    B. Selected by the local board of realtors.
    C. Appointed by the Governor.
    D. Appointed by the Commissioner.

14. When the Real Estate Commissioner requires legal advice, he consults with:

    A. The Attorney General.
    B. The State Legislature.
    C. The District Attorney.
    D. The Real Estate Advisory Commission.

15. The Commissioner's Ethics and Professional Conduct Code encourage:

    A. The broker to be honest and truthful with all parties of a transaction.
    B. The broker to maintain adequate, accurate, and complete records of all real estate transactions.
    C. The broker to attempt to settle disputes with licensees through arbitration.
    D. All of the above.

Answers may be found in Appendix C (Back of text)

REAL ESTATE LICENSING

The main purpose of the license law is to protect the general public by regulating those engaged in the real estate business as agents. A real estate license is required when an activity is performed for another person for compensation, or in expectation of compensation.

A. REQUIRED LICENSING ACTIVITIES - A real estate license is required by an individual who performs activities or negotiates for another person for compensation, or in expectation of compensation. These activities include:

1. Selling, buying, soliciting buyers and sellers, offering to sell or buy, obtaining listings, and negotiating the sale or exchange of real property or business opportunity.

2. Leasing, renting, collecting rent, offering to lease or rent, soliciting tenants, and negotiating a lease on real property or business opportunity.

3. Soliciting or negotiating loans on real property or business opportunity.

4. Buying, selling, exchanging, and servicing loans secured by real property or business opportunity.

5. Assisting in the filing of an application for purchasing, leasing, or locating government owned land.

6. Selling, listing, soliciting buyers and sellers, and negotiating the sale of a real estate syndication.

7. Charging an advance fee for selling, leasing, and obtaining a loan on real property or business opportunity.

B. EXEMPTIONS TO LICENSING - A real estate license is not required by the following:

1. **Principal** - An individual may sell any number of his own properties without a real estate license.

   a. An individual may sell seven (7) notes secured by a trust deed without a real estate license each year (Principal must have a license if, within one year, he sells eight (8) or more notes secured by a trust deed).

   b. A nonlicensed individual may buy property at a low price, even when he has received a higher offer for the same property.

c. A nonlicensed individual, knowing that he can sell property at $2,000 per acre, buys a property at $500 per acre and immediately resells it for $2,000 per acre. When the original owner learns of the second sale which was at a much higher price, he would not have any recourse against that individual.

2. **Corporation** - A corporation dealing with its own property does not require a real estate license. However, the transaction must be handled by a corporate officer and the officer can never receive any special compensation for selling the property.

3. **Attorney** - An attorney when performing his duties as an "attorney at law" may sell real property without a real estate license.

4. **Attorney-in-Fact** - A legally competent individual appointed to represent another person through a "Power of Attorney" may buy and sell real property for his principal without a real estate license. The instrument is referred to as a "Power of Attorney"; however, the individual delegated in the instrument, to act officially or to perform something legally for another in his stead, is referred to as an "Attorney-in-Fact".

   a. The "Power of Attorney" must be recorded to be effective in a real estate transaction.

   b. An Attorney-in-Fact may sign the name of his principal. An Attorney-in-Fact, when signing a document for his principal, signs his principal's name, and follows it with his own signature as "Attorney-in-Fact".

   c. An Attorney-in-Fact can perform certain activities under a general power of attorney.

   d. An Attorney-in-Fact may encumber his principal's property with a trust deed when the beneficiary is someone other than the Attorney-in-Fact. The Attorney-in-Fact can never be the beneficiary.

   e. An Attorney-in-Fact can never sell the property to himself, even when fair market value is paid for the property.

   f. When the Attorney-in-Fact is informed by the court that his principal has become incompetent, the Power of Attorney becomes ineffective.

5. **Appraiser** - An appraiser is not required to have a real estate license to appraise real property. A real estate salesperson may appraise real property and accept a fee from anyone, including a real estate broker who is not his employing broker. **EXAMPLE:** Salesperson Jones is employed by broker "A"; broker "B" may employ Jones to appraise real property. The reason why broker "B" can employ the salesperson is that appraising is a vocation which does not require a license.

6. **Trustee** - A trustee selling a property at a Trustee's Sale is not required to have a real estate license.

7. **Clerical Employee** - A receptionist, secretary, or bookkeeper employed by a real estate broker, is not required to have a real estate license. However, neither can they discuss properties nor quote prices and terms to customers and clients.

8. **Host/Hostess** - A host or hostess may greet potential buyers and answer the phone within the model homes of a new subdivision without a real estate license. However, when a host or hostess gives a potential buyer information on price and terms, or shows model homes, they must have a real estate license.

9. **Lending Institution Employees** - Employees of a bank, insurance company, trust company, credit union, and savings and loan are not required to have a real estate license to negotiate and to be compensated on loan transactions.

10. **Court Order** - Any individual acting under a court order is not required to have a real estate license to sell real property. This includes an administrator or executor, receiver, or trustee in a bankruptcy.

11. **Joint Venture** - A real estate license is not required when two or more persons want to purchase property as a joint venture. Neither is a license required when two licensed real estate brokers want to purchase property as a joint venture.

12. **Resident Property Manager** - When an apartment building contains sixteen (16) or more units, the owner must live on the premises or hire a resident property manager to live on the premises. A resident property manager is not required to have a real estate license. A resident property manager may only manage the property where he resides; he can never manage another property unless he has a real estate license.

C. VIOLATION OF LICENSING LAW

1. Any individual giving compensation to an unlicensed person for activities which require a real estate license may be fined $100 for each offense.

2. An unlicensed individual receiving compensation for activities which require a real estate license may either be placed in the county jail for a period of six months, be fined $10,000, or both. An unlicensed corporation may be fined $50,000.

D. SALESPERSON LICENSE REQUIREMENTS

1. Must be at least eighteen (18) years old.

2. Complete educational requirements.

3. Be honest and truthful.

4. Make application to the commissioner on an approved form.

5. Pass the qualifying examination.

E. SALESPERSON EDUCATIONAL REQUIREMENTS

1. To qualify to take an examination for a real estate salesperson license, an applicant must have completed a college-level **REAL ESTATE PRINCIPLES** course.

2. In addition to the real estate principles course, the applicant must also, either prior to issuance of the original license or within eighteen months after issuance, complete two additional basic real estate courses selected from among the following:

Real Estate Practice	**Legal Aspects of Real Estate**
Real Estate Appraisal	**Real Estate Financing**
Escrows	**Real Estate Economics**
Business Law	**Accounting**
Property Management	**Real Estate Office Administration**

These courses must be a three semester unit course, or the quarter equivalent, completed at an accredited institution of higher learning; or, be an equivalent course of study offered by a private vocational school approved by the Commissioner.

F. RENEWAL OF SALESPERSON LICENSE

1. On a first renewal of a salesperson license, those licensees who have met the above educational requirements will not be required to complete continuing education requirements except for a minimum three hour course in "Ethics and Legal Aspects of Real Estate" and a minimum three hour course in "Agency Relationships." Effective January 1, 1996, two additional three hour courses will be required in "Fair Housing" and "Trust Fund Handling."

2. Salespersons who qualify to take the examination by completing only the Real Estate Principles course shall have their licenses automatically suspended, effective eighteen months after issuance of the conditional license, unless the two additional courses mentioned above are completed within that time. The suspension will not be lifted until the licensee has submitted the required evidence of remaining course completion and the Commissioner has given written notice to the licensee of the lifting of the suspension.

G. SALESPERSON LICENSE FEE - The fee for a real estate salesperson license is $170 for those applicants who have completed three courses prior to issuance of the license. The fee for those who have not satisfied all of the educational requirements prior to the issuance of the license is $195.

H. BROKER LICENSE REQUIREMENTS

1. Must be at least eighteen (18) years old.

2. Two years full time experience or equivalent.

3. Complete educational requirements.

4. Be honest and truthful.

5. Make application to the Commissioner on the approved form.

6. Pass the qualifying examination.

I. BROKER EDUCATIONAL REQUIREMENTS - To qualify to take an examination for a real estate broker license, an applicant must have completed eight courses. These eight courses must include the following five:

Real Estate Practice   **Legal Aspects of Real Estate**
Real Estate Appraisal   **Real Estate Financing**
Real Estate Economics or Accounting

The remaining three courses may be selected from the following:

Real Estate Office Administration   **Real Estate Principles**
Advance Legal Aspects of Real Estate **Business Law**
Advance Real Estate Appraisal   **Property Management**
Advance Real Estate Finance   **Escrows**

These courses must be a three semester unit course, or the quarter equivalent, completed at an accredited institution of higher learning; or, be an equivalent course of study offered by a private vocational school approved by the Commissioner.

J. APPLICATION FOR LICENSE - After being notified of passing the real estate examination, an individual is required to file an application for a license within one year from the examination test date. When an individual fails to make application during this time period, he will have to take and pass another examination to obtain a real estate license.

K. TERM OF LICENSE

1. **Salesperson** - Four years (18 months to complete educational requirements on initial four year license or the license is suspended).

2. **Broker** - Four years.

L. RENEWAL OF LICENSE

1. **Continuing Education Requirements** - All broker and salesperson renewal applicants who have a four year license must complete forty-five clock hours of approved courses within the four year period preceding license renewal. This must include a three hour course in "Ethics, Professional Conduct and Legal Aspects of Real Estate," a three hour course in "Agency Relationships," and eighteen hours minimum in the category of "Consumer Protection." The remaining twenty-one hours may be in the any offering category. Effective January 1, 1996, two additional three hour courses will be mandatory in "Fair Housing" and "Trust Fund Handling."

2. **Late Renewal** - A real estate licensee who fails to renew his license prior to the expiration date may renew it within two years after the expiration date. The licensee must meet the continuing education requirements and pay a late renewal fee.

M. CLASSIFICATION OF LICENSES

1. **Corporation License** - When a corporation is performing activities which require a real estate license, the corporation must be licensed by the Department of Real Estate. Any real estate broker may qualify as the broker for the corporation.

105

2. **Partnership License** - A real estate license cannot be issued in the name of a partnership.

3. **Mineral, Oil, and Gas License** - A mineral, oil, and gas license is required by those individual real estate brokers who specialize in the sale of mineral, oil, and gas transactions. A licensed real estate broker is not required to have a mineral, oil, and gas license if he occasionally sells property where the mineral, oil, and gas rights are the major financial factor. However, the broker must secure a **PERMIT** from the Commission for each transaction and is limited to ten permits in one calendar year. The real estate broker must obtain a mineral, oil, and gas license if he wants to negotiate more than **ten** mineral, oil, and gas transactions within any one calendar year.

4. **Nonresident License** - Residency is not required to obtain a California real estate license. Nonresidents may qualify for a California real estate license if their resident state will reciprocate for California residents wishing to obtain a license in that state. When a nonresident licensee is required to appear for judicial process, a subpoena may be served by delivering the process to the California Secretary of State.

5. **Cancelled License** - The license of a real estate salesperson may be cancelled upon the death of his employing broker. Cancellation of a salesperson's license will also occur upon the expiration, suspension, or revocation of the employing broker's license. This does not mean that the salesperson loses his license; this means that the salesperson must place his license with a new employing broker.

6. **Restricted License** - A restricted license is issued to a licensee who is on probation with the Real Estate Commissioner for a specific reason.

   a. The license may be restricted by term or duration, employment to a specific broker, or type of activity the licensee may perform.

   b. The licensee may be required to file a surety bond.

   c. The licensee may be required to make detailed reports on all transactions to the Real Estate Commissioner.

   d. The Real Estate Commissioner may suspend a restricted license without a hearing.

7. **Suspended License** - A licensee will have a temporary loss of his license because of specific disciplinary action by the Department of Real Estate.

8. **Revoked License** - A licensee will have a complete loss of his license because of specific disciplinary action by the Department of Real Estate. The Real Estate Commissioner can never revoke a license without a hearing.

N. BROKER/SALESPERSON RELATIONSHIP

1. A real estate broker may receive compensation from anyone (buyer, seller, lender, borrower, owner, other brokers, etc.).

2. A real estate salesperson must be employed by a real estate broker and may only receive compensation from his employing broker.

3. **Employee** - Under the Real Estate License Law a salesperson is considered to be the employee and the broker is considered to be the employer. This means that the broker must supervise the activities of the salesperson.

   a. Real Estate Commissioner's Rules and Regulations require the broker to have a written employment agreement with a salesperson. This employment agreement must be retained by both the broker and the salesperson for three (3) years from the date of termination of employment.

   b. A real estate broker must review, initial and date all contracts made by the salesperson within five (5) days after they are signed by the parties to the contract, or prior to the close of escrow. The authority to review contracts may be delegated, in writing, to another broker or to a salesperson with two years recent full-time experience.

4. **Independent Contractor** - An independent contractor is an individual who is self-employed. An employer is only interested in the results achieved by an independent contractor. The independent contractor status may relieve the real estate broker from responsibility in reference to the salesperson's taxation and social security; however, the broker continues to be responsible for the salesperson and his activities under the real estate law.

5. A licensed real estate salesperson is required to notify his employing broker of any transaction where he is acting as a principal. This notification must be in writing and be within five days of execution of the agreement, or by the close of escrow, whichever occurs first.

6. A real estate salesperson may only be employed by one broker at a given time. A salesperson may transfer employment to another broker at any time. When a salesperson transfers his license, both brokers must immediately notify the Real Estate Commissioner of the transfer.

   a. Previous employing broker has ten (10) days to notify the Commissioner when using DRE Form 214.

   b. New employing broker has five (5) days to notify the Commissioner when using DRE Form 214.

   c. When a salesperson is discharged for a violation of the real estate law, the employing broker must immediately file a certified written statement of such facts with the Commissioner.

O. **FICTITIOUS BUSINESS NAME** (D.B.A., Doing Business As) - When an individual or corporation wishes to use any name other than its own, a fictitious business name statement must be filed with the county clerk in the county where the principal place of business of the individual or corporation is located. A fictitious business name statement must be renewed every five (5) years (the d.b.a. expires at the end of five years from December 31 in the year in which it was filed with the county recorder). An individual or corporate real estate license may be issued in one or more fictitious business names.

P. BUSINESS LICENSE TAX - A city may levy a tax based on the gross income of a business. A real estate company must pay a tax based on the gross receipts of the business.

Notes:
1. An individual licensed in the State of California may negotiate in California for the sale of property in another state.

2. An individual licensed in the State of California may negotiate a mortgage loan for a commission.

3. An individual licensed in the State of California may negotiate a lease for any length of time.

4. The minimum age to obtain a real estate license is eighteen (18).

5. United States citizenship is not a requirement to obtain a California real estate license. However, each salesperson applicant must provide to the Department of Real Estate his social security number which will be furnished to the Franchise Tax Board.

6. Residency is not a requirement to obtain a California real estate license.

7. The Real Estate Commissioner may deny a license to an applicant who cannot prove that he is honest and truthful.

8. A real estate license that is not renewed prior to the expiration date may be reinstated within the next two years.

9. Ethics refers to a branch of philosophy that deals with moral science and moral principles.

REVIEW QUIZ

SECTION I - **Matching** - Select the letter below which best describes, defines, or relates to the following numbered terms.

1. Attorney-in-Fact
2. Citizenship
3. Restricted License
4. Fictitious Business Name
5. Independent Contractor
6. Resident Property Manager
7. Revoked License
8. Cancelled License
9. Suspended License
10. Ethics

a. Employer is only concerned with the results of this person.
b. Does not require a real estate license.
c. A branch of moral science philosophy.
d. Temporary loss of license.
e. Status of a salesperson's license when his employing broker's license has expired.
f. A person delegated in writing to act officially or to perform something legally for another in his stead.
g. Commissioner may suspend without a hearing.
h. Complete loss of license.
i. Must be renewed every five years.
j. Not required to obtain a real estate license.

SECTION II - **True/False** - Select either true or false in response to the following statements.

1. The Real Estate Commissioner requires the broker to have a written employment agreement with all of his salespeople.
2. A nonresident may obtain a California real estate license.
3. After being notified of passing the real estate examination, an individual is required to file an application for a license within one year from the notification date.
4. A real estate license which is not renewed prior to the expiration date may be reinstated during the next five years.
5. A nonresident licensee may be issued a subpoena to appear for judicial process by delivering the process to the California Department of Real Estate.
6. The new employing broker has ten days to notify the Commissioner when a salesperson transfers his license.
7. The Commissioner may suspend a restricted license without a hearing.
8. The Commissioner cannot revoke a license without a hearing.
9. Nonresidents may qualify for a real estate license in California, but only if their states reciprocate for California residents.
10. An attorney-in-fact may sell the property to himself when fair market value is paid for the property.

SECTION III - Multiple Choice - Select the letter which best completes the statement or answers the question.

1. Which of the following statements is correct in reference to a restricted license issued by the Department of Real Estate?

   A. The licensee must post a surety bond with the Commissioner.
   B. The licensee may be required to make detailed reports to the Commissioner.
   C. It confers the property rights to the privileges exercised thereunder.
   D. The licensee may renew his license.

2. The written employment agreement required between a salesperson and his employing broker must be retained:

   A. By the salesperson for a period of three years from the date of execution.
   B. By the broker for a period of three years from the date of execution.
   C. By both the salesperson and broker for a period of three years from the date of termination.
   D. "A" and "B" are both correct.

3. A real estate salesperson's commission may be paid by:

   A. The seller.
   B. The broker.
   C. The escrow holder.
   D. Anyone.

4. To obtain a real estate salesperson's license, an individual must be:

   A. A citizen of the United States.
   B. A minimum age of twenty-one.
   C. A resident of the state of California.
   D. None of the above.

5. Which of the following would require a real estate broker's license?

   A. An attorney performing real estate services as a broker.
   B. A trustee selling under a deed of trust.
   C. An administrator acting under court order.
   D. An attorney-in-fact appointed to sell real property for another.

6. When a real estate licensee allows his license to expire, which of the following is true?

   A. He will be given a restricted license upon renewal.
   B. He has a two year period in which his license may be renewed.
   C. He must pay a fee and take a new examination.
   D. He must pay a renewal fee.

7. After taking the real estate examination, an individual must file an application for a license within:

   A. One year from notification of passing.
   B. Two years from notification of passing.
   C. One year from the test date.
   D. Two years from the date of application.

8. In reference to a restricted license issued by the Commissioner, all of the following are correct, except:

   A. The licensee may be required to give detailed reports of all transactions to the Commissioner.
   B. The licensee may be required to file a surety bond.
   C. The licensee has the right to renewal of his license.
   D. The Commissioner may suspend the restricted license without a hearing.

9. Mr. "A" and Mr. "B" are both licensed real estate brokers. They want to enter into a joint venture to purchase an office building. For this transaction:

   A. A license is not required.
   B. The real estate licenses they now possess must be used.
   C. A partnership license is required.
   D. A business opportunity license is required.

10. When the owner of an apartment building does not reside on the premises, he must have a resident property manager of the premises when the number of units is:

    A. Twelve or more.
    B. Fourteen or more.
    C. Sixteen or more.
    D. Twenty or more.

11. A real estate broker hired a hostess to work on weekends to show model homes and give prospective customers information on prices and terms of purchase. There was at least one licensed salesperson in the office at all times to write the transactions. Which of the following is correct?

    A. The broker was within his rights.
    B. The broker was within his rights as long as the salesperson was properly licensed.
    C. The broker was in violation of the real estate law.
    D. None of the above.

12. An individual is appointed by an insurance company to negotiate real estate loans and is compensated on a commission basis by the lending institution for each loan he procures. This requires:

    A. A real property security dealer's license.
    B. An active real estate broker's license.
    C. A $5,000 surety bond.
    D. None of the above.

13. A broker discharges a salesperson. That broker is then required to notify the commissioner:

    A. Immediately.
    B. Within ten days.
    C. When the license expires.
    D. Only if the salesperson was discharged for a violation of the real estate law.

14. A California real estate broker would be in violation of the real estate law if he did which of the following?

    A. Negotiated a lease for one year.
    B. Negotiated a mortgage loan for a fee.
    C. Negotiated in California for the sale of a ranch in Nevada.
    D. None of the above.

15. Keaton and Seaton are licensed real estate brokers who work in the same office; however, they are not partners. Truman works as a salesperson for Seaton. Which of the following activities could Truman perform for Keaton for a fee?

    A. Appraise property.
    B. Collect rent.
    C. Negotiate a loan.
    D. Lease property for recreational purposes.

Answers may be found in Appendix C (Back of text)

BROKER SPECIALIZATION

A. AGENCY - The relationship that exists when an individual is given the authority to both act and use discretion in business transactions for another person.

1. Parties to an Agency

    a. Principal (Employer) - The individual who gives the authority to act on his behalf in a real estate transaction. Examples include buyer, seller, lender, borrower, etc.

    b. Agent - An individual authorized to represent the activities which benefit another. In a real estate transaction the agent is the real estate broker.

    c. Subagent - An individual may authorize his agent to appoint a third party to perform activities in a business transaction. A salesperson's relationship to the principal is an example of a subagent. A cooperating broker is also an example of a subagency relationship.

2. Creation of an Agency Relationship

    a. Expressed Agreement - A principal may authorize an agent to perform activities before the fact. This expressed agency may be created in writing, orally, or by implication (the activities of the parties).

    b. Ratification - A principal may authorize an agent to perform activities after the fact.

        1. An individual performs an activity for Mr. Jones when he did not have the authorization to exercise such action. If Mr. Jones chooses to approve the activity of the individual and acknowledges that the individual is working on his behalf, an agency will be created through ratification.

        2. An individual may perform an activity in excess of his authority or without authorization. The alleged principal is not liable for any such action; however, the principal may approve the agency relationship and will, therefore, also become responsible for that previously performed activity.

3. Classification of Agent

    a. Actual - The agent is actually employed by the principal. This relationship may be established orally, in writing, or by the activities of both parties. A real estate broker is usually employed by a principal as an actual agent.

b. **Ostensible** - An ostensible agency is created when one individual intentionally, or through negligence, leads another individual to believe that he has the authority to perform activities for a third party, and the third party concurs with the first individual. **EXAMPLE:** Mr. "A" leads Mr. "B" to believe that he has the authority to act for Mr. "Y". If Mr. "Y" goes along with Mr. "A", the agency is created ostensibly.

c. **Dual Agency** - A real estate broker may represent and receive a commission from both parties in a real estate transaction. The broker is required to give knowledge and receive consent from both parties as to the dual agency. When the buyer and seller agree to a contract and neither party has knowledge of the dual agency, the broker may be subject to civil, criminal and administrative punishment. Disciplinary action may be taken by the Real Estate Commissioner and the agent cannot enforce the payment of his commission (the sale itself could be rescinded).

4. **Agency Disclosure** - Agency disclosure applies to real estate transactions involving the sale or lease of improved residential real property of one to four units. This includes mobile homes. Property may be either owner-occupied or non-owner-occupied. Agency disclosure is required if a lease is for more than one year.

   a. There are three steps in agency disclosure; disclosure, selection (election), and confirmation.

   b. The real estate agents and subagents are required to disclose the various agency relationships available to a buyer or seller as soon as their relationship becomes "more than casual."

   c. An Agency Disclosure Statement (Form) is required to familiarize the consumer with terminology and identify the role of agents, subagents, and principals in a real estate transaction.

   d. Agency disclosure is not required when a property is sold "For Sale by Owner" nor when selling an apartment complex of five or more units.

5. **Essential Elements of an Agency Relationship**

   a. Agreement between principal and agent.

   b. Competency of the principal and agent.

   c. Fiduciary relationship.

6. **Fiduciary Relationship** (Relationship of Trust) - An agent acting in a fiduciary relationship is obligated to inform his principal of any material facts he discovers in reference to a pending real estate transaction. The real estate broker has a primary fiduciary relationship with the seller. A broker must be fair and honest with a buyer when he has a fiduciary relationship with the seller.

   a. **Material Fact** - A material fact is any information which will influence the judgment or decision of the principal. This includes the sale of the property to a relative of the broker, the sale of the property to a friend of the broker, or the broker's knowledge of any existing offer.

b. A real estate broker is usually referred to as a fiduciary.

c. An agent is never allowed to profit at the expense of his principal.

d. The agent has the authority to act only as authorized by his principal.

e. The agent must comply with all lawful instructions received from his principal. **EXAMPLE:** A broker can never show the property to anyone when the seller is out of town if those are the instructions of the principal.

f. An agent is in violation of his fiduciary relationship if he acts in excess of the authority given to him by his principal. **EXAMPLE:** A real estate broker cannot tell a prospective purchaser that his principal will sell for an amount lower than the listed price.

g. When the real estate broker performs activities in excess of the authority given to him by the seller, he may be held liable by the buyer.

h. When an agent misleads a buyer without the knowledge of the seller, the buyer can sue both the agent and the seller.

i. An agent of the principal, without further authority, can never modify the terms of the sale nor cancel the sale for the buyer.

j. The agent can never enter into a contract to convey title to the buyer.

k. Examples of a fiduciary relationship include buying broker to buyer, selling broker to seller, lawyer to client, trustee to beneficiary, and an attorney-in-fact to principal under a power of attorney.

7. Duty to a Third Party (Buyer) - An agent must disclose all material facts to a prospective purchaser. This means that any item or information which affects the value of the subject property can never be withheld or concealed from a prospective purchaser.

    a. The broker and seller must disclose all material facts to a prospective buyer.

    b. All known defects must be disclosed to the buyer when a property is being purchased in "as is" condition.

    c. An offer to purchase a property in "as is" condition relieves the agent and seller from all liability for visible defects which can be seen by the buyer upon physical inspection of the property.

    d. When a buyer makes demands on the broker to replace a broken fixture, the broker may replace the fixture with his own funds to save his commission. However, the broker will be liable for this cost unless the seller agrees to reimburse the money to the broker.

8. Transfer Disclosure Statement - A seller (transferor) of real property containing one to four residential units must provide a prospective buyer (transferee) with a written disclosure statement in reference to the property.

    a. Transferor is responsible for the issuing of the Transfer Disclosure Statement.

b. The real estate agent is also required to inspect the accessible areas of the property, then disclose any material facts that affect the value of the property.

c. When an owner sells in "as is" condition, he is required to give a Transfer Disclosure Statement to the prospective buyer.

d. Transfer disclosure exemptions include a transfer between husband and wife, and sales by foreclosure, probate, bankruptcy, and REO's.

9. **Miscellaneous Required Disclosures** (MATERIAL FACTS)

   a. Knowledge of any imminent higher offer must be disclosed to the seller.

   b. All offers must be disclosed to the seller at the same time.

   c. A real estate licensee must submit all offers to the property owner. When two or more offers are received by the licensee, he must submit all offers at the same time, regardless of terms and conditions of a specific offer. The owner has the right to accept or reject any offer.

   d. A real estate broker must notify his principal if the cooperating broker has

   arranged for the buyer to purchase similar property at a considerably higher price prior to the close of escrow.

   e. The broker must disclose to the seller if he is going to give a portion of his commission to the buyer.

   f. The broker must disclose to both the buyer and seller any material facts about the property discovered during the escrow period (evidence of termite infestation).

10. **Termination of the Agency Relationship** - An agency agreement may be terminated by:

    a. Mutual agreement between principal and agent.

    b. Renunciation of the agreement by the agent.

    c. Destruction of the property by fire, earthquake or other hazard.

    d. Death of either party. The death of the principal (owner) immediately revokes the agent's authority to perform an activity for the principal. A tenant does not have to pay rent to a broker who represents a deceased principal (even if the rent is past due and the principal was alive when it was due).

Notes: 1. The Law of Agency is concerned with duties, liabilities, obligations, and responsibilities among and between the agent and his principal, the principal and a third party, and the agent and principal in their relationship to a third party.

2. Creation of an agency relationship does not require payment of consideration.

116

3. An expressed contract is usually used to create the agency relationship between the real estate broker and his client.

4. An agency for the sale of real property is legal and binding if it is in writing.

5. The broker's relationship to his principal may be that of a fiduciary, agent, or broker/client.

6. **Client** - The term client refers to the principal of a real estate agent. This is usually the seller.

7. **Customer** - The term customer refers to the buyer in a real estate transaction (the prospective purchaser to whom the broker shows property without a contract).

8. The relationship of a real estate agent to his principal is similar to the relationship between a trustee and his beneficiary.

9. Failure to disclose a material fact may cause the buyer to take legal action against both the broker and the seller.

10. Legal action may be taken against the seller for a material fact which was not disclosed to the buyer. If the buyer is successful in obtaining monetary damages from the seller, the seller could most likely receive the amount back from the broker because the broker failed to mention the material fact when negotiating the sale. The broker is also subject to disciplinary action by the Real Estate Commissioner.

B. PAPER TRANSACTIONS (Notes secured by Mortgages or Trust Deeds and Land Contracts) - A note secured by a mortgage or trust deed and a land contract are very valuable pieces of paper after they have been created. They are like stocks and bonds; they may be sold, traded, or used as collateral to borrow additional money.

1. Any individual lender (holder of paper) may sell seven (7) pieces of paper in one calendar year (January 1 to December 31).

2. Any individual lender who wants to sell eight (8) or more pieces of paper in a calendar year is required to sell these through a real estate broker.

3. When a real estate broker negotiates the sale of a note secured by a trust deed, the broker is required to make sure that the trust deed is properly assigned.

4. Exceptions to licensing requirements:

   a. An individual who sells one trust deed per month for twelve consecutive months through a real estate broker does not require a real estate license.

   b. An individual who purchases one trust deed per month for one year does not require a real estate license.

   c. When an investor purchases nine (9) notes secured by trust deeds, he may sell a maximum of seven (7) within one calendar year without having a real estate license.

d. A subdivider received ten (10) notes secured by trust deeds on ten individual properties in his subdivision eighteen months ago. He may sell a maximum of seven (7) trust deeds in one calendar year without having a real estate license.

C. REAL PROPERTY SECURITIES TRANSACTIONS - The sale to the public of a guaranteed note, out of state subdivision, promotional note, or promotional sales contract are considered real property securities transactions.

1. Guaranteed Note - This is a note secured by a trust deed in which the seller guarantees performance, a specific yield, or against any loss when selling the paper to the public. The requirements to sell a guaranteed note include:

a. The sale must be conducted by a **REAL ESTATE BROKER** who has a real property securities dealer endorsement on his license. To obtain a real property securities dealer endorsement a real estate broker must:

1. Post a $5,000 surety bond.

2. Pay a $100 fee.

3. Have his license endorsed.

b. The Real Estate Commissioner must issue a permit on each transaction.

2. Out of State Subdivision - In order to protect the public against fraud, an out of state subdivision is considered a real property securities transaction. The only requirement to sell an out of state subdivision in California is for the seller to obtain a permit from the Real Estate Commissioner.

3. Promotional Note - A promotional note is one of a series of notes not over three (3) years old secured by soft money trust deeds on separate parcels in one subdivision or contiguous subdivisions. This means that a promotional note is paper created where the subdivider is the lender in order to help promote the sale of this new subdivision. The three year distinction means that if the subdivider wants to sell the paper during the initial three years, he will have to obtain a permit from the Real Estate Commissioner. After three years, the paper is not considered a promotional note and the subdivider can sell the paper without any requirements. **EXAMPLE:** A subdivider sells twenty-five houses and receives a $7,500 note secured by a second trust deed on each house. If the subdivider sells any of the notes during the initial three year time period after creation of the note, he must obtain a real property securities permit from the Real Estate Commissioner.

4. Promotional Sales Contract - A promotional sales contract is one of a series of contracts not over three (3) years old on separate parcels in one subdivision or contiguous subdivisions. This means that the subdivider is the lender on a land contract to help promote the sale of his subdivision. The three year distinction means that if the subdivider wants to sell the paper during the initial three years, he will have to obtain a permit from the Real Estate Commissioner. After three years, the paper is not considered a promotional sales contract and the subdivider can sell the paper without any requirements (the requirements for the promotional sales contract are exactly the same as the promotional note).

5. Advertisement of Real Property Securities - Any advertisement used to promote the sale of real property securities must be filed with the Real Estate

Commissioner ten (10) days prior to its use. When the Commissioner does not disapprove of the advertisement within ten (10) days, it may be used by the dealer. A report must be made annually to the Commissioner in reference to the advertisement of real property securities.

6. **Real Property Security Statement** - A real property security statement is a disclosure statement which must be given to the prospective buyer of a real property security.

    a. A real property security statement is required in the purchase of one or more real property sales contracts created by a recent sale of homes in a new subdivision.

    b. A real property security statement is required when a real estate broker tells an investor that he will make up the difference if the trust deed investment does not show the required return. To buy back a trust deed in default requires a real property security statement.

7. **Appraisal** - The appraisal of the related real property is mandatory in a real property securities transaction. Any property requiring an appraisal will also require a real property security statement.

8. **Exemptions** - All of the above laws and requirements are not required in a real estate securities transaction which is sold to pension funds, corporations, institutional lenders, attorneys, real estate brokers, and contractors. This means that an individual can sell real property securities to these people, or to legal entities, without obtaining a permit from the Real Estate Commissioner.

9. **Annual Audit** - A real estate broker who deals in real property securities transactions is required to submit to the Real Estate Commissioner an annual audited report which includes:

    a. The total number of sales during the year.

    b. The total dollar volume from those sales.

Notes: 1. The Commissioner will review each real property security transaction to insure that it is fair, just, and equitable.
2. An endorsement as a real property securities dealer is good for the term of the broker's license.
3. The real estate broker who deals in real property securities transactions is required to maintain a $5,000 surety bond on file with the Commissioner.
4. The $5,000 surety bond is not required on each transaction.
5. The Real Estate Commissioner must issue a PERMIT on all real property securities transactions (also on all Mineral, Oil, & Gas transactions).
6. A lot in a Nevada subdivision being offered for sale in California requires a PERMIT from the Real Estate Commissioner prior to selling or offering to sell for the first time in California.
7. A PERMIT is not required in:
    a. The sale or purchase of state land.
    b. Promotional notes being used as collateral for a loan.
    c. Promotional notes being sold to a pension fund.
    d. Promotional notes being sold after the initial three (3) years.
8. A real estate broker who is qualified to perform activities as a real property securities dealer is also qualified to negotiate real estate loans. However, a

real estate broker can never perform activities as a real property securities dealer unless he has an endorsement on his license.

9. A real estate broker may buy back any trust deed which is in default if his license has a real property securities dealer endorsement.

D. SMALL LOAN TRANSACTIONS - The Loan Broker Law regulates the amount of commission and costs a borrower can be charged when a real estate broker arranges a loan between two private parties. The commission and costs are only controlled on small loans. Small loans refers to any first trust deed **LESS THAN $30,000** ($1 - $29,999) and any junior trust deed **LESS THAN $20,000** ($1 - $19,999).

1. Controlled Commission

a. First Trust Deeds (Less than $30,000) - The commission is controlled based on the duration of the loan.

1. Five **(5%)** percent is the maximum commission a broker can charge the borrower on any first trust deed paid off in less than three years.

2. Ten **(10%)** percent is the maximum commission a broker can charge the borrower on any first trust deed paid off in three years or more.

b. Junior Trust Deeds (Less than $20,000) - The commission is controlled based on the duration of the loan.

1. Five **(5%)** percent is the maximum commission a broker can charge the borrower on any junior trust deed paid off in less than two years.

2. Ten **(10%)** percent is the maximum commission a broker can charge the borrower on any junior trust deed paid off in two years but less than three years.

3. Fifteen **(15%)** percent is the maximum commission a broker can charge the borrower on any junior trust deed paid off in three years or more.

c. Any loan which is not in these controlled areas is not subject to the commission being regulated by law.

1. When a first trust deed is $30,000 or more, the real estate broker may arrange the loan and charge the borrower a commission based on whatever the competitive market will allow.

2. When a junior trust deed is $20,000 or more, the real estate broker may arrange the loan and charge the borrower a commission based on whatever the competitive market will allow.

2. Controlled Costs (Costs and Expenses) - The amount charged for costs and expenses on controlled loans can never exceed the actual costs. Excluding actual title charges and recording fees, the costs and expenses to arrange a small loan can never exceed five (5%) percent of the loan. When the costs and expenses are less than $390 the broker may charge up to the actual amount paid for services. The broker can never charge the borrower more than $700 on a small loan. The following will simplify how the costs and expenses are regulated under the Loan Broker Law:

a. **$390 Ceiling** - The maximum that may be charged on any loan that is less than $7,800 is $390. **EXAMPLE:** When a real estate broker arranges a $4,000 loan and the actual costs and expenses are $4.00, the broker can only charge the borrower $4.00. If the actual costs and expenses are $44.00, the broker can only charge the borrower $44.00. However, if the actual costs and expenses are $444.00 to arrange a $4,000 loan, then the broker can charge the borrower a maximum of $390.00.

b. **5% Control -** The maximum that may be charged on any loan that is between $7,800 and $14,000 is five percent. **EXAMPLE:** When a real estate broker arranges an $8,000 loan and the actual costs and expenses are $8.00, the broker can only charge the borrower $8.00. If the actual costs and expenses are $88.00, the broker can only charge the borrower $88.00. However, if the actual costs and expenses are $888.00 to arrange an $8,000 loan, then the broker can charge the borrower a maximum of $400.00 ($8,000 multiplied by the 5% control equals $400.00 maximum).

c. **$700 Maximum** - The maximum that may be charged on any controlled loan that is between $14,000 and $29,999 is $700. (Junior trust deeds to a maximum of $19,999 and first trust deeds to a maximum $29,999). **EXAMPLE:** When a real estate broker arranges a $20,000 first trust deed and the actual costs and expenses are $20.00, the broker can only charge the borrower $20.00. If the actual costs and expenses are $200.00, the broker can only charge the borrower $200.00. However, if the actual costs and expenses are $2,000.00 to arrange a $20,000 first trust deed, then the broker can charge the borrower a maximum of $700.00.

d. Any loan which is not in these controlled areas is not subject to costs and expenses regulated by the Loan Broker Law. This means that the broker may then charge the borrower any amount, based on whatever the market will allow.

3. **Miscellaneous Requirements for Loans Arranged by a Broker** - A real estate broker is required to comply with the following laws which regulate his activities on any loan he negotiates between private parties:

a. A mortgage loan broker is required to have a real estate license.

b. **Mortgage Loan Disclosure Statement** (Broker's Loan Statement) - The Mortgage Loan Disclosure Statement is used to provide the prospective borrower with information in reference to a loan being negotiated for him by a real estate broker. A real estate licensee negotiating or making a loan secured directly or collaterally by a lien on real property must obtain the signature of the prospective borrower on a completed Mortgage Loan Disclosure Statement prior to the time that the borrower becomes obligated to complete the loan transaction.

   1. When a broker negotiates a loan, he will most likely use a Broker's Loan Statement.

   2. The disclosure requirement does not apply when a real estate broker negotiates a loan for an institutional lender (Bank, Savings and Loan, or Insurance Company) and the broker receives a commission not in excess of 2%. The Mortgage Loan Disclosure Statement will be required in the negotiation of an $18,000 first trust deed loan secured from a Savings and Loan when the broker receives a ten (10%) percent commission.

3. The Mortgage Loan Disclosure Statement is not required either in the negotiation of a $20,000 purchase money trust deed, the sale of a $4,000 note secured by a trust deed, nor in the sale of a real property security.

4. The Broker's Loan Statement must be a form which has been approved by the Real Estate Commissioner.

5. The Broker's Loan Statement is designed for the protection and benefit of the trustor.

6. The Broker's Loan Statement must contain an estimate of the broker's commission, amounts to be paid on the instructions of the borrower, and the status of current loans of record.

7. The Broker's Loan Statement does not contain the buyer's credit rating.

8. The Mortgage Loan Disclosure Statement must be retained by the broker for a period of four (4) years.

9. Collaterally usually refers to liens secured by other loans.

c. **Exclusive Listing** - An exclusive agreement to negotiate a real estate loan of $2,000 or less, secured directly, or collaterally, by a lien on real property, cannot be for a period of more than forty-five (45) days. **EXAMPLE:** A broker cannot take a ninety day exclusive listing to arrange a $1,500 loan.

d. **Balloon Payment** - A balloon payment is an installment payment which is greater than twice the amount of the smallest installment payment.

1. A regulated small loan can never have a balloon payment if the term of the loan is less than three years.

2. A loan on an owner occupied dwelling can never have a balloon payment if the term of the loan is six years or less. This is not applicable to a loan of more than six years.

e. **Real Estate Broker Servicing Loans** - A real estate broker must have written authorization to service a loan secured directly or collaterally by real estate. Authorization may be given by either the beneficiary, borrower, or the holder of the note.

f. **Liability of Borrower** - A real estate broker may earn a commission and require payment for his expenses in a home loan transaction that is not consummated. When the loan is not consummated, because the borrower is at fault, the borrower is liable for one-half of the broker's commission, and any and all paid or incurred costs or expenses. Default may occur as a result of the borrower's failure to disclose liens on the property or faulty title as to his ownership of the property.

SITUATIONS:

1. When a real estate broker negotiates a new $5,000 second trust deed on a home for a term of two years, the maximum costs and commission the borrower will have to pay is $890.00.

   SOLUTION: Step 1 - The maximum commission on a junior trust deed loan for two years, but less than three years, is 10% (10% of $5,000 equals $500). Step 2 - The maximum costs on a junior loan less than $7,800 is $390. Step 3 - Maximum commission ($500) plus maximum costs ($390) equals $890.

2. The maximum commission and costs allowed when a real estate broker negotiates an $8,000 loan secured by a second trust deed for a period of four years is $1,600.

   SOLUTION: Step 1 - The maximum commission on a junior trust deed loan for three years or more is 15% (15% of $8,000 equals $1,200). Step 2 - The maximum costs on an $8,000 loan is 5% (5% of $8,000 equals $400). Step 3 - Maximum commission ($1,200) plus maximum costs ($400) equal $1,600.

3. Additional loans are treated the same as an original loan in order to determine the maximum costs and expenses to be charged by the broker. **EXAMPLE:** A broker negotiated an $8,000 junior loan on a home for two years and received the maximum fees and commission. After twenty-two months the owner wanted to borrow an additional $2,000 for eighteen months. When the broker arranges the additional $2,000 loan he may only charge the borrower $390 in costs and $100 for his commission. Maximum costs for any loan less than $7,800 is $390, and $2,000 multiplied by 5% equals $100 for commission (maximum commission on the additional loan is 5% because it is for less than two years).

4. When a real estate broker negotiates a $9,000 loan secured by a second trust deed for a period of two and a half years, the maximum commission allowed is $900.

   SOLUTION: The maximum commission on a junior trust deed for 2 years, but less than 3 years, is 10% ($9,000 multiplied by 10% equals $900).

5. When a real estate broker negotiates a $30,000 loan secured by a first trust deed for a period of three years, there is no maximum commission because the loan must be less than $30,000 for the commission to be controlled.

NOTES

REVIEW QUIZ

SECTION I - **Matching** - Select the letter below which best describes, defines, or relates to the following numbered terms.

1. Material Fact
2. Expressed Agency
3. Client
4. Dual Agency
5. Customer
6. Ratified Agency
7. Ostensible Agent
8. Guaranteed Note
9. Fiduciary
10. Promotional Note

a. One person leads another to believe that he has the authority to act for a third party.
b. An agent is authorized to perform activities after the fact.
c. A prospective purchaser to whom the broker shows property without a contract.
d. A note secured by a trust deed in which the seller guarantees a specific yield.
e. One of a series of notes, not over three years old, secured by trust deeds on separate properties in one subdivision.
f. Relationship of trust.
g. The principal of the real estate agent.
h. An agent is authorized to perform activities before the fact.
i. Any information which will influence the decision of the principal.
j. Broker represents and receives a commission from both parties.

SECTION II - **True/False** - Select either true or false in response to the following statements.

1. The real estate broker has a primary fiduciary relationship to the buyer.
2. The death of the principal immediately revokes the agent's authority to perform an activity for the principal.
3. An agent may act in excess of the authority given to him by the principal in order to consummate a transaction.
4. All offers must be disclosed to the seller at the same time.
5. The broker must disclose to the seller if he is going to give a portion of his commission to the buyer.
6. The broker's relationship to his principal is as an Attorney-in-Fact.
7. The relationship of a real estate agent to his principal is similar to the relationship between a trustor and his beneficiary.
8. The buyer could sue both the agent and the seller if an agent misleads a buyer without the seller's knowledge.
9. An endorsement as a real property securities dealer is good for four years.
10. The Broker's Loan Statement must contain the buyer's credit rating.

SECTION III - **Multiple Choice** - Select the letter which best completes the statement or answers the question.

1. A real estate broker must report all material facts to his principal. Which of the following is a material fact?

   A. Purchaser is of a specific ethnic group.
   B. Lender insists on an impound account.
   C. Knowledge that a higher offer is imminent.
   D. None of the above.

2. The Law of Agency is concerned with the duties, responsibilities, obligations, and liabilities between and among:

   A. The principal and a third party.
   B. The agent and his principal.
   C. The principal and his agent in his relationship to a third party.
   D. All of the above.

3. Which of the following is not an essential element to create an agency relationship?

   A. Fiduciary relationship.
   B. Agreement between agent and principal.
   C. Competency of the parties.
   D. An agreement to pay consideration.

4. The real estate broker has a fiduciary relationship with the seller. What responsibility does the broker have to the buyer?

   A. Disclosure of material facts which relate to the selling price.
   B. Honesty and fairness.
   C. Disclosure of only those material facts the buyer inquires about.
   D. Disclosure of nothing because he is paid by the seller.

5. The Real Estate Commissioner may issue a permit on all of the following, except:

   A. Purchase of state land.
   B. Out of state subdivision sales.
   C. Mineral, oil, and gas transactions.
   D. Real property securities transactions.

6. Which of the following forms would be required in the purchase of six real property sales contracts that were created by the recent sale of homes in a new subdivision?

   A. Receipt for Public Report.
   B. Real Property Securities Statement.
   C. Broker's Loan Statement.
   D. All of the above.

7. The possession of a valid real estate license is required by which of the following?

   A. A builder who sells one trust deed per month for twelve consecutive months through a real estate broker.
   B. An individual who purchases one trust deed a month for one year for investment purposes.
   C. An individual who has eight contracts of sale on which he has been collecting payments for four years and which he sells to eight individuals in one year.
   D. A contractor who sells five income properties in one year.

8. A real property securities dealer endorsement is good for:

   A. Four years.
   B. One year.
   C. The term of the broker's license to which the endorsement is affixed.
   D. As long as the broker's license is valid and does not need any further endorsements.

9. The real estate broker negotiates a second trust deed for $8,000. The maximum he can charge for costs and expenses is:

   A. $360.00.
   B. $390.00.
   C. $400.00.
   D. $700.00.

10. An exclusive agreement authorizing a real estate broker to negotiate a loan secured directly, or collaterally, by a lien on real property can never be for a term of longer than forty-five days if the amount of the loan is:

    A. More than $2,000.
    B. More than $2,500.
    C. $2,000 or less.
    D. $2,500 or less.

11. The maximum amount of commission and loan costs that may be charged on a $8,000 second trust deed for a period of four years is:

    A. $1,000.00.
    B. $1,100.00.
    C. $1,200.00.
    D. $1,600.00.

12. When a real estate broker wants to obtain a real property securities dealer's license, he must:

    A. Pay a $100 fee.
    B. Have his license endorsed.
    C. Post a $5,000 surety bond.
    D. All of the above.

13. Which of the following is not required by laws and regulations which regulate the sale of real property securities?

A. A report must be made annually to the Commissioner with respect to advertising.
B. Each transaction dealing with real property securities requires that a $5,000 surety bond be posted with the Secretary of State.
C. The Commissioner will review each offering to insure it is fair, just, and equitable.
D. A real property securities dealer must make an annual audited report to the Commissioner of the total number of sales and dollar volume of sales.

14. A permit must be secured from the Real Estate Commissioner in order to sell, or offer to sell, for the first time:

A. A lot in a Nevada subdivision being offered for sale in California.
B. A home that is purchased from the federal government.
C. A security of a corporation syndication.
D. A land project.

15. Mr. Smith is qualified to act as a real estate broker. Mr. Jones is qualified to act as a real property securities dealer. Which of the following statements is correct?

A. Jones may also negotiate real estate loans.
B. Smith may also act as a real property securities dealer.
C. Both may perform either of the activities mentioned above.
D. All of the above.

Answers may be found in Appendix C (Back of text)

REAL ESTATE CONTRACT LAW

A. CONTRACT DEFINITION - A contract is an agreement based upon consideration between two or more individuals who have the legal capacity to perform or abstain from any lawful activity. A simple contract does not have to be in writing.

B. ESSENTIAL ELEMENTS OF A VALID REAL ESTATE CONTRACT - It is essential to the existence of a valid real estate contract that there be Capable Parties, Mutual Consent, Lawful Object, Consideration, and a Proper Writing.

1. Capable Parties

a. Adult - Generally every adult in California is fully capable of contracting. An adult is any individual who is 18 years old.

b. Emancipated Minor - An emancipated minor is fully capable of contracting. An emancipated minor is any individual under 18 years of age who is:

1. Legally married or divorced.

   a. A married individual under 18 years of age may legally contract and create a valid deed.

   b. A deed signed by a married man under 18 years of age is considered to be valid.

   c. A real estate broker may take a listing from a 17 year old individual who is divorced.

2. On active duty in any branch of the armed forces.

3. Emancipated by court order (must be 14 or over) - A minor who is a ward of the court may legally contract.

c. Exceptions - Certain individuals are not capable of contracting. This includes:

1. Minors - A minor is any individual who is under the age of 18.

   a. A minor does not have the authority to enter into a contract for necessities. When a minor enters a contract, the individual with whom he contracts would risk having the minor disaffirm the contract prior to majority (18 years old), or within a reasonable time thereafter.

b. A deed is considered void when it is signed by a minor in the sale of real property. Should the grantee place improvements on the property received from a minor, the deed will still be considered void; however, the grantee would most likely be able to remove the improvements if the property reverted to the minor.

c. A minor is incapable of appointing an agent.

2. **Incompetents** - An incompetent is an individual who has been judicially determined to be of unsound mind (mentally insane).

   a. An individual is considered to be mentally incompetent when a conservator is appointed by the court to oversee the business affairs of that individual.

   b. A contract is void if an adjudged mentally incompetent individual enters into a real estate transaction without the knowledge of the other party.

3. **Convicts** - A convict is deprived of his civil rights and is incapable of contracting.

4. **Aliens** - A noncitizen or alien may be placed under certain restrictions to legally enter a contract to purchase real estate under Federal Law.

2. **Mutual Consent** - Mutual consent is a meeting of the minds by two or more individuals. This is usually evidenced by offer and acceptance. Mutual consent must be genuine and free of unfair influence. Unfair influence may be:

   a. **Fraud** - Intentionally deceiving or cheating to make an individual perform an activity which may result in the loss of property. When consent of the buyer is induced by fraud on the part of a real estate broker, the seller may still accept the offer; however, the transaction may be voidable on the part of the buyer.

      1. Fraudulent statements made by a real estate broker to induce a buyer to purchase real estate are reasons for the buyer to rescind the contract or to sue the broker and seller for fraud. The seller can be sued even if he was unaware of the statement made by the broker.

      2. **Negative Fraud** - Withholding of information which materially affected the desirability of a property. **EXAMPLE:** The owner and the broker were aware that a building was in a state of disrepair. Failure to disclose this information to the buyer would be negative fraud.

   b. **Duress** - To force an individual to perform an activity based on fear. A contract signed under duress may be accepted; however, it is voidable by the injured party.

   c. **Menace** - To threaten an individual to perform an activity based upon the possibility of duress. A contract signed under menace is voidable by the injured party.

d. Mistake - An error is made in reference to a material fact or its legal effect. The contract is usually void. **EXAMPLE:** When selling a property in another part of the State, neither party is aware that the improvements have been destroyed.

e. Undue Influence - To persuade an individual under weakness of mind to perform an activity of distress or necessity based upon a fiduciary or confidential relationship. A contract signed under undue influence is voidable by the injured party.

3. **Consideration** - Consideration is anything of value which causes an individual to enter into a contract. Consideration may be a promise, payment of money, or performance of an activity or service. Payment of money is not an essential element for a valid contract. A service already performed is not consideration in creating a valid contract. Examples of consideration include the following:

   a. Money to be paid ($1.00 or more).

   b. A promise for a promise.

   c. A promise to be performed.

   d. A service to be performed.

   e. Non-interest bearing note.

   f. A promise given in contemplation of marriage.

   g. A promise to paint improvements which have not yet been built.

4. **Lawful Object** - The object of a contract must be legal when the contract is made and cannot violate any specific law.

5. **A Proper Writing** - A proper writing is usually required for a valid real estate contract.

   a. Real estate contracts required to be in writing are:

      1. Any agreement which cannot be performed within one year.

      2. Any real estate lease agreement which is for longer than one year.

      3. Any agreement which employs a real estate broker to sell, exchange, or lease real property for longer than one year. A written employment contract between the broker and the principal is required in a transaction that includes title or any interest in real property.

      4. Any agreement to sell or exchange real property. A written instrument is required for a valid contract of sale in a real estate transaction.

      5. Any agreement to assume a loan secured by real property.

b. Contracts not required to be in writing include:

    1. Any agreement to be performed within one year.

        a. Leasing real property for one year or less.

        b. The employment of a real estate broker to lease property for one year or less.

    2. The employment of a real estate broker to sell personal property (Business Opportunity).

        a. The employment of a broker to find a business to purchase.

        b. The employment of a broker to sell stock-in-trade and goodwill of a business.

        c. The employment of a broker to negotiate one year leases on business property.

        d. An agreement to transfer personal property under $500.00.

    3. Oral agreements to split commissions between two or more real estate brokers. When two brokers orally agree to split a commission and one broker refuses to pay the other broker his share of the commission, the injured broker could initiate civil action against the other broker and would probably receive a judgment, and thereby receive his commission.

    4. A partnership agreement to buy and sell real property.

    5. An oral agreement for the sale of real property can be enforced when the buyer has taken possession, paid a portion of the purchase price, and made improvements on the property.

    6. An oral agreement for the exchange of real estate is enforceable under specific provisions of the law.

Notes:
1. A valid contract of sale in a real estate transaction does not have to be acknowledged, recorded, or covered by title insurance.
2. A valid real estate contract is required to be a written agreement that must include an accurate description of the property, a designated purchase price, the time and method of payments, and the names and signatures of both parties. Oral evidence of the description of the property will usually be accepted by the courts.
3. Performance is not an essential element of a contract.
4. A single unemancipated individual must be 18 years old to sign a valid contract in a real estate transaction.
5. Duress is most frequently associated with matters involving contracts.
6. Mutual consent may also be referred to as "mutual assent".
7. A contract to be performed beyond a period of one year must be in writing to be enforceable.
8. Actual fraud will occur when a broker does not advertise a property as promised when procuring a listing.

C. STATUTE OF FRAUDS - The Statute of Frauds is a law that requires certain contracts to be in writing to be legally enforceable in a court of law. The Statute of Frauds has nothing to do with the substantial validity of a contract. All it means is that if a contract is not in writing, an individual will not be able to pursue his legal rights. **EXAMPLE:** When an owner orally employs a real estate broker to sell his property, this can be a valid contract if, after the sale, the owner pays the broker his commission. However, an oral contract to sell real property is unenforceable. This means that if the broker procures a buyer in an oral contract and the owner does not pay the broker his commission, the broker could not prove that he had an employment agreement with the owner.

D. STATUTE OF LIMITATIONS - The Statute of Limitations is a law which will establish the time period within which an individual (plaintiff) can bring judicial action against another individual (defendant) for breach of contract.

1. When an individual does not pursue his legal rights within the Statute of Limitations, he is barred (outlawed) from any relief by this statute. This means that an individual must act within a specific time period or else he cannot bring civil action for a breach of contract. Statute of Limitations which relate to real estate include the following time periods for legal remedy:

   a. **Two (2) years** - Oral contracts.

   b. **Three (3) years** - Attachment, Encroachment, Fraud, Inverse Condemnation, and Trespass.

   c. **Four (4) years** - Written contracts. A buyer has four years to bring court action against a seller for failure to perform under the deposit receipt contract.

   d. **Five (5) years** - Adverse possession, prescription, and quiet title action.

   e. **Ten (10) years** - Judgment.

2. **Laches** - Laches is an inexcusable delay in asserting a legal right.

E. COPIES OF CONTRACTS

1. Any individual signing any instrument or contract in a real estate transaction must be given a copy of what he signs **IMMEDIATELY.**

2. Sales contracts must be retained by the broker for three (3) years.

   a. The broker must retain the deposit receipt for three (3) years from the closing date of escrow in a transaction in which a sale has resulted.

   b. The broker must retain the listing contract for three (3) years from the date of the listing in a listing agreement in which a sale has not resulted.

3. Loan documents must be retained for four (4) years. The broker must retain the Mortgage Loan Disclosure Statement for four (4) years.

F. PRIORITY OF CONTRACTS - Some contracts are handwritten and others are printed (prepared forms with blank spaces). Most contracts are a combination of handwritten and printed terms and conditions in which the handwritten portion always takes precedence over the printed portion. Any typed portion will also take precedence over the printed portion.

G. TRANSFER OF CONTRACT - All contracts may be assigned unless there is an agreement to the contrary. Contracts which cannot be assigned include:

1. Any contract which expressly prohibits assignment.

2. A deed can never be assigned.

3. Personal service contracts can never be assigned.

   a. A listing can never be assigned.

   b. Fire insurance usually requires some type of personal quality of the insured. If assigned without the consent of the insurance company, the coverage cannot be extended to the assignee.

4. An option in which the consideration is an unsecured promissory note can never be assigned.

H. BREACH OF CONTRACT - Breach of contract is an individual's failure to perform the terms and conditions of a contract, without legal excuse. Remedies for breach of contract include:

1. **Rescission** - A contract may be cancelled when each party restores the other party to his original position. This means to return everything of value, given or received in the contract, to the original party.

   a. **Unilateral rescission**

      1. The lack of mutual consent makes a contract voidable by the injured party. The injured party may unilaterally rescind the contract if he restores to the other party everything of value received under the contract.

      2. If the buyer defaults, the seller may agree to rescind the contract. This means that the seller must return any received cash deposit to the buyer if the buyer will restore seller to his original position. The buyer may have to pay some consideration to return the seller to his original position.

   b. **Mutual rescission** - Both parties may agree to release each other from the contract and restore each other to his original position.

2. Specific Performance - Specific performance is court action which compels an individual to perform pursuant to a valid contract. Since real property is unique in character and usually cannot be substituted for another property, the courts have made available the right to request specific performance for breach of contract.

   a. Specific Performance can be requested by the buyer or seller.

   b. The buyer of a property would most likely request an action for specific performance for breach of contract. The court would have the vendor or the seller execute a deed pursuant to a valid contract.

   c. The seller could request specific performance, but it would be difficult for the courts to use such action in favor of the seller because the court could not very easily make a buyer purchase a property.

   d. The broker acting as an agent for the seller cannot request specific performance in court. The request must be initiated by the seller.

3. Damages - A reasonable amount of money may be awarded by the court for a breach of contract.

4. Liquidated Damages - Buyer and seller may agree in a contract that the buyer will forfeit his deposit when the buyer does not perform as stated in the contract (buyer is in breach of contract). When the property is a dwelling with no more than four units, one of which the buyer intends to occupy as his residence, seller shall retain as damages the deposit actually paid, or an amount thereof, not more than three (3%) percent of the purchase price. Any excess must be returned to the buyer immediately. Liquidated damages received by the seller are usually divided equally with the listing broker.

I. CLASSIFICATION OF CONTRACTS

1. Valid Contract - A valid contract has all of the essential elements required by law. It is binding and enforceable in a court of law.

2. Void Contract - A contract that is missing one or more of the essential elements required by law. Technically, the term "void contract" is improper terminology because there never was a contract.

3. Invalid Contract - A contract that was initially valid, but is not valid any longer. **EXAMPLE:** An expired listing (after the expiration date on a valid listing, the initially valid listing contract becomes invalid).

4. Voidable Contract - A voidable contract is a contract that is valid and enforceable on its face, but one that may be rejected by one or more of the parties. It is good until it is avoided (rescinded) by the injured party. A contract is valid until some action is taken to make it void. **EXAMPLE:** The contract is voidable by the injured party when the mutual consent is not genuine (fraud, duress, menace, undue influence, etc.).

5. Unenforceable Contract - An unenforceable contract is a contract that can never be enforced in a court of law. **EXAMPLE:** An oral listing to sell real property is unenforceable.

6. **Bilateral Contract** - A bilateral contract is a contract in which the parties make a mutual agreement to perform an act. In a bilateral contract, the promise given in return for the offered promise is referred to as "consideration." **EXAMPLE:** A listing is a bilateral contract. There must first be a promise to act by the owner in order for the broker to be able to promise to act to create a bilateral listing contract. The broker agrees to use "diligence" in a listing contract. This phrase is required to create a bilateral listing contract between both the broker and the owner.

7. **Unilateral Contract** - A unilateral contract is a contract which will obligate only one of the parties to perform an act. **EXAMPLE:** An option. The optionor is the only party required to go through with the sale.

8. **Executory Contract** - An executory contract is a contract that is yet to be performed. **EXAMPLE 1:** A written contract between the employing broker and his salesperson is an executory contract (bilateral executory contract). **EXAMPLE 2:** A listing agreement where the owner states he will pay a commission on the sale of his property, and where the broker states he will use diligence in attempting to find a buyer, is an executory contract (bilateral executory contract).

9. **Executed Contract** - An executed contract is a contract which is completed and fully performed by both parties.

10. **Expressed Contract** - An expressed contract is a contract in which the terms of the contract are written or declared orally.

11. **Implied Contract** - An implied contract is created by performance of an activity or by law.

12. **Illegal Contract** - An illegal contract is a contract which has an unlawful objective.

13. **Parol Contract** - A parol contract is an oral contract. It may be entirely or partially oral.

J. MISCELLANEOUS CONTRACTUAL TERMS

1. **Bona Fide** - In good faith, without fraud. The opposite of collusion.

2. **Collusion** - An agreement between two or more individuals to either defraud or do something unlawful to another person that affects his legal rights.

3. **Novation** - An existing contract is replaced by an entirely new contract.

   EXAMPLE 1: Two individuals have a five year contract. After two years they agree to tear up this contract and replace it with a new ten year contract.

   EXAMPLE 2: A broker who is replaced by another broker in a listing.

4. **Privity** - Mutual relationship to the rights of property, such as ancestor to heirs and assignee to assignor. Privity will most likely exist in a contractual relationship.

5. **Rescind** - Rescind means to annul or terminate a contract.

6. **Rider** - A rider is an amendment to a contract.

7. **Tender** - Tender is an "offer to perform" as promised. An offer in a real estate transaction is tender. The offer of money or performance to fulfill an individual's part of the contract is tender. Tender is only an offer; it is not actually the money or performance of an act. If the offer is unjustifiably refused, it places the party who refuses in default and gives rise to an action for breach of contract.

8. **Waiver** - A waiver is a voluntary relinquishment of a known legal right, or a unilateral act with legal consequences.

NOTES

REVIEW QUIZ

SECTION I - Matching - Select the letter below which best describes, defines, or relates to the following numbered terms.

1. Negative Fraud
2. Consideration
3. Statute of Frauds
4. Statute of Limitations
5. Novation
6. Executed Contract
7. Rider
8. Void Contract
9. Voidable Contract
10. Executory Contract

a. An existing contract is replaced by a new contract.
b. Completed and fully performed.
c. Is yet to be performed.
d. Valid and enforceable on its face, but may be rejected.
e. Anything of value which causes a person to enter a contract.
f. Missing one or more of the legal essentials.
g. Creates the time period in which a person may pursue his legal rights.
h. Withholding information which materially affects the desirability of the property.
i. An amendment to a contract.
j. Requires certain contracts to be in writing to be enforceable in court.

SECTION II - True/False - Select either true or false in response to the following statements.

1. A simple contract does not have to be in writing.
2. A contract would be valid if an adjudged mentally incompetent person entered into a real estate transaction without the knowledge of the other party.
3. A minor that is a ward of the court may legally contract.
4. An alien cannot contract in certain real estate transactions.
5. The payment of money is an essential element for a valid contract.
6. The transfer of personal property which is valued under $500.00 does not have to be in writing.
7. A partnership agreement to sell real property must be in writing.
8. An oral agreement for the exchange of real estate is enforceable under specific provisions of the law.
9. A broker acting as an agent for the seller could request specific performance action in court.
10. Tender is only an offer, it is not actually the money or performance of an act.

SECTION III - Multiple Choice - Select the letter which best completes the statement or answers the question.

1. All of the following are essential elements of a simple contract, except:

    A. Mutual assent.
    B. Lawful object.
    C. Proper writing.
    D. Competent parties.

2. In a contract, consideration may be:

    A. A promise to perform an act.
    B. A promise for a promise.
    C. $1.00 or more.
    D. All of the above.

3. A remedy in court which compels a vendor to execute a deed pursuant to a valid contract is referred to as:

    A. Execution.
    B. Specific performance.
    C. Equity of redemption.
    D. Foreclosure.

4. In a bilateral contract, the promise given in return for an offered promise is referred to as:

    A. Acceptance.
    B. Mutual obligation.
    C. Partial performance.
    D. Consideration.

5. Which of the following would be considered an offer in a real estate transaction?

    A. Tender.
    B. Performance.
    C. Condition.
    D. Covenant.

6. Which of the following must be in writing to be enforceable?

    A. A commission agreement between two brokers.
    B. A general partnership.
    C. A lease for one year or less.
    D. A contract to be performed beyond a period of one year.

7. The law that establishes the time within which a plaintiff can bring suit is:

    A. The Business and Professions Code.
    B. The Statute of Limitations.
    C. The Statute of Frauds.
    D. The Real Estate Law.

8. Since land is unique in character and often cannot be substituted for another parcel, the courts have made available the right to request specific performance. Which of the following would most likely request such an action?

   A. The buyer of a single family residence.
   B. The seller of a single family residence.
   C. The seller of a large tract of land.
   D. The broker acting as agent for the seller.

9. Which of the following constitutes consideration?

   A. A promise given in contemplation of marriage.
   B. Non-interest bearing promissory note.
   C. A promise given to paint a building which has not yet been built.
   D. All of the above.

10. An oral agreement for the sale of real estate may be enforced when:

    A. The broker guarantees performance.
    B. Two neutral individuals witness the transaction.
    C. The consideration is less than $2,500.
    D. The buyer has gone into possession, paid a portion of the purchase price, and made improvements.

11. Rescind means to:

    A. Revise.
    B. Revoke.
    C. Annul.
    D. None of the above.

12. A voidable contract is:

    A. Enforceable.
    B. Illegal.
    C. Unenforceable.
    D. Valid until some action is taken to void it.

13. When an existing contract is replaced by an entirely new contract, this activity is referred to as:

    A. Rescission.
    B. Novation.
    C. Subrogation.
    D. Hypothecation.

14. An executed contract is a contract:

    A. Under the jurisdiction of the courts.
    B. Completed and fully performed by both parties.
    C. Yet to be performed.
    D. Signed, notarized, and recorded in the county where the property is located.

15. A "waiver" is legally defined as:

    A. An unstable individual.
    B. Detrimental justification.
    C. Estoppel.
    D. A unilateral act with legal consequences.

Answers may be found in Appendix C (Back of text)

REAL ESTATE CONTRACTS

A. LISTING

1. **Definition** - A listing is either an employment contract or personal service contract between the broker and the owner. The standard listing contract usually gives the broker authorization to find a buyer, obtain an offer from the buyer, fill out the deposit receipt, and present the offer to the property owner. A listing is always the property of the broker, even when taken by a salesperson who is employed by the broker.

2. **Valid Listing** - A valid listing contract is said to be a "meeting of the minds" of the broker and owner.

3. **Classification of Listings**

   a. **Exclusive Agency Listing** - An exclusive agency listing is a written instrument which gives one broker the right to sell the property for a specified time, but reserves the right of the owner to sell the property himself without paying a commission. The owner promises to pay a commission under all circumstances of sale, except if he sells the property himself.

      1. An exclusive agency listing must have a definite termination date.

      2. In an exclusive agency listing, the broker has a fiduciary relationship with the seller (owner).

      3. In an exclusive agency listing, if an individual owner sells to a friend, the broker will not receive a commission, even if he spent much time and money in a diligent effort to sell the property.

   b. **Exclusive Listing** (Exclusive Right to Sell, Exclusive Authorization to Sell, or Exclusive Authorization and Right to Sell) - An exclusive listing is a written authorization giving one broker the right to collect a commission if the property is sold by anyone during the term of the contract. It provides for payment of a commission to the broker no matter who sells the property. A real estate broker does not have to prove that he introduced the buyer to the seller to collect a commission in an exclusive authorization to sell listing.

      1. An exclusive listing must have a definite termination date. A real estate broker is not permitted to use an exclusive right to sell listing without a termination date.

      2. The exclusive right to sell listing cannot be revoked because it is a binding contract.

      3. In an exclusive listing, a broker cannot recover his expenses unless the seller had authorized the expenses.

c. **Open Listing** - An open listing is a written authorization given to a real estate broker wherein the said broker is given the right, along with other brokers, to secure a purchaser. If an owner lists his property with several brokers, the broker who sells the property is entitled to a full commission.

  1. An open listing does not require a definite termination date.

  2. In an open listing, if the broker shows the property to a prospective buyer, that broker should notify the seller, in writing, as to the identity of his prospective buyer.

  3. To earn a commission in an open listing, the individual must be a licensed real estate broker and produce a ready, willing, and able buyer, or be the procuring cause of the sale.

  4. The phrase "procuring cause" is very important to a broker in a dispute over the commission in an open listing. When two individual brokers have an open listing and they both show the property and report this to the owner, the broker who is able to take a deposit and have the buyer sign an offer will receive the full commission.

  5. An Exclusive Authorization to Sell agreement may be modified to create an Open Listing. A broker should modify the title of the document and any other clauses within the contract. If the broker only modifies the title of the contract, this indicates the intention of the broker to create an open listing and he will, thereby, be unable to claim a commission if the property is sold by another broker.

d. **Net Listing** - A net listing is a written agreement wherein a broker appointed in an exclusive capacity, may retain as compensation for his services, all sums received over and above the net price to the owner.

  1. In a net listing, the broker is required to notify the seller of the gross amount of the offer prior to acceptance by the seller.

  2. A net listing in which the broker does not disclose the amount of his compensation to the seller is unenforceable.

  3. The Real Estate Commissioner does not advocate the use of net listings.

4. **Multiple Listing Service (MLS)** - A multiple listing service is a central organization wherein a group of brokers cooperate with each other to sell each other's listings. When one broker takes a listing, he delivers information in reference to his listing to the central organization. The organization then distributes this information to all of the broker members. This gives greater exposure of the property to the general public and usually results in a faster sale. The commission earned on the sale of the property is then divided between the listing broker and the selling broker. Most listings used by the MLS are Exclusive Right to Sell listings.

5. **Listing with Option** - A real estate broker may have an option and a listing at the same time on one property. When the broker wishes to purchase the optioned property, he must first give notice to the parties that he holds an option and then disclose to the owner how much profit he is to receive by exercising his option.

6. **Provisions Upon Death** - A listing is automatically cancelled upon the death of either the agent (broker) or the principal (owner). Another broker must negotiate a new listing with the owner upon the death of the listing broker. This applies even if another broker inherits both the business and the assets of the deceased broker.

7. **Listing Contract Specifics**

   a. **Property Description** - A legal description is not required on a listing contract. Any accurate description is adequate. **EXAMPLE 1:** The vacant lot on the southwest corner of "J" Street and 23rd Avenue. **EXAMPLE 2:** An individual's residence on 10th Street in Los Angeles. This is adequate if the individual does not have any other property on 10th Street in Los Angeles. The significance of an accurate description on a listing is that it should be so specific that it can be distinguished from all other properties. This will make the contract enforceable, the conveyance effective, and will discourage litigation.

   b. **Deposit** - A real estate broker receives authorization to accept a deposit from the listing contract.

      1. In a listing contract, the owner may instruct the broker not to accept a deposit of less than a certain amount. If the buyer makes an offer with a smaller deposit than required by seller, the broker should present the offer, and if the seller accepts the offer, the broker will receive his full commission.

      2. When a prospective purchaser submits an offer without a deposit, the broker must present the offer and tell the seller that there is not a deposit with the offer.

      3. When a prospective purchaser submits an offer with a "pay to the order" note as the deposit, the broker must present the offer and tell the seller that the deposit is in the form of a note.

      4. Lost deposit:

         a. If there is a misappropriation of any deposit money, the owner/seller is liable because he gives authorization to the broker to accept a deposit when signing the listing.

         b. If the amount of the deposit is not designated and the broker accepts a $500 deposit and then misappropriates it, the seller is liable for the loss.

      5. If the clause "to accept a deposit" is deleted from the listing contract, the broker is not authorized by the owner to accept a deposit. If the broker accepts a deposit, he is acting as an agent for the buyer, but only in reference to the deposit.

6. The broker cannot deduct his previously agreed upon commission from a deposit if the seller has given the broker instructions to place the deposit in escrow.

7. It is illegal for a broker to cash a deposit check and place the money in his office safe. This illegal activity subjects the broker to disciplinary action by the Real Estate Commissioner.

c. **Safety Period** (Protection Period) - A safety period clause may be found in the listing contract. This means that an agent may collect a commission for a negotiated sale after the term of the contract expires if the contract provides a protection period. **EXAMPLE:** ". . if property is sold within 30 days after the termination of this contract to anyone with whom broker has had negotiations prior to the final termination, provided owner has received notice in writing, including the names of the prospective purchasers. .." This means that if a broker shows the property to a prospective purchaser and registers the name of the prospective purchaser with the owner, and then the prospective purchaser buys the property directly from the owner within the 30 day time period, the broker is entitled to his full commission. The protection clause provides that the broker is eligible for a commission after the termination of a listing.

d. **Commission** - A real estate broker is entitled to his full commission when he presents an offer from a buyer who is ready, willing, and able to purchase the property at the exact price and terms of the listing contract. The owner does not have to sell, but the broker can sue for his commission.

1. A broker is not entitled to his commission when he presents an offer at a different price and terms of the listing. **EXAMPLE:** A listing stated that the broker should not submit an offer where the seller will receive more than 25% of the sales price in the year of the sale. If the broker submits an all cash offer, he will not receive a commission.

2. When the broker brings in an offer with the price and terms different from those specified in the listing, the broker may earn a commission if the owner accepts the offer.

3. When a broker obtains an offer at the exact terms of the listing, but after the expiration date of the listing, the broker is not entitled to receive a commission.

4. When husband and wife own property as community property and either spouse signs a listing contract, this obligates the community property to pay a commission if the broker produces a ready, willing, and able buyer.

5. When husband and wife own property as joint tenants and the listing contract is signed by only the husband, this obligates the husband alone to pay a commission if the broker produces a ready, willing, and able buyer. The broker can bring court action against the one spouse who signs the listing contract.

6. The broker may collect a commission if the owner sells the property in the Exclusive Authorization to Sell. The broker cannot collect a commission if the owner sells the property in an Exclusive Agency.

7 . The broker does not have to be the procuring cause to collect a commission in the Exclusive Authorization to Sell. The broker does not have to be the selling agent to collect a commission in the Exclusive Authorization to Sell. Anyone selling the property produces a commission for the listing broker in the Exclusive Right to Sell.

8 . The terms of the listing do not provide for the broker to receive a commission if the buyer defaults. This provision is usually contained in the deposit receipt.

e . **Refusal to Proceed** - The real estate broker may consider the owner's refusal to show the property as a breach of contract and thus sue the owner for damages under an Exclusive Right to Sell listing. All exclusive listings are **IRREVOCABLE**. If the owner cancelled the contract he would still be liable to pay a full commission, even if a second broker both listed and sold the property during the time period of the initial agreement.

f . **Listing Purchased by Broker** - When a real estate broker makes an offer on his own listing, he must disclose to the seller that he is the buyer. This also applies when the broker is a member of a partnership or corporation that makes an offer on the broker's listing. Failure to meet this requirement will be considered improper conduct on the part of the broker on the grounds that he did not reveal his identity in the transaction.

Notes: 1. A listing cannot be recorded.

2. Death of the seller or broker automatically cancels the listing contract.

3. An authorization to sell is to both the seller and agent as a contract of sale is to both the vendor and vendee.

4. The clause "to use diligence in procuring a purchaser" is required to create a bilateral listing contract.

5. A listing signed by one spouse on community real property is enforceable.

6. When the listing states "single family residence", a lease can be written for a maximum of 99 years.

7. The payment of commission to a broker in an oral listing to sell real property, is permissible, if the seller elects to do so.

8. The Exclusive Agency Listing and the Exclusive Right to Sell Listing are similar because they both require a definite termination date.

9. Pocket Listing - A pocket listing exists when the listing agent does not expose the listing to the other agents in his office nor the multiple listing service. The agent keeps the listing to himself because he thinks that he can sell the property himself and receive a larger commission. It is unethical conduct for an agent to use a pocket listing.

ANALYSIS OF THE LISTING CONTRACT
(Use the following numbers to study contract on page 149)

1. Name of the broker.
2. Dates: The beginning date is not required by law, but should be filled in to indicate when the employment of the broker began. The real estate licensee is subject to disciplinary action if the termination date is not filled in on the contract.
3. Name of city.
4. Name of county.
5. Street address of property. A legal description is not required.
6. Write out the price in words.
7. Write the price in numerals.
8. Write the terms (All cash or the financing terms).
9. List any personal property included in the purchase price.
10. Write the name of the multiple listing service (Board of Realtors).
11. Write the name of the individual who will pay for the title insurance (buyer or seller).
12. Write the amount of commission as a percentage, and in dollar amounts.
13. Broker's Protection or Safety Clause - Broker or his salesperson must write in the number of days to be protected.
14. It authorizes the broker to accept a deposit.
15. Write any other terms or, if there is not enough space, refer to an attached addendum which becomes a part of the contract.
16. Write the date the contract is signed (Can be different from the beginning date. When the beginning date is left blank at the top of the contract, this date will be the beginning date).
17. Write the name of the city where the contract is signed.
18. Obtain the signature(s) of the owner(s).
19. Address and telephone number of the owner.
20. This clause creates a bilateral contract.
21. Name of broker.
22. Signature of the individual negotiating the contract (broker or salesperson).
23. Address of the broker.
24. Write the date.

EXCLUSIVE AUTHORIZATION AND RIGHT TO SELL
MULTIPLE LISTING AUTHORIZATION
THIS IS INTENDED TO BE A LEGALLY BINDING AGREEMENT–READ IT CAREFULLY.
CALIFORNIA ASSOCIATION OF REALTORS® STANDARD FORM

1. **EXCLUSIVE RIGHT TO SELL:** I hereby employ and grant _____ **(1)** _____
hereinafter called "Broker," the exclusive and irrevocable right commencing on _____ **(2)** _____, 19____, and expiring at
midnight on _____ **(2)** ____, 19____, to sell or exchange the real property situated in the City of _____ **(3)** _____,
County of _____ **(4)** _____, California described as follows: _____
_____ **(5)** _____
Information sheet ☐ is, ☐ is not attached as part of this agreement.

2. **TERMS OF SALE:** The purchase price shall be _____ **(6)** _____
_____ **(7)** _____($_____), to be paid as follows_____ **(8)** _____
_____
The following items of personal property are included in the above stated price: _____ **(9)** _____

3. **MULTIPLE LISTING SERVICE (MLS):** Broker is a participant of_____ **(10)** _____
_____BOARD OF REALTORS® Multiple Listing Service (MLS) to provide this listing information to the MLS to be published
and disseminated to its participants. The Broker is authorized to appoint subagents and to report the sale, its price, terms and financing for the
publication, dissemination, information and use by authorized Board members, MLS Participants and subscribers.

4. **TITLE INSURANCE:** Evidence of title to the property shall be in the form of a California Land Title Association standard coverage policy of title
insurance in the amount of the selling price, to be paid for by _____ **(11)** _____.

Notice: The amount or rate of real estate commissions is not fixed by law. They are set by each Broker individually and may be negotiable between the Seller and Broker.

5. **COMPENSATION TO BROKER:** I hereby agree to compensate Broker as follows:
(12)(a) _____ percent of the selling price, or $_____ if the property is sold during the term hereof, or any extension thereof, by
Broker on the terms herein set forth or any other price and terms I may accept, or through any other person, or by me, or _____ percent
of the price shown in 2, or $_____, if said property is withdrawn from sale, transferred, conveyed, leased, rented without
the consent of Broker, or made unmarketable by my voluntary act during the term hereof or any other extension thereof.

(b) the compensation provided for in subparagraph (a) above if property is sold, conveyed or otherwise tranferred within _____
calendar days after the termination of this authority or any extension thereof to anyone with whom Broker has had negotiations prior to final
termination, provided I have received notice in writing, including the names of the prospective purchasers, before or upon termination of this
agreement or any extension hereof. However, I shall not be obligated to pay the compensation provided for in subparagraph (a) if a valid listing
(13) agreement is entered into during the term of said protection period with another licensed real estate broker and a sale, lease or exchange of
the property is made during the term of said valid listing agreement.

(c) I authorize Broker to cooperate with other Brokers, to appoint subagents, and to divide with other Brokers such compensation in any manner
acceptable to Brokers.

(d) In the event of an exchange, permission is hereby given Broker to represent all parties and collect compensation or commissions from them,
provided there is full disclosure to all principals of such agency. Broker is authorized to divide with other brokers such compensation or commissions
in any manner acceptable to Brokers.

(e) If requested by Broker, Seller shall execute and deliver an escrow instruction irrevocably assigning Broker's compensation in an amount equal
to the compensation provided in subparagraph (a) (above) from the Seller's proceeds.

(14)6. **DEPOSIT:** Broker is authorized to accept and hold on sellers behalf a deposit on the account of the purchase price.

7. **HOME PROTECTION PLAN:** Seller is informed that home protection plans are available. Such plans may provide additional protection and benefit
to a Seller and Buyer. Cost and coverage may vary.

8. **KEYBOX:** I Authorize Broker to Install a KEYBOX: (Initial) **YES**(____/____) **NO**(____/____)
Refer to reverse side for important keybox information.

9. **SIGN:** I Authorize Broker to Install a FOR SALE/SOLD sign on the property: (Initial) **YES**(____/____) **NO**(____/____)

10. **STRUCTURAL MODIFICATIONS:** Seller shall comply with Civil Code Section 1134.5 by disclosing to Buyer in writing any known structural additions
or alterations, or the installation, alteration, repair, or replacement of significant components of the structures upon the property made with or
without appropriate permit(s).

11. **DISCLOSURE:** Seller's general disclosure obligations are set forth on the reverse side. Seller shall execute a disclosure statement concerning the
condition of the property. Broker is authorized to provide copies to prospective Buyers. I agree to save and hold Broker harmless from all claims,
disputes, litigation, and/or judgments arising from any incorrect information supplied by me, or from any material fact known to me which I fail
to disclose.   (Initial) (____/____)

12. **TAX WITHHOLDING:** Seller agrees to perform any act reasonably necessary to carry out the provisions of FIRPTA (IRC-1445) and regulations
promulgated thereunder. Refer to the reverse side for withholding provisions and exemptions.

13. **EQUAL HOUSING OPPORTUNITY:** This property is offered in compliance with state, local, and federal anti-discrimination laws.

14. **ATTORNEY'S FEES:** In any action or proceeding arising out of this agreement, the prevailing party shall be entitled to reasonable attorney's fees
and costs.

15. **ADDITIONAL TERMS:**_____ **(15)** _____

16. **ENTIRE AGREEMENT:** I, the Seller, warrant that I am the owner of the property or have the authority to execute this agreement. The Seller and
Broker further intend that this agreement constitutes the complete and exclusive statement of its terms and that no extrinsic evidence whatsoever
may be introduced in any judicial or arbitration proceeding, if any, involving this agreement.
I acknowledge that I have read and understand this agreement, including the important information on the reverse side, and have received a copy.

17. **CAPTIONS:** The Captions in this agreement are for convenience of reference only and are not intended as part of this agreement.
Dated_____ **(16)** _____, 19____ _____ **(17)** _____,California

Seller _____ **(18)** _____   Address _____ **(19)** _____

Seller_____ City_____ State_____ Phone_____

(20) In consideration of the above, Broker agrees to use diligence in procuring a purchaser.
Real Estate Broker _____ **(21)** _____ By _____ **(22)** _____
Address _____ **(23)** _____ City_____ _____ Date _____ **(24)** _____

A REAL ESTATE BROKER IS QUALIFIED TO ADVISE ON REAL ESTATE. IF YOU DESIRE LEGAL OR TAX ADVICE CONSULT AN APPROPRIATE PROFESSIONAL.

B. DEPOSIT RECEIPT (Real Estate Purchase Contract and Receipt for Deposit)

1. **Definition** - A deposit receipt is a sales contract between the buyer and seller.

2. **Valid Deposit Receipt** - A valid deposit receipt is said to be a "meeting of the minds" between the buyer and seller. To create a binding contract there must be both an offer and an acceptance.

3. **Parties to an Offer**

   a. **Offeror** - The individual making the offer (usually the buyer).

   b. **Offeree** - The individual receiving the offer (usually the seller).

4. **Presentation of Offer** - Any offer from a prospective purchaser must be presented through the listing broker.

5. **Offer and Acceptance** - A simple contract is an offer and acceptance.

   a. A written offer to purchase becomes a binding contract when the offer is accepted by the seller and the acceptance is communicated back to the buyer in writing. When the buyer revokes his offer prior to being accepted by the seller, the broker must refund to the buyer any earnest money deposit.

   b. An oral offer and acceptance is not a binding contract.

6. **Counter Offer** - A counter offer may be made on the back side of the deposit receipt or on a separate contract which makes reference to the initial contract. In either situation, when taking a counter offer from the seller, the broker must always leave a copy of the counter offer with the seller (immediately). A counter offer automatically terminates an offer.

7. **Termination of Offer** - An offer may be terminated by all of the following:

   a. Rejection by the offeree.

   b. A counter offer.

   c. Conditional acceptance of the offer by the offeree.

   d. Failure to accept the offer within the prescribed period of time.

   e. Revocation by the offeror. The offer may be revoked by the offeror at any time prior to communication of the acceptance by the offeree.

   f. Death or incompetency of either the offeror or offeree without notice thereof.

8. **Provisions Upon Death** - A deposit receipt is not automatically cancelled upon the death of either the buyer or seller. The heirs of the seller may be required to continue with the contract, but it would be difficult to make the heirs of the buyer purchase the property. Do not confuse the binding contract with the offer to purchase. The offer is automatically cancelled upon the death of either party.

9. Deposit Receipt Specifics

a. Property Description - A legal description is not required on a deposit receipt. Any accurate description is adequate.

b. Deposit

1. A deposit may be anything of value; it does not have to be money. The licensee must notify the seller as to the type of deposit prior to acceptance of an offer.

2. A broker may hold a deposit if the buyer stipulates that the broker is to hold the deposit until his offer is accepted by the seller.

3. A broker represents the buyer when a prospective buyer both signs a purchase agreement and gives the broker a deposit toward the purchase of a property on which the broker did not have any previous contract with the owner.

4. When a seller accepts an offer from a buyer and the broker does not have a signed listing contract with the seller, the broker must give the deposit to the seller upon demand.

5. A broker cannot return a deposit, after an offer has been accepted, without the expressed permission of the seller.

c. Commission - A real estate broker is entitled to receive a commission when he has communicated acceptance by the seller to the buyer.

1. If a seller decides not to sell his property while it is in escrow, the seller is usually liable to pay a commission to the real estate broker. **EXAMPLE:** Mr. Jones sells his house for $210,000, receiving a $1,000 deposit from the buyer. Mr. Jones agreed to pay the broker a six percent commission. If Mr. Jones decides not to sell during escrow, the broker is still entitled to a $12,600 commission ($210,000 multiplied by 6%).

2. When the deposit receipt and escrow instructions do not contain any mention of compensation for the broker, the broker will usually receive a commission in accordance with the listing contract.

3. The broker will not receive any commission when the buyer withdraws his offer prior to acceptance by the seller.

4. The terms of the deposit receipt usually provide for the broker to receive a commission if the buyer defaults. This provision is not on the listing contract.

5. A real estate broker is not entitled to receive a commission if an oral contract is not consummated.

d. Release of Obligation - When a purchaser wants to purchase a property contingent upon a certain event, he writes this into the offer. If the specific event(s) never occur, the buyer may cancel the offer and recover his entire deposit.

1. A clause that conditions the purchase of a property subject to the buyer obtaining satisfactory leases is enforceable.

2. When a purchaser wants to make an offer based on making a $1,000 deposit "subject to" the seller's acceptance of the offer, the buyer will write: "$1,000 will be deposited with the broker immediately upon acceptance by the seller".

3. When a buyer wants to purchase a property and protect his deposit --"in the event the escrow on the sale of his other property does not close"-- he inserts in his offer: "This contract is conditioned upon the close of escrow for the sale of the property at a specific address".

4. An owner knows that he can get a loan commitment on his property for $160,000 payable $1,410 per month including 9% interest per annum. The best wording to protect the potential buyer's deposit that is acceptable to the seller is: "Buyer to diligently seek a loan of $160,000 payable $1,410 per month including 9% interest. If buyer cannot qualify for the above described loan, he is released from his obligation to purchase".

e. Liquidated Damages - Most printed contracts have a liquidated damages clause. If the buyer and seller initial this clause, this establishes liquidated damages if the buyer defaults. There is usually an additional clause that will allow the broker to receive one half of the liquidated damages, but not to exceed his full commission. **EXAMPLE:** A $41,000 listing contract provided the broker with a six percent commission. The broker sold the property at the listed price with a three percent cash deposit. The purchase contract provided that the broker was to receive one half of the deposit if it was forfeited. The buyer later withdrew, and the seller accepted forfeiture. The broker received $615.00 ($41,000 X .03 = $1,230 X 1/2 = $615).

f. Acceptance Clause - The buyer does not have to purchase the property if the seller accepts the offer after the acceptance time period has elapsed. The contract is unenforceable and the buyer can demand the return of his deposit. The broker must communicate acceptance back to the buyer within the acceptance time period or else the contract is unenforceable, even if accepted prior to that time.

g. Possession - Possession of the property is usually established by an agreement between the buyer and seller in the deposit receipt.

1. If the time of possession is not stated in the contract, the seller must surrender possession of the property to the buyer at the close of escrow.

2. The real estate broker must obtain written permission from the seller to allow the buyer to enter the property for any reason (remodeling or redecorating) prior to the consummation of the transaction, or to the possession date agreed to in the contract.

h. **Additional Terms** - The signed deposit receipt is a binding contract between the buyer and seller. Any additional terms agreed upon by the two parties may be added to the contract. **EXAMPLE:** The printed deposit receipt does not usually mention discount points. If discount points are to be included in the terms of the contract, the licensee must write a clause to include the payment of discount points.

i. **Time is of the Essence** - Time is of the essence on all contracts. This is either said in words or implied by law. The phrase "time is of the essence" is usually found on the deposit receipt.

ANALYSIS OF THE DEPOSIT RECEIPT
(Use the following numbers to study contract on pages 156-159)

1. Name of city.
2. Date.
3. Name of the buyer (offeror).
4. Write the amount of the deposit in words.
5. Write the amount of the deposit in numerals.
6. Write the name that appears on the deposit check (usually the escrow company, title company, or the broker's trust fund account).
7. Write the amount of the price in words.
8. Write the amount of the price in numerals.
9. Name of city.
10. Name of county.
11. Street address of the property. A legal description is not required.
12. Name of escrow company (if unknown, write "any reliable escrow company").
13. Amount of deposit in numerals.
14. Write the number of days.
15. Name of escrow company.
16. Amount of increased deposit in numerals.
17. Name of escrow company.
18. Write date that the balance of down payment is to be deposited into escrow.
19. Write balance of down payment in numerals.
20. Paragraphs D, E, F, G, H, I, J, & K will be used when applicable based on the terms of the sale.
21. The summation of the Deposit, Increased Deposit, Balance of Down Payment, and Financing Terms (D-K), will equal the total purchase price.
22. Check appropriate box.
23. Name of escrow company.
24. Write number of days.
25. Write a "4" if the contract is four pages.
26. Have buyer(s) and seller(s) initial.
27. Write the existing liens on the property at the time of the offer (usually an expense of the seller, but could be negotiable).
28. Name of title company (if unknown, write "any reliable title company").
29. Write the name(s) of the buyer(s) and how the buyer(s) wish to take title.
30. Items to be prorated in escrow (a condominium will usually have a homeowner's association fee to be prorated).
31. Date of possession by the buyer.
32. List items of personal property to be included in the purchase of the property.
33. Buyer(s) and Seller(s) must both initial if they agree to paragraphs A, B, & C.
34. Write a "4" if the contract is four pages.
35. Have buyer(s) and seller(s) initial.
36. Buyer(s) and Seller(s) must both initial and check appropriate boxes if they agree to include a Pest Control Report with the purchase of the property.

ANALYSIS OF THE DEPOSIT RECEIPT Continued.

37. Buyer(s) and Seller(s) must both initial if they agree to include a Flood Hazard Area Disclosure with the purchase of the property.
38. Buyer(s) and Seller(s) must both initial if they agree to include a Special Studies Zone Disclosure with the purchase of the property.
39. Buyer(s) and Seller(s) must both initial if they agree to include a Energy Conservation Retrofit with the purchase of the property.
40. Buyer(s) and Seller(s) must both initial if they agree to include a Home Protection Plan with the purchase of the property.
41. Buyer(s) and Seller(s) must both initial if the property being purchased is located in a Condominium Project or Planned Unit Development.
42. Buyer(s) and Seller(s) must both initial if they agree to include a Liquidated Damages clause as part of this contract.
43. Write a "4" if the contract is four pages.
44. Have buyer(s) and seller(s) initial.
45. Buyer(s) and Seller(s) must both initial if they agree to include an Arbitration of Disputes clause as part of this contract.
46. Time is of the essence on all contracts. This is either said in words or implied by law. The phrase "time is of the essence" is usually found on the deposit receipt.
47. Write name of broker(s) and confirm representation.
48. Always write the number of days that the seller has to accept the offer.
49. Write the name of the selling broker and the salesperson will sign for his employing broker.
50. Signature(s) of the buyer(s).
51. Write the name of all brokers and the amount of commission.
52. Signature(s) of the seller(s).
53. Print name of broker(s) with signature of respective salespeople.
54. Write a "4" if the contract is four pages.

REAL ESTATE PURCHASE CONTRACT AND RECEIPT FOR DEPOSIT
THIS IS MORE THAN A RECEIPT FOR MONEY. IT IS INTENDED TO BE A LEGALLY BINDING CONTRACT. READ IT CAREFULLY
CALIFORNIA ASSOCIATION OF REALTORS' (CAR) STANDARD FORM

_____(1)_____ California, _____(2)_____ , 19___

Received from _____(3)_____(4)_____ Dollars $ ____(5)____

herein called Buyer, the sum of _____

evidenced by ☐ cash, ☐ cashier's check, ☐ personal check or ☐ _____ , payable to _____(6)_____

_____(7)_____ , to be held uncashed until acceptance of this offer as deposit on account of purchase price of

_____ Dollars $ ___(8)___

for the purchase of property, situated in _____(9)_____ , County of _____(10)_____ California,

described as follows: _____(11)_____

1. **FINANCING:** The obtaining of Buyer's financing is a contingency of this agreement.
   _____(12)_____

   A. DEPOSIT upon acceptance, to be deposited into _____ $ ___(13)___

   B. INCREASED DEPOSIT within __(14)__ days of acceptance to be deposited into _____(15)_____ (18) $ __(16)__

   C. BALANCE OF DOWN PAYMENT to be deposited into ___(17)___ on or before ___(18)___ $ __(19)__

   (20)

   D. Buyer to apply, qualify for and obtain a NEW FIRST LOAN in the amount of .... $ _____

   payable monthly at approximately $ _____ including interest at origination not to exceed _____%,

   ☐ fixed rate, ☐ other _____ all due _____ years from date of origination. Loan fee not to

   exceed _____ . Seller agrees to pay a maximum of _____ FHA/VA discount points.

   Additional terms _____

   E. Buyer ☐ to assume, ☐ to take title subject to an EXISTING FIRST LOAN with an approximate balance of .... $ _____

   in favor of _____ payable monthly at $ _____ including interest at _____% ☐ fixed rate,

   ☐ other _____ . Fees not to exceed _____ .

   Disposition of impound account _____

   Additional terms _____

   F. Buyer to execute a NOTE SECURED BY a ☐ first, ☐ second, ☐ third DEED OF TRUST in the amount of .... $ _____

   IN FAVOR OF SELLER payable monthly at $ _____ ☐ or more, including interest at _____% all due

   _____ years from date of origination, ☐ or upon sale or transfer of subject property. A late charge of _____

   _____ shall be due on any installment not paid within _____ days of the due date.

   ☐ Deed of Trust to contain a request for notice of default or sale for the benefit of Seller. Buyer ☐ will, ☐ will not execute a request

   for notice of delinquency. Additional terms _____

   G. Buyer ☐ to assume, ☐ to take title subject to an EXISTING SECOND LOAN with an approximate balance of .... $ _____

   in favor of _____ payable monthly at $ _____ including interest at _____%

   ☐ fixed rate, ☐ other _____ . Buyer fees not to exceed _____

   Additional terms _____

   H. Buyer to apply, qualify for and obtain a NEW SECOND LOAN in the amount of .... $ _____

   payable monthly at approximately $ _____ including interest at origination not to exceed _____% ☐ fixed rate,

   ☐ other _____ , all due _____ years from date of origination.

   Buyer's loan fee not to exceed _____ . Additional terms _____

   I. In the event Buyer assumes or takes title subject to an existing loan, Seller shall provide Buyer with copies of applicable notes and Deeds

   of Trust. A loan may contain a number of features which affect the loan, such as interest rate changes, monthly payment changes, balloon

   payments, etc. Buyer shall be allowed _____ calendar days after receipt of such copies to notify Seller in writing of disapproval.

   FAILURE TO NOTIFY SELLER IN WRITING SHALL CONCLUSIVELY BE CONSIDERED APPROVAL. Buyer's approval shall not be

   unreasonably withheld. Difference in existing loan balances shall be adjusted in ☐ Cash, ☐ Other _____

   J. Buyer agrees to act diligently and in good faith to obtain all applicable financing. _____

   _____

   K. ADDITIONAL FINANCING TERMS: _____

   _____

   (21) L. TOTAL PURCHASE PRICE .... $ _____

(22) 2. **OCCUPANCY:** Buyer ☐ does, ☐ does not intend to occupy subject property as Buyer's primary residence.

3. **SUPPLEMENTS:** The ATTACHED supplements are incorporated herein:
   ☐ Interim Occupancy Agreement (CAR FORM IOA-11)   ☐ _____
   ☐ Residential Lease Agreement after Sale (CAR FORM RLAS-11)   ☐ _____
   ☐ VA and FHA Amendments (CAR FORM VA/FHA-11)   ☐ _____

4. **ESCROW:** Buyer and Seller shall deliver signed instructions to _____(23)_____ the escrow holder, within __(24)__ calendar days

   of acceptance of the offer which shall provide for closing within _____ calendar days of acceptance. Escrow fees to be paid as follows: _____

   _____

(25)
(26)

Buyer and Seller acknowledge receipt of copy of this page, which constitutes Page 1 of _____ Pages.

Buyer's Initials (_____) (_____)   Seller's Initials (_____) (_____)

OFFICE USE ONLY
Reviewed by Broker or Designee _____
Date _____

REAL ESTATE PURCHASE CONTRACT AND RECEIPT FOR DEPOSIT (DLF-14 PAGE 1 OF 4)

Subject Property Address: _____

(27) 5. **TITLE:** Title is to be free of liens, encumbrances, easements, restrictions, rights and conditions of record or known to Seller, other than the following: (a) Current property taxes, (b) covenants, conditions, restrictions, and public utility easements of record, if any, provided the same do not adversely affect the continued use of the property for the purposes for which it is presently being used, unless reasonably disapproved by Buyer in writing within _____ calendar days of receipt of a current preliminary report furnished at _____ expense, and (c) _____
_____

Seller shall furnish Buyer at _____**(28)**_____ expense a California Land Title Association policy issued by _____
_____ Company, showing title vested in Buyer subject only to the above. If Seller is unwilling or unable to eliminate any title matter disapproved by Buyer as above, Buyer may terminate this agreement. If Seller fails to deliver title as above, Buyer may terminate this agreement; in either case, the deposit shall be returned to Buyer.

(29) 6. **VESTING:** Unless otherwise designated in the escrow instructions of Buyer, title shall vest as follows: _____
_____ .

(The manner of taking title may have significant legal and tax consequences. Therefore, give this matter serious consideration.)

(30) 7. **PRORATIONS:** Property taxes, payments on bonds and assessments assumed by Buyer, interest, rents, association dues, premiums on insurance acceptable to Buyer, and _____ shall be paid current and prorated as of ☐ the day of recordation of the deed; or ☐ _____ . Bonds or assessments now a lien shall be ☐ paid current by Seller, payments not yet due to be assumed by Buyer; or ☐ paid in full by Seller, including payments not yet due; or ☐ _____ . County Transfer tax shall be paid by _____ . The _____ transfer tax or transfer fee shall be paid by _____ . **PROPERTY WILL BE REASSESSED UPON CHANGE OF OWNERSHIP. THIS WILL AFFECT THE TAXES TO BE PAID.** A Supplemental tax bill will be issued, which shall be paid as follows: (a) for periods after close of escrow, by Buyer (or by final acquiring party if part of an exchange), and (b) for periods prior to close of escrow, by Seller. TAX BILLS ISSUED AFTER CLOSE OF ESCROW SHALL BE HANDLED DIRECTLY BETWEEN BUYER AND SELLER.

(31) 8. **POSSESSION:** Possession and occupancy shall be delivered to Buyer, ☐ on close of escrow, or ☐ not later than _____ days after close of escrow, or ☐ _____ .

9. **KEYS:** Seller shall, when possession is available to Buyer, provide keys and/or means to operate all property locks, and alarms, if any.

(32) 10. **PERSONAL PROPERTY:** The following items of personal property, free of liens and without warranty of condition, are included: _____
_____

11. **FIXTURES:** All permanently installed fixtures and fittings that are attached to the property or for which special openings have been made are included in the purchase price, including electrical, light, plumbing and heating fixtures, built-in appliances, screens, awnings, shutters, all window coverings, attached floor coverings, TV antennas, air cooler or conditioner, garage door openers and controls, attached fireplace equipment, mailbox, trees and shrubs, and _____ except _____

12. **SMOKE DETECTOR(S):** State law requires that residences be equipped with an operable smoke detector(s). Local law may have additional requirements. Seller shall deliver to Buyer a written statement of compliance in accordance with applicable state and local law prior to close of escrow.

13. **TRANSFER DISCLOSURE:** Unless exempt, Transferor (Seller), shall comply with Civil Code §§1102 et seq., by providing Transferee (Buyer) with a Real Estate Transfer Disclosure Statement: (a) ☐ Buyer has received and read a Real Estate Transfer Disclosure Statement; or (b) ☐ Seller shall provide Buyer with a Real Estate Transfer Disclosure Statement within _____ calendar days of acceptance of the offer after which Buyer shall have three (3) days after delivery to Buyer, in person, or five (5) days after delivery by deposit in the mail, to terminate this agreement by delivery of a written notice of termination to Seller or Seller's Agent.

14. **TAX WITHHOLDING:** Under the Foreign Investment in Real Property Tax Act (FIRPTA), IRC §1445, *every* Buyer of U.S. real property *must*, unless an exemption applies, deduct and withhold from Seller's proceeds 10% of the gross sales price. Under California Revenue and Taxation Code §§18805 and 26131, the Buyer must deduct and withhold an additional one-third of the amount required to be withheld under federal law. The primary FIRPTA exemptions are: No withholding is required if (a) Seller provides Buyer with an affidavit under penalty of perjury, that Seller is not a "foreign person," or (b) Seller provides Buyer with a "qualifying statement" issued by the Internal Revenue Service, or (c) Buyer purchases real property for use as a residence and the purchase price is $300,000 or less and Buyer or a member of Buyer's family has definite plans to reside at the property for at least 50% of the number of days it is in use during each of the first two twelve-month periods after transfer. Seller and Buyer agree to execute and deliver as directed any instrument, affidavit, or statement reasonably necessary to carry out those statutes and regulations promulgated thereunder.

15. **MULTIPLE LISTING SERVICE:** If Broker is a Participant of an Association/Board multiple listing service ("MLS"), the Broker is authorized to report the sale, its price, terms, and financing for the publication, dissemination, information, and use of the authorized Board members, MLS Participants and Subscribers.

16. **ADDITIONAL TERMS AND CONDITIONS:**

(33) **ONLY THE FOLLOWING PARAGRAPHS 'A' THROUGH 'K' *WHEN INITIALLED BY BOTH BUYER AND SELLER* ARE INCORPORATED IN THIS AGREEMENT.**

Buyer's Initials   Seller's Initials

_____ / _____   _____ / _____   **A. PHYSICAL AND GEOLOGICAL INSPECTION:** Buyer shall have the right, at Buyer's expense, to select a licensed contractor and/or other qualified professional(s), to make "Inspections" (including tests, surveys, other studies, inspections, and investigations) of the subject property, including but not limited to structural, plumbing, sewer/septic system, well, heating, electrical, built-in appliances, roof, soils, foundation, mechanical systems, pool, pool heater, pool filter, air conditioner, if any, possible environmental hazards such as asbestos, formaldehyde, radon gas and other substances/products, and geologic conditions. Buyer shall keep the subject property free and clear of any liens, indemnify and hold Seller harmless from all liability, claims, demands, damages, or costs, and repair all damages to the property arising from the "Inspections." All claimed defects concerning the condition of the property that adversely affect the continued use of the property for the purposes for which it is presently being used (☐ or as _____) shall be in writing, supported by written reports, if any, and delivered to Seller within _____ calendar days FOR "INSPECTIONS" OTHER THAN GEOLOGICAL, and/or within _____ calendar days FOR GEOLOGICAL "INSPECTIONS," **of acceptance of the offer.** Buyer shall furnish Seller copies, at no cost, of all reports concerning the property obtained by Buyer. When such reports disclose conditions or information unsatisfactory to the Buyer, which the Seller is unwilling or unable to correct, Buyer may cancel this agreement. Seller shall make the premises available for all Inspections. BUYER'S FAILURE TO NOTIFY SELLER IN WRITING SHALL CONCLUSIVELY BE CONSIDERED APPROVAL.

Buyer's Initials   Seller's Initials

_____ / _____   _____ / _____   **B. CONDITION OF PROPERTY:** Seller warrants, through the date possession is made available to Buyer: (1) property and improvements, including landscaping, grounds and pool/spa, if any, shall be maintained in the same condition as upon the date of acceptance of the offer, and (2) the roof is free of all known leaks, and (3) built-in appliances, and water, sewer/septic, plumbing, heating, electrical, air conditioning, pool/spa systems, if any, are operative, and (4) Seller shall replace all broken and/or cracked glass; (5) _____

Buyer's Initials   Seller's Initials

_____ / _____   _____ / _____   **C. SELLER REPRESENTATION:** Seller warrants that Seller has no knowledge of any notice of violations of City, County, State, Federal, Building, Zoning, Fire, Health Codes or ordinances, or other governmental regulation filed or issued against the property. This warranty shall be effective until the date of close of escrow.

(34)
(35)   Buyer and Seller acknowledge receipt of copy of this page, which constitutes Page 2 of _____ Pages.

Buyer's Initials (_____) (_____)   Seller's Initials (_____) (_____)

REAL ESTATE PURCHASE CONTRACT AND RECEIPT FOR DEPOSIT (DLF-14 PAGE 2 OF 4)

Subject Property Address _____

(36)

Buyer's Initials   Seller's Initials

____ / ____   ____ / ____   D. PEST CONTROL: (1) Within _____ calendar days of acceptance of the offer, Seller shall furnish Buyer at the expense of ☐ Buyer, ☐ Seller, a current written report of an inspection by _____ , a licensed Structural Pest Control Operator, of the main building, ☐ detached garage(s) or carport(s), if any, and ☐ the following other structures on the property:
_____

(2) If requested by either Buyer or Seller, the report shall separately identify each recommendation for corrective measures as follows:
   "Section 1": Infestation or infection which is evident.
   "Section 2": Conditions that are present which are deemed likely to lead to infestation or infection.
(3) If no infestation or infection by wood destroying pests or organisms is found, the report shall include a written Certification as provided in Business and Professions Code § 8519(a) that on the date of inspection "no evidence of active infestation or infection was found."
(4) All work recommended to correct conditions described in "Section 1" shall be at the expense of ☐ Buyer, ☐ Seller.
(5) All work recommended to correct conditions described in "Section 2," if requested by Buyer, shall be at the expense of ☐ Buyer, ☐ Seller.
(6) The repairs shall be performed with good workmanship and materials of comparable quality and shall include repairs of leaking showers, replacement of tiles and other materials removed for repairs. It is understood that exact restoration of appearance or cosmetic items following all such repairs is not included.
(7) Funds for work agreed to be performed after close of escrow, shall be held in escrow and disbursed upon receipt of a written Certification as provided in Business and Professions Code § 8519(b) that the inspected property "is now free of evidence of active infestation or infection."
(8) Work to be performed at Seller's expense may be performed by Seller or through others, provided that (a) all required permits and final inspections are obtained, and (b) upon completion of repairs a written Certification is issued by a licensed Structural Pest Control Operator showing that the inspected property "is now free of evidence of active infestation or infection."
(9) If inspection of inaccessible areas is recommended by the report, Buyer has the option to accept and approve the report, or within _____ calendar days from receipt of the report to request in writing further inspection be made. BUYER'S FAILURE TO NOTIFY SELLER IN WRITING OF SUCH REQUEST SHALL CONCLUSIVELY BE CONSIDERED APPROVAL OF THE REPORT. If further inspection recommends "Section 1" and/or "Section 2" corrective measures, such work shall be at the expense of the party designated in subparagraph (4) and/or (5), respectively. If no infestation or infection is found, the cost of inspection, entry and closing of the inaccessible areas shall be at the expense of the Buyer.
(10) Other _____
_____
_____

(37)

Buyer's Initials   Seller's Initials

____ / ____   ____ / ____   E. FLOOD HAZARD AREA DISCLOSURE: Buyer is informed that subject property is situated in a "Special Flood Hazard Area" as set forth on a Federal Emergency Management Agency (FEMA) "Flood Insurance Rate Map" (FIRM), or "Flood Hazard Boundary Map" (FHBM). The law provides that, as a condition of obtaining financing on most structures located in a "Special Flood Hazard Area," lenders require flood insurance where the property or its attachments are security for a loan.
   The extent of coverage and the cost may vary. For further information consult the lender or insurance carrier. No representation or recommendation is made by the Seller and the Broker(s) in this transaction as to the legal effect or economic consequences of the National Flood Insurance Program and related legislation.

(38)

Buyer's Initials   Seller's Initials

____ / ____   ____ / ____   F. SPECIAL STUDIES ZONE DISCLOSURE: Buyer is informed that subject property is situated in a Special Studies Zone as designated under §§ 2621-2625, inclusive, of the California Public Resources Code; and, as such, the construction or development on this property of any structure for human occupancy may be subject to the findings of a geologic report prepared by a geologist registered in the State of California, unless such a report is waived by the City or County under the terms of that act.
   Buyer is allowed _____ calendar days from acceptance of the offer to make further inquiries at appropriate governmental agencies concerning the use of the subject property under the terms of the Special Studies Zone Act and local building, zoning, fire, health, and safety codes. When such inquiries disclose conditions or information unsatisfactory to the Buyer, which the Seller is unwilling or unable to correct, Buyer may cancel this agreement. BUYER'S FAILURE TO NOTIFY SELLER IN WRITING SHALL CONCLUSIVELY BE CONSIDERED APPROVAL.

(39)

Buyer's Initials   Seller's Initials

____ / ____   ____ / ____   G. ENERGY CONSERVATION RETROFIT: If local ordinance requires that the property be brought in compliance with minimum energy Conservation Standards as a condition of sale or transfer, ☐ Buyer, ☐ Seller shall comply with and pay for these requirements. Where permitted by law, Seller may, if obligated hereunder, satisfy the obligation by authorizing escrow to credit Buyer with sufficient funds to cover the cost of such retrofit.

(40)

Buyer's Initials   Seller's Initials

____ / ____   ____ / ____   H. HOME PROTECTION PLAN: Buyer and Seller have been informed that Home Protection Plans are available. Such plans may provide additional protection and benefit to a Seller or Buyer. The CALIFORNIA ASSOCIATION OF REALTORS® and the Broker(s) in this transaction do not endorse or approve any particular company or program:
a) ☐ A Buyer's coverage Home Protection Plan to be issued by _____
Company, at a cost not to exceed $_____ , to be paid by ☐ Buyer, ☐ Seller; or
b) ☐ Buyer and Seller elect not to purchase a Home Protection Plan.

(41)

Buyer's Initials   Seller's Initials

____ / ____   ____ / ____   I. CONDOMINIUM/P.U.D.: The subject of this transaction is a condominium/planned unit development (P.U.D.) designated as unit _____ and _____ parking space(s) and an undivided interest in community areas, and _____ . The current monthly assessment charge by the homeowner's association or other governing body(s) is $_____ . As soon as practicable, Seller shall provide Buyer with copies of covenants, conditions and restrictions, articles of incorporation, by-laws, current rules and regulations, most current financial statements, and any other documents as required by law. Seller shall disclose in writing any known pending special assessment, claims, or litigation to Buyer. Buyer shall be allowed _____ calendar days from receipt to review these documents. If such documents disclose conditions or information unsatisfactory to Buyer, Buyer may cancel this agreement. BUYER'S FAILURE TO NOTIFY SELLER IN WRITING SHALL CONCLUSIVELY BE CONSIDERED APPROVAL.

(42)

Buyer's Initials   Seller's Initials

____ / ____   ____ / ____   **J. LIQUIDATED DAMAGES: If Buyer fails to complete said purchase as herein provided by reason of any default of Buyer, Seller shall be released from obligation to sell the property to Buyer and may proceed against Buyer upon any claim or remedy which he/she may have in law or equity; provided, however, that by initialling this paragraph Buyer and Seller agree that Seller shall retain the deposit as liquidated damages. If the described property is a dwelling with no more than four units, one of which the Buyer intends to occupy as his/her residence, Seller shall retain as liquidated damages the deposit actually paid, or an amount therefrom, not more than 3% of the purchase price and promptly return any excess to Buyer. Buyer and Seller agree to execute a similar liquidated damages provision, such as CALIFORNIA ASSOCIATION OF REALTORS® Receipt for Increased Deposit (RID-11), for any increased deposits. (Funds deposited in trust accounts or in escrow are not released automatically in the event of a dispute. Release of funds requires written agreement of the parties, judicial decision or arbitration.)**

(43)
(44)

Buyer and Seller acknowledge receipt of copy of this page, which constitutes Page 3 of _____ Pages.

Buyer's Initials (_____) (_____)   Seller's Initials (_____) (_____)

┌─────── OFFICE USE ONLY ───────┐
│ Reviewed by Broker or Designee _____ │
│ Date _____ │
└──────────────────────────────┘

EQUAL HOUSING OPPORTUNITY

Subject Property Address _____

K. ARBITRATION OF DISPUTES: Any dispute or claim in law or equity arising out of this contract or any resulting transaction shall be decided by neutral binding arbitration in accordance with the rules of the American Arbitration Association, and not by court action except as provided by California law for judicial review of arbitration proceedings. Judgment upon the award rendered by the arbitrator(s) may be entered in any court having jurisdiction thereof. The parties shall have the right to discovery in accordance with Code of Civil Procedure § 1283.05. The following matters are excluded from arbitration hereunder: (a) a judicial or non-judicial foreclosure or other action or proceeding to enforce a deed of trust, mortgage, or real property sales contract as defined in Civil Code § 2985, (b) an unlawful detainer action, (c) the filing or enforcement of a mechanic's lien, (d) any matter which is within the jurisdiction of a probate court, or (e) an action for bodily injury or wrongful death, or for latent or patent defects to which Code of Civil Procedure § 337.1 or § 337.15 applies. The filing of a judicial action to enable the recording of a notice of pending action, for order of attachment, receivership, injunction, or other provisional remedies, shall not constitute a waiver of the right to arbitrate under this provision.

Any dispute or claim by or against broker(s) and/or associate licensee(s) participating in this transaction shall be submitted to arbitration consistent with the provision above only if the broker(s) and/or associate licensee(s) making the claim or against whom the claim is made shall have agreed to submit it to arbitration consistent with this provision.

"NOTICE: BY INITIALLING IN THE SPACE BELOW YOU ARE AGREEING TO HAVE ANY DISPUTE ARISING OUT OF THE MATTERS INCLUDED IN THE 'ARBITRATION OF DISPUTES' PROVISION DECIDED BY NEUTRAL ARBITRATION AS PROVIDED BY CALIFORNIA LAW AND YOU ARE GIVING UP ANY RIGHTS YOU MIGHT POSSESS TO HAVE THE DISPUTE LITIGATED IN A COURT OR JURY TRIAL. BY INITIALLING IN THE SPACE BELOW YOU ARE GIVING UP YOUR JUDICIAL RIGHTS TO DISCOVERY AND APPEAL, UNLESS THOSE RIGHTS ARE SPECIFICALLY INCLUDED IN THE 'ARBITRATION OF DISPUTES' PROVISION. IF YOU REFUSE TO SUBMIT TO ARBITRATION AFTER AGREEING TO THIS PROVISION, YOU MAY BE COMPELLED TO ARBITRATE UNDER THE AUTHORITY OF THE CALIFORNIA CODE OF CIVIL PROCEDURE. YOUR AGREEMENT TO THIS ARBITRATION PROVISION IS VOLUNTARY."

"WE HAVE READ AND UNDERSTAND THE FOREGOING AND AGREE TO SUBMIT DISPUTES ARISING OUT OF THE MATTERS INCLUDED IN THE 'ARBITRATION OF DISPUTES' PROVISION TO NEUTRAL ARBITRATION."

Buyer's Initials   Seller's Initials

(45)   _____ / _____   _____ / _____

17. OTHER TERMS AND CONDITIONS: _____
_____
_____
_____
_____

18. ATTORNEY'S FEES: In any action, proceeding or arbitration arising out of this agreement, the prevailing party shall be entitled to reasonable attorney's fees and costs.

(46) **19. ENTIRE CONTRACT:** Time is of the essence. All prior agreements between the parties are incorporated in this agreement which constitutes the entire contract. Its terms are intended by the parties as a final expression of their agreement with respect to such terms as are included herein and may not be contradicted by evidence of any prior agreement or contemporaneous oral agreement. The parties further intend that this agreement constitutes the complete and exclusive statement of its terms and that no extrinsic evidence whatsoever may be introduced in any judicial or arbitration proceeding, if any, involving this agreement.

20. CAPTIONS: The captions in this agreement are for convenience of reference only and are not intended as part of this agreement.

(47) **21. AGENCY CONFIRMATION:** The following agency relationship(s) are hereby confirmed for this transaction:

LISTING AGENT: _____ is the agent of (check one):
(Print Firm Name)

☐ the Seller exclusively; or ☐ both the Buyer and Seller

SELLING AGENT: _____ (if not the same as Listing Agent) is the agent of (check one):
(Print Firm Name)

☐ the Buyer exclusively; or ☐ the Seller exclusively; or ☐ both the Buyer and Seller.

22. AMENDMENTS: This agreement may not be amended, modified, altered or changed in any respect whatsoever except by a further agreement in writing executed by Buyer and Seller.

(48) **23. OFFER:** This constitutes an offer to purchase the described property. Unless acceptance is signed by Seller and a signed copy delivered in person, by mail, or facsimile, and received by Buyer at the address below, or by _____ who is authorized to receive it, on behalf of Buyer, within _____ calendar days of the date hereof, this offer shall be deemed revoked and the deposit shall be returned. Buyer has read and acknowledges receipt of a copy of this offer. This agreement and any supplement, addendum or modification relating hereto, including any photocopy or facsimile thereof, may be executed in two or more counterparts, all of which shall constitute one and the same writing.

(49) REAL ESTATE BROKER _____   BUYER _____ **(50)**

By _____   BUYER _____

Address _____   Address _____

_____   _____

Telephone _____   Telephone _____

ACCEPTANCE

The undersigned Seller accepts and agrees to sell the property on the above terms and conditions and agrees to the above confirmation of agency relationships

(51) (☐ subject to attached counter offer).

Seller agrees to pay to Broker(s) _____

compensation for services as follows: _____.

Payable: (a) On recordation of the deed or other evidence of title, or (b) if completion of sale is prevented by default of Seller, upon Seller's default, or (c) if completion of sale is prevented by default of Buyer, only if and when Seller collects damages from Buyer, by suit or otherwise, and then in an amount not less than one-half of the damages recovered, but not to exceed the above fee, after first deducting title and escrow expenses and the expenses of collection, if any. Seller shall execute and deliver an escrow instruction irrevocably assigning the compensation for service in an amount equal to the compensation agreed to above. In any action, proceeding, or arbitration between Broker(s) and Seller arising out of this agreement, the prevailing party shall be entitled to reasonable attorney's fees and costs. The undersigned has read and acknowledges receipt of a copy of this agreement and authorizes Broker(s) to deliver a signed copy to Buyer.

(52) Date _____ Telephone _____   SELLER _____

Address _____

_____   SELLER _____

Real Estate Broker(s) agree to the foregoing.

(53) Broker _____ By _____ Date _____

Broker _____ By _____ Date _____

(54) This form is available for use by the entire real estate industry. The use of this form is not intended to identify the user as a REALTOR®. REALTOR® is a registered collective membership mark which may be used only by real estate licensees who are members of the NATIONAL ASSOCIATION OF REALTORS® and who subscribe to its Code of Ethics.

Page 4 of _____ Pages

┌─ OFFICE USE ONLY ─┐
Reviewed by Broker or Designee _____
Date _____

REAL ESTATE PURCHASE CONTRACT AND RECEIPT FOR DEPOSIT (DLF-14 PAGE 4 OF 4)

C. OPTION - An option is a contract to keep an offer open for a specified period of time. The buyer, in effect, purchases an agreed amount of time in which to accept or reject the seller's underlying offer in reference to the property. The offer to sell is irrevocable when an individual owner receives consideration and agrees to keep the offer open for a certain period of time.

1. Parties to an Option

    a. Optionor (Seller) - The optionor is the only party required to go through with the sale.

    b. Optionee (Buyer) - The optionee does not have an estate or interest in the property.

2. Valid Option
- An optionee must give valuable consideration to create a valid option. Consideration of $1.00 is sufficient for a valid option, if the $1.00 is actually given to the optionor. An option given without consideration is invalid.

3. Transfer of Option
- An option may be sold or assigned. The individual optionee (assignor) transfers all of his rights to the assignee. The assignee may exercise the contract based on the original terms of the option.

4. Exercise of the Option
- To exercise an option means that the optionee performed and completed the transaction. The optionee has a choice. He may walk away from the transaction and forfeit his consideration or he may complete the transaction (exercise his option).

    a. When the buyer gives full payment within the specified time period, the option then becomes a binding sales contract.

    b. When the optionor states that he does not want to sell prior to the expiration of the option, this does not terminate the option. The optionee, or his assignee, has a good chance, in court, to have the optionor sell the property to him, if the option is exercised prior to its expiration date.

    c. If the optionee does not exercise the option, he forfeits the thing of value given to the optionor as consideration.

Notes:
1. An option is an offer which expresses contractual intent that cannot be revoked for a specified period of time.
2. It is not necessary to write a separate sales agreement within the option period to have a valid option. The sales agreement is written as a part of the original option contract.
3. A deed in the exercise of an option relates back to the date of the option, and any subsequent interests lose their priority with knowledge of the option.
4. An option on a Business Opportunity may also include the property on which the business operates.
5. A real estate broker may have an option in a sale, provided he discloses that he is a principal in the transaction.
6. The most recognized difference between an option and a land sales contract is the lack of mutual obligation.

REVIEW QUIZ

SECTION I - Matching - Select the letter below which best describes, defines or relates to the following numbered terms.

1. Deposit Receipt
2. Offeror
3. Exclusive Listing
4. Optionor
5. Exclusive Agency Listing
6. Offeree
7. Open Listing
8. Optionee
9. Net Listing
10. Option

a. To keep an offer open for a specified period of time.
b. Usually the seller in a deposit receipt.
c. Broker to receive a commission over and above the amount received by owner.
d. Usually the seller in an option.
e. The broker who sells the property receives the commission.
f. A sales contract between buyer & seller.
g. Broker receives commission if anyone sells the property during the listing.
h. Usually the buyer in an option.
i. Owner may sell the property during the term of the listing & not pay the broker.
j. Usually the buyer in a deposit receipt.

SECTION II - True/False - Select either true or false in response to the following statements.

1. In an exclusive agency listing, the broker has a fiduciary relationship with the buyer.
2. Most listings used by the multiple listing service, are exclusive right to sell listings.
3. A broker does not have to prove that he introduced the buyer to the seller to collect a commission in an exclusive listing.
4. A listing is automatically cancelled upon the death of the agent or the principal.
5. It is legal for a real estate broker to cash a deposit check and place the money in his office safe.
6. A listing cannot be recorded.
7. An offer may be terminated when there is a rejection by the offeree or a revocation by the offeror.
8. A real estate broker is entitled to receive a commission when he has communicated acceptance by the seller to the buyer.
9. A clause that conditions the purchase of a commercial building, subject to the buyer obtaining satisfactory leases, is unenforceable.
10. The optionee is the only party required to go through with the sale in an option.

SECTION III - Multiple Choice - Select the letter which best completes the statement or answers the question.

1. A broker who has an exclusive listing would not be able to recover his expenses unless:

    A. He was acting in the best interest of the seller.
    B. The expense was required to protect the property.
    C. The buyer demanded that the broker spend the money.
    D. The seller had authorized them.

2. A broker has a property listed for $114,000 and submits an offer of $112,000. There is a three day acceptance period in the offer. One day after the acceptance period, the seller accepts the buyer's original offer of $112,000. But the buyer decides that he does not want the property. In this situation, the acceptance is:

    A. Not a contract.
    B. Void.
    C. Voidable.
    D. Enforceable because of the original offer.

3. All of the following are methods by which an offer to purchase real estate will be terminated, except:

    A. Conditional acceptance of the offer by the offeree.
    B. Failure to communicate revocation of the offer before the other party communicates his acceptance.
    C. Incompetency or death of either offeror or offeree without notice thereof.
    D. Failure to accept the offer within a prescribed period of time.

4. An offer is terminated by:

    A. Revocation by the offeror.
    B. Revocation by the offeree.
    C. Rejection by the offeror.
    D. When the contract is changed by the offeror.

5. An offer is terminated by:

    A. Rejection by the offeror.
    B. Rejection by the offeree.
    C. Revocation by the offeree.
    D. When the contract is changed by the offeror.

6. Under a purchase contract, if the buyer defaults and the seller agrees:

    A. Seller may sue for damages.
    B. Seller may advertise the default in a local newspaper and proceed against the buyer.
    C. Seller must place the property back on the market to keep the damages to a minimum.
    D. Seller may agree to return deposit monies to the buyer and the buyer will restore the seller to his original position.

7. A prospective buyer signed an offer to purchase and gave the broker a deposit toward the purchase of the property on which the broker did not have the authorization to sell, nor have any prior contact with the present owner. In this situation, the broker:

   A. Would be representing the buyer, not the seller.
   B. Would be guilty of conversion.
   C. Would be liable to the owner if a civil suit were filed against him.
   D. Cannot legally accept a deposit.

8. In an open listing, a broker earns his commission when:

   A. He is a licensed broker.
   B. He is the procuring cause of the sale.
   C. He produces a buyer who is ready, willing, and able to purchase the property.
   D. All of the above.

9. A normal listing contract allows the real estate broker to:

   A. Convey title to the property.
   B. Guarantee the purchaser will accept.
   C. Find a purchaser, fill out the deposit receipt, obtain an offer, and present it.
   D. Find a purchaser, obtain an offer, and bind the principal to that offer.

10. An individual entered a contract to purchase a commercial building but conditioned his purchase on obtaining satisfactory leases. This contract is:

    A. Enforceable.
    B. Unenforceable under the statute of frauds.
    C. A combination bilateral and unilateral contract.
    D. Illusory.

11. An authorization to sell is to both the seller and agent as a:

    A. Bill of sale is to both the vendor and a secured party.
    B. Sheriff's deed is to both the trustee and beneficiary.
    C. Contract of sale is to both the vendor and vendee.
    D. Sublease is to both the lessee and the trustee.

12. Which of the following is true in reference to an option?

    A. The optionee does not have an interest or estate in the property.
    B. Only the optionor must go through with the transaction.
    C. A deed received in an option relates back to the date of the option and any intervening interests lose their priority.
    D. All of the above.

13. A broker obtains an offer from a buyer who does not have any cash. As a result, the buyer offers a deposit of $1,000 in the form of a promissory note, payable in thirty days. Which of the following is correct?

    A. A broker may accept a note if it is made in favor of the broker to cover his expenses.
    B. A broker may accept a promissory note as deposit if he advises the seller of this prior to acceptance.
    C. This is unacceptable because the deposit must be either cash or check.
    D. The form of the deposit is immaterial as long as the $1,000 amount appears on the deposit receipt.

14. Which of the following is required to create a bilateral listing contract?

    A. The signature of both the husband and wife if the property is community property.
    B. A promise to act by owner for a promise to act by broker.
    C. A promise by owner for monetary consideration, to be paid to the broker.
    D. All of the above.

15. A client's property is listed with a broker under an open listing. After the broker shows the property to a prospective purchaser, the broker should:

    A. Notify the seller in writing as to the prospect's identity.
    B. Confirm the showing to the buyer with a written memo.
    C. Make an official record for the office.
    D. Wait until the prospect contacts the owner before giving any notice.

Answer may be found in Appendix C (Back of text)

REAL ESTATE VALUATION

A. VALUE (WORTH) - Value means the same as worth. A property that has a value of $100,000 is also said to be worth $100,000; therefore, the terms have the same meaning. Value may be thought of as any of the following:

1. The relationship between the thing desired to a potential buyer.

2. The ability of one commodity to command other commodities in exchange.

3. The present worth of all rights to future benefits arising out of the ownership of property.

B. TYPES OF VALUE

1. Market Value - Market value is best described as a concept of both a willing buyer and seller, where neither is under any abnormal influence to act.

   a. In determining market value, an appraiser considers both the tangible and intangible aspects of the property, which include bundle of rights, utility of the property, as well as the physical aspects of the land or any improvements to it.

   b. Definitions of market value are concerned with an open market, value in exchange, and objective value. Definitions of market value are least concerned with material cost.

   c. Market value appraisals assume that a typical purchaser will be able to obtain normal financing.

   d. Market value is most closely related to market price. **MARKET PRICE** is the price that a property actually sells for on the open market.

      1. An offer to buy real estate tends to set the bottom, or floor, on the market price.

      2. An offer to sell real estate tends to set the ceiling, or top, of the market price.

      3. The offer to sell real estate is also the listed price. The listed price of the property usually sets the ceiling on the market value.

   e. Market value is least concerned with material cost.

   f. Reproduction cost will establish a ceiling on market value.

2. Improved Value - Improved value is the market value of the land and the improvements.

3. **Subjective Value** - The value in use, which is value directed toward a specific use. Determines the value of property for a specific purpose or for a specific individual. **EXAMPLE:** Listed price.

4. **Objective Value** - The value which is not subject to restrictions of a given property. **EXAMPLE:** Market Value.

5. **Assessed Value** - The value placed on the property as a basis for property tax.

6. **Book Value** - The value placed on the property for income tax calculations.

7. **Loan Value** - The value placed on the property by lenders when making a loan on a specific property.

8. **Insurance Value** - The value placed on the property by insurance companies.

C. ESSENTIAL ELEMENTS OF VALUE

1. **Utility** - To create value, the item must be useful. The maximum utilization of an available resource is the basic economic factor that best expresses why real estate has value. Functional utility in a dwelling is dependent upon what the occupant desires.

2. **Scarcity** (Supply) - A small supply (greater scarcity) of desirable property will increase values. A large supply of desirable property will decrease values. A commodity can never have value unless it possesses, to some degree, the elements of "utility" and "scarcity". Land is the basic means for all productivity. However, land is a limited resource.

3. **Demand** - The value of property is best determined by the demand of qualified buyers. In order for demand to be effective, it must be implemented by purchasing power.

   a. Increase in demand is usually followed by increases in construction and price. Increase in demand does not increase the quality of construction.

   b. The expansion and contraction of available space to meet demand is stipulated most by market fluctuations of prices and rents. When prices to build are relatively low and rents are high, builders will usually expand the space to meet the demand.

   c. The supply of housing units, versus their demand, influences the vacancy factor in apartment buildings.

   d. There has recently been an increased demand for residential lots with wider front footage.

4. **Transferability** - A property must be able to be transferred from one individual to another to create value . Any real property that has the title restricted or clouded will have a lower value.

D. SPECIAL GREAT FORCES OF VALUE - The value of real property is created maintained, modified, and destroyed by the following four great forces:

1. **Physical Characteristics** - Physical characteristics can be created either by nature or man. Natural characteristics which influence the value of property include: climate, soil type, topography (contour of the land), and natural boundaries for future development, such as oceans, rivers, lakes, mountains, swamps, etc. Improvements created by man which influence the value of property include: the quality of conveniences, public transportation, shopping areas, the availability of schools, churches, etc.

2. **Social Ideas and Standards** - The competition for housing will influence the value of property. This is created by population size and ideas. Population size is influenced by size of family, age, marriage, divorce, birth, death, etc. Social and aesthetic standards are created by both individuals and groups who desire privacy, prestige, recreation, cultural opportunities, etc.

3. **Economic Fluctuations** - The economy of the nation, state, or city will influence the value of property. The economy may fluctuate based on industrial and commercial trends, employment trends, wage levels, price levels, interest rates, the availability of money or credit, the economic base of the community, new developments, natural resources, etc.

4. **Governmental Regulations** - Government regulations will influence the value of property. Federal, state and local governments preserve value through building codes, zoning laws, public health laws, fire regulations, rent control, government housing, government loans, monetary policies, etc.

E. ECONOMIC PRINCIPLES OF VALUE - An individual should understand some basic economic principles which are essential to create value.

1. **Supply and Demand** - The principle of supply and demand involves the inter-relationship of economic forces which affect market value. An increasing supply or declining demand will affect adversely the market value of the property. The opposite is also true; however, the relationship may not be directly proportional.

   a. **Buyer's Market** - Many properties for sale with few buyers.

   b. **Seller's Market** - Fewer properties for sale with many buyers.

2. **Change** - Change is constantly occurring. Social and economic trends will affect the value of property. Value is not permanent; it is always in transition. A change in property value may result from the principles of progression, regression, or integration and disintegration.

   a. **Progression** - The value of a lesser property is increased because of its proximity to similar properties with greater value. **EXAMPLE:** A $30,000 house is built in a neighborhood of $80,000 houses. The value of the $30,000 house may increase 10% because of the better neighborhood.

b. **Regression** - The value of a greater property is decreased because of its proximity to similar properties with lesser value. **EXAMPLE:** A $150,000 house is built in a neighborhood of lower priced houses. The value of the $150,000 house may decrease in value because of the poorer neighborhood. The economic principle is regression; however, the effect the location has on the $150,000 house is economic obsolescence.

c. **Integration/Disintegration** - All property is characterized by three distinct life cycles. Individual properties, neighborhoods, and communities tend to follow the following patterns:

　1. **Integration** (Development) - The development or growth of property.

　2. **Equilibrium** (Maturity) - The stability of property. Property reaches maximum value.

　3. **Disintegration** (Old age) - Property declines in value.

3. **Conformity** - Conformity to land use objectives will maintain values in a community which is properly developed. Zoning ordinances usually help to develop a compatible community. Minor zoning changes do not usually affect the value of the neighborhood. Conformity of houses in a neighborhood usually contribute to the stability of the neighborhood. Residents with similar income tend to stabilize the neighborhood. Most families that are from the same religious or ethnic group tend to stabilize the value of the neighborhood. An introduction of medium priced homes to an area of higher priced homes would probably cause the single family neighborhood to lose value (regression).

4. **Contribution** - The principle of contribution will evaluate an improvement and its influence on the entire property. This means that an individual owner will be interested in what a new improvement will contribute to the amount of his net return on his invested dollar. **EXAMPLE 1:** When an individual wishes to make extensive repairs to an older building, the most important thing for him to take into consideration is how the improvements will influence his net income. **EXAMPLE 2:** The economic feasibility of construction of a swimming pool relates to the principle of contribution. When the owner of an apartment building wishes to build a swimming pool, he calculates what the new pool will contribute to his net income.

5. **Diminishing Returns** - On a given site, at some amount of capital investment or improvements, expenditures for furnishings, or services rendered in management, the maximum return is reached and additional amounts will yield a lesser return.

6. **Highest and Best Use** - Highest and best use is that which is the most profitable likely use of the property -- "the use which results in the highest net income attributable to the land". The recognized definition of highest and best use includes the words "net return". The first logical step in the appraisal of vacant land is to determine the highest and best use of the property.

7. **Substitution** - The principle of substitution holds that the value of a property is based on the ability to acquire an equally desirable property. The substitution of one property for another property may be measured by earnings, structural design, and use of the property. A decision not to buy a property because of the asking price is usually based on the principle of substitution. The principle of substitution may also be defined as:

   a. The cost of producing, through new construction, an equally desirable comparable property, usually sets the upper limit of value.

   b. The value of a property tends to coincide with the value indicated by the activity of informed buyers in the market for comparable properties.

   c. The compensation to which an owner is entitled when deprived of the use of his property is based on the value indicated by the activities of informed buyers in the market for comparable properties.

8. **Anticipation** - The principle of anticipation affirms that value is created by the expectation of future benefits in the property (present worth of future benefits).

9. **Competition** - The principle of competition comes from the fact that profit tends to breed competition, and excessive profit tends to breed ruinous competition.

10. **Surplus Productivity and Balance** - Surplus productivity is defined as the net income remaining after the costs of labor, capital (the investment in the building or equipment), coordination (the management contribution), and land have been paid. Surplus productivity is dependent upon the principle of balance. The maximum value of a property depends on the balance of labor, capital, coordination, and land costs. An imbalance of any of these four agents may decrease value.

F. MISCELLANEOUS ITEMS WHICH INFLUENCE VALUE

1. **Location** - Location is the most important factor to consider in the value of property. Location will influence the demand for a property. The prudent buyer will most likely choose a home that is located in the center of a new subdivision.

2. **Directional Growth** - Property in the path of progress will tend to increase in value. This is especially true if the growth is steady and rapid.

3. **Assemblage** - The process of combining two or more contiguous parcels into one larger parcel which makes the one parcel more valuable than the separate parcels.

4. **Plottage** - The result of assemblage. Plottage is an increase in value resulting from improved usability where two or more contiguous properties are joined together to form a single property under one ownership. Plottage value consists of the increase in front foot or square foot value where several properties are combined to form a single property.

5. **Unearned Increment** - An increase in real estate value without any effort on the part of the individual property owner. Unearned increment may result from increased population, lower taxes, or a change in zoning. Unearned increment is the increase in value of property due primarily to the operation of special forces.

6. **Trend** - A series of related changes brought about by a chain of causes and effects. The trend of employment in the community will affect the value of property.

7. **Amenities** - Amenities are the attractive or beneficial features to be enjoyed by a home or a neighborhood. Those conditions, settings, or improvements to property which increase the enjoyment of living on the property. Amenities are not measured as monetary considerations; however, they are measurable on the market based on pride of ownership for well maintained properties in a neighborhood, and proximity to desirable elements. A nice yard, beautiful trees, and good neighbors are amenities that usually increase the value of residential property. Amenity type properties are usually appraised by the market data approach.

8. **Anchor Tenant** - A business (large department store) that is well known, leases space in a large commercial development. This makes the shopping center more desirable for other small businesses. An anchor tenant will usually stabilize the value of the property. An anchor tenant is the most important factor to a lender considering a loan to a developer of a shopping center.

9. **Fertility of the Soil** - The fertility of the soil is important when selecting land for agricultural purposes. It is not important when selecting land for industrial use.

10. **Sun/Shade Exposure** - The southwest corner of a building is the warmest in the afternoon. A retail merchant prefers to be in a certain location based on the shade from the late afternoon sun.

   a. A retail merchant prefers to be on the south and west sides of the street. The north and east sides of the street are the least desirable sides because a clothing retailer does not like to display samples in the show windows. The bright sun will fade the fabric.

   b. A retail merchant prefers to be on the southwest corner of an intersection.

   c. A retail merchant prefers to be on the northeast corner of a city block. The northeast corner of a city block is the exact same location as the southwest corner of an intersection.

11. **Orientation** - The value of a property may be influenced by the placement of the structure on the lot in reference to the exposure of the sun, wind, privacy, and protection from noise.

12. **Lot Size** - As a lot increases in depth, its value increases and the front foot value increases.

13. **Blighted Area** - An area which is deteriorating because of extreme environmental changes or economic conditions. Deterioration of a residential neighborhood is usually prevented when the neighborhood has artificial or natural barriers, all the families have a similar income, and when the neighborhood is in the path of the directional growth of the city. Deterioration usually occurs when a residential neighborhood is only partially built-up.

14. **Public Transportation** - The lack of public transportation will affect the value of property in the community.

G. MISCELLANEOUS TERMS

1. **Commercial Acre** - An acre of land minus the alleys and streets.

2. **Corner Influence** - The increase in value of a property because of its location on a corner lot.

3. **Depth Table** - A depth table is used by appraisers to estimate the value of commercial property where lots vary in depth (4-3-2-1 Rule). A depth table has nothing to do with water.

4. **Forecasting** - Taking the past as a guide to the future together with both present conditions and the appraiser's judgment for the projection of the future.

5. **Key Lot** - A lot which is located so that one side adjoins the rear of the other lots. This is usually the least desirable lot in the subdivision.

6. **Megalopolis** - A heavily populated urban area which includes many cities.

Notes: 1. Stabilized values are usually created when there is a high percentage of owner occupied dwellings in a neighborhood.

2. The terms and conditions of the sale will affect the price of the subject property.

3. A home may be worth less than it cost if it is an over improvement.

4. Private restrictions are not great forces that influence value.

5. The cost of real property will most likely equal its value if the property is new, or, if the improvements represent the highest and best use of the land.

6. Cost is not an element of value. Original cost is not important when making an appraisal of an old house.

7. The Principle of Contribution may be used with all methods of appraisal (market data, cost and capitalization).

8. The Principle of Substitution will apply to the market data, cost, and capitalization approaches.

NOTES

REVIEW QUIZ

SECTION I - **Matching** - Select the letter below which best describes, defines, or relates to the following numbered terms.

1. Market Value
2. Plottage
3. Improved Value
4. Forecasting
5. Subjective Value
6. Progression
7. Commercial Acre
8. Regression
9. Trend
10. Unearned Increment

a. An acre of land minus the alleys and streets.
b. A series of related changes brought about by a chain of causes and effects.
c. The value of a lesser property increases because of its proximity to properties with greater value.
d. An increase in value resulting from improved usability where one or more properties are joined together to form a single property under one ownership.
e. The value of a greater property decreases because of its proximity to properties with lesser value.
f. A willing buyer, willing seller concept.
g. Value in use for a specific individual.
h. Market value of the land & improvements.
i. An increase in property value without any effort on the part of the owner.
j. Taking the past as a guide to the future.

SECTION II - **True/False** - Select either true or false in response to the following statements.

1. Market value is most closely related to market price.
2. Reproduction cost establishes a ceiling on market value.
3. Private restrictions are great forces which influence value.
4. Definitions of market value are most concerned with material cost.
5. Subjective value is the price that a property actually sells for on the open market.
6. The listed price of property will usually establish the ceiling on market value.
7. Cost is an element of value.
8. The south and west sides of the street are the least desirable for a retail store.
9. As a lot increases in depth, its value increases and the front foot value decreases.
10. Original cost is important when making an appraisal of an old house.

SECTION III - Multiple Choice - Select the letter which best completes the statement or answers the question.

1. The term value is most nearly the same as:

   A. Price.
   B. Cost.
   C. Worth.
   D. Utility.

2. Which of the following groups of words is the best definition for value?

   A. Utility, cost, demand, transferability.
   B. Transferability, utility, scarcity, demand.
   C. Transferability, cost, utility, scarcity.
   D. Utility, scarcity, cost, demand.

3. Which of the following best defines market value?

   A. Cost concept.
   B. Directional growth.
   C. Market price.
   D. Willing buyer-willing seller concept.

4. In order for demand to be effective, it must be implemented by:

   A. Purchasing power.
   B. Reliability.
   C. Transferability.
   D. Objectivity.

5. In reference to a residential neighborhood, which of the following offers the least protection against blighting influences on future development?

   A. When all the families have similar incomes.
   B. Natural or artificial barriers.
   C. Partially built-up neighborhood.
   D. New neighborhood in the path of the directional growth of the city.

6. As a lot increases in depth:

   A. The lot's value decreases and the front footage value decreases.
   B. The lot's value decreases and the front footage value increases.
   C. The lot's value increases and the front footage value increases.
   D. The lot's value increases and the front footage value decreases.

7. When purchasing a home in a new subdivision, a prudent buyer will most likely select a home which is located:

   A. Near a bus stop.
   B. On a key lot.
   C. In the center of the tract.
   D. Across the street from a shopping center.

8. Which of the following is not one of the four great forces which influence the value of real property?

   A. Economic fluctuations.
   B. Private restrictions.
   C. Government regulations.
   D. Social ideas and standards.

9. In the appraisal of real property, the Principle of Substitution applies to:

   A. Cost.
   B. Capitalization.
   C. Market data approach.
   D. All of the above.

10. All of the following are important in the appraisal of an old house, except:

   A. Original cost.
   B. Suitability of the site.
   C. Purpose of the appraisal.
   D. Physical condition of the buildings.

11. "Highest and best use" of the land is best described as that use which:

   A. Creates the highest total gross annual income.
   B. Is in compliance with deed and zoning restrictions.
   C. Is the best in terms of the welfare of the community.
   D. Results in the highest net income attributable to the land.

12. Which of the following is improved value?

   A. Market value divided by the total rents.
   B. Cost of replacement, less depreciation.
   C. Market value of the land and improvements.
   D. The difference between contract and economic rent.

13. Increased demand is usually followed by an:

   A. Increase in the quality of construction.
   B. Increase in price.
   C. Increase in construction.
   D. Both B and C.

14. Definitions of market value are least concerned with:

   A. An open market.
   B. Material cost.
   C. Objective value.
   D. Value in exchange.

15. When there is a high percentage of owner occupied dwellings in a neighborhood, there is usually:

   A. A low rate of turnover.
   B. A high cost of financing.
   C. High rents.
   D. Stabilized values.

Answers may be found in Appendix C (Back of text)

REAL ESTATE APPRAISAL

A. **DEFINITION** - An appraisal is an expert's opinion as to the value of property. Appraisal is considered to be an art, not a science. All appraisals must be in writing and dated. An appraisal is good for one day; however, FHA and VA appraisals are good for six months.

B. **APPRAISER** - A real estate appraiser is not required to have a real estate license. However, federal and state laws require any individual who appraises federally related transactions to be a licensed appraiser or certified appraiser. Federally related transactions include any property purchased with a loan that has federal assistance or federal insurance. Appraisers must be licensed or certified through the Office of Real Estate Appraisers. Appraisal licenses and certificates are not real estate licenses. Real estate licenses are issued by the Department of Real Estate. An appraiser should have a basic knowledge of building design and construction. The Code of Ethics for appraisers includes:

1. The appraiser may only discuss the details of the appraisal with the individual who hired him.

2. The appraisal fee is based on an agreement between the appraiser and his client. An organization such as the Appraisal Institute does not set standardized appraisal fees.

3. When there is a question as to the legality of the improvements on a property, the appraiser should assign a value to the improvements and also state the circumstances in his report.

4. An appraiser may perform an appraisal and collect a fee for his services on a property in which he has an interest, as long as full disclosure is made to his client in the appraisal report (Appraising property for a corporation in which the appraiser owns stock).

5. An appraiser can never charge an appraisal fee which is based on a percentage of the estimated value of the property.

6. An appraiser can never pay a fee to an individual for referring appraisal clients.

7. An appraiser can never accept an assignment without previous knowledge or experience which qualifies the appraiser for the assignment.

8. When an appraiser is employed by a lender to estimate the value of an apartment building, he must determine the value of the property in an identifiable market. The appraiser is not concerned with the requirements of the borrower. The appraiser does not attempt to create a value based on the selling price. He will be conservative in his approach in order to establish a lower value to protect the interest of the lender.

C. THE APPRAISAL PROCESS - An appraisal is made to solve a specific problem. The appraisal process is not an exact science, but a concise, systematic procedure to estimate the value of the property. The orderly step-by-step process to solve the problem is the following:

1. Definition of the problem. To develop a concise statement as to the definition of the problem, an appraiser must understand the precise nature of the real estate to be appraised, the property rights involved, the specific date to which the appraisal applies, the objective of the appraisal report, and a definition of the type of value to be estimated.

2. Make a preliminary survey of the basic problem to estimate the character, the scope, and the amount of work required to solve the problem.

3. Collection and analysis of data. Appraisal data may be divided into general and specific classifications. General data relates to the economy, region, city, and neighborhood. Specific data relates to the property being appraised.

4. Application of the three approaches. The appraiser will attempt to estimate the value based on the comparison, income, and cost approaches. Whenever possible, the value indicated from one approach is compared to the other approaches. If an appraiser decided that one of the appraisal methods was not applicable to the subject property, he would state why it is not a reliable solution to the specific appraisal problem.

5. Reconciliation (correlation) of value. The appraiser will take into consideration the indicated value based on the three approaches. The three approaches are never averaged to estimate value. Major emphasis will be given on one or more approaches which appear to produce the most reliable and applicable solution to the specific appraisal problem.

6. Written appraisal report. The appraiser will make a final estimate of value and prepare the appraisal report. The final estimate of value of a single family residence is ascertained and limited by the market value.

D. THE APPRAISAL REPORT - An appraisal report is good for only one day, which is the date of the appraisal. The appraisal form usually includes an analysis of the property, the site, and the improvements. It does not include the amount and the terms of the loan.

1. **Letter Form** - Consists of a brief description and analysis of the property. It is used when the client is familiar with the area.

2. **Short Form** - Consists of checklists or specific spaces to be filled in about the property. It is used by lending institutions and government agencies.

3. **Narrative Form** - A narrative appraisal is the most comprehensive and complete type of appraisal. It gives the appraiser an opportunity to discuss certain evidence which supports his conclusion. The form is usually divided into an introduction, description of the general neighborhood, market value, economic characteristics, and a final estimate of value. In a narrative appraisal, the property value will be stated under the purpose of the appraisal. It is used by the courts or out-of-town clients who require factual data about the property.

E. APPRAISAL METHODS - Real estate may be appraised by the comparison, income, gross multiplier, or cost approaches.

    1. Comparison Approach (Market Data Approach) - Comparing property to the recent sales prices of similar properties. Sales prices of comparable properties are adjusted to designate what those properties may have sold for if they had been more closely identical to the subject property, or if they had similar prominent characteristics of the subject property. The appraiser will make the properties almost identical by adjusting comparables to the subject property. To establish a basis for a sales price of a 15 year old owner-occupied single family residence in a good neighborhood, emphasis should be placed on the careful analysis of the property in comparison with information related to other selected properties having comparable characteristics.

        a. The market data approach is the oldest, easiest, and quickest method used to calculate the present value of a property.

        b. The market data approach is the easiest method for a beginner to use when appraising property.

        c. When establishing the value of a single family residence using the market comparison approach, the appraiser will be concerned with the neighborhood, living area of the home, and the sales prices of similar properties. The appraiser is not interested in rents being paid for similar properties in the neighborhood.

        d. The terms sales, substitution, comparative, and comparable are related to each other.

        e. The appraiser will usually refer to the selling price of comparable properties in the appraisal of a residential property.

        f. The value of land is usually based on the sales prices of comparable sites. In the appraisal of vacant land, a licensee will be concerned with the highest and best use of the land, and comparable sales to similar properties. When there is a building that does not have any value, it is best to appraise for the highest and best use of the land and then deduct the cost of demolition of the improvements.

        g. When estimating value based on the selling prices of comparable properties, an appraiser is most interested in the date the purchase contract was signed. The date of acceptance of an offer on a comparable property is important to indicate the prevailing market conditions at the time of the sale.

        h. In relation to comparable sales, assessed value, and replacement costs, the appraiser is least concerned with the sales price. This is because the sales price may deviate from actual value based on unequal motivation of sellers, unusual terms, or even a poor negotiating position.

        i. The appraiser gives the most consideration to marketability and acceptability in the appraisal of residential property.

2. **Income Approach** (Capitalization of Net Income Approach) - This is used to appraise income property (any property producing money). The capitalization method of appraisal bases the present value of the property on the anticipated future benefits of ownership in dollars, and discounts them to present worth at a rate which is attracting purchasing capital to similar investments.

   a. Capitalization is the process by which an appraiser converts income to value.

   b. The value of investment property is most dependent upon the capitalization of future net income.

   c. When making an appraisal of an income property, the appraiser considers rent and other charges, date, parties, security and term, covenants, rights of assignment, option for renewal, and provisions for disaster, condemnation, improvements and repairs.

   d. FORMULA - Gross income minus all allowable expenses equals net income. Net income divided by the capitalization rate equals value.

      1. **Gross Income** - Gross income is the sum of all the rent for the entire property for one year. Gross income is always figured on an annual basis. The maximum amount of income an income property may yield is gross scheduled income. Rental schedules in an apartment building or commercial building are best determined by market comparison.

         a. Contract Rent - The actual amount of the bargained rent paid between the landlord and the tenant.

         b. Economic Rent - The expected rent a property may yield if it were available for rent at the time of the appraisal (the portion of the total net income that the land will bring on the open market). Also, rent available to comparable properties in the open market.

         c. An increase in the economic rent which is over and above the contract rent is economically advantageous to the tenant on a long term lease. The tenant can sublease the property at a profit.

         d. When appraising income property, income is based upon the quantity, quality, and durability of income. Quantity of income refers to the amount of rent earned in a year. Quality of income depends on the financial responsibility of the tenant. The appraiser will take into account the quality of income by means of the interest rate used for capitalization. Durability of income refers to the duration or term of the tenancy. The quality and durability of the income affect the risk.

         e. The productivity of real estate is the income the property will produce. There is a direct and proportional variation between income and value. Therefore, productivity is a direct function of value.

2. **Allowable Expenses** - When itemizing the expenses, provisions can be made to allow for taxes, allowances for vacancy and collection losses, insurance, management costs (management agent fee), reserves for replacement, maintenance expenses, and utilities (water and electricity). Expenses that can never be deducted to establish net income include finance charges (cost of payment for principal or interest), building depreciation, capital improvements, federal tax payments, reserves for depreciation of the improvements, remodeling, and business license fees.

   a. Fixed Expenses - These expenses continue regardless of any factors. Fixed expenses include real estate taxes, insurance, mortgage interest, and licenses.

   b. Variable Expenses - These expenses exist in direct proportion to the rental factors. They are at their highest when there is a zero percentage vacancy factor, and at their lowest when there is a large vacancy factor (Maintenance, Management, Utilities, Etc.).

   c. Operating Expenses - These expenses are a combination of the fixed and variable expenses.

3. **Net Income** - The value of income property is most dependent upon net income. The difference between net income as calculated for appraisal purposes, and net income as calculated for investment purposes, is best described as the difference between actual expenses and attributable expenses. Net income calculated for appraisal purposes is based on actual expenses. Net income calculated for investment purposes is based on attributable expenses.

4. **Capitalization Rate** - The capitalization rate is the rate of return demanded by the individual investor. The capitalization rate represents a ratio of income to market value. Capitalization is a process which converts income into value.

   a. Quality, quantity, and duration are considered in the appraisal of an income property. The appraiser takes into consideration the quality of the income by means of the capitalization rate.

   b. Quality of income establishes the interest rate portion of the capitalization rate.

   c. The greater the risk, the higher the capitalization rate. Higher risk is the reason one appraiser may choose a higher capitalization rate.

   d. Taxes are not included in the capitalization rate.

   e. When interest rates on loans increase, the capitalization rate will tend to increase and the value of the property will decrease.

   f. When interest rates go up and the income of a property is fixed, the capitalized value of the property will decrease and the equity in the property will decrease.

g . When the net income is constant, but interest rates increase, the value of the owner's equity will decrease (use a teeter totter).

h . When property taxes increase and all other items remain the same, an income property will decrease in value by more than the amount of the taxes.

i . A decrease in the capitalization rate creates an increase in the value of the property.

j . Service buildings with an income from a government tenant (post office, city hall, etc.) have a lower risk than commercial buildings which receive an income from a commercial tenant (department store, hardware store, etc.). The service type tenant is not as risky as a commercial tenant. Therefore, a property rented to a public service will have a lower capitalization rate than if it were rented to a commercial tenant.

k . The capitalization rate usually provides for return on investment (yield), return of investment (depreciable portion of the property), and depreciation. The return of investment is important in the appraisal of commercial, industrial, and residential income property. The return of investment is not important in the appraisal of farm lands.

l . There are three ways to calculate a capitalization rate; market comparison, summation, and band of investment. The only one that needs to be explained is band of investment.

m. Band of Investment - The theory used to establish a capitalization rate. To arrive at a capitalization rate, the appraiser may use the band of investment approach. The capitalization rate developed by the band of investment theory is a synthesis of trust deed and equity interest rates. The trust deed(s) and equity each represent a specific portion of the entire property --Trust Deed(s) + Equity = 100%. Each portion has its own rate of return. Multiply each portion by its own rate of return to find its product. Then, add the individual products to figure the capitalization rate.

EXAMPLE 1: The first trust deed represents 75% of the property and has a 7% interest rate. The remaining equity demands a 9% return. What is the capitalization rate? **Answer: 7.5%**

Solution:

	PORTION		RATE		PRODUCT
First Trust Deed	.75	X	.07	=	.0525
Equity	.25	X	.09	=	.0225
	1.00				
			Capitalization Rate		.0750 = 7.5%

EXAMPLE 2: The first trust deed represents 50% of the property and has a 6% interest rate. The second trust deed represents 25% of the property and has an 8% interest rate. The remaining equity demands a 10% return. What is the capitalization rate? **Answer: 7.5%**

Solution:

	PORTION		RATE		PRODUCT
First Trust Deed	.50	X	.06	=	.0300
Second Trust Deed	.25	X	.08	=	.0200
Equity	.25	X	.10	=	.0250
	1.00				

Capitalization Rate   .0750 = 7.5%

e. Shortened Formula - Gross income minus all allowable expenses equals net income. Net income divided by the capitalization rate equals value. This formula may be shortened to read: **INCOME** divided by **RATE** equals **VALUE** $(I \div R = V)$. **Variations** can now be made to this formula. Value can be determined by dividing the income by the rate. But, what if rate or income are unknown? When the basic formula is known, it can be changed to figure the rate or the income. The easiest method to change a formula is to substitute simple numbers into the formula that make a new correct formula. Each number will then represent a specific letter in the formula $(I \div R = V)$ can be substituted by $(6 \div 3 = 2)$.

1. Make a new formula to solve for rate. Rate has been substituted by the number three. The new formula must be equal to three. Using the other numbers (6 & 2), make another formula to equal three. Three is equal to six divided by two $(3 = 6 \div 2)$. Now, resubstitute the letters for the corresponding numbers $(R = I \div V)$.

2. Make a new formula to solve for income. Income has been substituted by the number six. The new formula must be equal to six. Using the other numbers (3 & 2), make another formula to equal six. Six is equal to two times three $(6 = 2 \times 3)$. Now, resubstitute the letters for the corresponding numbers $(I = V \times R)$.

f. Variations - The basic capitalization formula can be changed to calculate either the effective gross income or the net spendable income.

1. **Effective Gross Income** - The supply of housing, versus the demand, will most likely influence the vacancy factor of apartment buildings during a period of normal competitive conditions. The vacancy factor of an apartment building is influenced by the availability of other apartment houses in the neighborhood. A variation in the vacancy factor will occur, based on the location of the property, as well as any different time periods (from time to time). The effective gross income reflects both the vacancy factor and the credit losses and may be expressed as any of the following:

a. A deduction of vacancies from gross income is used to arrive at an effective gross income.

b. To determine effective gross income, an appraiser deducts vacancy factors, rental concessions, and collection losses. A rental concession is a reduction in rent for a certain period of time to attract tenants. Rental concessions are most frequently used in shopping centers and commercial buildings.

c. Effective gross income remains after deducting the vacancy and collection losses. Past contractual rent can never be deducted when establishing an effective gross income.

2. Net Spendable Income (Cash Flow) - Net spendable income is the maximum possible income a property can yield. It may be expressed as any of the following:

a. Gross income minus all actual operating expenses of operation, but prior to the deduction of depreciation.

b. Monies left after deducting principal and interest payments and operating expenses from the gross income.

c. Gross income minus principal and interest, actual personal expenses due to investment, and attributable income tax.

d. Gross income minus all actual operating expenses and maintenance, principal and interest payments, and accrued personal expenses due to investment and attributable income tax.

g. Capitalization Rate Mathematics

1. Two individual investors wished to purchase separate properties. Each property had a net income of $30,000. What is the difference in the value of these properties if one investor used a capitalization rate of 5% and the other investor used a capitalization rate of 6%.

SOLUTION: The basic formula is $I \div R = V$. Find the value of each property using the specified rate.

Property 1: $I \div R = V$ or $30,000 ÷ .05 = \quad$ 600,000 Value
Property 2: $I \div R = V$ or $30,000 ÷ .06 = \quad$ <u>500,000 Value</u>
$\qquad\qquad\qquad\qquad\qquad\qquad$ **Answer:** $\quad$ 100,000 Difference

2. Two appraisers were hired to estimate the value of an apartment house. Over the last few years the net income has been quite constant at $9,020. One appraiser used a 10% capitalization rate and the other appraiser used an 11% capitalization rate. The estimated value by the appraiser using the higher capitalization rate will be approximately how much higher or lower in percentage terms than the estimated value of the other appraiser?

SOLUTION: The basic formula is $I \div R = V$. Find the value of each property using the specified rate.

Property 1: $I \div R = V$ or $9,020 ÷ .10 = \quad$ 90,200 Value
Property 2: $I \div R = V$ or $9,020 ÷ .11 = \quad$ <u>82,000 Value</u>
$\qquad\qquad\qquad\qquad\qquad\qquad\qquad\qquad$ 8,200 Difference

ANALYSIS: $8,200 divided by $82,000 equals .10 or 10% ($82,000 is 10% lower than $90,200).

ANSWER: The 11% capitalization rate created a value in the property that is almost 10% lower than the value created by the 10% rate.

3. An apartment building was appraised at $100,000 using an 8% capitalization rate. The value of the property based on a capitalization rate of 10% will be:

SOLUTION: The basic formula is $I \div R = V$. The unknown in this question is the income. Determine the income using $100,000 and 8%. Then use the income with the 10% capitalization rate to find the value of the property.

Step 1: Change the formula to solve for income.

$I \div R = V$ or
$6 \div 3 = 2$ (Substitute numbers).
$6 = 3 \times 2$ or
$I = R \times V$ (Resubstitute letters).

Step 2: Determine the income from the question.

$I = R \times V$ or
$I = .08 \times \$100,000$ or
$I = \$8,000$.

Step 3: Determine the value of the property using the $8,000 income and the 10% rate.

$I \div R = V$ or
$\$8,000 \div .10 = \mathbf{\$80,000}$ **(Answer).**

4. An apartment building with a 6.5% return on its $46,500 value will have a monthly return of:

SOLUTION: The unknown in this question is the income (monthly). Solve for income using the formula in example 3 above, then divide by 12 months.

Step 1: Determine the income.

$I = R \times V$ or
$I = .065 \times \$46,500$ or
$I = \$3,022.50$.

Step 2: Divide the income by twelve months.

$\$3,022.50 \div 12 = \$251.875$ or **$251.88(Answer).**

5. A freeway was recently constructed adjacent to a 24 unit apartment building. If the new freeway causes a loss of $180.00 per month to an owner who uses a capitalization rate of 10%, the loss of value to the property will be:

SOLUTION: The unknown is value (loss of value). Solve for value using the basic formula $I \div R = V$.

Step 1: Convert monthly income to annual income.

$180 x 12 months = $2,160 annual income loss.

Step 2: Solve for value.

$I \div R = V$ or
$2,160 \div .10 = $21,600 **(Answer)**.

h. Residual Techniques - When estimating the value of income property, an appraiser may use the building residual technique, the land residual technique, or the property residual technique.

1. Building Residual Technique - In the building residual technique, the unknown and desired result is the value of the building. The building value is computed by capitalizing the net income after deducting interest on the land value.

2. Land Residual Technique - In the land residual technique, the unknown and desired result is the value of the land.

a. When using the land residual technique the appraiser is primarily concerned with the net return.

b. An appraiser who has many comparables on land values of similar properties will least likely use the land residual technique.

3. Property Residual Technique - In the property residual technique, the unknown and desired result is the value of the property. To establish value by the property residual technique, the appraiser adds the land and the building to establish value of the entire property. The property residual technique uses an overall capitalization rate which applies to the net income. Land residual applies only to the land, and building residual applies only to the building.

i. Percentage Return Rule - The percentage return rule can be used to figure the return (yield) on the purchase price, down payment, or equity. The basic capitalization formula will be used to calculate the percentage return of an item (price, down payment, or equity). Value in the formula will be represented by the individual item. Change the formula to solve for rate ($R = I \div V$). The percentage return formula for the purchase price is $R = I \div$ **Price**. The percentage return formula for the down payment is $R = I \div$ **Down Payment**. The percentage return formula for the equity is $R = I \div$ **Equity**.

EXAMPLE: An investor purchased a property for $10,000. The property returned an annual gross income of 8%. The investor's only expense was 6% interest per year on a $9,000 trust deed. What percentage of return did the investor receive on his equity?

Step 1: Solve for the amount of the equity.

Price	10,000
Trust Deed	9,000
Equity	1,000

Step 2: Determine the gross income.

$10,000 x .08 = $800.00 gross income

Step 3: Determine the expense.

$9,000 x .06 = $540.00 interest expense

Step 4: Use the above three items in the formula.

Gross income	$800.00
Interest expense	- $540.00
Net income	$260.00 divided by (rate) equals $1,000 equity.

Step 5: Rate is the unknown. Change formula to solve for rate (I ÷ R = V) becomes (R = I ÷ V).

R = I ÷ V (Value is replaced by the equity)
R = $260 ÷ $1,000
R = .26 or **26% (Answer).**

3. **Gross Multiplier Approach (Rent Multiplier)** - The gross multiplier approach is a quick one-step appraisal if the gross income of the property is known. It is used in the appraisal of older apartment buildings. The value of the property is based on the relationship between rental value and the sales price of comparable properties. The gross multiplier approach can be used to appraise commercial buildings, residential apartment buildings, industrial properties, and residential properties. The gross multiplier is least likely to be used to appraise public buildings and vacant land. The gross multiplier approach is least concerned with the value of the land.

   a. The gross multiplier is a currently acceptable number used to establish value based on the income of the property.

   b. **Formula** - Gross income multiplied by the gross multiplier equals value (GI x GM = V).

   c. Variations can be made of this formula. The easiest method to change a formula is to substitute simple numbers into the formula that make a new correct formula. Each number will then represent a specific letter in the formula: (GI x GM = V) can be substituted by (2 x 4 = 8).

      1. Make a new formula to solve for the gross multiplier. Gross multiplier has been substituted by the number 4. The new formula must equal four. Four is equal to eight divided by two (4 = 8 ÷ 2). Now, resubstitute the letters for the corresponding numbers (GM = V ÷ GI). The gross multiplier is calculated by dividing the value (sales price) by the gross monthly income.

2. Make a new formula to solve for the gross income. Gross income has been substituted by the number 2. The new formula must equal two. Two is equal to eight divided by four ($2 = 8 \div 4$). Now, resubstitute the letters for the corresponding numbers (GI = V ÷ GM).

d. Gross Multiplier Mathematics

1. A property was rented for $125 per month. An appraiser used the gross multiplier approach to estimate the value of $18,000. The gross multiplier used by the appraiser was:

SOLUTION: Change the formula to solve for the gross multiplier.

(GI x GM = V) becomes (GM = V ÷ GI).
GM = V ÷ GI or
GM = $18,000 ÷ $125 or
GM = **144 (Answer).**

2. When appraising a single family dwelling which is renting for $345 per month, the comparable data of the neighborhood indicates that a similar house across the street recently sold for $39,000 and it had been rented at the time of sale for $300 per month. Based on this information, the value of the dwelling is $44,850.

SOLUTION: Determine the gross multiplier of the comparable property, then use the gross multiplier to determine the value of the dwelling.

Step 1: Solve for gross multiplier of the comparable property.

(GI x GM = V) becomes (GM = V ÷ GI).
GM = V ÷ GI or
GM = $39,000 ÷ $300 or
GM = 130.

Step 2: Use the gross multiplier approach to determine the value of the dwelling.

GI x GM = V or
$345 x 130 = **$44,850 (Answer).**

Notes: 1. The gross multiplier approach is a rough estimate of value.

2. The gross multiplier approach is not as accurate as the capitalization approach.

3. A separate site analysis is not required when using the gross multiplier approach.

4. **Cost Approach** (Replacement, Reproduction, Summation) - The cost approach is used to appraise a special purpose type of property which does not sell very often and where the net income of the property is difficult to calculate (public buildings or utility buildings). The cost approach is concerned with land value, cost per square foot, and depreciation; it is not concerned with the estimated rentals of the property.

   a. In the cost approach, the value of land and improvements is created separately by more than one method.

   1. The market data approach is used to determine the value of the land.

   2. The cost per square foot is used to determine the value of the improvements. The shape of a residence will affect the value of the property in reference to its replacement cost. To determine the square footage of a house, use the outside measurements of the house.

   b. The replacement cost value, plus the value of the land will establish the final value of a single family residence.

   c. The reproduction cost approach is a valid method on new properties where both the cost of building replacement and the value of the land can be ascertained.

   d. The cost approach tends to set the upper limits on value, and the ceiling on market value. It may be used to check the value created by the other appraisal methods.

   e. The cost approach is difficult to use because knowledge of current economic factors is required by an appraiser.

   f. The replacement cost method is most accurate in the appraisal of real property when the improvements are new. This is because there is not any depreciation to be calculated on a new building. Therefore, the cost approach is most effective on new buildings. The cost approach is most appropriate to use in the appraisal of a new single family residence.

   g. The replacement cost method is more difficult to use in the appraisal of older properties because the depreciation schedule is more difficult to calculate on older buildings.

   h. FORMULA

   1. The value of the land.

   2. Compute the value of the improvements.

   3. Subtract the accrued depreciation.

   4. Add the value of the land.

i. EXPANDED FORMULA

1. The value of the land (Comparison Approach) - Separate the land from the entire property.

2. Compute the value of the improvements (structure) brand new today. Always use the exterior dimensions. In the appraisal of a home, the square footage for replacement cost purposes will be calculated by measuring the outside dimensions of the house and the garage.

3. Calculate the depreciation for one year (Annual Depreciation). Use the **EVA** formula.

$$\text{Economic Life} \,) \, \overline{\text{Value of the Improvements}} \quad = \quad \text{Annual Depreciation}$$

OR

Value ÷ Economic Life = Annual Depreciation (V ÷ E = A)

4. Calculate the accrued depreciation. Multiply the annual depreciation by the actual age of the improvements.

   Note: If an **EFFECTIVE AGE** is given, it must be used in place of the actual age to calculate accrued depreciation. Effective age is the age given by the appraiser (the opinion of the appraiser) based on the physical condition of the improvements. The effective age may be shorter or longer than the actual age, depending on the physical condition of the property. **EXAMPLE 1:** The appraisal estimate is 8 years old for depreciation when a 15 year old building has been maintained in exceptional condition. **EXAMPLE 2:** At the time of the appraisal, a building is 15 years old. The building was so well maintained that the appraiser assigned a 6 year life to the building. The 6 year effective age will be used to calculate the accrued depreciation.

5. Subtract the accrued depreciation from value of the improvements. An improvement is the only item that can be depreciated. Land can never be depreciated. Subtract the accrued depreciation from number two above.

6. Add the value of the land plus any landscape, if given. Add number one above to the remainder of number five to estimate the value of the property.

j. Reproduction Cost Mathematics

1. The cost of the land was $22,500. After construction, the property was valued at $131,000. If the economic life was 50 years, what would the property be worth after seventeen years?

SOLUTION:

Value of the land =	$ 22,500
Value of improvements (separate land from entire property - $131,000 - $22,500 = $108,500) =	$108,500

EVA becomes V ÷ E = A ($108,500 ÷ 50 years = $2,170 Annual Depreciation)

$2,170 x 17 years = $36,890 Accrued Depreciation =	- $ 36,890
Depreciated Value of the Improvements =	$ 71,610
Add the land =	$ 22,500
Value =	**Answer: $ 94,110**

2. The owner of a 20 unit apartment building installed two water heaters at a cost of $200 each, a new roof at a cost of $1,500, and awnings at a cost of $800. The useful life of these items is: water heater - 10 years; new roof - 15 years; and awnings - 8 years. What is the total accrued depreciation if the awnings are three years old and the water heaters and the roof are four years old?

SOLUTION: Compute the annual depreciation of each item, multiply by its respective age, and then total the accrued depreciation.

Water heaters ($200 each)

EVA becomes V ÷ E = A ($200 ÷ 10 years = $20 Annual Depreciation)
$20 x 4 years = $80 Accrued Depreciation (One heater) x 2 = $160

Roof ($1,500)

EVA becomes V ÷ E = A ($1,500 ÷ 15 years = $100 Annual Depreciation)
$100 x 4 years = $400 Accrued Depreciation = $400

Awnings ($800)

EVA becomes V ÷ E = A ($800 ÷ 8 years = $100 Annual Depreciation)
$100 x 3 years = $300 Accrued Depreciation = $300

Total accrued depreciation =   **Answer: $860**

F. APPRAISAL MISCELLANEOUS

1. **Urban Commercial Property** - When analyzing the data to estimate the value of urban commercial property, the most important factor is location. Both the lack of public transportation and the trend of community employment will affect property values.

2. **Leased Property** - In making a complete analysis of a leased property, the appraiser will consider the date, the rent and other charges, the parties of the lease, the security and term of the lease, covenants of the lease, options and renewal or assignment of the lease, maintenance of the property, and provisions for destruction or condemnation of the property.

3. **Cost** - The expenditure of money required for the creation of an improvement on a property. The cost of real property will most likely equal its value if the property is new or if the improvements represent the highest and best use of the land.

4. **Management Costs** - In the appraisal of income property, management costs will be considered when the owner manages the property, when a tenant manages for free rent, or when the tenant manages the property without any cost to the owner. If any cost is overlooked when listing an income property, it is usually the cost of management.

5. **Hoskold and Inwood** - Hoskold and Inwood are two appraisers who developed appraisal handbooks. Therefore, the terms Hoskold and Inwood relate to estimating value. The significant difference between Hoskold and Inwood appraisal methods is the use of the **SINKING FUND** concept. A sinking fund is money which is set aside from the income of an income producing property to replace the improvements on the property as needed. A sinking fund is similar to **DEPRECIATION RESERVES.** Depreciation reserves occurs when the investor creates a reserve savings account to protect his invested capital.

6. **Deferred Maintenance** - Deferred maintenance is the negligent or postponed repair of property. Deferred maintenance is best represented in a building that requires rehabilitation.

7. **Economic Life** (Useful Life, Theoretical Life) - The period over which a property will yield a return on the investment over and above the economic or ground rent due to land. Economic life is the period in which the improvements are worth being maintained. Economic life depends on the owner's repair policy, and the age, use, and condition of the improvements. The average economic life of a frame structure is forty years. The buyer of a property will be concerned with the future economic life of the building.

8. **Physical Life** - The period over which an improvement will be functional or will remain standing. The economic life of an improved property is always shorter than the physical life of an improved property.

Notes: 1. The first step of the appraisal process is to define the problem.
2. The final step of the appraisal process is to make a final estimate of value.
3. To appraise a vacant parcel of land, the first logical step is to determine the highest and best use of the property.
4. The Comparative Analysis Approach is used to appraise unimproved land for the purpose of building a single family residence.

4. Accrued Depreciation - Accrued depreciation is past depreciation. It is an appraiser's estimate of accumulated age depreciation, with allowances for conditions based on the effective age of the property. Accrued depreciation is best estimated by the approved appraisal methods. Direct or indirect methods may be used to compute accrued depreciation.

5. Direct Methods of Depreciation - Direct methods of depreciation include age life, engineering, and breakdown techniques.

    a. Age Life (EVA) - The age life method is based on the assumption that depreciation will occur at a constant average annual rate over the estimated economic life of the improvements. Depreciation will accumulate at the same percentage each year.

    b. Engineering - The engineering method is computed exactly the same as the age life method; however, it considers the individual component parts of the building. It requires a more complete inspection of the improvements and is based upon a reasonably comprehensive cost analysis, such as a quantity survey or unit-in-place cost method.

        1. Quantity Survey - A detailed estimate of all labor and materials is compiled for each component of the building. The quantity survey is the most expensive and difficult type of appraisal. Real estate appraisers seldom use this method.

        2. Unit-in-Place Cost Method - The cost of units of the building (walls, foundations, floors, windows, ceilings, roof, etc.) as installed is computed and applied to the entire structure. Real estate appraisers seldom use this method.

    c. Breakdown (Observed Condition, Cost to Cure) - The breakdown method is computed by making an analysis of physical deterioration, functional obsolescence, and economic obsolescence. The curable and incurable deficiencies are then translated into a monetary estimate for accrued depreciation.

6. Indirect Methods of Depreciation - Indirect methods of depreciation include capitalized income and market data.

    a. Capitalized Income - The capitalized income method is computed by taking the difference between the reproduction cost (new) and the capitalization approach to determine the accrued depreciation.

    b. Market Data - The market data method is computed by taking the difference between the reproduction cost (new) and the market data approach to determine the accrued depreciation.

Notes: 1. The greatest cause of depreciation is obsolescence.

2. Normal wear and tear due to use do not contribute to obsolescence.

3. The impairment of both desirability and usefulness of real property by economic changes is brought about by obsolescence.

4. When itemizing expenses in the Capitalization Approach, provisions can be made for the return of the investment (depreciation).

5. Quantity survey, comparative square foot, or cubic foot methods are used by appraisers, architects, and contractors to estimate the cost in reproducing the construction of improvements.

6. Quantity survey, unit-in-place, comparative square foot, and cubic foot measurements are used in the cost approach. All of these methods are considered comprehensive methods of estimating building costs to include labor, material, overhead, and profit.

7. On a unit cost per square foot basis, a small house will cost more than a large house.

8. The appraiser and accountant are interested in the depreciation of real estate for two different reasons. The appraiser is interested in actual depreciation and the accountant is interested in the book value of depreciation.

9. An appraiser will not normally use the Cost Approach to appraise an old house with a great amount of functional obsolescence.

10. A "fee appraiser" is usually self-employed and charges a fee for each appraisal.

11. An appraiser may be found guilty of a felony if improper techniques are used to appraise property that is financed with a government insured or guaranteed loan.

REVIEW QUIZ

SECTION I - Matching - Select the letter below which best describes, defines, or relates to the following numbered terms.

1. Effective Age
2. Market Data Approach
3. Accrued Depreciation
4. Physical Life
5. Gross Income
6. Cost Approach
7. Net Spendable
8. Capitalization Approach
9. Effective Gross Income
10. Economic Life

a. Sets the upper limits on value.
b. The sum of all the rent for the entire property for one year.
c. Bases present value on future benefits.
d. Useful life of the building.
e. Past depreciation with allowances for conditions based on the effective age.
f. Gross income minus vacancy factor.
g. Appraiser assigns to a well maintained building to compute accrued depreciation.
h. Monies left after deducting principal and interest payments and operating expenses from the gross income.
i. The easiest method for a beginner to use when appraising property.
j. Period during which property will remain functional.

SECTION II - True/False - Select either true or false in response to the following statements.

1. An appraiser may pay a fee to a broker for referring clients to him.
2. The final step of the appraisal process is to define the problem.
3. A narrative appraisal is the most comprehensive and complete type of appraisal.
4. When appraising a building without any value, the appraiser should appraise for highest and best use and add the cost of demolition.
5. The value of income properties is most dependent upon net income.
6. The maximum amount of income an income property may yield is gross scheduled income.
7. The theory to establish a capitalization rate is referred to as band of investment.
8. The gross multiplier approach is least likely to be used to appraise public buildings.
9. The cost approach is most effective in older buildings.
10. Normal wear and tear contribute to obsolescence.

SECTION III - Multiple Choice - Select the letter which best completes the statement or answers the question.

1. Which of the following is the first step in the appraisal process?

   A. Classify the data.
   B. Organize the data process.
   C. Define the problem.
   D. Make a preliminary survey and appraisal plan.

2. Which of the following approaches to value tends to set the upper limit of value?

   A. Comparative sales.
   B. Market data.
   C. Income.
   D. Replacement.

3. Which of the following types of depreciation is the most difficult to eliminate?

   A. Functional obsolescence.
   B. Economic obsolescence.
   C. Physical depreciation.
   D. Physical deterioration.

4. Functional obsolescence is a decrease in value due to:

   A. Being outdated.
   B. Decline in neighborhood.
   C. Wear and tear.
   D. Adverse zoning.

5. Which of the following is an example of economic obsolescence?

   A. Architectural design.
   B. Termite infestation.
   C. Negligence of tenant.
   D. Legislative regulations.

6. Which of the following could be considered functional obsolescence?

   A. Oversupply.
   B. Private restrictions.
   C. Lack of air conditioning.
   D. Insufficient parking available.

7. In the appraisal of residential property, the cost approach is most appropriate in the case of:

   A. Older property.
   B. New property.
   C. Middle aged property.
   D. Multi-family property.

8. Which approach to value is given most consideration in an appraisal of a shopping center?

   A. Market data.
   B. Construction cost.
   C. Summation.
   D. Income.

9. An appraiser received a $175 fee from Mr. Brown for appraising Mr. Jones' property. The appraiser may discuss the details of the appraisal with:

   A. Anyone.
   B. Jones.
   C. Brown.
   D. No one.

10. In analyzing the data to establish the value of urban commercial property, the most important factor is the:

   A. Topography.
   B. Size of parcel.
   C. Depth of parcel.
   D. Location.

11. Productivity is a direct function of:

   A. Value.
   B. Use.
   C. Supply.
   D. Demand.

12. An appraiser using the cost method may use the unit cost per square foot or per cubic foot in his computations. On a unit cost per square foot basis:

   A. A small house will cost more than a large house.
   B. A small house will cost less than a large house.
   C. A large house will cost more than a small house.
   D. The cost of a large house and a small house will be the same.

13. Depreciation of real estate may be the result of:

   A. Reserves for replacement.
   B. Plumbing repairs.
   C. Increase in amenities.
   D. Poor architectural design.

14. Economic obsolescence is not affected by:

   A. Zoning changes.
   B. Income of the area.
   C. Neighborhood influence.
   D. Failure of heating and air conditioning system.

15. A definition of value to an appraiser is:

A. The ability of one commodity to command other commodities in exchange.
B. The present worth of all rights to future benefits arising out of the ownership of property.
C. The relationship between the thing desired and the potential purchaser.
D. All of the above.

Answers may be found in Appendix C (Back of text)

REAL ESTATE FINANCE

The real estate industry is dependent upon financing. The extension of credit on suitable terms is essential in order to purchase or to develop real property. Real estate financing constitutes the largest use of funds that flows into financial institutions and money markets.

A. FEDERAL RESERVE BANKING SYSTEM - The Federal Reserve Banking System was created in 1913. It is the nation's central bank and consists of 12 regional banks (Federal Reserve Banks) which are controlled through the Federal Reserve Board. The Federal Reserve Board (FED) may control the supply of money in our economy by regulation of the reserve requirements of the member banks, adjustment of the discount rate, or participation in the Government Bond market.

    1 . Reserve Requirement - Each member bank must maintain cash reserves on account based on a certain percentage of its deposits.

        a . Increased Reserves - An increase in the reserve requirement will decrease the amount of money which is available for real estate financing. The Federal Reserve Board raises reserve requirements to curb inflation.

        b . Decreased Reserves - A decrease in the reserve requirement will increase the amount of money which is available for real estate financing. The Federal Reserve Board lowers the reserve requirements to increase the availability of money in our economy.

    2 . Discount Rate - The discount rate is the interest rate charged by a Federal Reserve Bank (FED) to its member banks.

        a . Increased Rate - An increase in the discount rate will increase the cost of money for financing and slow the flow of money. Raising the discount rate to borrowers makes less money available in our economy. The Federal Reserve Board raises the federal discount rate to curb inflation.

        b . Decreased Rate - A decrease in the discount rate will decrease the cost of money for financing and stimulate the economy.

    3 . Government Bond Market - The Federal Reserve Board may expand open market conditions with the sale or purchase of U. S. Government Securities through the Federal Open Market Committee.

        a . Sale of Bonds - The sale of government bonds will remove funds from the money market. The Federal Reserve Board sells bonds to curb inflation. When the FED feels there is an inflationary trend developing in the United States, they can enter into the government bond market in a selling capacity. This will decrease the supply of money for financing and creates a "tight money market".

1. A conventional loan costs the most in a tight money market.

2. The seller pays higher discount points under an FHA or VA loan in a tight money market.

3. A tight money market in which the FED has taken action to reduce the money supply will most likely result in an increase in new second trust deeds and mortgages, a decrease in new first trust deeds and mortgages, a decrease in new home construction, and a decrease in real estate sales.

4. A real estate licensee would be least affected if he was active with exchange transactions during a tight money market.

b. **Purchase of Bonds** - The purchase of government bonds will release funds into the money market and supplement the money supply for real estate financing.

B. FEDERAL HOME LOAN BANK SYSTEM

B. FEDERAL HOME LOAN BANK SYSTEM - The Federal Home Loan Bank System was created in 1932. It consists of a Federal Home Loan Bank Board and the Federal Home Loan Bank (FHLB). The Federal Home Loan Bank Board supervises the activities of the Federal Home Loan Banking System. The primary purpose of the Federal Home Loan Bank is to establish a credit reserve for Savings and Loan Associations. The FHLB is the organization that has given the most assistance to provide mortgage funds for home loans on a national scale.

C. MORTGAGE MARKETS (Money Markets)

1. **Primary Mortgage Market** (Primary Money Market) - The primary money market is where loans are created by lenders for qualified borrowers. An increase in the availability of funds in the real estate mortgage market comes from both individuals placing more money or household savings into savings institutions and from individuals saving more for old age retirement. The desire by people for more liquid assets does not increase the availability of funds for the real estate mortgage market. Increased rates on corporate and government bonds is least likely to increase the availability of funds for residential financing.

2. **Secondary Mortgage Market** (Secondary Money Market) - The secondary money market is where loans are purchased and sold between lenders to provide for more funds in the primary market. Liquidity and marketability are important in the secondary mortgage market. The secondary money market creates a market-place for loans to be transferred between mortgagees and mortgagees.

a. **Federal National Mortgage Association** (FNMA.) "Fannie Mae" - Under Title III of the National Housing Act of 1934, the Federal National Mortgage Association was initially created primarily for the purpose of providing housing credit for the economy. This means that FNMA was created to provide more credit in the secondary mortgage market. FNMA was created primarily to purchase FHA and VA loans from the lending institutions to stabilize the mortgage market.

b . Federal Home Loan Mortgage Corporation (FHLMC) "Freddie Mac" -
The Federal Home Loan Mortgage Corporation was established by Congress to
increase the availability of mortgage credit for needed housing. FHLMC has
the authority to buy and sell conventional, FHA, and VA loans in the secondary
money market.

c . Government National Mortgage Association (GNMA.) "Ginnie Mae"-
The Government National Mortgage Association was established under the
Housing and Urban Development Act to purchase FHA loans on low income
housing from the lending institutions to stabilize the mortgage market when
FNMA considered the loans too risky.

D . CONVENTIONAL LOAN - A conventional loan is any loan made by an
institutional lender without being insured or guaranteed by the government. When
considering a loan, a conventional lender is concerned with government regulations,
the economic and financial condition of the nation, and the amount of funds available
for lending. However, the lender is most concerned with the degree of risk involved
in making the loan.

E . FEDERAL HOUSING ADMINISTRATION LOAN (FHA) - The National
Housing Act of 1934 created the FHA loan in order to insure lenders against loss.
FHA was originally created to provide insurance for lenders, but in addition to
providing for the insuring of loans, it has had some secondary benefits which include
establishing minimum standards for construction, a comprehensive system for valuing
property and rating mortgage risk, stimulating mortgage investment on a national basis,
and scientific subdivision planning to reduce neighborhood deterioration. FHA does
not loan money. A buyer seeking an FHA loan applies to an institutional lender who
provides FHA financing. The buyer (borrower) would not apply at the FHA office.

1 . Lender Considerations - Prior to making an FHA loan, a lender must consider
the supply and demand of mortgage funds, equity of the borrower in the investment, and the current discount rate. The interest rate and mortgage insurance rate
are least likely to be considered by the lender when making an FHA loan. The
equity position of the borrower is not a primary concern of the lender on an FHA
loan because if there is a default, the loan is insured by the federal government.

2 . Types of Loans

a . Title I - May be used for alteration or repair of existing home improvements.
The purpose cannot be for the purchase of a home.

b . Title II (Section 203b) - The basic insured loan used for the construction or
purchase of residential property (1 - 4 units).

c . Title III - Used to provide additional credit in the secondary money market.

3 . Minimum Property Requirements (MPR's) - The FHA specifies certain
minimum construction standards on home loans insured by FHA. These standards control material, products and construction methods, plot and building plans,
internal and external finishes, mechanical equipment, individual water supply,
sewage disposal and plot development. The minimum ceiling height on an FHA
loan is 7 1/2 feet, however, a home purchased using FHA financing will usually
have a ceiling height of eight (8) feet in California.

4 . Down Payment - The down payment on an FHA loan will always be different because it is calculated on the amount borrowed. To calculate the down payment, take 3% of the first $25,000 of the appraisal, plus 5% of any excess over $25,000 of the appraisal, and 100% of excess of the purchase price over the appraisal.

EXAMPLE: What is the down payment on a house with a $60,000 appraisal.

Solution:	Appraisal	$60,000		
	3% of first	$25,000	=	$ 750
	5% of balance	$35,000	=	$1,750
		Down payment	=	$2,500

5 . Loan Fee - A possible 1% service charge may be charged to the borrower on an FHA loan. The FHA loan fee, which is paid by the borrower, is referred to as an origination fee.

6 . Discount Points - The discount points on an FHA loan are equivalent to prepaid interest. The discount points usually charged on an FHA loan may be paid by either the buyer or seller.

7 . Prepayment Penalty - A prepayment penalty is never charged when paying off an FHA loan.

8 . Insurance - Mutual mortgage insurance is required by FHA. Mutual mortgage insurance protects the lender in the event of default on an FHA loan.

9 . Secondary Financing - Secondary financing is not allowed when buying a property using an FHA loan. A real estate licensee can refuse to accept an offer when the buyer wants to submit the offer using FHA financing and secondary financing. Secondary financing may be added at a later date.

10. Loan Assumption - An FHA loan does not contain an alienation clause; therefore, it may be assumed. It is usually easier to assume an FHA loan than a conventional loan or insurance company loan. The fee paid by a buyer who takes over an existing FHA loan is referred to as an assumption fee.

11. Rental of the Property - A house purchased to rent may be financed with an FHA loan.

12. Comparison to a Conventional Loan

	FHA	CONVENTIONAL
Processing	Slower	Faster
Terms	Less flexible	More flexible
Interest Rate	Lower	Higher
Down Payment	Smaller	Larger
Principal Payment	Smaller	Larger
Loan To Value Ratio	Larger	Smaller
Impound Account	Required	Not always required
Maturity Date	Longer	Shorter
Assumption of loan	Easiest	Not always easy

1. FHA loans usually require an improvement in housing standards.
2. When a lender chooses to make an FHA loan instead of a conventional loan, the determining factor will be the degree of risk.
3. The FHA loan requires a loan impound account for property taxes and insurance.

F. VETERANS ADMINISTRATION LOAN (VA) **"G. I. Loan"** - The Serviceman's Readjustment Act of 1944 created the VA loan in order to guarantee lenders against loss. The VA loan was originally created to provide a guarantee for lenders, but in addition to providing for the guarantee of loans, the VA is concerned with the development of new neighborhoods. The VA has jurisdiction over the development of subdivisions where homes are purchased using VA loans. A buyer seeking a VA loan normally applies to an institutional lender who provides VA financing.

1. **Lender Considerations** - The amount of a GI loan to purchase a home is directly limited by the lender's requirements and the buyer's capacity to pay.

2. **Certificate of Eligibility** - A veteran must obtain a Certificate of Eligibility to be qualified for a VA loan. This can be obtained by submitting the proper forms and discharge papers (DD Form 214) to the VA. The Certificate of Eligibility indirectly limits the amount of the GI loan.

3. **Certificate of Reasonable Value** (CRV) - The Certificate of Reasonable Value is issued by the VA. This is the VA's appraisal. The maximum amount of the federally approved VA loan is the amount stated in the CRV. The amount of a GI loan to purchase a home is directly limited by the CRV.

4. **Down Payment** - A down payment may be required by a lender; however, a down payment is only required when the purchase price exceeds the amount stated in the CRV. **EXAMPLE:** A home being purchased for $80,000 has a $77,500 CRV. If the lender is willing to loan the maximum allowed by VA, the lender would loan $77,500. The GI buyer will be required to pay a cash down payment for the difference or $2,500.

5. **Discount Points** - Lenders continue to charge points on VA loans to close the gap between the market rates and the fixed rates. This will equate the yield and provide the lender with a competitive yield. The discount points charged on the VA loan may be paid by either the veteran buyer or the seller.

6. **Prepayment Penalty** - A prepayment penalty is never charged when paying off a VA loan.

7. **Guarantee** - The guarantee will vary depending on the loan amount. Check with lender. In the event of default on a VA loan, the property will be sold. A veteran is liable if the government has to advance funds under the guarantee. Liability continues if the veteran sells the property and allows a non-veteran to purchase the property "subject to" the existing VA loan. The federal government is allowed to seek a deficiency judgment against the veteran's purchase money trust deed if they advance money under the guarantee. The VA may also offset any such claims against any benefits that the veteran can claim in the future from the government.

8. **Secondary Financing** - Secondary financing is allowed when buying a property using a VA loan.

9. **Loan Assumption** - A VA loan does not contain an alienation clause; therefore, it may be assumed. A VA loan may be taken over by anyone, including veterans and non-veterans. When the veteran sells his house "subject to" the existing VA loan, the guarantee continues, even if the new owner is not a veteran.

10. **Rental of the Property** - A house that was purchased for rental purposes can never be financed with a VA loan.

11. **Comparison to Conventional Loan**

	VA	CONVENTIONAL
Processing	Longer	Shorter
Terms	Less flexible	More flexible
Interest Rate	Lower	Higher
Down Payment	Smaller	Larger
Loan to Value Ratio	Larger	Smaller
Maturity Date	Longer	Shorter

G. CAL-VET LOAN - The California Farm and Home Purchase Act created the Cal-Vet loan in order to assist California veterans with farm and home purchases. Currently, any veteran who can qualify for a VA loan may also qualify for a Cal-Vet loan. The Cal-Vet loan is administered by the California Department of Veterans Affairs (DVA). A qualified veteran who wishes to purchase a home under the Cal-Vet program must file an application with the California Department of Veterans Affairs (DVA).

1. **Lender Considerations** - The funds for a Cal-Vet loan come from the sale of State Bonds. A trust deed is not used in a Cal-Vet loan. The California Farm and Home Purchase Act provides that the buyer acquires possession through the use of a land contract. When a qualified veteran purchases a home using a Cal-Vet loan, title is held by the DVA.

2. **Down Payment** - The down payment on a Cal-Vet loan will be 3% for a home of $35,000 or less and 5% on homes over $35,000.

3. **Discount Points** - Discount points can never be charged on a home loan created under DVA. Excluding any down payment, the Cal-Vet loan will involve the least amount of closing costs for the buyer when compared to other loans.

4. **Interest Rate** - The Cal-Vet loan may have a variable amortization rate.

5. **Prepayment Penalty** - The Cal-Vet loan provides for a prepayment penalty if the loan is paid off during the first five (5) years. There is a prepayment penalty based on six (6) months interest on 80% of the loan balance when a Cal-Vet loan is paid off within the first five years.

6. **Insurance** - The borrower is required to apply for term life insurance and disability insurance under the Cal-Vet loan.

7. **Rental of the Property** - A California veteran can never rent his house without obtaining permission from the DVA.

8. Loan Assumption - A Cal-Vet loan may be assumed; however, it is not easy to assume because it may only be assumed by a California veteran.

Notes: 1. FHA and VA do not loan money. FHA insures the loan. VA guarantees the loan.

2. The assumption of loans is usually easiest when the existing loan is an FHA or VA loan.

3. The buyer in an FHA loan agrees to pay mutual mortgage insurance and to make amortized payments.

4. Included in an FHA loan is a "schedule of payments". An FHA loan does not have secondary financing, a prepayment penalty, or mortgage life insurance.

5. Points - Points means the same as percentages. When a lender states that he will charge two (2) points, this means that he will charge 2% of the loan. Points paid in advance are equivalent to prepaid interest.

6. Discount Points - Used by lenders in FHA and VA loans to adjust their effective interest rate so that it is equal to the prevailing market rate. This means that the loan amount may be discounted in order to provide the lender with a higher current market yield. The rule of thumb is that every 1/8 percent difference is equal to one discount point.

7. Impounds - The real estate finance term "impound" means the same as reserves. The lender may require reserves for fire insurance, property taxes, and assessment bond payments when making a loan. Mortgage interest is least likely to be a part of impound deposits.

   IMPOUND MATH: A $24,500 building is insured at $0.16 per hundred per annum. The premium for three years is two and one-half times the annual rate. How much would the lender require per month for an impound account to cover the cost of the insurance? **Answer: $2.72 per month.**

   SOLUTION: $0.16 x 245 hundreds = $39.2 per annum. $39.2 x 2 1/2 years = $98.00 for 3 years. $98.00 divided by 36 months = $2.72.

8. Loan Origination Fee - A fee paid to the lender for the preparation of loan documents.

9. The Soldiers and Sailors Civil Relief Act limits foreclosures on veterans.

	FHA	**VA**	**CAL-VET**
Government Agency	Federal Housing Administration	Veterans Administration	Department of Veterans Affairs
Source of Funds	Institutional Lender	Institutional Lender	State Bonds
Security Device	Trust Deed	Trust Deed	Land Contract
Purpose of Loan	Housing (1-4 Units) Mobile Home	Housing Mobile Home	Housing Mobile Home
Term	35 years	30 years/House 20 years/Mobile Home	25 years/House 15 years/Single Mobile Home 20 years/Dual Mobile Home
Maximum Price	None	None	None
Maximum Loan	Home: 124,875 2 Units: 140,600 3 Units: 170,200 4 Units: 197,950 Condo: 124,850 (High Cost Area)	Certificate of Reasonable Value (CRV)	Home: 125,000 Farm: 200,000 Fee Title Mobile Home: 90,000 Rental Mobile Home: 70,000
Down Payment	3% - 1st $25,000 of appraisal; 5% - of the balance; 100% of any excess	Yes - When the price is more than the CRV	3% - $35,000 or less 5% - More than $35,000
Monthly Payment	Level (Equal)	Equal or Unequal	Equal or Unequal
Interest Rate	Fixed	Fixed	Variable
Discount Points	Paid by Buyer or Seller	Paid by Buyer or Seller	None
Origination Fee	Buyer-1 pt. maximum	Buyer-1 pt. maximum	None
Prepayment Penalty	None	None	6 months interest-80% of principal balance during the first 5 years.
Insurance	Mutual Mortgage Insurance	Guaranteed (Variable)	Disability and Term Life
Secondary Loan (Financing)	Original sale - No Resale - Yes	Original sale - Yes Resale - Yes	Yes - 90% of Value
Loan Assumption	Yes	Yes	Yes - Cal-Vet only.

REVIEW QUIZ

SECTION I - **Matching** - Select the letter below which best describes, defines or relates to the following numbered terms.

1. CRV
2. Term Life Insurance
3. FHA Loan
4. Secondary Money Market
5. VA Loan
6. Decreased Reserves
7. Increased Discount Rate
8. Tight Money Market
9. Federal Home Loan Bank
10. Primary Money Market

a. Created in 1932.
b. Loans are transferred between mortgagees and mortgagees.
c. Increases the availability of money.
d. A curb against inflation.
e. Loans are created by lenders for qualified borrowers.
f. Does not require a prepayment penalty.
g. There is a decrease in construction and real estate sales.
h. Requires a Certificate of Eligibility.
i. The appraisal by the VA.
j. Required in a Cal-Vet loan.

SECTION II - **True/False** - Select either true or false in response to the following statements.

1. The primary purpose of the Federal Home Loan Bank was to establish a credit reserve for Savings and Loan Associations.
2. Fannie Mae was created primarily to purchase FHA and VA loans from lending institutions to stabilize the mortgage market.
3. The interest rate is the most likely consideration by a lender when making an FHA loan.
4. A prepayment penalty is usually charged when paying off an FHA loan.
5. Secondary financing is not allowed when purchasing a property using an FHA loan.
6. Terms on an FHA loan are usually more flexible than a conventional loan.
7. An FHA loan would usually have a higher interest rate than a conventional loan.
8. The maximum amount of a federally approved VA loan is the amount stated in the CRV.
9. Discount points are not allowed on a Cal-Vet loan.
10. A trust deed is used in a Cal-Vet loan.

SECTION III - Multiple Choice - Select the letter which best completes the statement or answers the question.

1. In the purchase of property using Cal-Vet financing, which of the following is permitted that is not permitted with FHA financing?

   A. Purchase of a four unit apartment complex as an investment property.
   B. Prepayment penalty if the loan is paid off in the first five years.
   C. Discount points are paid to the lender.
   D. All of the above.

2. The National Housing Act created the FHA to insure loans and secondarily to provide all of the following, except:

   A. Minimum standards for construction.
   B. Scientific subdivision planning to protect against neighborhood deterioration.
   C. Long term interest rate mortgages.
   D. A comprehensive system for evaluating property and rating mortgage risk.

3. Historically, VA financing compared to conventional financing will have:

   A. Lower interest rate.
   B. Higher interest rate.
   C. More flexible terms.
   D. Shorter loan processing time.

4. Discount points under the California Home Purchase Act are paid by:

   A. Seller.
   B. Buyer.
   C. The State.
   D. No one.

5. The California Farm and Home Purchase Act provides that the buyer acquires possession through:

   A. Land contract.
   B. Quitclaim deed.
   C. Grant deed.
   D. California State deed.

6. All of the following are incorrect, except:

   A. The buyer must live in one-half of a duplex to obtain an FHA loan.
   B. A Cal-Vet cannot rent his home without written permission.
   C. A veteran cannot use a VA loan to purchase a mobile home.
   D. FHA does not make any distinction between income property and single family home purchases.

7. Excluding the down payment, which type of loan will have the least amount of closing costs for the buyer?

   A. FHA.
   B. GI.
   C. Cal-Vet.
   D. Conventional.

8. The Certificate of Reasonable Value is issued by:

   A. Veterans Administration.
   B. Federal Housing Administration.
   C. Department of Veterans Affairs.
   D. Federal National Mortgage Association.

9. Points cannot be charged on which of the following types of home loans?

   A. FHA.
   B. DVA.
   C. VA.
   D. None of the above.

10. FHA Title I loans:

   A. Are the same as Title II loans.
   B. Can be used for alterations or repair of existing home improvements.
   C. Are for home purchase only.
   D. None of the above.

11. Discount points on an FHA loan are usually equivalent to:

   A. Prepaid interest.
   B. Prepaid taxes.
   C. A prepayment penalty.
   D. A discount to the buyer.

12. Under which of the following loans is the buyer required to apply for term life insurance?

   A. FHA.
   B. VA.
   C. Cal-Vet.
   D. Savings and Loan Association.

13. Points on a VA loan are charged to:

   A. Provide a competitive yield.
   B. Equate the yield.
   C. Close the gap between the market rates and the fixed rates.
   D. All of the above.

14. In a tight money market, the type of loan that will cost the most points is:

    A. VA.
    B. Conventional.
    C. Cal-Vet.
    D. None of the above.

15. When a qualified buyer purchases a home under the California Farm and Home Purchase Act, title is held by the:

    A. DVA.
    B. FHA.
    C. VA.
    D. Buyer.

Answers may be found in Appendix C (Back of text)

REAL ESTATE LENDING

A. LENDERS - Real estate loans are made either by institutional lenders or noninstitutional lenders. Institutional lenders consist of Savings and Loan Associations, Insurance Companies, Commercial Banks, Mutual Savings Banks, and Federal Land Banks. The institutional lenders provide the principal source of funds for real estate mortgage lending. Noninstitutional lenders consist of Mortgage Companies, Pension Funds, Credit Unions, Trust Funds, Finance Companies, and Private Individuals.

1. **Savings and Loan Association** - The Savings and Loan specializes in real estate loans that are not insured or guaranteed by the government. It makes many medium and long term loans, services its own loans, allows a higher loan-to-value ratio, and usually charges a higher interest rate than other conventional lenders.

   a. The Savings and Loan invests most of their assets into home loans. The Federal Savings and Loan Association is the primary source of funds for residential financing.

   b. The Savings and Loan receives most of their funds for making real estate loans from the individual savings accounts.

   c. **Savings Association Insurance Fund** (SAIF) - The Savings Association Insurance Fund will provide for insurance on deposits up to $100,000. SAIF is a division of the Federal Deposit Insurance Corporation.

2. **Life Insurance Company** - Life Insurance Companies prefer to invest their assets into long term, large real estate loans on large housing developments and commercial properties without geographical limitations.

   a. A Life Insurance Company is the best source of funds for a large loan on a shopping center.

   b. Life Insurance Companies do not like to service their own loans.

   c. An Insurance Company either makes a direct loan to borrowers or invests its funds indirectly through a Mortgage Banker (Mortgage Company). Mortgage Bankers act as loan correspondents by making loans in their specific geographical location and when completed, deliver these loans to the Insurance Company.

   d. A Life Insurance Company is least likely to make a residential construction loan, an interim loan during construction, or a short term loan on a single family residence ($19,000 first trust deed for 5 years).

3. **Commercial Bank** - Commercial Banks prefer to invest their assets into short term real estate loans where they have a past association with the borrower and the financed property is in close proximity to the bank.

a. Both liquidity and marketability are of great importance to a commercial bank when making real estate loans. Therefore, a commercial bank must be aware of the activities of the secondary mortgage market. The secondary money market provides the marketplace for the loans the commercial bank may wish to sell. Their ability to sell in the secondary mortgage market provides a ready source of cash and maintains liquidity.

b. A Commercial Bank would be the least likely lender to make a take-out loan.

c. **Federal Deposit Insurance Corporation** (FDIC) - The Federal Deposit Insurance Corporation will provide of insurance on deposits up to $100,000.

4. **Mutual Savings Bank** - A Mutual Savings Bank is mutual in character as the depositors share in the earnings of the bank. Mutual Savings Banks both originated and operate in the northeastern United States. They are occasionally represented by loan correspondents in California.

5. **Federal Land Bank** - A Federal Land Bank will make loans directly to farmers and ranchers. These loans are then serviced by the local branch of the National Farm Loan Association.

6. **Mortgage Company** - Mortgage Companies are the source for a substantial amount of funds used to finance California real estate. Mortgage Companies will usually solicit loans from just about anyone while representing other lending institutions. They initiate many new loans and then sell the loans to other lenders rather than holding them in their own portfolio.

a. A Mortgage Company (Mortgage Banker) will act as a loan correspondent by making loans in their specific geographical location and when completed, deliver these loans to Insurance Companies, Mutual Savings Banks, and other lenders. Mortgage Companies are regulated by State Law.

b. A Mortgage Company will participate and supervise construction loans.

c. A Mortgage Company will usually contract to service the loan with the lending institution for whom they originate the loan . A Mortgage Company will usually service the loan for one-half of one percent of the outstanding loan balance. A good portion of the income of a Mortgage Company comes from servicing loans. Servicing a loan usually includes collecting payments, paying taxes, providing for continuous insurance coverage, and general protection of the property.

d. A Mortgage Company prefers loans which are salable on the secondary mortgage market.

e. **Warehousing** - Warehousing operations takes place when a Mortgage Banker collects and packages many loans prior to being sold to other lenders in the secondary mortgage market. The warehoused loans can be used as collateral for other loans prior to being sold on the secondary mortgage market.

7. **Pension Funds and Credit Unions** - Pension Funds and Credit Unions are a growing source of funds for real estate loans. They usually operate through a Mortgage Banker and prefer to make first trust deed loans, but will make second trust deed loans.

8. **Trust Funds** - Some estate funds administered by the bank are used for real estate loans.

9. **Finance Company** - A Finance Company will make loans that use both real and personal property as collateral (Package Mortgage). The Finance Company has a P.P.B. (Personal Property Broker) license and is under the jurisdiction of the Corporation Commissioner.

10. **Private Individuals** - Most junior loans are secured through private lenders. These junior loans can be in the form of a seller carry back (purchase money trust deed) or loans arranged by a Mortgage Loan Broker under Article 7 of the Real Estate Law. These private loans are usually for a short period and contain interest rates that are higher than normal.

B. TYPES OF LOANS

1. **Construction Loan** (Interim Loan) - Short-term financing used for real estate construction. In a construction loan, the lender will usually release the final payment to the borrower when the lien period has expired. When there is an unspecified maturity date on a construction loan, the time begins to run from the date the signature is obtained on the note. A construction loan is usually obtained from a Commercial Bank. An Insurance Company is least likely to make residential construction loans; however, Savings and Loans, State Banks, and Federal Banks will make residential construction loans.

   a. **Obligatory Advances** - The terms of the original loan requires the lender to release a set amount of additional money at a later date. Lenders use advances with developers and subdividers when making construction loans. They will advance funds with the progression of construction. Money is released to the general contractor at various stages of construction.

   b. **Completion Bond** - It may be required that the builder post a completion bond to obtain a construction loan. This will assure completion of the building. If there is a default, the lender will have the property with the completed improvements as security for the loan. In this example the completion bond is for the benefit of the lender. A completion bond may also be used to benefit the owner of the property.

2. **Take-Out Loan** - Long term financing after the construction is completed. Issued upon the completion of the interim construction financing. A take-out loan is usually obtained from a Mortgage Company, Insurance Company, or a Savings and Loan. A Commercial Bank does not usually make a take-out loan.

3. **Participation Loan** (Co-venture Loan) - A lender may reduce the interest rate of the loan in exchange for a percentage of ownership interest in the acquired property. This loan is occasionally used in large commercial developments.

4. **Compensating Balance Loan** - An individual borrows money from a bank, but must leave a certain amount of money on deposit with the bank for the entire length of the loan.

5. **Seasoned Loan** - A loan in the lender's portfolio held for a period of time. It is dependent on the pattern of payments of the borrower (trustor) over a period of time. A seasoned loan is usually a loan with an excellent payment record.

C. MORTGAGE EVALUATION - A mortgage evaluation is a summary prepared by a loan officer which correlates the characteristics of the borrower, the property, and the offered loan. The most difficult item for the lender to evaluate when negotiating a loan is the risk.

1. **Borrower** - The adequacy of the borrower's income is a significant factor to qualify for a loan to purchase real estate. A general rule of thumb is that the price of a home should not exceed two and one half times the annual income of the average family. Credit characteristics of the borrower include the salary of the husband and wife and their outstanding debts. The husband's overtime is given the least consideration by the lender when evaluating a borrower for a loan (FHA). Any individual who is refused credit is entitled to see a copy of an unfavorable credit report. If the credit bureau will not deliver a copy of this report, the applicant may sue for a copy of the report and eligible damages. The least likely qualifications include the ethnic background of the borrower, marital status of the borrower, and purchase price of the property.

2. **Property** - A lender will give consideration to the value of the property in relation to the loan prior to approval of a loan. The value of the property gives the lender the best protection in case of default.

3. **Offered Loan** - A lender will give consideration based on the amount of the down payment and the income ratio of the borrower prior to approval of a loan. The borrower's need for financial assistance is not as important as the amount of the down payment, the loan-to-value ratio, or the income ratio of the borrower.

D. PRIVATE MORTGAGE INSURANCE (Private Mortgage Guaranteed Insurance) **P.M.I.** - Private Mortgage Insurance is an insurance policy which is given to the lender to insure against loss. Lenders have recently become more confident and have been lending up to 95% on residential mortgages due to the availability of Private Mortgage Insurance.

E. LOAN COMMITMENT - A lender makes a written promise or agreement as to the specific terms of a mortgage loan it will make on the property. A prudent lender will gather information on the property, the borrower, and the type of loan in order to determine the loan commitment. The lender considers the ability of the borrower to pay, the market value of the property that is security for the loan, and the free and clear title of the property.

1. **Conditional Commitment** - An owner may arrange to finance the property with a lender prior to obtaining a buyer. A written promise or agreement is given to the property owner based on the property value, without having knowledge of a purchaser or borrower.

   a. The conditional commitment is contingent upon the borrower meeting the requirements set by the lender.

   b. An owner will apply for a conditional commitment to assure that the buyer receives the highest possible loan.

2. **Firm Commitment** - A written promise or agreement is given to the borrower after he has qualified for the loan.

3. **Standby Commitment** - A written promise given to a builder to provide a future loan at a specific interest rate.

F. LOAN-TO-VALUE RATIO (LTV) - A percentage of the appraised value of the property that a lender will loan to a borrower. The lending policy is usually based on a LTV ratio that does not exceed a percentage of the appraised value and which is less than the market value of the property. The LTV ratio cannot exceed the ability of the borrower to repay the debt. The lower the LTV ratio, the higher the equity interest.

G. EQUITY - Equity is the value of real estate over and above the existing loans against the property. Value minus all liens equals the equity. Real estate purchased for an investor's own use or for the income it may yield may be classified as equity.

1. Large equities bring about specific trends in real property. These trends are: the owner will take better care of the property, the borrower will receive better financing terms, and the installment payment will usually be paid on time.

2. The owner's loss of interest on his equity is considered to be a cost of ownership; however, 100% equity in a personal residence is most advantageous to the owner because it allows for greater flexibility of his personal income.

3. Equity may be expressed as the down payment, the difference between market value and the loan amount, or the difference between the market value and the outstanding liens against the property.

4. **Trading of Equity** - Trading of equity means to borrow money at an interest rate that is less than an investor's net return.

H. USURY - Usury means that a ceiling is set on interest rates. If the lender charges an illegal rate of interest on a loan, it is considered usurious. Usury is charging interest in excess of the provisions provided for under law.

1. The interest rate charged by banks and savings and loans is governed by the financial code.

2. Individual lenders are limited as to the amount of interest they may charge on real estate loans.

   a. The interest rate charged by individuals on loans arranged by a real estate broker is exempt from the usury law (Article 7).

   b. The interest rate charged by individuals on purchase money loans taken back as part of the purchase price is exempt from the usury law.

   c. The interest rate charged by individuals on owner occupied residential property is limited to 10%.

   d. The interest rate charged by individuals on investment property is limited to five percent above the federal discount rate.

I. AMORTIZATION - Amortization is the liquidation of a financial obligation on an installment basis with level payments. Level means to express the payment on a loan where the monthly sum of the principal and interest is always the same. The interest portion will decrease and the principal portion will increase on a long term amortized loan which has level payments. (Amortization of a loan is probably the most significant factor determining why there have been fewer foreclosures in recent years).

1. **Fully Amortized** - Consists of level payments including principal and interest, at an interest rate which will be completely paid off at maturity.

2. **Partially Amortized** - Consists of level payments including principal and interest, but requires a balloon payment because the maturity date is prior to the time allowed for total amortization.

3. **Straight** - Consists of interest payments only over the duration of the loan and requires all of the principal to be paid at maturity with a balloon payment. A straight note accrues more interest than an installment note when the interest rate and duration of the loans are identical. The terms and conditions of a straight note are negotiable as long as the interest rate is not usurious. The interest may be payable monthly, yearly, or in one payment on the due date.

4. **Negative Amortization** - Consists of level payments that are less than interest only. This means that the principal balance on the loan will increase with each payment.

AMORTIZATION TABLE

TABLE OF MONTHLY PAYMENTS TO AMORTIZE A $1,000 LOAN

Term of years	5%	5-1/2%	6%	6-1/2%	6.6%	7%	7-1/2%	8%	8-1/4%	8-1/2%	8-3/4%	9%	9-1/4%	9-1/2%	9-3/4%	10%
5....	18.88	19.11	19.34	19.57	19.62	19.81	20.04	20.28	20.40	20.52	20.64	20.76	20.88	21.01	21.13	21.25
6....	16.11	16.34	16.58	16.81	16.86	17.05	17.30	17.54	17.66	17.78	17.90	18.03	18.15	18.28	18.40	18.53
7....	14.14	14.38	14.61	14.85	14.90	15.10	15.34	15.59	15.71	15.84	15.96	16.09	16.22	16.35	16.47	16.61
8....	12.66	12.90	13.15	13.39	13.44	13.64	13.89	14.14	14.27	14.40	14.52	14.66	14.78	14.92	15.04	15.18
9....	11.52	11.76	12.01	12.26	12.31	12.51	12.77	13.02	13.15	13.28	13.41	13.55	13.68	13.81	13.94	14.08
10....	10.61	10.86	11.11	11.36	11.41	11.62	11.88	12.14	12.27	12.40	12.53	12.67	12.80	12.94	13.08	13.22
11....	9.87	10.12	10.37	10.63	10.68	10.89	11.15	11.42	11.55	11.69	11.82	11.97	12.10	12.24	12.38	12.52
12....	9.25	9.51	9.76	10.02	10.08	10.29	10.56	10.83	10.96	11.11	11.24	11.39	11.52	11.67	11.81	11.96
13....	8.74	8.99	9.25	9.52	9.57	9.79	10.06	10.34	10.47	10.62	10.75	10.90	11.04	11.19	11.33	11.48
14....	8.29	8.55	8.82	9.09	9.14	9.36	9.64	9.92	10.06	10.20	10.34	10.49	10.64	10.79	10.93	11.09
15....	7.91	8.17	8.44	8.72	8.77	8.99	9.28	9.56	9.70	9.85	10.00	10.15	10.29	10.45	10.59	10.75
16....	7.58	7.85	8.12	8.40	8.45	8.63	8.96	9.25	9.40	9.55	9.69	9.85	10.00	10.15	10.30	10.46
17....	7.29	7.56	7.84	8.12	8.17	8.40	8.69	8.99	9.13	9.29	9.44	9.59	9.74	9.90	10.05	10.22
18....	7.04	7.31	7.59	7.87	7.93	8.16	8.45	8.75	8.90	9.06	9.21	9.37	9.52	9.68	9.84	10.00
19....	6.81	7.08	7.37	7.65	7.71	7.95	8.25	8.55	8.70	8.86	9.01	9.17	9.33	9.49	9.65	9.82
20....	6.60	6.88	7.17	7.46	7.52	7.76	8.06	8.37	8.52	8.68	8.84	9.00	9.16	9.33	9.49	9.66
21....	6.42	6.70	6.99	7.29	7.35	7.59	7.90	8.21	8.36	8.53	8.68	8.85	9.01	9.18	9.34	9.51
22....	6.26	6.54	6.84	7.13	7.19	7.44	7.75	8.07	8.22	8.39	8.55	8.72	8.88	9.05	9.21	9.39
23....	6.11	6.40	6.69	7.00	7.06	7.30	7.62	7.94	8.10	8.27	8.43	8.60	8.76	8.93	9.10	9.28
24....	5.97	6.27	6.56	6.87	6.93	7.18	7.50	7.83	7.99	8.16	8.32	8.49	8.66	8.83	9.00	9.18
25....	5.85	6.15	6.45	6.76	6.82	7.07	7.39	7.72	7.88	8.06	8.22	8.40	8.56	8.74	8.91	9.09
26....	5.74	6.04	6.34	6.65	6.72	6.97	7.30	7.63	7.79	7.96	8.14	8.31	8.48	8.66	8.83	9.01
27....	5.64	5.94	6.24	6.56	6.62	6.88	7.21	7.55	7.71	7.88	8.06	8.23	8.41	8.58	8.76	8.94
28....	5.54	5.84	6.16	6.48	6.54	6.80	7.13	7.47	7.64	7.81	7.99	8.16	8.34	8.52	8.70	8.88
29....	5.45	5.76	6.08	6.40	6.46	6.73	7.06	7.40	7.57	7.75	7.92	8.10	8.28	8.46	8.64	8.82
30....	5.37	5.68	6.00	6.33	6.39	6.66	7.00	7.34	7.51	7.69	7.87	8.05	8.23	8.41	8.59	8.68
35....	5.05	5.38	5.71	6.05	6.13	6.39	6.75	7.11	7.29	7.47	7.65	7.84	8.03	8.22	8.41	8.68
40....	4.83	5.16	5.51	5.86	5.93	6.22	6.59	6.96	7.14	7.33	7.52	7.71	7.91	8.10	8.30	8.49

Term of years	10-1/4%	10-1/2%	10-3/4%	11%	11-1/4%	11-1/2%	11-3/4%	12%	12-1/4%	12-1/2%	12-3/4%	13%	13-1/4%	13-1/2%	14%	15%
5....	21.37	21.49	21.62	21.74	21.87	21.99	22.12	22.25	22.37	22.50	22.63	22.75	22.88	23.01	23.27	23.79
6....	18.65	18.78	18.91	19.04	19.16	19.29	19.42	19.55	19.68	19.81	19.94	20.07	20.21	20.34	20.61	21.15
7....	16.73	16.86	16.99	17.12	17.25	17.39	17.52	17.65	17.79	17.92	18.06	18.19	18.33	18.47	18.74	19.30
8....	15.31	15.44	15.57	15.71	15.84	15.98	16.12	16.25	16.39	16.53	16.67	16.81	16.95	17.09	17.37	17.95
9....	14.21	14.35	14.49	14.63	14.76	14.90	15.04	15.18	15.33	15.47	15.61	15.75	15.90	16.04	16.33	16.92
10....	13.35	13.49	13.63	13.78	13.92	14.06	14.20	14.35	14.49	14.64	14.78	14.93	15.08	15.23	15.53	16.13
11....	12.66	12.80	12.95	13.09	13.24	13.38	13.53	13.68	13.83	13.98	14.13	14.28	14.43	14.58	14.89	15.51
12....	12.10	12.24	12.39	12.54	12.68	12.83	12.98	13.13	13.29	13.44	13.59	13.75	13.90	14.06	14.37	15.01
13....	11.63	11.78	11.92	12.08	12.23	12.38	12.53	12.69	12.84	13.00	13.15	13.31	13.47	13.63	13.95	14.60
14....	11.23	11.38	11.54	11.69	11.85	12.00	12.16	12.31	12.47	12.63	12.79	12.95	13.11	13.28	13.61	14.27
15....	10.90	11.05	11.21	11.37	11.52	11.68	11.84	12.00	12.16	12.33	12.49	12.65	12.82	12.98	13.32	14.00
16....	10.62	10.77	10.93	11.09	11.25	11.41	11.57	11.74	11.90	12.07	12.23	12.40	12.57	12.74	13.08	13.77
17....	10.37	10.53	10.69	10.85	11.02	11.18	11.35	11.51	11.68	11.85	12.02	12.19	12.36	12.53	12.87	13.58
18....	10.16	10.32	10.49	10.65	10.82	10.98	11.15	11.32	11.49	11.66	11.83	12.00	12.18	12.35	12.70	13.42
19....	9.98	10.14	10.31	10.47	10.64	10.81	10.98	11.15	11.33	11.50	11.67	11.85	12.03	12.20	12.56	13.28
20....	9.82	9.98	10.15	10.32	10.49	10.66	10.84	11.01	11.19	11.36	11.54	11.72	11.89	12.07	12.44	13.17
21....	9.68	9.85	10.02	10.19	10.36	10.54	10.71	10.89	11.06	11.24	11.42	11.60	11.78	11.96	12.33	13.07
22....	9.55	9.73	9.90	10.07	10.25	10.42	10.60	10.78	10.96	11.14	11.32	11.50	11.69	11.87	12.24	12.99
23....	9.44	9.62	9.79	9.97	10.15	10.33	10.51	10.69	10.87	11.05	11.23	11.42	11.60	11.79	12.16	12.92
24....	9.35	9.52	9.70	9.88	10.06	10.24	10.42	10.60	10.79	10.97	11.16	11.34	11.53	11.72	12.10	12.86
25....	9.26	9.44	9.62	9.80	9.98	10.16	10.35	10.53	10.72	10.90	11.09	11.28	11.47	11.66	12.04	12.81
26....	9.19	9.37	9.55	9.73	9.91	10.10	10.28	10.47	10.66	10.84	11.03	11.22	11.41	11.60	11.99	12.76
27....	9.12	9.30	9.49	9.67	9.85	10.04	10.23	10.41	10.60	10.79	10.98	11.17	11.37	11.56	11.95	12.73
28....	9.06	9.25	9.43	9.61	9.80	9.99	10.18	10.37	10.56	10.75	10.94	11.13	11.32	11.52	11.91	12.70
29....	9.01	9.19	9.38	9.57	9.75	9.94	10.13	10.32	10.52	10.71	10.90	11.09	11.29	11.48	11.88	12.67
30....	8.96	9.15	9.33	9.52	9.71	9.90	10.09	10.29	10.48	10.67	10.87	11.06	11.26	11.45	11.85	12.64
35....	8.79	8.98	9.18	9.37	9.56	9.76	9.96	10.16	10.35	10.55	10.75	10.95	11.15	11.35	11.76	12.57
40....	8.69	8.89	9.08	9.28	9.48	9.68	9.88	10.09	10.29	10.49	10.69	10.90	11.10	11.30	11.71	12.53

J. AMORTIZATION MATHEMATICS (Use chart on previous page).

1. Mr. Jones borrowed $10,000 for twenty years including 12% interest, what is the monthly payment? **Answer: $110.10**

   SOLUTION: From the amortization chart find the monthly payment for $1,000 for 20 years at 12% interest ($11.01). Multiply the $11.01 (payment per thousand) times the number of thousands (10). $11.01 x 10 = $110.10.

2. Mr. Smith pays $167.40 per month on $12,000, which includes interest at 14% per annum. How many years will it take to amortize the loan? **Answer: 13**

   SOLUTION: Divide the $167.40 payment by twelve to determine the payment per thousand ($167.40 ÷ 12 = $13.95). Look down the 14% column to find $13.95. The $13.95 monthly payment appears in the row for 13 years.

3. Mr. Able borrowed $50,000 for twenty years. He made level monthly payments including 12% interest until paid. What is the amount of interest he will pay on this loan? **Answer: $82,120**

   SOLUTION: From the amortization chart find the monthly payment for $1,000 for 20 years at 12% interest ($11.01). Multiply the $11.01 (payment per thousand) times the number of thousands (50). $11.01 x 50 = $550.50. Calculate the total amount paid over the duration of the loan ($550.50 x 240 months), then subtract the original principal amount from the total amount paid to determine the interest paid.

   $550.50 x 240 months = $132,120
   Less principal   - $ 50,000
                             $ 82,120 Interest.

4. Two individuals each borrow $80,000 with payments which include 13% interest. Mr. "A" amortized his loan for twenty years. Mr. "B" amortized his loan for thirty years. The total interest paid by Mr. "A" is what percent of the total interest paid by Mr. "B"? **Answer: 60.8%.**

   SOLUTION:

   Mr. "A" - 13% for 20 years = $11.72 per $1,000 (From chart). $11.72 x 80 = $937.60 per month x 240 months = $225,024 Total Paid by Mr. "A".
   $225,024 - $80,000 Original Principal = $145,024 Interest Paid by Mr. "A".

   Mr. "B" - 13% for 30 years = $11.06 per $1,000 (From chart). $11.06 x 80 = $884.80 per month x 360 months = $318,528 Total Paid by Mr. "B".
   $318,528 - $80,000 Original Principal = $238,528 Interest Paid by Mr. "B".

   Mr. "A's" interest ($145,024) is what percent of Mr. "B's" interest ($238,528)? Divide Mr. "B's" interest into Mr. "A's" interest to find the percentage.

   $145,024 divided by $238,528 = .6079957 = 60.8%

K. INTEREST FORMULA - Interest is equal to the Principal multiplied by the Annual Interest Rate, multiplied by the Time (In years) or **(I = PRT)**. This formula can be changed to solve for Principal, Rate, or Time. To change the basic formula you must recognize that every formula has an equal (=) sign. The amount on the left side of the equal sign is always equal to the amount on the right side of the equal sign. If you were to add an amount to the left side of the equal sign, you would also have to add the same amount to the right side of the equal sign in order for the formula to remain equal.

1. **Variation #1:** Change the basic formula I=PRT to solve for the Principal **(P)**.

   SOLUTION: In order to isolate the letter "P", you must divide the right side by "RT". You must also divide the left side by "RT" to keep the formula equal.

   $$I = PRT \text{ becomes } \frac{I}{RT} = \frac{PRT}{RT} \text{ becomes } \frac{I}{RT} = P \text{ or } \mathbf{P} = \frac{I}{\mathbf{RT}}$$

2. **Variation #2:** Change the basic formula I=PRT to solve for the Rate **(R)**.

   SOLUTION: In order to isolate the letter "R", you must divide the right side by "PT". You must also divide the left side by "PT" to keep the formula equal.

   $$I = PRT \text{ becomes } \frac{I}{PT} = \frac{PRT}{PT} \text{ becomes } \frac{I}{PT} = R \text{ or } \mathbf{R} = \frac{I}{\mathbf{PT}}$$

3. **Variation #3:** Change the basic formula I=PRT to solve for the Time **(T)**.

   SOLUTION: In order to isolate the letter "T", you must divide the right side by "PR". You must also divide the left side by "PR" to keep the formula equal.

   $$I = PRT \text{ becomes } \frac{I}{PR} = \frac{PRT}{PR} \text{ becomes } \frac{I}{PR} = T \text{ or } \mathbf{T} = \frac{I}{\mathbf{PR}}$$

   NOTE: Time is always calculated on a annual basis. Monthly interest is always calculated by dividing the annual rate by twelve months. Monthly will be represented by 1/12th in the formula. Three months is 3/12ths or 1/4th. Six months is 6/12ths or 1/2. Nine months is 9/12ths or 3/4ths, etc. *A banker's year is normally used to compute interest at a commercial bank. A banker's year consists of 360 days per year, or 30 days per month.*

L. PLUS OR INCLUDING INTEREST - There is a definite difference in cost to the borrower between "plus" and "including" interest.

1. **Including Interest** - When an individual borrows $10,000 that is payable $100 per month **including** interest at 6% per annum, this means that a portion of the $100 is allocated for interest while the balance is principal.

2. **Plus Interest** - When an individual borrows $10,000 that is payable $100 per month **plus** interest at 6% per annum, this means that the $100 is all principal and the monthly interest must be added to the principal to calculate the total payment.

221

3. Comparison Chart

Including Interest		Plus Interest
	Including Interest	**Plus Interest**
$10,000	Principal	$10,000
x .06	Rate	x .06
$600.00	Annual Interest	$600.00
50.00	Monthly Interest	50.00

PAYMENT ANALYSIS

$100	Total Payment	$150
$50	Interest Payment	$50
$50	Principal Payment	$100

PRINCIPAL BALANCE CALCULATIONS

$10,000	Beginning Balance	$10,000
- $50	1st Months Principal	- $100
$9,950	Still Owed After One Month	$9,900

SECOND MONTHS INTEREST CALCULATIONS

$9,950	Principal	$9,900
x .06	Rate	x .06
$597.00	Annual Interest	$594.00
$49.75	Monthly Interest	$49.50

SECOND MONTHS PRINCIPAL CALCULATIONS

$100.00	Total Payment	$149.50
$49.75	Interest Payment	$49.50
$50.25	Principal Payment	$100.00

PRINCIPAL BALANCE CALCULATIONS

$9,950.00	Principal Balance	$9,900.00
-$50.25	2nd Months Principal	-$100.00
$9,899.75	Still Owed After Two Months	$9,800.00

M. TYPES OF INTEREST

1. **Simple Interest** - Simple interest is calculated on the principal balance. Simple interest is usually charged on home loans.

2. **Compound Interest** - The rate or premium paid by the borrower, per unit of time, for the use of borrowed funds which is periodically added to the unit charge. This means that interest is paid on the principal and the amount of accrued simple interest.

3. **Nominal Rate** - The interest rate specified in the promissory note.

4. **Effective Rate** - The actual interest rate paid by the borrower.

5. **Variable Interest Rate** - The interest rate of the loan is allowed to change. This is used because there is often a change in the money market.

N. **INTEREST RATE** - The price or rate of premium per unit of time paid on conventional real estate loans by borrowers for the use of borrowed funds.

1. Interest rates on home loans are usually established by the length of time for repayment. A longer term usually means a higher interest rate.

2. The factor which exerts the greatest influence on real estate mortgage interest rates is the condition of the money market; more specifically, the availability of loan funds. Interest rates usually decline when there is an excess of mortgage funds available.

3. The level and movement of mortgage rates is directly influenced by inflation, a tight money market, and the demand for funds. Unemployment does not usually influence mortgage rates.

4. A reduction in the interest rates may create a beneficial situation for the borrower. The borrower could refinance a loan to lower his monthly payments.

O. **INTEREST MATHEMATICS**

1. If an individual borrowed $2,500 at 9% interest for three years, ten months, and twenty days, the total interest paid would be: **Answer: $875.00**

SOLUTION: Calculate the interest for one year, then divide by 12 months to calculate the monthly interest. Divide the monthly interest by 30 days to calculate daily interest. Multiply each amount (Yearly, monthly, and daily) by the specific times stated in the question and add their products to calculate the total interest.

$I = P x R x T$
$I = \$2,500 x .09 x 1$ (1 represents annual interest). $I = \$225.00$

$I = \$225.00$ per year. $I = \$18.75$ per month. $I = \$0.625$ per day.

| x 3 years | | x 10 months | | x 20 days | |
| $675.00 | + | $187.50 | + | $12.50 | = $875.00. |

2. If an individual borrowed $5,000 at 9% interest for three years, ten months, and twenty days, the total interest paid would be: **Answer: $1,750**

SOLUTION: Calculate the same as number one.

$I = P x R x T$
$I = \$5,000 x .09 x 1$
$I = \$450.00$ per year. $I = \$37.50$ per month. $I = \$1.25$ per day.

| x 3 years | | x 10 months | | x 20 days | |
| $1,350 | + | $375.00 | + | $25.00 | = $1,750.00. |

3. One month's interest on a straight note amounted to $45.00. What is the face amount of the note at a 4 1/2% interest rate? **Answer: $12,000**

SOLUTION: Change the basic formula I=PRT to solve for the face amount ("P"). Use $45.00 for the amount of Interest. Use .045 for the 4.5% Rate. And use 1/12 of a year for the Time.

I = PRT becomes

$$P = \frac{I}{RT} \quad \text{or} \quad P = \frac{\$45}{.045 \times 1/12} \quad = \quad \frac{\$45}{0.00375} \quad = \quad \$12,000$$

OPTIONAL SOLUTION: $45 per month multiplied by 12 months equals $540 annual interest. Now use $540 for Interest, .045 for Rate, and 1 year for Time.

4. The amount of investment required to earn $75.00 per month at 5% per annum is: **Answer: $18,000**

SOLUTION: Change the basic formula I=PRT to solve for "P". Use $75.00 for the amount of Interest. Use .05 for the 5% Rate. And use 1/12 of a year for the Time.

I = PRT becomes

$$P = \frac{I}{RT} \quad \text{or} \quad P = \frac{\$75}{.05 \times 1/12} \quad = \quad \frac{\$75}{0.0041666} \quad = \quad \$18,000.288$$

OPTIONAL SOLUTION: $75 per month multiplied by 12 months equals $900 annual interest. Now use $900 for Interest, .05 for Rate, and 1 year for the Time.

5. An individual paid $180 interest on an $8,000 straight note for 90 days. What was the interest rate? **Answer: 9%**

SOLUTION: Change the basic formula I=PRT to solve for "R". Use $8,000 for the amount of Principal. Use $180 for the Interest. And use 1/4 of a year for the Time.

I = PRT becomes

$$R = \frac{I}{PT} \quad \text{or} \quad R = \frac{\$180}{\$8,000 \times 1/4} \quad = \quad \frac{\$180}{\$2,000} \quad = \quad .09 \quad = 9\%$$

OPTIONAL SOLUTION: $180 for 90 days may be expressed as $720 Interest per year. Now use $720 for Interest, $8,000 for Principal, and 1 year for Time.

6. Mr. Jones paid $150 interest in eight months on a $2,500 straight note. What is the interest rate on the note? **Answer: 9%**

SOLUTION: Change the basic formula I=PRT to solve for "R". Use $2,500 for the amount of Principal. Use $150 for the Interest. And use 2/3 of a year for the Time.

I = PRT becomes

$$R = \frac{I}{PT} \quad \text{or} \quad R = \frac{\$150}{\$2,500 \times 2/3} = \frac{\$150}{1666.6666} = .09 = 9\%$$

OPTIONAL SOLUTION: $150 Interest for 8 months may be expressed as $225 Interest per year ($150 divided by 8 = 18.75 interest/month x 12 months = 225). Now use $225 for Interest, $2,500 for Principal, and 1 year for Time.

7. Mr. Smith paid $945 interest on a $7,000 straight note. What is the term of the loan if the annual rate of interest is 9%? **Answer: 18 Months**

SOLUTION: Change the basic formula I=PRT to solve for "T". Use $7,000 for the Principal. Use $945 for the Interest. And use .09 for the Rate.

I = PRT becomes

$$T = \frac{I}{PR} \quad \text{or} \quad T = \frac{\$945}{\$7,000 \times .09} = \frac{\$945}{\$630.00} = \begin{array}{l} \text{1.5 Years or} \\ \text{(18 months)} \end{array}$$

P. TRUTH-IN-LENDING (Regulation Z) - The principal purpose of Truth-in-Lending is to provide a meaningful disclosure of credit terms to a potential borrower.

1. **Creditor** - Regulation Z applies to individual or business creditors who offer or extend credit more than twenty-five times per year, or more than five times per year for transactions secured by a dwelling which is subject to a finance charge.

2. **Exemptions**

   a. Credit extended primarily for business, commercial, or agricultural purposes is an exemption to Regulation Z. When property is not intended to be owner-occupied, and the creditor extends credit, regardless of the number of units, the transaction is considered to be for business purposes. Extension of credit to acquire, improve, or maintain a rental property is exempt from this law.

   b. Credit extended over $25,000 which is not secured by real property or a principal residential dwelling is exempt from Regulation Z.

3. **Disclosures**

   a. **Finance Charge and Annual Percentage Rate** (APR) - The finance charge and APR are considered to be the most important of the required disclosures and must be more visible than other required disclosures. This is usually accomplished by printing the finance charge and APR in different type styles, bold print, by dividing lines, or by a colored background. Real estate licensees should be most aware of the finance charge and the APR.

1. Finance Charge

    a. The charges which make up the finance charge include:

        1. Loan fees (Interest rates, buyer's points, discount points paid by the borrower, assumption fees, commissions or buyer's points, finder's fees and similar fees for finding lenders).

        2. Time price differential.

        3. Mortgage insurance or mortgage guarantee required by the lender.

    b. The charges which do not make up the finance charge include:

        1. Appraisal, credit report, notary, and title insurance fees.

        2. Points paid by the seller.

        3. Fees for the preparation of documents (deeds, mortgages, trust deeds, reconveyance, settlement, etc.).

    2. Annual Percentage Rate (APR) - It is intended under Truth-in-Lending that the cost of credit be expressed as an APR. APR is best defined as all loan costs, direct or indirect, expressed as a percentage rate.

b. Prepayment Penalty - A prepayment penalty must be disclosed by the creditor.

4. Advertisement - The advertisement requirement under Regulation Z applies to anyone who uses advertisements for consumer credit. The correct method of advertising under Regulation Z is that the lender must state the finance charge expressed as an Annual Percentage Rate. **EXAMPLE:** Assume an 8% Annual Percentage Rate. Truth-in-Lending advertising which states, "Graduated Monthly Payments", should also include a "schedule" of the monthly payments. Real estate brokers and home builders who place advertisements containing financing must comply with this law even if they are not the "creditor" in the available financing which is being advertised.

5. Right of Rescission - The consumer has the right to rescind until midnight of the third business day. The three day right to rescind usually begins on the date the note is signed by the borrower (trustor). However, if this date is different from the date that the disclosure statement is delivered, then the three day period begins on the date the disclosure statement is delivered.

a. Exemptions

    1. The right to rescind does not apply to transactions made to finance the acquisition or initial construction, if the security is the consumer's personal dwelling. An individual purchasing a home as a personal residence, who finances the property with a purchase money trust deed from a federal savings and loan, never has the right to rescind the transaction under Truth-in-Lending.

2. An individual purchasing a home with a new first trust deed does not have the right to rescind. This exemption applies to first trust deeds used to purchase a home with conventional, FHA, or VA financing, a first trust deed used to purchase a new business or commercial property, or a first trust deed loan used to purchase a rental house.

3. An individual refinancing an existing first trust deed loan on his home with the proceeds being used to purchase a business does not have the right to rescind.

b. The right to rescind does apply to a new second trust deed loan against a home.

c. The right to rescind is not one of the many disclosures required by Truth-in-Lending. The right to rescind applies only to the extension of credit that creates a security interest in real estate (A lien against the principal dwelling of the consumer).

6. **Administration** - Truth-in-Lending is administered and enforced by the Federal Trade Commission.

Q. REAL ESTATE SETTLEMENT PROCEDURE ACT (RESPA) - The primary purpose of RESPA is to give the buyer the opportunity to shop around for settlement services. The lender must supply the borrower with a Uniform Settlement Form at or before closing the transaction. This form provides a complete breakdown of the escrow costs involved in a real estate transaction.

1. **Application** - RESPA sets forth special disclosure requirements for nonexempt lenders who provide loan funds in transactions involving an initial lien on a one-to-four unit family dwelling. This means that a lender whose deposits are insured by a federal agency and loans funds on an owner-occupied one-to-four unit dwelling must comply with RESPA. A private lender making a loan or a seller taking back a note secured by a trust deed are not required to comply with RESPA.

2. **Information Booklet** - Lenders are required to provide the borrower with a consumer pamphlet authorized by the U. S. Department of Housing and Urban Development (HUD). This will explain closing costs incurred by the principals in the transaction. The lender can never charge a fee for pamphlets or documents furnished to a potential borrower.

3. **Good Faith Estimate** - When a real estate licensee sells a house and a loan for the buyer is secured through a Savings and Loan, the lender must provide the buyer (borrower) with a good faith estimate of settlement costs within three (3) days of the loan application.

4. **Uniform Disclosure Statement** - Lenders are required by HUD to provide both the buyer and seller with a Uniform Settlement Statement. In order to close an escrow, an individual borrower may waive his right to a Uniform Settlement Statement prior to the close of escrow. If the lender receives a written waiver from the borrower, the lender must supply the Uniform Settlement Statement to the borrower as soon as is practical after the close of escrow.

5 . **Violations** - All of the following are prohibited under RESPA.

    a . The seller can never condition the sale of a property upon the buyer purchasing the title policy from a specific title insurance company. This is a violation of the federal law and the seller could be liable to pay three times the cost of the policy of title insurance to the buyer.

    b . Kickbacks, unearned fees, and referral fees are not allowed between real estate agents and nonlicensees. This means that a real estate agent can never accept a fee from a title insurance company for the referral of his clients and customers.

R. FINANCE MISCELLANEOUS

1 . Insurance companies usually invest their assets in real estate investments, which include large commercial loans, new housing developments, and FHA insured loans.

2 . A loan that is acquired with a low down payment and easy terms usually results in increased financing costs.

3 . If the borrower had a choice of 25 years or 30 years to repay a loan at the same interest rate, the longer term would most likely provide for smaller monthly payments.

4 . The historical average term of home ownership is 5 to 8 years.

5 . When an individual borrows money at 7.2% interest per annum, the quickest method used to compute interest for one month is to multiply the principal balance by .006 (7.2% equals .072; .072 divided by 12 months equals .006).

6 . The buyer designating the lender is not a violation of RESPA.

7 . The term "interim loan" means the same as "construction loan".

8 . The lower the loan to value ratio, the higher the equity interest.

9. Deregulation means that there will be an easing and relaxing of rules and regulations with lending institutions.

10. Debt-Income Ratio (Income-Debt Ratio) - A ratio established between the income and long-term debt of a prospective borrower to determine if a borrower is able to qualify for a loan.

11. Mortgage Yield is the interest that a lender receives from a mortgage. Mortgage yield may also be the rate of return for the buyer of an existing loan that takes into consideration the interest rate, discount rate, loan servicing fees, and the term of the loan.

12. Interest on a construction loan is usually calculated from the date the funds are placed into escrow.

13. Service debt or debt service refers to the monthly payments on the mortgage. When the service debt of a loan is not sufficient to cover the interest amount of the loan, the result is Negative Amortization.

REVIEW QUIZ

SECTION I - **Matching** - Select the letter below which best describes, defines, or relates to the following numbered terms.

1. Life Insurance Company
2. Savings & Loan Association
3. Commercial Bank
4. Mortgage Company
5. Institutional Lenders
6. Amortization
7. Firm Commitment
8. Obligatory Advances
9. Compensating Balance Loan
10. Conditional Commitment

a. The terms of the original loan requires the lender to release additional funds at a later date.
b. A written promise is given to the owner without the knowledge of a borrower.
c. The principle source of funds for real estate mortgage lending.
d. Liquidation of a financial obligation on an installment basis with level payments.
e. Make real estate loans where they have a past association with the borrower and the property is close to the bank.
f. Prefers to make long term real estate loans on large commercial properties.
g. To borrow money from a bank and leave a certain amount of money on deposit with the bank for the duration of the loan.
h. Acts as a loan correspondent by making loans in their area and delivering these loans to other lenders.
i. A written promise is given to a borrower after he has qualified for a loan.
j. The principle source of funds for residential financing.

SECTION II - **True/False** - Select either true or false in response to the following statements.

1. A partially amortized loan will have a balloon payment.
2. Compound interest is usually charged on home loans.
3. A Commercial Bank is the least likely lender to make a take-out loan.
4. The take-out loan is the same as the interim loan.
5. The lender in a "Participation Loan" will increase the interest rate and take a percentage of the acquired property.
6. Risk is the most difficult item for the lender to evaluate when making a loan.
7. Insurance Companies are most likely to make residential construction loans.
8. Individual lenders are not limited as to the amount of interest they may charge on real estate loans.
9. The main reason for Truth-in-Lending is to provide a meaningful disclosure of credit terms.
10. An appraisal fee is to be included in the finance charge under Regulation Z.

SECTION III - **Multiple Choice** - Select the letter which best completes the statement or answers the question.

1. Because of the nature of their assets, which of the following would be interested in long term real estate loans?

    A. Private parties.
    B. Insurance Companies.
    C. National Banks.
    D. Credit Unions.

2. Savings and Loan institutions obtain most of their money for making loans from:

    A. Federal National Mortgage Association.
    B. Corporation profits.
    C. Corporate savings.
    D. Individual savings.

3. Commercial Banks consider both liquidity and marketability of paramount importance when making loans on real property. Such banks are interested in which of the following?

    A. Security given by the Federal Deposit Insurance Corporation.
    B. Activities of the secondary mortgage market.
    C. Home resales.
    D. Credit of the borrower.

4. Which of the following lenders participates and supervises construction loans, solicits loans from anyone, involves itself in the secondary money market, and represents other lenders?

    A. Commercial Bank.
    B. Savings and Loan Association.
    C. Mortgage Company.
    D. Insurance Company.

5. The hardest thing for the lender to evaluate at the time the loan is negotiated is the:

    A. Risk.
    B. Total cost of the loan.
    C. Value of the property.
    D. Interest to be charged.

6. A private individual charging interest in excess of the provisions provided under law, is guilty of which of the following?

    A. Perjury.
    B. Usury.
    C. Penury.
    D. All of the above.

7. Mutual Savings Banks are effective in the area of the United States in which they operate. They originated in the:

A. Southeast.
B. Northeast.
C. Northwest.
D. West.

8. Mortgage Companies are private lenders that are regulated by state law. They provide a source of substantial funds used in the financing of real property and therefore, are considered advantageous to the financial world. Which of the following best describes the function of a Mortgage Company?

A. They acquire loans in a secondary mortgage market and hold them to maturity for a gain on the money invested.
B. They make a subjective analysis of a loan with a view toward the optimistic value of the investment to the investor.
C. They initiate new loans and sell them to other investors and service them for a fee, not holding these loans in their own portfolio.
D. They encourage thrift and savings in the working man to provide for old age.

9. An owner wishes to sell his home and has arranged with a lender to finance the purchase, but has not yet obtained a buyer. This situation would be referred to as:

A. An option.
B. A conditional commitment.
C. A firm commitment.
D. An interim commitment.

10. Mortgage Companies which act as loan correspondents:

A. Do not as a rule service their loans.
B. Do not as a rule deal in government insured or guaranteed loans.
C. Deal only in FHA insured loans.
D. Prefer loans which are salable on the secondary money market.

11. An individual secured a loan on an unmortgaged property. His interest payment was less than his total net return. This is an example of:

A. Band of Investment.
B. Deficit financing.
C. Capital turnover.
D. Trading of Equity.

12. A prudent lender would take into consideration which of the following prior to making a loan?

A. Clear title of the property.
B. Borrower's ability to repay.
C. The market value of the property that is security for the loan.
D. All of the above.

13. A Mortgage Company gives the least consideration to which of the following when granting a loan?

    A. Borrower's need for financial assistance.
    B. Amount of down payment.
    C. Value of the property in relation to the loan.
    D. Borrower's income ratio.

14. In reference to Truth-in-Lending, which of the following applies only to the extension of credit that creates a security interest in real estate?

    A. Right of rescission.
    B. Prepayment penalty.
    C. Annual percentage rate.
    D. Total finance charge.

15. A lender making loans subject to RESPA must do all of the following, except:

    A. Provide a HUD consumer pamphlet explaining closing costs.
    B. Provide the HUD Uniform Settlement Disclosure Statement to both the buyer and seller.
    C. Impose a charge of not more than $10.00 per document furnished.
    D. Give the borrower a good faith estimate of closing costs within three days of the loan application.

Answers may be found in Appendix C (Back of text)

REAL PROPERTY TAXATION

A. REAL PROPERTY TAX - The money from real property taxes is used to support the State government. Real property taxes are usually the largest expenditure for the owner of an apartment building.

   1. Ad Valorem - "Ad valorem" means according to value. Real property taxes in California are based on the value of the individual property. The consistency of the tax burden on an individual property is related to the assessment of similar properties in the surrounding neighborhood. In determining real property taxes, the land and improvements are assessed separately and then taken as one figure times the tax rate. Tax assessments on real property consider all improvements on the property. A water well and pump on the property are considered to be improvements on the property.

   2. Parcel Number - Real property taxes in most counties are assessed by locating the property by the parcel number. This is not a legal description.

   3. County Assessor - The County Assessor's Office is responsible for determining property values for real property taxes. The Assessor maintains a tax roll of all the assessed properties in the county. The tax roll is used to establish a tax base.

     a. The annual residential tax obligation is determined by the County Assessor's Office. Property is assessed at 100% of value.

     b. A residential property is reassessed every time the property is sold. This requires a supplemental tax bill.

     c. An individual owner is required to file a change of ownership statement with the County Recorder or County Assessor within forty-five (45) days of any change of ownership (Recordation). Failure to file this statement could result in a penalty of $100.00 or 10% of the taxes, whichever is greater.

     d. The age of a single family residence is best determined by the records in the County Assessor's Office.

   4. County Board of Supervisors - The Board of Supervisors will establish the real property tax rate which is limited to one percent of assessed value, plus an amount for existing bond debts.. The term **"MILL"** is used with the real property tax rate. One mill is equivalent to one-tenth of a cent ($.001).

   5. State Board of Equalization - The State Board of Equalization will appraise all public utility properties for tax assessments. The Assessor's Office and the Board of Equalization are responsible for assessing real property for income tax purposes. **LOCAL BOARD OF EQUALIZATION** (County Board of Supervisors) - The Local Board of Equalization will listen to complaints and appeals in reference to property taxes.

6 . Formula - Assessed Value x Tax Rate = Annual Property Tax.

7 . Tax Fiscal Year - The State tax fiscal year is July 1 through midnight June 30. It is sometimes expressed as July 1 to July 1. Real property taxes are paid in two installments.

    a. First Installment - First installment due date is **November 1st.** First installment delinquent date is **December 10th.**

    b. Second Installment - Second installment due date is **February 1st.** Second installment delinquent date is **April 10th.**

8 . Delinquent Property Tax - When an individual owner is delinquent with his property taxes, the property is sold to the State. The sale is usually on or before June 30 and is referred to as a Tax Stamp Sale. It receives this name because the County will stamp its records "Sold to the State".

    a . The significant factor of the Tax Stamp Sale is to immediately initiate the sequence for the redemption period.

    b . The delinquent owner has a five (5) year redemption period. The delinquent owner may continue with an undisturbed possession of the property during the redemption period.

    c . Real property that has been sold because of delinquent taxes may be redeemed upon payment of delinquent taxes, costs, interest, and redemption penalties. The State then releases the property by issuing a paid receipt from the State Controller, which is unofficially referred to as a Controller's Deed.

    d . Real property that is not redeemed during the five year redemption period will be sold by the State at a public auction. The State will issue a tax deed to the highest bidder. Title is free of all previous liens on the property.

9 . Lien Priority - Real property taxes become a lien on March 1st, prior to the tax fiscal year. This means that the real property taxes for fiscal year 1985-1986 are considered a lien on the property when an individual purchases a property on May 1, 1985.

    a . Real property tax liens are always superior liens. This means that they take priority over all other liens on the property, contrary to the time of recordation or creation of the lien.

    b . A real property tax lien is a specific lien on an individual property; therefore, real property taxes can never be a blanket encumbrance.

10. Special Tax Exemptions - There are many properties that are assessed but are partially or totally tax-exempt. These exemptions include:

    a . Homeowner's Exemption - $7,000 of the assessed value.

    b . Veterans Exemption - $4,000 of the assessed value.

c . Senior Citizen Tax Exemption - For an individual who is 62 years of age or older with a household income of $24,000 or less. They may defer their taxes until the property is sold or until the claimant does not occupy the property, or does not meet the above requirements. Senior citizens should contact the State Controller's Office for complete information.

d . Blind and Disabled Exemption - For an individual who is blind or disabled.

e . Church Exemption - Churches and other religious organizations are usually entitled to property tax exemptions.

11 . Assessment Appeals Board - The Assessment Appeals Board will listen to complaints in reference to over assessed property taxes.

B. SPECIAL ASSESSMENTS - The money raised from special bond assessments is used for local improvements. Special assessments are similar to real property taxes because they are always superior liens. They always take priority over all other liens contrary to the time of recordation or creation of the lien. The owner shall have thirty days to pay special assessments prior to becoming a lien. The significant difference between real property taxes and assessment bonds is that special assessments are used for local improvements and taxes are used to support the State government.

1 . Street Improvement Act of 1911 - The Street Improvement Act of 1911 is utilized for street improvements in the State. It may be used in any county or city in California. Assessments are levied for the cost of specific local improvements such as streets, sidewalks, curbs, drainage, sewers, and water systems.

a . Assessments can never be levied for the purchase of land for development nor to finance the construction of a home.

b . When a city has sold assessment bonds for street improvements, properties within that specific area are usually assessed in proportion to services or benefits which are received by those properties. An individual property owner will be assessed based on the front footage of his property when streets are constructed or repaired.

2 . A street assessment bond assumed in the purchase of real property is considered to be part of the cost of the property.

3 . An assessment bond can lower the value of a specific property.

EXAMPLE: When an appraiser discovers a $4,000 assessment bond on a property subject to appraisal and a comparable property recently sold for $50,000 without an assessment bond, the appraised value of the subject property will be $46,000.

4 . An assessment bond assumed by a buyer will increase the cost basis of the property for income tax purposes.

C. INCOME TAX - Income tax is an important item to consider in the acquisition, ownership, and disposition of real property. Tax consciousness in reference to real estate should take place prior to the acquisition of the property. The theory of our federal income tax is that it is a progressive system. This means that as taxable income increases, the rate of taxes increases.

1. **Taxable Income**

   a. **Ordinary Income** - Ordinary income is money received in the form of wages, commissions, interest, or business profits.

      1. Interest is the return on the investment and is taxable as ordinary income. The holder of bonds is not required to declare interest income on his federal income tax return. All interest earned on state, local, and municipal bonds is exempt from federal income tax.

      2. Prepaid rent received is reported on the owner's income tax return in the year collected. **EXAMPLE:** An individual signed a lease on December 15, 1990 and collected the rent in advance for the last two months. The term of the lease is from January 1, 1991 to December 31, 1993. The payment of the rent for the last two months will be declared as income in 1990.

      3. Any profit from the sale of homes in a subdivision is considered to be ordinary income. Property held for sale to customers will usually result in a payment of the most federal tax on the gain.

      4. Any profit from property held for investment purposes, property held for an investment, or a personal residence is considered ordinary income.

   b. **Capital Gains Income -** A capital gain is any profit from the sale of an asset. These profits are taxed as ordinary income based on the individual's income tax bracket. There are two basic tax brackets, 15% and 28%, with a phantom 33% tax bracket.

2. **Taxable Deductions**

   a. Interest paid on trust deeds and mortgages is a deductible item for first and second homes. It may be interest on any primary or secondary trust deeds and home-equity lines of credit, without any restriction on the use of the money as long as the total borrowed does not exceed the purchase price plus the cost of improvements. Interest paid on equity loans up to $100,000 is fully deductible.

   b. A prepayment penalty is a deductible interest expense.

   c. The owner of income property, who actively participates in the management of the property, may deduct $25,000 per year from his ordinary income. Investor's adjusted gross income cannot exceed $100,000 for entire deduction.

   d. The owner of income property may deduct a salary given for management.

   e. The owner of a business may deduct 100% of the rent paid as a business expense on his income tax return.

   f. The cost to remodel or redecorate vacant units in an apartment building is deductible. Redecoration expenses are not improvements; therefore, they are usually deducted as operational expenses in the year of the expense. Remodeling is an improvement; therefore, an individual owner of income property will be allowed to **CAPITALIZE** the cost of remodeling. To capitalize for income tax purposes means to add the expenditure to the owner's cost basis. The item is then depreciated and cannot be used as a deduction in the year of the expense.

g. Points paid in obtaining a loan are a proper deduction on an individual's federal income tax return. The manner in which they are treated depends upon the transaction and their use.

1. Points paid for a *service* are usually deductible over the term of the loan. Points paid by the buyer as an origination fee on an FHA or VA loan are a nondeductible finance charge. This means that they cannot be deducted as interest during the year of purchase. They must be spread out over the term of the loan.

2. Points paid as *interest* are usually deductible in the year paid. Points paid by the buyer on a first trust deed to purchase property can usually be deducted in full the first year as long as the points do not exceed a reasonable normal charge and are usually charged in the area. A prepayment penalty is usually an interest expense for income tax purposes.

h. Depreciation is deductible on income producing property (even when the property appreciates in value).

3. Nondeductible Items

a. Loss of rental fees because of a vacancy factor cannot be deducted on an individual's income tax.

b. Making an improvement (building a fence) is not deductible on an individual's income tax; however, the cost of the improvement can be used to adjust the cost basis of the property.

4. Depreciation - Depreciation is the return of the investment and is tax exempt. This means that real property held for use in a business or trade is given special treatment by the Internal Revenue Service. Real property held for use in a trade or a business is usually given the greatest preferential tax treatment by the Internal Revenue Service.

a. Property must be *improved* to qualify for a real property depreciation deduction on an income tax return. The entire value of the improvements may be depreciated.

b. A new building is depreciated based on what it cost for construction.

c. When an owner of an apartment building deducts depreciation on his income tax, this deduction will reduce his annual income by the amount of the depreciation. It does not reduce his tax payment by the amount of the depreciation, only his annual income.

d. Depreciation over the period of ownership will adjust the cost basis down. If a property does not go up in value over the period of ownership, the investor must pay capital gains tax on the depreciation amount. **EXAMPLE:** An individual purchased an apartment building for $200,000. Ten years later he sells the property for $200,000. During the ten year period of ownership he depreciated the building $60,000. Therefore, he must pay capital gains tax on the $60,000 depreciation.

e. The accountant and the appraiser are interested in the depreciation of real estate for two different reasons. The accountant is interested in the book value of the depreciation and the appraiser is interested in the actual depreciation.

f. Any property which produces an income may be depreciated. This includes, but is not limited to, an orchard, a vacant duplex, an unoccupied apartment unit, and a rented single family dwelling. A home may be rented to anyone, including a friend or a welfare recipient.

g. Depreciation is not allowed on all capital assets. Properties that can never be depreciated include:

   1. Vacant land. Vacant land held for an investment cannot be depreciated.
   2. Land rented for a parking lot cannot be depreciated.
   3. An owner-occupied farm residence cannot be depreciated.
   4. An individual's personal residence cannot be depreciated.

h. Depreciation over the period of ownership will decrease the cost basis of the property.

i. When a real estate licensee and investor speak about a tax shelter, this usually refers to depreciation.

j. A tax shelter from a real estate investment may legally decrease an individual's income tax. A real estate investment has an advantage over a stock market investment because the owner may depreciate the real estate investment.

k. Obsolescence does not provide for depreciation. It is a type of depreciation.

l. The owner of an income property must take depreciation for each year of ownership. Depreciation cannot be deferred to offset a higher income in a future year.

5. Methods of Depreciation (Depreciation Schedules) - Each individual owner must establish his own depreciation schedule. When an investor buys a used apartment building he will ignore the depreciation schedule of the previous owner. The new owner's depreciation schedule will be based on his purchase price (cost basis) of the property. Depreciation schedules include Straight Line Depreciation, 125% Declining Balance Method, 150% Declining Balance Method, 175% Declining Balance Method, 200% Declining Balance Method, and Sum-of-the-Years' Digits Method. These depreciation schedules cannot all be used today; however, a real estate licensee may encounter any of these accounting systems in his daily practice.

   a. Straight Line (EVA) - Straight line depreciation provides an equal amount of depreciation each year. It offers the greatest amount of depreciation in the later years when compared to the other depreciation schedules.

   Economic Life) Value of Improvements = Annual Depreciation
   (Useful Life)

b. Declining Balance Methods (125%, 150%, 175%, 200%) - These methods of accelerated depreciation are based on a percentage of straight line. It is best to determine straight line as a "percentage", and then to multiply the straight line percentage by the declining balance percentage. **EXAMPLE:** If straight line is 5%, then the annual depreciation for the respective declining balance method will be:

1. **125%** - **6.25%** (125% of 5% equals 6.25%).
2. **150%** - **7.50%** (150% of 5% equals 7.50%).
3. **175%** - **8.75%** (175% of 5% equals 8.75%).
4. **200%** - **10.00%** (200% of 5% equals 10.00%).

In each of these methods, the depreciation rate will be the greatest in the first year and decreases each year thereafter. The amount of depreciation taken each year is subtracted from the cost of the property before the next year's depreciation is computed. The same depreciation rate will apply to the smaller or declining balance each year. This results with a larger deduction for depreciation in the first year and a gradually smaller deduction in each succeeding year. In a declining balance method, the amount of depreciation reduces each year because the basis for depreciation is less in the later years. The basis is depreciated less in the later years. Salvage value will be disregarded in this method of depreciation.

c. Sum-of-the-Years' Digits - This method of accelerated depreciation is based on a different fraction each year. The sum of the annual fractions must equal one (1) at the end of the depreciation schedule.

EXAMPLE: If a building has an economic life of five (5) years, what is the depreciation schedule using the sum-of-the-years' method?

Step 1: Determine the common denominator for the annual fractions. The digits which represent the numbers of each year will be added to determine the common denominator. When a building has a economic life of five (5) years, there are five digits (1, 2, 3, 4, & 5). 1 + 2 + 3 + 4 + 5 = 15. Fifteen is the common denominator.

Step 2: Determine the numerator (top number) for the annual fractions. The digits (1, 2, 3, 4, & 5 are reversed in order (5, 4, 3, 2, & 1) to determine the numerator for the annual fractions.

Step 3: Write the depreciation schedule from the information in the previous two steps.

Year:	1	2	3	4	5	
Depreciation Schedule	$\frac{5}{15}$ +	$\frac{4}{15}$ +	$\frac{3}{15}$ +	$\frac{2}{15}$ +	$\frac{1}{15}$ =	$\frac{15}{15}$

Using the sum-of-the-years' digits method of depreciation on a building with a five year useful life results in 1/3rd depreciation the first year. The 5/15ths fraction may be reduced to 1/3rd.

6. Depreciation Provisions

a. Prior to 1981 - A <u>new</u> residential property purchased between July 25, 1969 and December 31, 1980 could be depreciated by straight line, 125% declining, 150% declining, 200% declining, or the sum-of-the-years' methods of depreciation.

b. 1981 through 1986 - Depreciation options under the former law were replaced in 1981 by the **ACCELERATED COST RECOVERY SYSTEM (ACRS)** and further modified in 1984. A <u>new</u> residential property purchased after 1980 could be depreciated by straight line or 175% declining method of depreciation. Low income housing may still be depreciated using the 200% declining method. Salvage value is not considered in this process. ACRS provides for improvements to be depreciated:

1. Over a fifteen (15) year period for property acquired from January 1, 1981 through March 15, 1984.

2. Over an eighteen (18) year period for property acquired after March 15, 1984.

A table for the accelerated depreciation under ACRS was created to simplify the calculations using declining percentages each year. This table makes it easier to calculate the depreciation allowance. When the table is unavailable, the owner may use the regular declining balance method.

c. (1987 -   ) - Straight line depreciation has been mandated for residential and non-residential properties.

1. Residential property may be depreciated over a period of 27.5 years.

2. Non-residential property may be depreciated over a period of 39 years.

7. Sinking Fund
- Depreciation may be provided for by a Sinking Fund. This means that money is placed into a special account or investment to be used to replace the improvements as required. The Sinking Fund is usually established from the income of the income producing property.

8. Calculation of a Capital Gain or Loss
- A capital gain or loss may be taken when the market value of the property changes at the time of sale. A capital gain occurs if the market value increases from the purchase price. A capital loss occurs if the market value decreases from the purchase price.

a. Capital Gain - The owner has a capital gain when the adjusted sales price is more than the adjusted cost basis.

b. Capital Loss - The owner has a capital loss when the adjusted cost basis is more than the adjusted sales price. A deduction may be taken for a loss on the sale of a farm, property held for investment, and property held for productive use in business. An investment in land can never be depreciated; however, a capital loss may be taken if the selling price is less than the original cost basis. *A deduction cannot be taken for a loss on the sale of a personal residence.*

c. Terminology

1. **Cost Basis** - The cost basis is the price paid for the property regardless of the appraised, assessed, or loan market value. The cash down payment does not affect the cost basis of a property. The unadjusted basis of the taxpayer's property is referred to as the original cost.

   a. The cost basis is determined by the method of acquisition of the property -- the actual cost to purchase the property. This is used to determine a capital gain or loss.

   b. An estimated low cost basis will result in maximum future taxes.

   c. An estimated high cost basis will result in minimum future taxes.

   d. The cost basis of a property may be increased by installation of a capital improvement, increased amenities, or installation of a new roof.

   e. Regular maintenance does not increase the cost basis of a property.

   f. Depreciation will decrease the cost basis of an income producing property.

2. **Adjusted Cost Basis** - The adjusted cost basis is calculated by adding any improvements to the original cost basis and subtracting the amount of depreciation taken during ownership (depreciation may only adjust the cost basis on income producing property). New improvements will increase the adjusted cost basis on any property. *Operating expenses are a tax expense during the year of the expense, they do not adjust the cost basis of the property.*

3. **Adjusted Sales Price** - The adjusted sales price is calculated by deducting commission and other expenses of a sale from the sales price. Payment of a real estate commission is considered to be a selling expense.

4. **Capital Gains Formula** - To calculate a capital gain on the sale of real property, find the difference between the Adjusted Sales Price and the Adjusted Cost Basis.

   ```
        Cost Basis (Purchase Price)
      + Improvements
      - Depreciation
        Adjusted Cost Basis

        Sales Price
      - Commissions
      - Escrow Fees
        Adjusted Sales Price

      - Adjusted Sales Price
      - Adjusted Cost Basis
        Capital Gain
   ```

241

5. **Salvage Value** - Salvage value is the fair market value of the improvements at the end of its useful life. An estimation of salvage value is based upon the individual's policy for disposing of assets. The salvage value must be subtracted from the cost basis of the improvements in order to establish the amount to be depreciated over the useful life of the property. When figuring depreciation by the straight line method, an individual owner is to estimate the amount of salvage value that will be realized upon the sale of an asset. Real property with a provision for salvage value will decrease the depreciation allowance on the owner's income tax return. **EXAMPLE:** An individual purchased an apartment building for $300,000. The land was valued at $50,000 and the owner established a salvage value of $15,000 on the improvements. If the owner was to use the straight line method of depreciation, he would depreciate $235,000 over the useful life of the property.

      SOLUTION: $300,000 Cost basis
                             - $ 50,000 (Cannot depreciate land)
                              $250,000 Improvements
                             - $ 15,000 Salvage value
                              $235,000 To depreciate

6. **Book Value** - Book value is used for accounting purposes to establish the current value of an asset. It is computed by taking the original cost, plus capital improvements (additions), minus accumulated depreciation. $20,000 worth of depreciation will decrease the book value of the property by $20,000.

9. Methods to Defer (Put-Off) Taxes

a. Personal Residence

1. Annual itemized deductions by the owner-occupant of a single family residence include real property taxes, interest paid on the trust deed or mortgage, and the unreimbursed portion of a casualty or theft loss.

2. The cost of painting a room does not qualify for itemized deductions by the owner-occupant of a single family residence.

3. Depreciation cannot be used as a deduction on a personal residence. An individual purchaser of a personal residence is least concerned with depreciation.

4. The cost basis of a personal residence may be adjusted by the addition of capital improvements. The addition of a concrete patio increases the cost basis of a personal residence.

5. **Deferred Capital Gain** - The owner of a personal residence is allowed to defer the capital gain from the sale of an owner-occupied single family residence if another residence is acquired or built within **TWENTY-FOUR (24) MONTHS.** Acquisition of the new property may be within twenty-four months preceding or following the sale. The price of the new residence must be equal to, or in excess of, the adjusted sales price of the initial residence. **EXAMPLE:** An individual purchased a $120,000 home in 1983. He sold it for $149,000 in September 1985 after making capital

improvements of $20,000. He purchased a $154,000 home in March 1986. What amount of taxable gain will be reported on his 1986 tax return?
Answer: Nothing

SOLUTION:

$120,000 Cost Basis	$149,000 Sales Price
$ 20,000 Capital Improvement	-$140,000 Adjusted Cost Basis
$140,000 Adjusted Cost Basis	$ 9,000 Capital Gain

There is a $9,000 capital gain on the sale of the house. This does not have to be reported because the individual purchased another house of equal or greater value ($154,000) within 24 months of the sale.

Note: Deferred Capital Gain Rule may be used over and over again; however, it cannot be used more often than once every 24 months, unless the owner qualifies for the moving expense tax deduction. Moving expense deduction requires a new job location to be at least 35 miles further away from your prior residence than was your old job location.

6. **Capital Loss** - A capital loss cannot be taken on the sale of a personal residence; however, a capital loss may be taken to reduce or offset any deferred capital gain on a personal residence. **EXAMPLE:** Mr. Smith has an adjusted cost basis of $45,000 on a house which he sold for $50,000. He immediately purchased another house for $60,000 and later resold it for $58,000. What is his reportable capital gain in this situation?
Answer: $3,000

SOLUTION:

FIRST HOUSE	SECOND HOUSE
$50,000 Sales Price	$60,000 Cost Basis
-$45,000 Adjusted Cost Basis	-$58,000 Sales Price
$ 5,000 Deferred Capital Gain	$ 2,000 Capital Loss

The $5,000 deferred capital gain on the first house may be offset by the $2,000 capital loss on the second house ($5,000 - $2,000 = $3,000).

7. **Exclusion** - An individual age 55 and over may have a once in a lifetime exclusion of up to **$125,000** on the sale of his personal residence. The property must have been owned for five years and occupied as a personal residence for three of the five years preceding the sale. This exclusion can only be taken once by married couples. Only one spouse has to be age 55 to qualify the community property for the exclusion.

b. **Installment Sale** - An installment sale is the sale of property which is reported over a number of years. When an individual sells his property on terms, rather than all cash, he may elect to pay taxes on his capital gain on an installment basis. The advantage of an installment sale is that the capital gains tax may be spread over several years. An installment sale may apply to any type of property.

c. Tax-Free Exchange - A tax-free exchange usually means that there will be "deferred taxes". A tax-free exchange is a contract of conveyance of real property. Two or more properties are transferred pursuant to an agreement or contract. An oral agreement for the exchange of real estate may be enforceable under specific provisions of the law. An exchange agreement gives the broker the right to perform activities for all principal parties involved in the transaction. A broker is most likely to receive a commission from both parties in a tax-free exchange.

1. Requirements

a. Like for Like - To qualify for a tax deferred exchange, the eligible property must be exchanged for a property of a "like kind". The term "like kind" is defined by the IRS to mean "the character or nature of the property". Examples of "like kind" are any combination of investment property (including vacant land), income producing property, and trade or business property.

b. Even or Up Basis - The owner will usually trade up in value to dispose of income property without having to pay any income tax at the time of the transaction.

2. Boot

Boot - Boot is anything of value given or received in an exchange. Boot may be in the form of cash, securities, loan relief, or personal property. Loan relief may be referred to as "mortgage boot" or "net mortgage relief". Net mortgage relief is the reduction of loan liability when exchanging properties.

a. Boot received in an exchange may be offset by or netted against Boot given in the exchange. In calculating the realized gain of the transaction, an owner may offset the liabilities of the property transferred against the liabilities of the property acquired. Cash consideration in an exchange may be offset by consideration received in the form of an assumption of liabilities.

b. Boot received is a recognized gain (taxable when received). In order to defer any gain in a tax-free exchange the individual should assume a higher loan and pay boot.

c. In an exchange transaction, the cost basis of the property transferred becomes the cost basis of the property which is acquired or received. Certain adjustments are required based on the terms of the exchange.

d. The cost basis of a property in an exchange will decrease by the amount of money received and increase by the amount of the recognized gain. When an individual does not pay any Boot in a tax-free exchange, the book value of the second property will be identical to the book value of the property exchanged. **EXAMPLE:** An individual owned a property free and clear valued at $320,000 with a book value of $220,000. If he exchanged for a property valued at $365,0000 which was also free and clear and did not pay any Boot, the book value of the second property will be $220,000.

e. An individual investor will usually be able to create a tax-free exchange by trading his mortgaged income property for a like property with a slightly higher loan and giving cash consideration to balance the equities.

f. Mortgage Boot is received when the loans on the property acquired in an exchange are less than the loans on the property transferred. Mortgage Boot is the relief from indebtedness.

g. A real estate broker will most likely encounter the term "Boot" when considering a situation involving income tax.

h. Calculation of the Cash Boot

    1. Calculate the equity of both properties.

PROPERTY "A"		PROPERTY "B"
$75,000	Market Value	$100,000
$50,000	Loans	$ 50,000
$25,000	Equity	$ 50,000

    2. Calculate the difference in equity between the properties. $50,000 - $25,000 = $25,000. The individual owner with the lesser equity owes the other owner the difference in equities. There are many alternatives for balancing the equities. The easiest method is for the owner with the lesser equity to give consideration in the form of cash for the difference in equities. Cash given as consideration is referred to as Boot.

3. Tax Consequences

    a. Boot - The first step in determining the tax consequences of an exchange is to calculate the boot.

    b. Realized Gain (Actual Gain) - The second step in determining the tax consequences of an exchange is to calculate the realized gain of the taxpayer. Realized gain is the total consideration received minus the adjusted cost basis of the transferred (given) property. Total consideration received is the value of the like property acquired (received) added to any boot received (cash and net mortgage relief).

    c. Recognized Gain (Taxable Gain) - The third step in determining the tax consequences of an exchange is to calculate the recognized gain of the taxpayer. Any boot received is usually the recognized gain and is taxable in the year received; however, if the boot is $30,000 and the realized gain is only $20,000, the recognized gain will be $20,000. The recognized gain can never be more than the realized gain.

    d. Deferred Gain - The last step in determining the tax consequences of an exchange is to calculate the deferred gain of the taxpayer. Deferred gain is the difference between the realized gain and the recognized gain (Realized Gain - Recognized Gain = Deferred Gain).

4. **Delayed Tax-Free Exchange** - A simultaneous exchange is not required to defer a capital gain. Requirements for a delayed exchange include:

   a. A replacement property must be identified within 45 days from the closing date of escrow of the sold property.

   b. Replacement property must be acquired within 180 days from the closing date of escrow of the sold property.

   c. Proceeds from the sold property must be given to an accommodator to hold pending the purchase of the replacement property.

5. **Exchange Mathematics**

   a. Mr. Austin owned an apartment valued at $225,000 with an adjusted cost basis of $185,000 which was mortgaged for $137,000. He exchanged for a commercial building valued at $198,000 with a $125,000 mortgage. Austin received $25,000 cash in the exchange.

   Question 1: What is Mr. Austin's actual gain?

   Answer: $50,000

   Step 1: $ 25,000 Cash
              $ 12,000 Net Mortgage Relief ($137,000 - $125,000)
              $ 37,000 Boot

   Step 2: $198,000 Value of the Commercial Building Received
              $ 37,000 Boot
              $235,000 Total Received
            - $185,000 Adjusted Cost Basis of Apartment Building
              $ 50,000 Actual Gain (Realized Gain)

   Question 2: What is Mr. Austin's recognized or taxable gain?

   Step 3:   **Answer: $37,000** Same as Boot above.

   Question 3: What is Mr. Austin's deferred gain?

   Step 4:   **Answer: $13,000**

              $ 50,000 Realized Gain
            - $ 37,000 Recognized Gain
              $ 13,000 Deferred Gain

b. Mr. Baker owned an apartment building with an adjusted cost basis of $175,000. His property was encumbered with a $147,000 first trust deed. He exchanged this property for a commercial building valued at $187,000 and $18,000 in cash. The commercial building was encumbered with a $143,000 first trust deed which he assumed in the exchange.

Question 1: What is Mr. Baker's actual gain?

Answer: $34,000

Step 1. $ 18,000 Cash
$\underline{\$\;\;4,000}$ Net Mortgage Relief ($147,000 - $143,000)
$ 22,000 Boot

Step 2: $187,000 Value of the Commercial Building Received
$\underline{\$\;22,000}$ Boot
$209,000 Total Received
- $\underline{\$175,000}$ Adjusted Cost Basis of Apartment Building
$ 34,000 Actual Gain (Realized Gain)

Question 2: What is Mr. Baker's recognized or taxable gain?

Step 3: **Answer: $22,000** Same as Boot above.

Question 3: What is Mr. Baker's deferred gain?

Step 4: **Answer: $12,000**

$ 34,000 Realized Gain
- $\underline{\$\;22,000}$ Recognized Gain
$ 12,000 Deferred Gain

Notes: 1. The IRS requires 80% of the gross income to be from residential rentals in order to depreciate a residential rental property.

2. A real estate salesperson who specializes in the exchange of income property should know that his best prospective client is an individual who is in a high income tax bracket with income property that he has owned for many years. The real estate salesperson may be able to show a potential client that he has enjoyed many years of depreciation and the advantage of exchanging for a new property is to create a new cost basis on a different property for a greater depreciation tax shelter.

3. In a Sale-Leaseback the owner of the property sells the property, but retains possession and use, by leasing it from the purchaser. The purchaser is least concerned with the depreciated book value of the property because he will establish his own book value based on what he paid for the property. The seller (tenant) will be able to deduct his rental payments as an ordinary business expense.

4. To borrow money on real estate is not a taxable transaction. There is not any tax due on the transaction even if the amount borrowed exceeds the cost basis of the property.

5. A tax advantage on an individual's federal income tax return may be achieved by using a tax-free exchange, an installment sale, or a depreciation deduction on income producing property.

6. Voluntary sale of an income producing property must be taxed in the year of sale, even if the seller purchases another income property in the same year.

7. The purchase of a vacant lot held for an investment, and its exchange for another vacant lot held for an investment, is not taxable in the year of the exchange.

8. Depreciation may be provided by Straight Line Depreciation, Accelerated methods of Depreciation (125%, 150%, 175%, 200% Declining and Sum-of-the-Years' Digits) and Sinking Fund.

9. 200% Declining Method gives the greatest amount of depreciation in the first year.

10. Unsecured personal property taxes are assessed and due when they become a lien.

11. A tax shelter allows you to defer taxes on current income to a later year.

12. Security deposits and other fees received in advance must be reported as income in the year received.

13. Low income families do not have a property tax exemption.

14. Marginal Tax Rate - The tax rate on the next dollar earned.

15. Capital Improvement - Money spent to physically improve a property. It may be for remodeling, building a wall, or the addition of a new air conditioning or heating system. Capital improvements are not deductible during the year of the expense. Capital improvements have to be added to the cost basis and are depreciable (27 1/2 or 39 years).

16. The escrow agent is responsible for reporting the sale to the Internal Revenue Service.

REVIEW QUIZ

SECTION I - Matching - Select the letter below which best describes, defines, or relates to the following numbered terms.

1. March 1st
2. Cost Basis
3. Recognized Gain
4. April 10th
5. Boot
6. Adjusted Cost Basis
7. Realized Gain
8. February 1st
9. Long Term Capital Gain
10. Ad Valorem

a. Anything of value given or received in an exchange.
b. Boot received which is taxable in the year received.
c. Is calculated by adding improvements and deducting depreciation.
d. Means according to value.
e. Second installment of taxes is delinquent on this date.
f. Taxes become a lien on this date.
g. Any profit made from an asset in a period which is longer than six months.
h. The purchase price of the property.
i. Second installment of taxes is due on this date.
j. Total consideration received minus the adjusted cost basis of the given property.

SECTION II - True/False - Select either true or false in response to the following statements.

1. The age of a single family residence is best determined by the records in the county recorder's office.
2. The annual residential tax obligation is determined by the County Assessor's Office.
3. A residential property is reassessed every time the property is sold.
4. The Board of Supervisors establishes real property tax rates.
5. An assessment bond assumed by a buyer will decrease the cost basis of the property for income tax purposes.
6. The owner of income property may deduct an operational loss in the full amount from his ordinary income.
7. Depreciation may be used as a deduction on a personal residence.
8. Regular maintenance will increase the cost basis of an apartment building.
9. "Like kind" is defined by the IRS to mean the character or nature of the property.
10. Cash Boot received is a recognized gain and is taxable when received.

1. Which of the following is the minimum age for a once in a lifetime free exemption for capital gains?

    A. 50.
    B. 55.
    C. 60.
    D. 65.

2. One of the qualifications for a real property depreciation deduction on an income tax return is that the property is required to be:

    A. Encumbered.
    B. Unencumbered.
    C. A personal residence.
    D. Improved.

3. The purchaser in a sale-leaseback would be least concerned with the:

    A. Depreciated book value of the property.
    B. Condition of the improvements.
    C. Location of the property.
    D. General credit of the lessee.

4. Federal income tax in theory is a:

    A. Proportional tax.
    B. Regressive tax.
    C. Progressive tax.
    D. Percentage tax.

5. When a real estate licensee speaks of tax shelter, he is referring to:

    A. Net income.
    B. Real property tax.
    C. Financial loss.
    D. Depreciation.

6. Tax consciousness in reference to real estate should take place:

    A. Six months after taking possession.
    B. Prior to acquisition.
    C. At the close of escrow.
    D. At the time of sale.

7. A tax-free exchange usually means that there will be:

    A. No gain.
    B. No taxes.
    C. An even exchange.
    D. Deferred taxes.

8. A deduction for depreciation on an individual's income tax return can be taken on:

    A. An apartment unit that is not occupied.
    B. Land leased for a parking lot.
    C. Land held for an investment.
    D. Vacant land.

9. The unadjustable basis of a taxpayer's property is best defined as:

    A. Original cost.
    B. Original cost plus capital improvements, less depreciation.
    C. Original cost plus capital improvements.
    D. Original cost minus allowable depreciation.

10. For income tax purposes, which of the following can be depreciated?

    A. An owner-occupied single family residence.
    B. A peach tree orchard.
    C. Vacant land.
    D. An owner-occupied farm residence.

11. An owner of income property will be able to capitalize which of the following for income tax purposes?

    A. Taxes.
    B. Maintenance.
    C. Plumbing repairs.
    D. Cost of remodeling.

12. Which method would give the greatest amount of depreciation in the first year?

    A. Sum-of-the-years' digits.
    B. Straight line.
    C. 150% declining balance.
    D. 200% declining balance.

13. Which of the following is correct in reference to income tax?

    A. Depreciation is the return of the investment and is tax exempt.
    B. Interest is a return on the investment and is taxable as ordinary income.
    C. Both "A" and "B".
    D. Neither "A" nor "B".

14. A taxpayer may adjust the cost basis of his personal residence on his income tax records for which of the following?

    A. Interest on the first trust deed.
    B. A paid fire insurance premium.
    C. The addition of a concrete patio.
    D. Depreciation.

15. A real estate licensee would most likely encounter the term "Boot" when considering a problem involving:

A. Income tax.
B. Water rights.
C. Depreciation.
D. A legal description.

Answers may be found in Appendix C (Back of text)

REAL ESTATE DESCRIPTIONS

In theory, a legal description is only required on title insurance. However, in real life, both a deed and escrow instructions usually contain a legal description. The one item that usually never has a legal description is a real property tax bill. The least likely place to obtain a legal description is the real property tax bill. The methods used to legally describe property in California are U. S. Government Survey (Townships and Sections), Recorded Lot, Block, and Tract (Subdivision), and Metes and Bounds.

A. **U. S. GOVERNMENT SURVEY** - The U. S. Government Survey is a legal description which refers to fractionalized sections, townships, and ranges. The U. S. Government description of property in California starts at three (3) different points (Points of beginning). At each point of beginning there is a **base line and meridian intersection.** Base lines run East and West. Meridians run North and South. The base line and meridian intersections in California are referred to as:

   Humboldt Base Line and Meridian Intersection.

   Mount Diablo Base Line and Meridian Intersection.

   San Bernardino Base Line and Meridian Intersection.

Legal descriptions are created by the same method at each base line and meridian intersection.

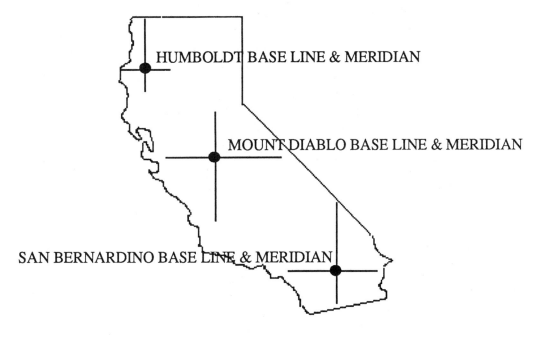

1. **Township** - Township lines and range lines cross to form a parcel of land which is six (6) miles square, and contains thirty-six square miles. Each parcel is referred to as a township. Townships are bordered by township and range lines. The description of a township is numbered by its location North and South of the base line and its location East and West of the meridian.

   a. **Township Lines** - Proceeding North and South from the base line at every six (6) mile interval, there are parallel East-West Township Lines. Township lines are six (6) miles apart, run East and West, and are located North and South of the base line.

   b. **Range Lines** - Proceeding East and West from the meridian at every six (6) mile interval, there are parallel North-South Range Lines. Range lines are six (6) miles apart, run North-South, and are located East and West of the meridian.

2. **Section** - Within a township there are parallel North-South lines and parallel East-West lines at every one (1) mile interval, which divide the township into smaller parcels that are one (1) mile by one (1) mile square and contain one (1) square mile. Each of these smaller parcels is referred to as a section. There are thirty-six sections in a township.

   a. All sections are considered to be equal in size. Each section is one (1) mile square and contains one (1) square mile. Each section contains **640 ACRES.**

   b. **Fractionalized Sections** - All townships are identical in size; however, some townships are smaller in land area because of the curvature of the earth. This will affect eleven (11) sections on the North and West sides of a township. Sections 1, 2, 3, 4, 5, 6, 7, 18, 19, 30, & 31 are considered fractionalized sections within these smaller townships.

   c. A section may be divided into smaller fractionalized parcels. This division is based on dividing a section into smaller parcels with each new parcel given a name based on its location to the points on a compass. Quarter sections are referred to as Northeast, Northwest, Southwest, and Southeast. Half sections may be referred to as North, South, East, and West. Quarter and half sections may be further divided into smaller fractions using similar names based on the points of a compass. These smaller parcels may also be divided into even smaller fractions using similar names based on the points of a compass, etc. When dividing a section into fractionalized parcels, it is necessary to follow the description backwards from right to left. Begin by locating the center of the section. Then, draw the next description within the section. Locate the center of the smaller parcel, and then draw the next description within the previously newly drawn parcel until you draw the last description. When working the description backwards, if you encounter the word "and" or a "semicolon", begin once again with the entire section. Draw this new description and add it to the description which the word "and" separated.

TOWNSHIP NAMES
(NUMBERING)

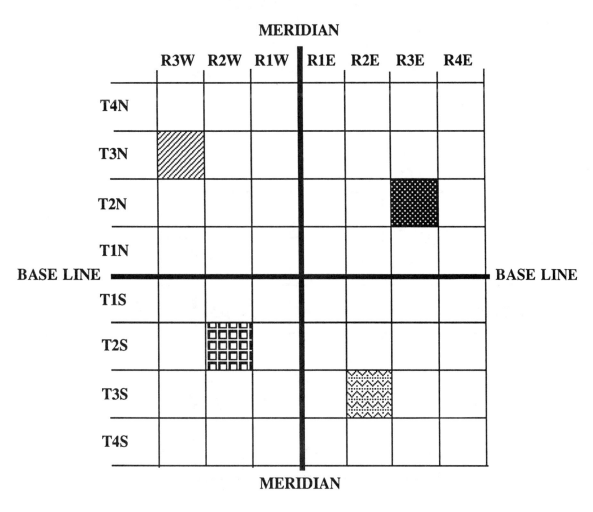

 Description of Township 3 North, Range 3 West

 Description of Township 2 North, Range 3 East

 Description of Township 2 South, Range 2 West

 Description of Township 3 South, Range 2 East

SECTION NUMBERING
(WITHIN A TOWNSHIP)

| 32 | | | | | |

6	5	4	3	2	1
7	8	9	10	11	12
18	17	16	15	14	13
19	20	21	22	23	24
30	29	28	27	26	25
31	32	33	34	35	36

7

13

3

NOTE: There are four sections outside of the township (3, 7, 13 & 32). These are sections in other contiguous townships.

256

Quarter Sections

NW	NE

SW	NW / NE
	nw ne / sw se

One Section - 640 Acres

160	160

160	40	40
	40	10 10 / 10 10

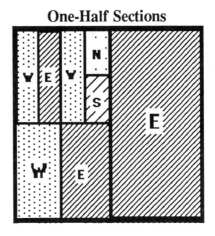

Northwest 1/4 of Section or Northwest 1/4 of Southeast 1/4 of Section

Southwest 1/4 of Section or Southwest 1/4 of Southeast 1/4 of Section

Northeast 1/4 of Section or Northeast 1/4 of Southeast 1/4 of Section

One-Half Sections

N

N / S / W E / S / N / S

One-Half Sections

W E / W N / S / E / W E / E

North 1/2 of Section or North 1/2 of 1/4 & 1/2 Sections

South 1/2 of Section or South 1/2 of 1/4 & 1/2 Sections

East 1/2 of Section or East 1/2 of 1/4 & 1/2 Sections

West 1/2 of Section or West 1/2 of 1/4 and 1/2 Sections

One Section = 640 Acres

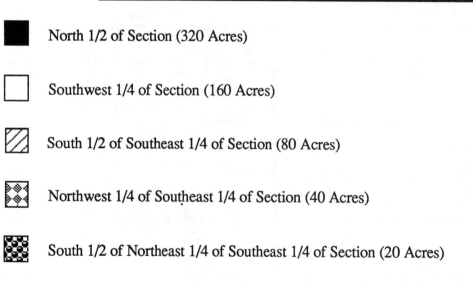

North 1/2 of Section (320 Acres)

Southwest 1/4 of Section (160 Acres)

South 1/2 of Southeast 1/4 of Section (80 Acres)

Northwest 1/4 of Southeast 1/4 of Section (40 Acres)

South 1/2 of Northeast 1/4 of Southeast 1/4 of Section (20 Acres)

Northwest 1/4 of Northeast 1/4 of Southeast 1/4 of Section (10 Acres)

East 1/2 of Northeast 1/4 of Northeast 1/4 of Southeast 1/4 of Section (5 Acres)

Southwest 1/4 of Northeast 1/4 of Northeast 1/4 of Southeast 1/4 of Section (2.5 Acres)

B. RECORDED LOT, BLOCK, AND TRACT - The recorded lot, block, and tract is a legal description which refers to properties which have been subdivided. The map shows the relationship of the subdivision to other subdivisions. Each parcel in the new subdivision is outlined and is given a name or number for identification.

C. METES AND BOUNDS (Measures and Angles) - Metes and Bounds is a legal description which refers to a property that is irregular in shape. It is similar to a treasure map because it is created by making a description of the boundaries by the use of lines or by a number of feet from one point to another. The Metes and Bounds procedure is usually a very long, wordy, and complicated description. It usually commences with "beginning at a point . . ." or "start at a point . . ."

1. **Definitions**

   a. **Metes** - Metes refers to the length or measurement in a description.

   b. **Bounds** - Bounds refers to the boundaries in a description.

2. Metes and Bounds descriptions are measured in degrees, minutes, and seconds from the North and South points on a compass.

   a. There are 360 degrees in a circle.

   b. There are 60 minutes in one degree.

   c. There are 60 seconds in one minute.

3. A proper Metes and Bounds description should contain:

   a. A definite point of beginning and definite corners of the property.

   b. The specific length and directions of the side of a property.

   c. The area in accepted units of measure contained within the described boundary lines.

4. Metes and Bounds is often used to describe a property where a map has not been recorded.

5. Metes and Bounds may be used even when other types of descriptions are available to legally describe a property.

6. A monument is an undesirable element in a legal description because a monument may be destroyed or lost. Artificial monuments include streets, canals, fences, etc. Natural monuments include trees, rocks, etc.

7. A neighbor's property line may be used as a boundary in a Metes and Bounds legal description.

8. Metes and Bounds is not a method used to measure land and buildings. Land and buildings may be measured by acre, square foot, or cubic foot.

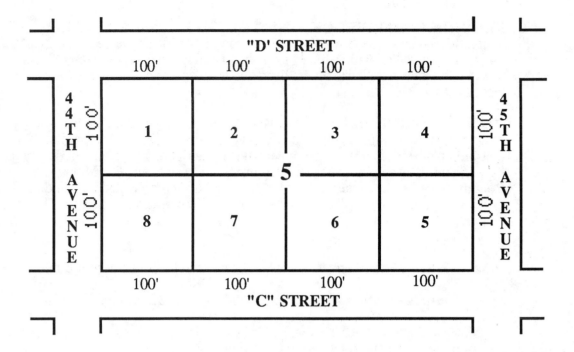

The legal description for the above diagram is Lots 1, 2, 3, 4, 5, 6, 7, and 8, Block 5, Tract 1086, as recorded in Book 44, Page 42 of Maps, County of Los Angeles, in the State of California.

Question - Draw the following Metes and Bounds description on the above diagram.

Metes and Bounds Description: Start at a point on the South side of "D" Street, 250 feet West of the Southwest corner of 45th Avenue and "D" Street. Thence in a Southerly direction to the North side of "C" Street, thence 100' West, thence parallel to the first course 200' in a Northerly direction, thence to the starting point.

Solution: Do the first sentence backwards to find the starting point (point of beginning), then follow the remainder of the description forward to enclose the described parcel.

1. What lots are included in the outlined Metes and Bounds description?

    (A) 2, 3, 6, & 7; (B) 1, 2, 5, & 6; (C) 3, 4, 7, & 8; (D) 1, 2, 7, & 8.

2. What is the cost of the outlined parcel at $120.00 per front foot?

    (A) $6,000; (B) $12,000; (C) $24,000; (D) $48,000.

3. What lots are contiguous to lot 5 in the diagram?

    (A) 4 & 6; (B) 6, 7, & 8; (C) 3, 4, & 6; (D) None of the above.

4. How much building area will be permitted on lot 5 if there is a 10' setback on 45th Avenue and a 10' setback on "C" Street?

    (A) 10,000 square feet; (B) 9,000 square feet; (C) 8,700 square feet; (D) 8,100 square feet.

Continue on next page. . .

5. Consider that there is an alley 20 feet wide halfway between "D" Street and "C" Street. Lot 8 has a setback of 15 feet on 44th Street and a 10 foot setback on "C" Street. How many square feet are available for building on lot 8?

    (A) 6,000 square feet; (B) 6,800 square feet; (C) 7,200 square feet; (D) 7,225 square feet.

Answer the following questions based on the drawing to the immediate left of the question.

6. How many feet of single strand wire are required to place a fence around the shaded portion of the section?

7. How many rods of single strand wire are required to place a fence around the shaded portion of the section?

8. How many acres in the shaded portion of the section?

9. How many acres in the shaded portion of the section?

Answers: 1 - D; 2 - B; 3 - C; 4 - D; 5 - B; 6 - 15,840 feet; 7 - 960 rods;

8 - 160 acres; 9 - 280 acres.

LAND MEASUREMENTS

TOWNSHIP

6 miles on each side.
6 miles square.
24 miles around the perimeter.
36 square miles.
Contains 36 Sections.
Contains 23,040 Acres.
24 miles square is equivalent to 16 Townships.

SECTION

1 mile on each side.
1 mile square.
4 miles around the perimeter.
1 square mile.
Contains 640 Acres.
24 miles square is equivalent to 576 Sections.
A quarter Section is 1/2 mile by 1/2 mile square (160 Acres).

CONVERSIONS

1 Acre = 43,560 square feet = 160 square rods = 10 square chains.
1 mile = 5,280 feet = 1,760 yards = 320 rods = 80 chains.
1 square acre has 208.71 lineal feet on each side.
1 rod = 16.5 feet.
1 chain = 4 rods = 66 feet.
1 square yard = 9 square feet.
1 cubic yard = 27 cubic feet.

6 MILES

```
36
SQUARE
MILES
```

TOWNSHIP

1 MILE

```
1
SQUARE
MILE
```

SECTION

262

REVIEW QUIZ

SECTION I - **Matching** - Select the letter below which best describes defines, or relates to the following numbered terms.

1. Base Line
2. Acre
3. Rod
4. Township
5. Bounds
6. Meridian
7. Range Lines
8. Metes
9. Section
10. Quarter Section

   a. 43,560 square feet.
   b. Contains 640 acres.
   c. Sixteen and one-half feet.
   d. Dimensions are one-half mile by one-half mile.
   e. Runs North and South.
   f. Refers to the length or measurement in a description.
   g. Approximately six miles apart.
   h. Refers to boundaries in a description.
   i. Runs East and West.
   j. Six miles square.

SECTION II - **True/False** - Select either true or false in response to the following statements.

1. The one item that usually never has a legal description is title insurance.
2. All townships do not have the same land area.
3. Section 7 is part of the West boundary of a township.
4. The number of the section in a township which is due North of section 4 in the lower township is 34.
5. Metes and Bounds is often used to describe a property where a map has not been recorded.
6. Metes and Bounds is used for the description of townships and sections.
7. A monument is a desirable element in a legal description.
8. Metes and Bounds is a method used to measure land and buildings.
9. Metes and Bounds descriptions are measured in degrees, minutes and seconds from North and South points.
10. Metes refers to boundaries in a legal description.

SECTION III - **Multiple Choice** - Select the letter which best completes the statement or answers the question.

1. The imaginary lines used in the government survey system for legally describing property, which are six miles apart are referred to as:

   A. Longitude and latitude lines.
   B. Base and meridian lines.
   C. Township and range lines.
   D. None of the above.

2. The South 1/2 of the Northeast 1/4 of Section 14, Township 3 North, Range 4 East, San Bernardino Base Line and Meridian Intersection is an example of a legal description by:

   A. Record of Survey.
   B. U. S. Government Survey.
   C. Reference to Recorded Map.
   D. Metes and Bounds.

3. Which of the following is considered an artificial monument?

   A. Fences and rocks.
   B. Streets and trees.
   C. Trees and fences.
   D. Streets and canals.

4. How many square miles in a section?

   A. One.
   B. Four.
   C. Six.
   D. Thirty-six.

5. The dimensions of a quarter section are:

   A. One-half mile by one mile.
   B. One-half mile by one-half mile.
   C. One-quarter mile by one-quarter mile.
   D. One-quarter mile by one-half mile.

6. How many acres are contained in a parcel of land 1,320' x 2,640'?

   A. 20.
   B. 40.
   C. 60.
   D. 80.

7. Metes and Bounds is used:

   A. With townships and ranges.
   B. Only on government land.
   C. For description of boundaries.
   D. On unsurveyed land.

8. The least desirable feature of using a monument as part of a legal description is:

   A. Monuments are specific.
   B. Monuments may be difficult to find.
   C. Monuments may be destroyed or lost.
   D. A title insurance policy will not be issued on property which is described by monuments.

9. In government survey, the North-South lines identified as range lines are how many miles apart?

   A. One.
   B. Six.
   C. Twelve.
   D. Thirty-six.

10. A parcel of land which measures one-half mile by one-half mile contains:

    A. 40 acres.
    B. 80 acres.
    C. 120 acres.
    D. 160 acres.

11. Metes and Bounds descriptions are measured in degrees, minutes, and seconds from:

    A. East and West points.
    B. North and South points.
    C. South and East points.
    D. North and West points.

12. Which of the following is incorrect in reference to a Metes and Bounds description?

    A. You may use a neighbor's property line as a boundary.
    B. You may use lines or a number of feet from one point to another.
    C. Metes means boundaries and bounds means measurements.
    D. You may use a tree or permanent fence as a boundary.

13. The survey, which refers to fractional sections, townships, and ranges, is a legal description by:

    A. Recorded Map.
    B. U. S. Government Survey.
    C. Metes and Bounds.
    D. None of the above.

14. The following statements are all correct in reference to a township, except:

    A. All standard townships contain 36 square miles.
    B. All townships have the same land area.
    C. A standard township is 6 miles square.
    D. Townships are bordered by township and range lines.

15. All of the following statements in reference to a Metes and Bounds description are true, except that it:

    A. Is beneficial for its brevity, simplicity, and ease of interpretation.
    B. Is often used to describe irregularly shaped properties.
    C. Is often used for property for which a map has not been duly recorded.
    D. May be used even when other types of legal descriptions are possible.

Answers may be found in Appendix C (Back of text).

REAL ESTATE DEVELOPMENT

A. DEFINITIONS

1. **Cul-De-Sac** - A cul-de-sac is a street that is closed at one end (a dead end street). The closed end usually has a large rounded area to allow for U-turns. The cul-de-sac street is frequently used by a developer in planning new subdivisions.

2. **Redevelopment** - The existing structures are demolished and new buildings are immediately constructed. Redevelopment is usually associated with Urban Renewal Programs.

3. **Rehabilitation** - The restoration of an old house to its original condition without making any changes in the style or the floor plan.

4. **Remodeling** - To alter the floor plan or structure to correct functional deficiencies or modernize the style of the improvements.

5. **Strip Commercial Development** - A commercial development in a straight line along a major arterial street.

B. DEVELOPER (SUBDIVIDER) - The developer or subdivider creates new residential, commercial, and industrial properties. His primary objective is to supply a product in a price range that will meet the required demand of the marketplace.

C. LOCATION OF DEVELOPMENT - Subdividers and land developers prefer to work in suburban areas. A suburban area tends to offer the developer a strong labor force at competitive prices and moderate costs for building materials. This will assure lower development costs. A severe or heavy tax burden in a city will cause new construction to move to other communities. This additional tax burden is very important to an appraiser as well as to both developers and builders. When planning a commercial shopping center in a suburban community, the most important consideration is purchasing power. In the analysis of a commercial district the emphasis is placed upon the quantity and quality of the purchasing power in the shopping area. Purchasing power is determined by the population. Shopping center considerations based on population are as follows:

1. **Neighborhood Shopping Center** (5 - 10 Stores) - Requires a 5,000 to 10,000 population within a one mile radius.

2. **Community Shopping Center** (10 - 20 Stores) - Requires a 30,000 population within a four mile radius.

3. **Regional Shopping Center** (40 - 100 or more Stores) - Requires a 300,000 population within a six mile radius.

D. FEASIBILITY STUDY - A developer will always consider the condition of the national economy when making a feasibility study for a new development. He will make a market analysis of the economic base, the local zoning ordinances, and the target markets. The feasibility study does not include specific data in reference to the proposed project.

E. MARKET ANALYSIS - A market analysis indicates whether the proposed subdivision will sell in the area he plans to develop. The developer or subdivider makes a market analysis prior to purchasing land for development.

F. TOPOGRAPHY - Topography is the contour of the surface of the land. A developer must give consideration to the topography of the proposed subdivision land because it is desirable to have some irregularities in the surface of the land. Perfectly flat land will create a monotonous (lack of variation) neighborhood. Hilly or irregularly shaped lots increase the cost of construction.

G. SOIL TYPES - The type of soil may affect construction costs. Extensive foundations are usually required when the soil is soft. Adobe, alkaline, and expansive are types of soil. Deciduous is not a type of soil. Deciduous refers to trees which lose their leaves.

H. SUBDIVISION CONSIDERATIONS - When planning a subdivision, the developer must consider that long blocks are more economical than short blocks, excessively deep lots are wasteful, sharply angled land usually creates engineering problems, and minor streets entering major streets should be at right angles. The developer is responsible for the installation of streets, curbs, and public utilities in a new subdivision.

I. SUBDIVISION RESTRICTIONS - A developer may place certain restrictions on a new subdivision. These restrictions include the limitations as to lot size, minimum square footage of a house, and total height of the improvements. The developer can never enforce restrictions as to the amount of dollars allowed for improvement of each lot.

J. SUBDIVISION MAP ACT - The Subdivision Map Act is regulated by the city and county planning commissions. It gives them the authority to standardize the regulations which govern the physical aspects of subdivision. The planning commission will make recommendations to the legislative body (City Council or Board of Supervisors) on subdivisions, zoning, use permits, and variances. This is to develop and maintain the local general plan. The local planning commission is responsible for the alignment of streets within the new subdivision (street design) and the design and improvement for drainage and sewers.

1. Definition of Subdivision - Dividing improved or unimproved land into *two or more* parcels. This includes condominiums, community apartment projects, or five or more existing dwelling units converted into a stock co-operative for the immediate sale, lease, or financing.

2. Exemption - A lease of agricultural land for any purpose is exempt from the Subdivision Map Act regardless of size.

3. Map Requirements - A subdivider filing under the Subdivision Map Act is required to file his map with the city or county officials.

a. Tentative Map - The subdivider must prepare and submit a tentative map to the local planning commission.

b. Final Map - Recordation of the final subdivision map completes the process which then allows the city or county to acquire the streets as an easement in the new subdivision.

4. **Statutory Dedication** - Giving land for public use. Recordation of the final subdivision map completes the process of statutory dedication or donation of land to the City, County, or State. A Certificate of Dedication is given by the subdivider and a Certificate of Acceptance is signed by the local authorities.

   a. Maintenance of the streets and curbs in a new subdivision become the responsibility of the city or county.

   b. The original grantor has the right to claim abandoned public streets which he gave to the city through statutory dedication.

K. SUBDIVIDED LANDS LAW - The subdivided lands law is regulated by the Real Estate Commissioner. Its purpose is to prevent fraud and misrepresentation in the sale of subdivisions in California. This applies to subdivisions located within or outside the boundaries of the State. A subdivision cannot be offered for sale in California until it has been approved by the Real Estate Commissioner. The subdivider must furnish documented evidence that each property can be used for its intended purpose. This is usually covered when the subdivider files a Notice of Intention to Sell and Questionnaire with the Commissioner. The Commissioner will issue a subdivision public report upon approval of a subdivision.

1. **Definition of Subdivision** - Dividing improved or unimproved land into *5 or more* parcels for immediate or future sale, leasing, or financing. Five or more homes on a parcel of land which are sold to the tenants requires the seller to make an application for a subdivision.

2. **Exemptions**

   a. Industrial and commercial subdivisions.

   b. Standard residential subdivisions within the city limits in which the improvements are completed or financial arrangements for completion have been approved by the city.

   c. Offerings by local or state public entities, including the University of California.

3. **Financial Arrangements** - The subdivision public report will not be issued until the Commissioner is satisfied that the subdivider has met all statutory requirements with special emphasis that financial arrangements have been made to assure the completion of the improvements and facilities included in the new subdivision.

   a. If a subdivider intends to offer lots for sale in a subdivision in which he plans to include any community recreational facilities, he must furnish documented evidence to the Real Estate Commissioner showing that financing is available for any community recreational facilities included in the offering.

b. The Real Estate Commissioner has the principal authority to assure the financial arrangements for completion of the community facilities. The Real Estate Commissioner will refuse the issuance of a final public report if recreational facilities are planned without adequate financing.

4. **Preliminary Public Report** - It could take many months to obtain a final public report from the Real Estate Commissioner when a subdivider files his Notice of Intention to Sell and Questionnaire. The subdivider may want to start his marketing plan prior to the issuance of the final public report. In this situation, a preliminary public report may be requested and issued if a minimum package is submitted to the Commissioner for approval.

   a. A preliminary public report does not allow the subdivider to sell the lots in his subdivision. It only allows the subdivider to take **RESERVATIONS**.

   b. Any good faith deposit taken by the subdivider under a preliminary public report is completely refundable prior to the issuance of the final public report.

   c. The preliminary public report expires one (1) year after issuance, or any time during the one year period when the final public report is issued by the Real Estate Commissioner, or on the occurrence of any material change in the physical aspects of the subdivision.

5. **Final Public Report** - A subdivider can never sell property in a new subdivision prior to receiving the final public report from the Department of Real Estate, giving the final public report to the prospective purchaser, and receiving a receipt for the final public report from the purchaser.

   a. Issuance of the final public report by the Real Estate Commissioner makes information available to a potential purchaser as to sewer assessments, liens, utilities to the property, blanket encumbrance, maintenance of the streets, etc.

   b. The final public report expires five (5) years after issuance or upon the occurrence of any material change in the physical aspects of the subdivision.

   c. Failure to show that all lots can be used for the purpose for which they are being offered will result in denial of the Commissioner's Public Report.

   d. Violations of the Commissioner's Regulations or provisions of the final public report will result in the issuance of a **DESIST AND REFRAIN ORDER** by the Real Estate Commissioner. This prevents any further sales activities by the subdivider.

   e. When a final public report has not been issued on a property that an individual wants to purchase, he can ask the local title insurance company to perform a preliminary title search to determine the possibility of a blanket encumbrance, deed restrictions, utility easements, street maintenance, financing, etc.

6. **Receipt for Public Report** - The buyer's receipt for public report is required to be reported on a special form with prescribed wording approved by the Real Estate Commissioner.

a . The receipt for public report cannot be made part of the deposit receipt or final public report, and it is not required to be signed on a registered prenumbered receipt.

b . The subdivider or his agent must retain a copy of the receipt for the final sub-division public report for three (3) years.

7 . Material Change - Any material change in the subdivision must be reported to the Real Estate Commissioner.

    a . Material change includes:

        1 . Change in the size of the lots.
        2 . Change in the method in which title will be conveyed.
        3 . Change in ownership of the subdivision. The sale or option of five (5) or more lots to one individual. Resale of five (5) units in a condominium or stock cooperative.
        4 . A change in the proposed use of the lots being sold.
        5 . An increase in services which would create additional values to the lots being sold.

    b . Material change does not include:

        1 . Change in market price (increase or decrease).
        2 . Signing a listing contract with a broker.

8 . Blanket Encumbrance - In a subdivision which is financed using a blanket encumbrance without partial release clauses, the subdivider must deposit all monies received into an impound account to protect the interest of the individual lot purchasers.

9 . Sales Contract - A sales contract relating to the purchase of property in a new subdivision must include a legal description of the property, the terms of the sale, and a statement of the existing encumbrances against the property.

    a . The contract does not require a statement that the buyer will receive a copy of the public report.

    b . A clause in the sales contract which prohibits the purchaser from placing a "for sale" sign of reasonable size on his property until all the remaining properties are sold is illegal.

    c . A contract for the purchase of a property in a subdivision does not become binding until the final report is received by the purchaser, read, and receipt is received by the purchaser.

L . INTERSTATE LAND SALES FULL DISCLOSURE ACT - The Interstate Land Sales Full Disclosure Act is administered by a division of Housing and Urban Development. Its purpose is to control the sale of large (25 or more lots) vacant lot subdivisions which are sold interstate.

M. TYPES OF SUBDIVISIONS

1. **Standard Subdivision** - Land is divided into five (5) or more parcels and there is not any common or mutual interest among the individual owners.

2. **Planned Development** - Land is divided into five (5) or more parcels and there is a common or mutual interest among the individual owners in lots or areas which may be used by some or all of the individual owners. A planned development may be a subdivision in a residential, commercial, or industrial zoned area.

3. **Condominium** - An estate in real property consisting of an undivided interest in common, within a portion of a parcel of real property, together with five (5) or more separate interests of space in either a residential, commercial, or industrial building. This means that a condominium may be in an office building.

   a. **Ownership Interest** - An individual may do anything with his individual unit interest. Individual interest may be transferred by conveyance or will.

   b. **Common Areas** - Common areas in a condominium project are items in which a unit owner will have an in-common interest with others. These include bearing walls, elevators, sidewalks, and the central heating system.

   c. **Conversion** - When converting an apartment building to a condominium project, each tenant must receive 180 days advance notice prior to vacating the premises. An owner of a four-plex may sell the units to his tenants and an undivided interest in the common area if he complies with the Subdivision Map Act. This is less than five (5) units, therefore he does not have to comply with the Subdivided Lands Law.

   d. Seller is required to give the buyer a copy of the CC&R's, by-laws, and a financial statement from the homeowner's association.

4. **Community Apartment Project** - A subdivision which consists of five (5) or more apartments. Each owner has an undivided interest in the land, together with the right of exclusive occupancy of an apartment unit located thereon.

5. **Stock Cooperative Project** (CO-OP) - A corporation which consists of five (5) or more stockholders. The corporation owns the real property while each stockholder will have the right of exclusive occupancy of an apartment unit located in the real property. It is similar to the corporation being the landlord (lessor) and the stockholders being the tenant (lessee).

   a. The proprietary lessees usually make monthly payments which include principal, interest, taxes, insurance, maintenance, and association fees. If a few of the lessees fail to make their payments, the other owners could lose their equity position through a foreclosure sale.

   b. An individual owner is not issued a separate tax bill; however, an individual owner may deduct the amount of his share of the property taxes on his own income tax return.

   c. An individual owner is not responsible for the cost of an assessment bond against the property.

6. Land Project - A land project is a division of unimproved property (land) into fifty (50) or more parcels, offered for sale for residential purposes located in a sparsely populated area housing less than 1,500 registered voters. Advertisements for a land project must be approved in advance by the Department of Real Estate. An individual purchaser has the right to unilaterally rescind his offer to purchase property in a land project by midnight of the **14TH CALENDAR DAY** following the day the purchaser received a copy of the final public report.

7. Timeshare Project - A timeshare project is the division of real estate into twelve (12) or more estates of five years or more or twelve (12) or more estates of less than five years with an option to renew. Each estate is for a period of time in which the estate holder may occupy and use the property.

N. CONSTRUCTION - An individual land owner should consult with an architect to insure proper plans and specifications when constructing a new building. This should include the possibility of building on or near earthquake fault lines. The **Alquist-Priolo Act** provides for the disclosure of earthquake fault lines on a map.

1. Construction Costs - Direct costs of construction include material, labor, and subcontractors. An indirect cost that is usually overlooked in construction costs is the building permit.

2. Construction Terminology

Anchor Bolt - A large bolt used to fasten the mud sill to the foundation.

Backfill - Dirt used to replace earth (ground) into a hole or against a structure which was removed by excavation for construction. The backfill will fill in the excavation or will help to brace the foundation.

Bearing Wall - A wall which supports the building. A bearing wall is usually constructed stronger than other walls and may be constructed at any angle to doors and windows. A bearing wall is best noticed when remodeling a building.

Bench Mark - Used by a surveyor to mark the elevation in a topographical survey or tidal observations.

Board Foot - A unit of measure for lumber equivalent to **144 cubic inches** (12" x 12" x 1" = 144 cubic inches).

QUESTION: 2" x 12" x 36" = How many board feet? **Answer: 6.**

SOLUTION: 2" x 12" x 36" = 864 cubic inches.
864 cubic inches divided by 144 cubic inches = 6 board feet.

Bracing - A diagonal board placed across a framed wall to prevent the wall from swaying. It makes the wall stronger.

Bridging - Wood or metal placed between the joists to make the floor or ceiling stronger.

B. T. U. (British Thermal Unit) - A standard unit of heat measurement used to rate the capacity of heating systems.

Building Paper - A waterproof paper used for insulation between sheathing when constructing the roof or wall.

Compaction - To compress the dirt so that the ground will be able to bear the weight of new construction.

Conduit - A metal pipe in which electric wiring is installed in a new building. A conduit is usually installed by an electrician.

Crawl Space - The area below the building between the ground and the first floor. The minimum size is 18 inches. The **CRAWL HOLE** is the opening to the crawl space. The crawl hole requires a minimum size of 18 inches by 18 inches.

Cripple - A stud which is above or below a window or door opening.

Drywall - The wall is attached in a dry condition, usually as sheet material. Examples include plywood, fiberboard, and gypsum board. Plaster is applied wet; therefore, it is not considered to be drywall.

Eaves - The protruding underpart of the roof that hangs over the exterior walls.

Elevation Sheet - A drawing showing the front and side views of a building as it appears after the structural work has been completed. The details of the drawing will indicate openings, such as doors, windows, vents, and skylights.

Energy Efficiency Rating (EER) - Measures the efficiency of air-conditioners. The higher the EER, the higher or greater efficiency of the air-conditioner.

Flashing - A piece of metal which protects the structure from water seepage.

Footing - The expanded portion of a concrete foundation.

Header (Lintel) - A horizontal member over a doorway or window.

Joist - The parallel beams or parallel timbers which support the load of the floor and the ceiling in a frame house.

Kiosk - A small, free standing information booth or sales stall in a shopping mall.

Off-site Improvements - Improvements which are not on the property, such as streets, curbs, sewers, and street lights.

Penny - A measurement of length which is used in reference to nails.

Percolation Test - Is used to indicate the ability or capacity of the soil to absorb water. Usually made prior to installing a septic tank.

Pitch - The slope or angle of the roof. The life expectancy of the roof depends on the pitch of the roof. The lower the slope, the lower the life. The steeper the slope, the longer the life. A Gable Roof has two sloping sides. A Hip Roof has four sloping sides.

Plot Plan - A guide to the placement of the improvements on the property. The primary purpose of the plot plan is to show the lot dimensions and lot improvements scaled in proportion to the boundary lines.

Potable - Water that is suitable for drinking.

Ridge - Horizontal line, meeting, or junction of edges of two sloping roof surfaces.

Ridgeboard - The uppermost or highest member of a frame house.

"R" Rating - "R" is the resistance to heat transfer. It is used to measure the quality of insulation. The higher the "R" rating, the better the insulation. It does not mean that the insulation is thicker, it means that it is a better quality of material that will resist the heat or cold. When it is very cold outside and you touch the outside wall of a building and it is as warm as the inside temperature, the reason is **poor insulation**.

Settling - The compacting of the soil caused by the weight of the building. A crack that is creeping up the wall of a house means that the building is settling. When there is a crack in the wall or the foundation, and the windows and doors do not hang properly, this may mean that the building is settling. You or the appraiser should request a **Soil Engineer Report** from a registered civil engineer.

Sill (Mud Sill) - The lowest member of a frame house resting on the foundation.

Soil Pipe - A sewer pipe from the building to the sewer main.

Sole Plate - A horizontal member which is usually at the level of the floor. Wall studs are placed on and secured to the sole plate.

Studs - Vertical supports in the walls and partitions. Usually made with two-by-fours which are spaced 16" on center.

Subflooring - The underflooring laid on the joists, over which the flooring is laid. The subflooring is usually found in the foundation plans.

Termites - Insects which are similar to ants that feed on wood. Subterranean termites are the most destructive insects in a building.

Toxic Waste Report - Used to evaluate the condition of the soil when appraising a property next to an abandoned service or gas station.

Turnkey Project - Fully completed houses in a new subdivision. This means that the houses are ready for occupancy when the buyer purchases from the builder.

Walkup - An apartment with two or more floors without an elevator.

NOTES

REVIEW QUIZ

SECTION I - Matching - Select the letter below which best describes, defines, or relates to the following numbered terms.

1. BTU
2. Studs
3. Flashing
4. Joist
5. Rehabilitation
6. Remodeling
7. Conduit
8. Ridgeboard
9. Sole Plate
10. Redevelopment

a. Wall studs are placed on & secured to this.
b. The restoration of an old house to its original condition without changing the floor plan.
c. The uppermost member of a frame house.
d. To alter the floor plan or structure to correct functional deficiencies.
e. Usually installed by an electrician.
f. Existing structures are demolished & new buildings are immediately constructed.
g. Vertical supports in walls & partitions.
h. Parallel timbers which support the floor and ceiling.
i. A standard measurement of heat used to rate the capacity of heating systems.
j. A piece of metal which protects the structure from water seepage.

SECTION II - True/False - Select either true or false in response to the following statements.

1. Deciduous is a type of soil.
2. The Subdivision Map Act is regulated by the Real Estate Commissioner.
3. A tentative map is prepared & filed with the City or County Planning Commission.
4. Recordation of the final subdivision map completes the process of statutory dedication or donation of land to the City, County, or State.
5. Maintenance of streets and curbs in a new subdivision is the responsibility of the subdivider.
6. The subdivider must furnish documented evidence that each property can be used for its intended purpose.
7. The preliminary public report expires three years after it is issued.
8. Receipt for public report must be retained on file by the subdivider or his agent for three years.
9. Market price increase is a material change.
10. A planned development may be defined as a subdivision.

1. An individual purchasing property in a California land project may unilaterally rescind his offer to purchase within:

   A. 3 days.
   B. 10 days.
   C. 14 days.
   D. Never.

2. The subdivider must notify the Commissioner of any material change in the subdivision which occurs after issuance of the Commissioner's final public report. Which of the following constitutes a material change?

   A. Change in ownership of the subdivision.
   B. Change in the size of the lots.
   C. Change in the manner by which title is to be transferred.
   D. All of the above.

3. Which of the following is the best definition of a land project?

   A. A condominium or community apartment project.
   B. The division of land into 50 or more parcels, offered for sale for residential purposes, located in a sparsely populated area housing less than 1,500 registered voters.
   C. The division of land into 5 or more lots in an urban area.
   D. A subdivision of land into 5 or more parcels, located in a sparsely populated area having less than 1,500 registered voters.

4. The Real Estate Commissioner has primary authority over subdivision matters involving:

   A. Financial arrangements to insure the completion of community facilities.
   B. Design of improvements for drainage.
   C. Alignment of streets within the tract.
   D. All of the above.

5. In reference to a property that is not exempt under the Subdivision Map Act, a subdivider must:

   A. Submit purchase contract forms to local authorities.
   B. Submit a tentative map to local authorities.
   C. Obtain a release clause on all blanket encumbrances.
   D. Deliver the Commissioner's final public report to each prospective buyer.

6. When a subdivision has been developed, the responsibility for the maintenance of the streets and curbs is placed on the:

   A. Real Estate Commissioner.
   B. City and county departments.
   C. City and Real Estate Commissioner.
   D. Developer or subdivider.

7. All of the following in reference to a condominium are correct, except:

   A. An owner's interest may be willed.
   B. Unit owners have an in-common interest with others.
   C. An owner of a condominium may hold property only as an estate for years, regardless of how title is conveyed.
   D. A condominium may be in an office building.

8. The preliminary public report issued by the Real Estate Commissioner on a California subdivision expires:

   A. One year after issuance.
   B. When the final Commissioner's public report is issued.
   C. When a material change in any physical aspect occurs.
   D. When any of the above occur.

9. When a subdivider intends to offer lots for sale in a subdivision in which he plans to include recreational facilities, he is required to furnish documented evidence to the Real Estate Commissioner showing:

   A. That financing is available for any community recreational facilities included in the offering.
   B. That land fill will not exceed 20 feet in depth in any parcel in the subdivision.
   C. The exact size of each lot in the subdivision.
   D. That all utilities are installed to each lot, including sewer, water, telephone, etc.

10. The subdivider can never sell property in a subdivision prior to:

    A. Receiving receipt for report from purchaser.
    B. Receiving final public report.
    C. Giving report to prospective purchaser.
    D. All of the above.

11. The Real Estate Law defines a planned development as which of the following?

    A. A subdivision.
    B. A cooperative apartment project.
    C. A community apartment project.
    D. A condominium project.

12. The receipt for a subdivision final public report must be retained on file by the subdivider or his agent for a period of:

    A. One year.
    B. Two years.
    C. Three years.
    D. Four years.

13. The resale of which of the following would not require any notice to the Real Estate Commissioner?

   A. Two lots in a planned development.
   B. Five lots in a subdivision.
   C. Five units in a stock cooperative.
   D. Five units in a condominium.

14. The right of a buyer to rescind his purchase agreement by midnight of the 14th calendar day following the day the buyer received a copy of the Commissioner's final report applies to the purchase of a:

   A. Unit in a community apartment project.
   B. Unit in a condominium project.
   C. Parcel in a land project.
   D. All of the above.

15. Subdividers and land developers prefer to work in suburban areas:

   A. To provide lower cost single family dwelling units.
   B. To make well organized, integrated communities.
   C. Because of lower costs for development.
   D. Because it raises the value of adjacent land.

Answers may be found in Appendix C (Back of text)

REAL ESTATE MATHEMATICS

A. EQUIVALENT FRACTIONS, PERCENTAGES, & DECIMAL POINTS.

FRACTION	PERCENTAGE	DECIMAL POINTS
1	100.00%	1.00
3/4	75.00%	.75
2/3	66.67%	.6667
1/2	50.00%	.50
1/3	33.33%	.33
1/4	25.00%	.25
1/6	16.67%	.1667
1/8	12.50%	.125
1/15	6.67%	.0667

To change a fraction into a decimal point you must divide the bottom number (denominator) into the top number (numerator). Examples include:

$$1/2 = 2 \overline{)\ 1.00} = .50; \quad 1/4 = 4 \overline{)\ 1.00} = .25; \quad 3/4 = 4 \overline{)\ 3.00} = .75$$

To change a decimal point into a fraction you must move the decimal point two places to the right and divide by 100. Then reduce the fraction to the lowest common denominator. Examples include:

.50 is equivalent to 50/100ths; 50/100 can be reduced to 1/2.
.25 is equivalent to 25/100ths; 25/100 can be reduced to 1/4.
.75 is equivalent to 75/100ths; 75/100 can be reduced to 3/4.

To change a percentage into a decimal point, remove the percentage sign and move the decimal point two places to the left. Examples include:

50% = .50;   25% = .25;   75% = .75

To change a decimal point into a percentage, move the decimal point two places to the right and add the percentage symbol. Examples include:

.50 = 50%;   .25 = 25%;   .75 = 75%

Optional Conversion Rule: Decimal points are similar to money. Writing from one penny to one dollar is a similar method to write percentages as decimal points. Examples include:

1 cent = .01 = 1%;   6 cents = .06 = 6%;   9 cents = .09 = 9%;

50 cents = .50 = 50%;   75 cents = .75 = 75%;   1 dollar = 1.00 = 100%

B. PERCENT, PAID, & MADE FORMULA - The Percent, Paid, & Made Formula is used to interpret a word question. Usually two items are given and the question asks for a third item. The Percent, Paid, & Made formula will assist by showing where to place the given items. The answers for the unknown item can be found by placing the given items into the formula, and then by following the formula to solve for the answer. PLACE SOMETHING LIKE A COIN OVER ONE OF THE WORDS IN THE DIAGRAM; THE REMAINING ITEMS WILL INDICATE WHETHER TO DIVIDE OR MULTIPLY.

SOLUTIONS:

1. Made divided by Paid equals Percent.
2. Made divided by Percent equals Paid.
3. Percent multiplied by Paid equals Made.

$$\frac{\%}{\text{PAID}} \Big| \text{MADE}$$

MISCELLANEOUS APPLICATIONS OF FORMULA - The Percent, Paid, & Made formula can be used in most math questions by substituting other terminology for the terms Percent, Paid, & Made. Acceptable substitutes include:

PERCENT	PAID	MADE
Commission Rate	Selling Price	Amount of Commission
Rate of Return	Amount Invested	Profit
Percent of Gross Profit	Selling Price	Amount of Profit
Percent of Net Profit	Cost	Amount of Profit
Interest Rate	Principal	Interest
Capitalization Rate	Value	Net Income

Examples:

1. Mr. Jones purchased a $1,500 note at a 20% discount. He received payments of $131.00 per month, including 9% interest for one year. What was the percent of return on his investment? **Answer: 31%**

   SOLUTION: Step 1: Determine how much was Paid for the note (A 20% discount means that he paid 80% of face value for the note--$1,500 x 80% = $1,200 Paid). **Step 2:** Determine how much was Received in one year ($131.00 x 12 months = $1,572 Received). **Step 3:** Determine how much was Made on the investment (Received - Paid = Made--$1,572 - $1,200 = $372 Made). **Step 4:** Place the dollar amounts of Paid and Made into the basic formula to solve for Rate of Return on the investment (Made ÷ Paid = Percent or $372 ÷ $1,200 = 0.31 or 31%).

2. Mr. Smith purchased two lots for $18,000 each and divided them into three lots which he sold for $15,000 each. What was his percent of profit? **Answer: 25%**

   SOLUTION: Step 1: Determine how much was Paid for the property ($18,000 x 2 lots = $36,000 Paid). **Step 2:** Determine how much was Received from the sale of the property ($15,000 x 3 lots = $45,000 Received). **Step 3:** Determine the Profit (Received - Paid = Profit--$45,000 - $36,000 = $9,000 Profit). **Step 4:** Place the dollar amounts for Paid and Made into the basic formula to solve for Percent of Profit (Made ÷ Paid = Percent or $9,000 ÷ $36,000 = 0.25 or 25%). **NOTE:** Remember that the Profit is the same as Made.

C. SELLING PRICE VARIATIONS

Gross Selling Price - The entire selling price is equivalent to **100%**. Commissions, escrow fees, cash received, loans, etc., are usually a portion of the selling price; therefore, they will be a portion of the 100% Price. Always relate to the entire price as 100% by drawing a circle. Any other items can be drawn as a portion of the entire circle. These items can be shown either in percentages or dollar amounts.

Gross Selling Price   **Example # 1 Below**

After placing all the items in the circle, add up the dollar amounts. Then add up the percentages. Subtract the given percentages from 100% to determine the percentage for the dollar amounts. Place the percentage of the dollar amount and the total dollar amount into a sentence. EXAMPLE: _____% of Price = $_____. To change the basic formula you must recognize that every formula has an equal (=) sign. The amount on the left side of the equal sign is always equal to the amount on the right side of the equal sign. If you were to add an amount to the left side of the equal sign you would also have to add the same amount to the right side of the equal sign in order for the formula to remain equal.

Examples:

1. Mr. Nelson sold his property and received $15,238 at the close of escrow. If escrow deducted a 6% commission from the selling price and $215.60 for miscellaneous expenses, what is the gross selling price of the property?

   SOLUTION: The entire price is made up of $15,238 received, $215.60 in expenses, and a 6% commission. **Step 1:** 100% - 6% = 94% for the total dollar amount. **Step 2:** $15,238 + $215.60 = $15,453.60 total dollar amount. **Step 3:** Place the percentage of the dollar amount and the total dollar amount into a sentence (94% of Price = $15,453.60). **Step 4:** Divide both sides of the formula by 94%. This changes the formula to (Price = $15,453.60 ÷ 94%)

   94% of Price = $15,453.60   **becomes**

   $\frac{94\% \text{ of Price}}{94\%} = \frac{\$15,453.60}{94\%}$ **becomes**   Price = $\frac{\$15,453.60}{94\%}$ = $16,440

283

2. After deducting a 6% commission from the selling price and $403.50 for other expenses, the seller received a $37,187.10 check from escrow. What was the gross selling price of the property?

SOLUTION: The entire price is made up of $37,187.10 received, $403.50 in other expenses, and a 6% commission. **Step 1:** 100% - 6% = 94% for the total dollar amount. **Step 2:** $37,187.10 + $403.50 = $37,590.60 total dollar amount. **Step 3:** Place the percentage of the dollar amount and the total dollar amount into a sentence (94% of Price = $37,590.60). **Step 4:** Divide both sides of the formula by 94%. This changes the formula to (Price = $37,590.60 ÷ 94%).

94% of Price = $37,590.60 BECOMES

$$\frac{94\% \text{ of Price}}{94\%} = \frac{\$37,590.60}{94\%} \quad \text{BECOMES} \quad \text{Price} = \frac{\$37,590.60}{94\%} = \textbf{\$39,990}$$
Answer

Original Price - The original price is equivalent to 100%.

A profit is more than the original price. When the profit is expressed as a percentage, it must be added to the original 100% price in order to equal a percentage of the selling price. Place the percentage of the selling price and the total dollar amount into a sentence. **EXAMPLE:** ____% of Price = $_____. Change the formula as in the above Gross Selling Price examples.

Examples:

1. Mr. Jones sold his property for $35,200 and made a 10% profit over what he paid for the property. How much was his profit?

SOLUTION: The profit is a portion of the $35,200. Determine the original price, then subtract the original price from the $35,200 to calculate the profit. **Step 1:** 100% Original Price + 10% Profit = 110% Received. **Step 2:** Place the 110% and the $35,200 into a sentence (110% of the Original Price = $35,200). **Step 3:** Divide both sides of the formula by 110% to calculate the Original Price. This changes the formula to (Original Price = $35,200 ÷ 110%). **Step 4:** Sales Price minus Original Price = Profit.

110% of Original Price = $35,200 BECOMES

$$\frac{110\% \text{ of Original Price}}{110\%} = \frac{\$35,200}{110\%} \quad \text{BECOMES} \quad \text{Original Price} = \frac{\$35,200}{110\%}$$

BECOMES Original Price = $32,000

$35,200 Sales Price - $32,000 Original Price = **$3,200 Profit - Answer**

2. An individual sold his property for $17,200. This is 9% more than he paid for the property. What was his original cost?

SOLUTION: $17,200 is 9% more than the original cost. Original cost is 100%. Therefore, $17,200 is equivalent to 109%. **Step 1:** Place the 109% and $17,200 into a sentence (109% of the Original Cost = $17,200). **Step 2:**

Divide both sides of the formula by 109% to calculate the Original Cost. This changes the formula to (Original Cost = $17,200 ÷ 109%).

109% of Original Cost = $17,200 **BECOMES**

$\frac{109\% \text{ of Original Cost}}{109\%} = \frac{\$17,200}{109\%}$ **BECOMES** Original Cost $= \frac{\$17,200}{109\%}$

BECOMES Original Cost = $15,779.816 or approximately **$15,780**
Answer

D. AREA (Square Footage)

1. Rectangle

a. Formulas

1. **Base x Height = Area**
2. **Area ÷ Base = Height**
3. **Area ÷ Height = Base**

Note: The term Height may be expressed as Depth or Length. The term Base may be expressed as Width or Frontage. Area may be expressed as Acreage, Square Feet, or Square Yards. Lineal measurements may be expressed as Miles, Rods, Yards, or Feet.

b. Examples

1. A rectangular parcel of land contains 540 square yards and has a 45 foot frontage. The length of the parcel is how many feet?

   SOLUTION: Given is the area of the parcel and the frontage. To calculate the length of the parcel use Formula # 2 above. **Step 1:** Convert the 540 square yards to an area of square feet. **Step 2:** Place the square foot area and the frontage (base) into the formula. **Step 3:** Divide to solve for the height (length) of the parcel.

   Measurement conversion (1 square yard = 9 square feet)
   540 square yards x 9 = 4,860 square feet.
   Area ÷ Base = Height **BECOMES** 4,860 ÷ 45' = **108' Answer**

2. An easement running the entire length of a section contains five acres. How wide is the easement?

   SOLUTION: The area of the rectangle is given as acres; therefore, it must be converted to square feet. The length of the rectangle is the side of a section (1 mile), it must be converted to feet. Make the conversions and use formula # 3 above.

   Measurement conversions (1 acre = 43,560 square feet) (1 mile = 5,280').
   43,560 x 5 acres = 217,800 square feet.
   Area ÷ Length = Width
   217,800 ÷ 5,280 = **41.25' Answer**

2. **Rectangle Variations Using SETBACKS and SIDEWALKS** - The previously stated area formulas can be used to calculate the square footage of a property minus the setbacks on the property, or to calculate the square footage of a sidewalk around the outside edges of the property.

   a. **Setback** - A setback is determined for each lot when the subdivider's map is approved by the local planning commission. A setback on a lot regulates the distance that the improvements can be constructed inside the boundary lines. This means that if there is an eighteen foot setback on the front of the lot, the improvements have to be built at least eighteen feet back from the front boundary line.

   Example: The dimensions of a city lot are 50' x 150'. There is a 20' setback in the front, and a 4' setback on each side and at the rear of the lot. If all of the area available for the building is used, what is the maximum square footage of the building?

   SOLUTION: Subtract the setbacks from the front and rear of the lot from the length of the lot to determine the length within the setbacks (150' minus 20' front setback, minus 4' rear setback equals 126'). Subtract the setbacks from each side of the lot from the width of the lot to determine the width within the setbacks (50' minus 4' left side, minus 4' right side equals 42'). The dimensions within the setbacks are 42' x 126'.

   42' x 126' = **5,292 Square Feet - Answer**

   b. **Sidewalk** - An individual wants to build a 7' wide sidewalk around two outside edges of a corner lot that measures 60' x 90'. How many square feet will the sidewalk contain?

   SOLUTION: A sidewalk the width of the lot will measure 7' x 60'. At the corner there is now a sidewalk which adds 7' to the length of the lot. This means that a sidewalk the length of the lot will measure 7' x 97'. Find the area of the two sidewalks and add them together to calculate the total square footage.

   $$7' \times 60' = 420 \text{ Square Feet}$$
   $$7' \times 97' = \underline{679 \text{ Square Feet}}$$
   $$\mathbf{1,099 \text{ Square Feet - Answer}}$$

3. **Triangle** - In real estate mathematics a triangle is usually one-half of a rectangle. Usually there are two boundary lines that meet at right angles and a diagonal third boundary line that encloses the triangle.

   a. **Formula**

   $$\mathbf{Area = \frac{Base \times Height}{2}}$$

b. Examples

1. A triangle has a base of 1,320' and a height of 660'. How many acres are in the triangle?

   SOLUTION: Multiply the base by the height and divide by two to calculate the square feet in the triangle. Convert the square feet to acreage. **Step 1:** 1,320' x 660' = 871,200 Square Feet. **Step 2:** 871,200 divided by two = 435,600 Square Feet. **Step 3:** Convert 435,600 Square Feet to Acreage (1 Acre = 43,560 Square Feet).

   435,600 ÷ 43,560 = **10 Acres - Answer**

2. A triangle has a base of 2,640' and a height of 1,320'. How many acres are in the triangle?

   SOLUTION: Multiply the base by the height and divide by two to calculate the square feet in the triangle. Convert the square feet to acreage. **Step 1:** 2,640' x 1,320' = 3,484,800 Square Feet. **Step 2:** 3,484,800 divided by two = 1,742,400 Square Feet. **Step 3:** Convert 1,742,400 Square Feet to Acreage (1 Acre = 43,560 Square Feet).

   1,742,400 ÷ 43,560 = **40 Acres - Answer**

E. DEPRECIATION

1. **Straight Line** - An equal amount of depreciation is deducted each year.

   a. **Formula (EVA)** $E \overline{)V} = A$

   Value of Improvements ÷ Economic Life = Annual Depreciation

   b. **Example:** If a building is valued at $6,000,000 and has a useful life of 50 years, how much depreciation can be taken each year using the straight line method?

   SOLUTION: Divide the value of the improvements by the useful life to calculate the annual depreciation.

   $6,000,000 ÷ 50 = **$120,000 Annual Depreciation (2% per year).**

2. **Declining Balance Method** - An accelerated method to calculate depreciation in which the depreciation declines (gets smaller) each year. Declining balance methods include 125%, 150%, 175%, and 200%. To calculate the depreciation by a declining balance method, you must first determine straight line depreciation (as a percentage). Then multiply the straight line percentage by the declining balance percentage. This means that if straight line is 2% per year:

125%	= 2.5%	(125% x 2%)
150%	= 3.0%	(150% x 2%)
175%	= 3.5%	(175% x 2%)
200%	= 4.0%	(200% x 2%)

Examples

a. A building has a useful life of 50 years and is valued at $6,000,000.

    1. Using the 150% Declining Method, how much depreciation can be taken the first year?

    SOLUTION: From the straight line example above, straight line was equal to 2% per year. 2% x 150% = 3%

    $6,000,000 x 3% = **$180,000 - 1st year depreciation**

    2. Using the 150% Declining method, how much depreciation can be taken the second year?

    SOLUTION: In any declining balance method the depreciation for the previous year must be deducted prior to calculating the depreciation for the next year ($6,000,000 - $180,000 = $5,820,000 to be depreciated the second year).

    $5,820,000 x 3% = **$174,600 - 2nd year depreciation**

    3. Using the 150% Declining method, how much depreciation can be taken the third year?

    SOLUTION: Calculate the depreciation from the previous balance. (5,820,000 - $174,600 = $5,645,400 to be depreciated the third year).

    $5,645,400 x 3% = **$169,362 - 3rd year depreciation**

b. An investor has a property with a cost basis of $52,000. Using the 175% declining balance method of depreciation for a 15 year period, how much depreciation can be taken the first year?

SOLUTION: Determine the straight line depreciation, then multiply by 175%.

Value ÷ Years = Annual Depreciation (Straight Line or EVA)

Straight Line: $52,000 ÷ 15 = $3,466.6666;

Multiply by 175%: $3,466.6666 x 1.75 = $6,066.6666

1st year depreciation - $6,066

REVIEW QUIZ

SECTION I - Matching - Select the letter below which best describes, defines, equals, or relates to the following numbered terms.

1. Calculate Made
2. Area of Rectangle
3. Straight Line
4. Calculate Paid
5. Profit
6. Depth of Rectangle
7. Commission & Escrow Fees
8. Calculate Percent
9. Area of Triangle
10. Frontage of Rectangle

a. Area divided by length.
b. Base multiplied by height and then divided by two.
c. A portion of the 100% Selling Price.
d. Made divided by Percent.
e. Base x Height.
f. A percentage that is more than the Original Price.
g. Made divided by Paid.
h. An equal amount of depreciation is deducted each year.
i. Percent multiplied by Paid.
j. Area divided by Base.

SECTION II - True/False - Select either true or false in response to the following statements.

1. To change a fraction to a decimal point you must divide the top number into the bottom number.
2. The fraction 1/6 is equal to sixteen and two-thirds percent.
3. Commissions, escrow fees, cash received, and loans are usually a portion of the 100% Selling Price.
4. Profits must be subtracted from the 100% Original Price.
5. Lineal measurements are expressed as acreage, square feet or square yards.
6. A setback on a lot regulates the distance that the improvements can be constructed inside the boundary lines.
7. The amount of commission made divided by the selling price equals the commission rate.
8. The amount of profit divided by the percent of net profit equals the cost.
9. Straight line is an accelerated method in which to calculate depreciation.
10. Declining balance methods provide for the same amount of depreciation each year.

SECTION III - **Multiple Choice** - Select the letter which best completes the statement or answers the question.

1. A road consisting of a total of three acres runs along the northern boundary of a section. Which of the following is most likely the width of the road?

    A. 23 feet.
    B. 25 feet.
    C. 30 feet.
    D. 35 feet.

2. A building that has interior dimensions of 26' by 30' and has 6" walls would cover how many square feet of land?

    A. 744.
    B. 755.
    C. 775.
    D. 837.

3. A rectangular parcel of land which measures 1,780' x 1,780' contains approximately how many acres?

    A. 20.
    B. 40.
    C 60.
    D. 73.

4. A rectangular parcel containing 540 square yards which has a frontage of 45' would have a depth of how many feet?

    A. 108'.
    B. 144'.
    C. 176'.
    D. 216'.

5. Mr. Jones owns a property which has a 2,640' frontage on one road and a 1,320' frontage on another road meeting at right angles. A third boundary parallels the shorter road and extends 2,640'. How many acres are in this property?

    A. 80.
    B. 120.
    C. 140.
    D. 160.

6. A rectangular parcel measures 760' x 950' and is divided diagonally by a concrete irrigation canal. How many acres are contained in each parcel?

    A. 5.3.
    B. 8.3.
    C. 10.6.
    D. 16.6.

7. How many 50' x 100' lots can be created from one acre?

   A. 6.
   B. 7.
   C. 8.
   D. 9.

8. A home sold for $33,700 which was 7% less than the original purchase price. What was most nearly the original cost to the sellers?

   A. $36,260.
   B. $36,059.
   C. $31,290.
   D. $31,059.

9. Mr. and Mrs. Duncan sold their home for $36,850 which represents a 17% profit over the original price. How much was the original price?

   A. $30,250.
   B. $30,495.
   C. $31,495.
   D. $33,495.

10. A depreciable asset which cost $6,000,000 had a useful life of 50 years. If the owner used the 150% declining balance method, how much depreciation could be taken in the third year?

    A. $115,248.
    B. $120,000.
    C. $169,362.
    D. $180,000.

11. Mr. Smith sold his house for $17,950 which was 11% more than he paid for it. The original selling price was most nearly:

    A. $15,430.
    B. $15,800.
    C. $16,170.
    D. $19,925.

12. A parcel of land measures 220 yards by 220 yards. How many acres are in the parcel?

    A. 1.11 acres.
    B. 3.33 acres.
    C. 5 acres.
    D. 10 acres.

13. Mr. Smith purchased a $1,700 promissory note at a 20% discount. The note is to be repaid in monthly payments of $155 including interest at 9% per annum over a period of one year. Mr. Smith's rate of return on his investment would be:

   A. 24%.
   B. 26%.
   C. 31%.
   D. 36%.

14. Mr. Jones purchased two lots for $18,000 each and divided them into three equal lots which sold for $15,000 each. What was his percent of profit?

   A. 15%.
   B. 20%.
   C. 25%.
   D. 30%.

15. Construction was started on a lot which cost $22,500. After completion the property was valued at $131,000. If the economic life was 50 years, what is the value of the property after seventeen years?

   A. $71,610.
   B. $86,460.
   C. $94,110.
   D. $95,600.

Answers may be found in Appendix C (Back of text)

BUSINESS OPPORTUNITIES

A Business Opportunity is the sale or lease of a business. A business is personal property and may or may not include real property.

A. LICENSE REQUIREMENT - An individual must have a valid real estate license in order to negotiate and receive commission in a business opportunity transaction. An authorization to sell a business opportunity that is taken by the real estate broker, making himself the optionee, is a perfectly valid contract.

B. DEFINITIONS

1. **Advance Fee** - A charge by a broker in the sale of a Business Opportunity to pay for promotional services for advertising in a newspaper listing businesses which are "For Sale" or "Wanted" by the client. The broker may take a fee for advertising Business Opportunities in a pamphlet he publishes without taking a listing on the property. The broker must furnish the business owner with a verified accounting of the use of the fee charged or collected.

2. **Bill of Sale** - The instrument which is used to transfer title to personal property. A bill of sale is required when the value of the personal property transferred is $500 or more. A bill of sale used in the transfer of a retail merchandising business will usually include inventory, goodwill, fixtures, and equipment. The bill of sale will not include the leasehold. In a Business Opportunity transaction, the instrument which is similar to a deed is the bill of sale.

   a. **Parties to a Bill of Sale** - The seller in the bill of sale is referred to as the **VENDOR**. The buyer in the bill of sale is referred to as the **VENDEE**.

   b. **Valid Bill of Sale** - A valid bill of sale must contain the name of the buyer (vendee), signature of the seller (vendor), and a description of the property. Consideration is usually stated, but it is not required to create a valid bill of sale. A date usually appears on a bill of sale, but it is not required to make it valid. A bill of sale is not usually recorded; therefore, an acknowledgement is even less required than a date.

3. **Goodwill** - Goodwill is the expectation of continued public patronage. Goodwill is created by long-term advertisements, habits of the customers who patronize the business, and pleasant association by the customers because of past excellent service. Modern fixtures and adequate inventory do not contribute to goodwill.

4. **Inventory** - Inventory is a detailed list which includes stock-in-trade and trade fixtures.

5. **Turnover** - Turnover is the number of times a given amount of inventory sells over a specific period of time.

C. FINANCIAL STATEMENT - A financial statement is supported by a Balance Sheet and a Profit and Loss Statement.

1. **Balance Sheet** - A balance sheet indicates the financial status of a business as of a specific date. It consists of assets, liabilities, and net worth.

    a. **Assets** - Assets are items of value which are owned by the business.

    b. **Liabilities** (Accounts Payable) - Liabilities are claims of creditors against the business. Accounts payable are a liability on the balance sheet. Accounts payable are subtracted from the assets when establishing a net worth of a business.

    c. **Net Worth** - Net worth is the difference between the assets and liabilities of a business (Assets minus Liabilities equals Net Worth).

2. **Profit and Loss Statement** - A profit and loss statement will indicate the profit or loss of a business over a definite period of time. It consists of Gross Income, Expenses, and Net Income.

    a. **Gross Income** - Gross income is the actual revenue received from the sale of goods or services in a business. Gross sales means the same as gross income and always appears on the Profit and Loss Statement. Gross sales will not appear on the Balance Sheet.

    b. **Expenses** - Expenses of a business may be the cost of goods and operational expenses.

    c. **Net Income** - Net income is the difference between the gross income and the expenses of a business (Gross Income minus Expenses equals Net Income). The net income is the most important item considered by a lender when making a loan to a business.

D. PARTIES TO A BUSINESS OPPORTUNITY

1. **Transferor** (VENDOR) - The seller in a Business Opportunity is referred to as the transferor or vendor.

2. **Transferee** (VENDEE) - The buyer in a Business Opportunity is referred to as the transferee or vendee.

E. UNIFORM COMMERCIAL CODE (UCC) - The Uniform Commercial Code was created to modify and make uniform the Uniform Sales Act and the Negotiable Instrument Act. It provides notification to the transferor's creditors of a bulk transfer and establishes a comprehensive scheme for the regulation of security transactions involving personal property. It protects the buyer, seller, and creditors.

1. **Bulk Sales Law** (Division 6) - Division 6 of the Uniform Commercial Code is referred to as the Bulk Sales Law. It is designed primarily to protect creditors.

    a. **Notice of Sale** - When a business is sold, the transferee (buyer) must give proper notice by recordation and publication of the proposed sale. A notice to creditors of a bulk sale contains the names of the transferee and transferor, the addresses of the transferee and the transferor, location and general description of the goods being transferred, and the location and date on or after which the transaction will be consummated.

b. Requirements - In the sale of a Business Opportunity with stock-in-trade, the transferee is required to:

1. Publish a notice of sale (bulk transfer) in a newspaper of general circulation in the county where the business is located **12 BUSINESS DAYS** prior to the sale.

2. Record a notice of sale (bulk transfer) in the county **12 BUSINESS DAYS** prior to the sale.

3. Send a notice of sale (bulk transfer) to the County Tax Collector by certified or registered mail **12 BUSINESS DAYS** prior to the sale.

c. Noncompliance - The transferee is responsible for publishing and recording the notice of sale. Noncompliance of the recordation and publication requirement make the sale void and fraudulent against the existing creditors of the seller. This means that if the transferee (buyer) does not publish and record the notice of sale, the seller remains primarily liable for the debts of the business.

2. Personal Property Loans (Division 9) - Division 9 of the Uniform Commercial Code is entitled "Secured Transaction, Sale of Accounts, Contract Rights and Chattel Paper". It is designed primarily to regulate and control the sale, creation, and priority of liens and security interests in personal property.

a. Security Interests - A business loan may be secured by a security agreement on furniture and fixtures, accounts receivable, or a personal guarantee. A business loan cannot be secured by stock-in-trade (inventory) if the individual unit price of the item is less than $500. All items used to secure a personal property loan in a Business Opportunity are referred to as security interests.

b. Loan Documents

1. Note - A promissory note is given as evidence of the debt.

2. Security Agreement - A security agreement is used to create a security interest in the personal property that is financed. It describes the creditor's interest in the personal property.

3. Financing Statement - A financing statement is required to be filed with personal property security transactions. It is used to protect or "PERFECT" the interest created by the security agreement and is filed with the Secretary of State or the County Recorder. It gives constructive notice that the personal property is being used as security for a loan.

a. Secretary of State - Most financing statements are filed with the Secretary of State due to the movable status of the personal property.

b. County Recorder - Financing statements used to perfect the security interest of consumer goods, uncut timber, or growing crops are filed with the County Recorder.

c. A chattel lien search for claims of possible creditors is made at either the Offices of the County Recorder, or the Secretary of State.

    1. Stock in Trade is filed with the County Recorder.

    2. Fixtures are filed with the Secretary of State.

d. When a farmer requires additional working capital and wants to encumber his crops, he will have to sign a financing statement to complete the loan.

4. **Termination Statement** - A termination statement is issued when an individual has satisfied his debts and wishes to release a previously recorded financing statement.

F. CALIFORNIA SALES AND USE TAX PROVISIONS - The Sales and Use Tax Law is important to a real estate licensee in connection with a Business Opportunity transaction that includes the sale of tangible personal property. A sales tax must be collected on both retail and wholesale sales.

1. **Seller's Permit** - Every wholesale and retail business is required to obtain a seller's permit from the State Board of Equalization.

2. **Administration** - The State Board of Equalization will collect the sales tax collected by the owner of the business. The buyer of a Business Opportunity that is subject to successor's liability must account to the State Board of Equalization.

3. **Penalty** - A business owner may be subject to a penalty of not more than 10% when filing a late sales tax return. A penalty of 25% is added to the sales tax if the return is fraudulent. The maximum penalty is 35%.

4. **Business Opportunity Transaction** - In the sale of a business, sales tax is paid on the tangible assets, such as the trade fixtures. Sales tax is not paid on intangible assets, such as goodwill, inventory and accounts receivable. The State sales tax due on fixtures may be paid by the buyer to the seller together with the purchase price. It is then remitted by the seller to the State Board of Equalization and a Certificate of Clearance is issued.

5. **Certificate of Clearance** - A Certificate of Clearance is issued to indicate that the seller has paid all of the sales tax which is due in a Business Opportunity transaction.

6. **Successor's Liability** - Unpaid sales tax in the sale of a Business Opportunity can be determined by consulting with the State Board of Equalization. The buyer of the business will be secondarily liable if the seller does not pay the taxes (If the Certificate of Clearance receipt is not obtained). A real estate broker should not allow funds to be released from escrow until a tax clearance has been received. This will protect the buyer of a Business Opportunity.

G . ALCOHOLIC BEVERAGE CONTROL ACT - A Business Opportunity transaction may include the sale of a liquor license. A real estate licensee negotiating the sale of a business which also includes a liquor license must have a basic knowledge of the laws which govern the issuance of a license to engage in the sale of alcoholic beverages.

1 . **Administration** - The Alcoholic Beverage Control Board (ABC) has jurisdiction over the Alcoholic Beverage Control Act.

2 . **License Classifications** - A license may be issued for the sale of alcohol that is consumed either on or off of the premises. A license may be issued to sell all types of alcohol or limited to the sale of beer and wine. A special license may be issued for the sale of alcohol at a seasonal resort.

3 . **Original License Fee** - The fee for an original on-sale or off-sale general liquor license is $6,000. The fee for a seasonal on-sale liquor license is $3,500. Beer and wine license fees are $100 for an off-sale license and $300 for an on-sale. A fee for a special on-sale beer license is $200.

4 . **Transfer of License**

   a . A general on-sale or off-sale license cannot be sold for more than $6,000 during the initial five years. However, it may be sold for less than $6,000 during the initial five years ($1 - $5,999). The liquor license may be sold for any price after the initial five years.

   b . Transfer of an unlike license is not allowed. This means that an owner of an unconditional off-sale general license cannot trade with the holder of an off-sale beer and wine license.

   c . A buyer of a liquor license cannot transfer the license to a county which has a population of less than 35,000.

5 . **Community Property License Requirements**

   a . A liquor license is required to be issued in the names of both the husband and wife.

   b . A married man or woman who wishes to purchase a liquor license must make application with his or her spouse.

   c . Married individuals do not have to apply with their spouse if the spouse is unavailable (out of State for a prolonged period) or if the spouse is physically disabled.

6 . **License Refusal**

   a . A liquor license may be refused if the intended location is in close proximity to a school, church, park, public playground, or hospital.

   b . A liquor license may be refused to a club which has been in operation for less than one year. This means that a newly formed club cannot qualify for a liquor license. A club in existence for six months is considered newly formed; therefore, it cannot qualify for a liquor license.

H. FRANCHISE INVESTMENT LAW - A Business Opportunity transaction may include the sale of a franchise. A real estate licensee negotiating the sale of a business that includes a franchise must have a basic knowledge of the laws which govern the franchise. The California Franchise Law is designed to protect the potential franchisee. This is the person who is contemplating the purchase of a franchise.

1. **Definition** - A franchise is a marketing or distribution system under which a large company (franchisor) gives an exclusive dealership to a smaller company (franchisee). The larger company grants the smaller company the right to sell, offer to sell, or exchange goods or services under a marketing plan designed by the larger company (grantor).

2. **Trademark** (Trade Name) - The franchisee is allowed to use the franchisor's trademark, trade name, service mark, logo, etc.

3. **Administration** - The Department of Corporations has jurisdiction over the Franchise Investment Law.

4. **Registration** - Any franchise offered for sale in California must be registered with the Corporation Commissioner.

5. **Exemption** - A franchise offered for sale in California does not have to be registered with the Corporation Commissioner if:

   a. The franchisor has a net worth on a consolidated basis of more than $5,000,000.

   b. The franchisor has twenty-five franchises consistently conducting business during the five-year period immediately preceding the sale.

REVIEW QUIZ

SECTION I - **Matching** - Select the letter below which best describes, defines, or relates to the following numbered terms.

1. Turnover
2. Bill of Sale
3. Security Agreement
4. Net Income
5. Goodwill
6. Inventory
7. Net Worth
8. Seller's Permit
9. Certificate of Clearance
10. Financing Statement

a. Expectation of continued public patronage.
b. Used to perfect the security agreement.
c. The difference between assets and liabilities.
d. A detailed list which includes trade fixtures and stock-in-trade.
e. Used to secure a loan when personal property is financed.
f. A statement showing that the sales tax has been paid.
g. Used to transfer the title to personal property.
h. Required by every business that sells wholesale and retail goods.
i. The number of times a given amount of inventory sells over a specific period of time.
j. The most important item considered by a lender when making a loan to a business.

SECTION II - **True/False** - Select either true or false in response to the following statements.

1. A real estate license is required in order to negotiate and receive commission in the sale of a Business Opportunity transaction.
2. Consideration is usually required to create a valid bill of sale.
3. Adequate inventory and modern fixtures do not contribute to goodwill.
4. Proper notice of a bulk sale should be published as provided for in the U.C.C.
5. Filing a financing statement is required to perfect the security agreement.
6. The transferor is responsible for publishing the notice of sale.
7. A business loan cannot be secured by stock-in-trade if the individual unit price of the item is less than $500.
8. Unpaid sales tax in a business can be determined by consulting with the Department of Corporations.
9. The Alcohol Beverage Control Board may approve the issuance of an on-sale license to a seasonal resort.
10. The California Franchise Law is designed to protect the potential franchisor.

SECTION III - Multiple Choice - Select the letter which best completes the statement or answers the question.

1. The party responsible for publishing the notice of intention to sell is the:

   A. Transferee.
   B. Transferor.
   C. Seller.
   D. Creditors of the seller.

2. The number of times per year that a given inventory sells is referred to as:

   A. Net worth.
   B. Turnover.
   C. Assets.
   D. Short rate.

3. A valid bill of sale need not contain any of the following, except:

   A. Mention of consideration.
   B. An acknowledgement.
   C. A description of the property.
   D. A date.

4. The Uniform Commercial Code tends to modify or make uniform which of the following?

   A. Negotiable Instrument Act.
   B. Uniform Sales Act.
   C. Neither "A" nor "B".
   D. Both "A" and "B".

5. In reference to a financial statement, accounts payable would appear on the:

   A. Profit and loss statement.
   B. Asset side of the balance sheet.
   C. Liability side of the balance sheet.
   D. None of the above.

6. If an individual sells a business, sales tax would be paid on which of the following?

   A. Goodwill.
   B. Trade fixtures.
   C. Accounts receivable.
   D. Inventory of goods on hand.

7. Under the Uniform Commercial Code, the instrument that best describes the creditor's interest in personal property is a:

   A. Chattel mortgage.
   B. Hypothecated agreement.
   C. Security agreement.
   D. Pledge.

8. Division 6 of the Uniform Code in reference to the Bulk Sales Law is to protect primarily:

   A. Buyers.
   B. Partners.
   C. Creditors.
   D. Patrons.

9. A Certificate of Clearance is issued by the:

   A. County Board of Equalization.
   B. State Board of Equalization.
   C. Franchise Tax Board.
   D. Secretary of State.

10. How much would be paid to secure an original on-sale general liquor license?

    A. $250.
    B. $500.
    C. $5,000.
    D. $6,000.

11. In establishing the net worth of a Business Opportunity, accounts payable is an account which is:

    A. Added to the net worth.
    B. Added to the assets.
    C. Subtracted from the assets.
    D. Subtracted from the liabilities.

12. In the sale of a business, which of the following would contribute the least to goodwill?

    A. Adequate stock and modern fixtures.
    B. Pleasant association in the customer's mind because of past service.
    C. Advertising over a period of time.
    D. Habit of customer patronage of the establishment.

13. The State sales tax due on the fixtures in the sale of a Business Opportunity is:

    A. Paid before the Certificate of Clearance is issued.
    B. Paid by the buyer to the seller together with the purchase price.
    C. Remitted by the seller to the State Board of Equalization.
    D. All of the above.

14. In the sale of a business, a Clearance Receipt is issued by the State Board of Equalization to protect the:

    A. Purchaser of the business.
    B. Successor's liability.
    C. Secured creditors.
    D. Unsecured creditors.

15. The California Franchise Law protects:

   A. The purchaser of the franchise if he is from out of state.
   B. New franchisees preparing to purchase a franchise.
   C. Only the franchisor who has a net worth of $5,000,000.
   D. The general public on a fair, just, and equitable basis.

Answers may be found in Appendix C (Back of text)

REAL ESTATE PRACTICE

A. REAL ESTATE MARKET - The real estate market is affected by the economy of the United States.

1. **Gross National Product** (Gross Domestic Product) - The Gross National Product is the measure of total goods and services in the United States during one calendar year. When the Gross Domestic Product rises, both personal income and home sales will also rise.

2. **Business Cycle** - The business cycle may have phases of recession, depression, expansion, and progression (prosperity).

   a. When the business cycle is in the prosperity phase, it is usually followed by a real estate cycle of a high level of sales transactions, construction, and borrowing.

   b. The prosperity phase of the business cycle is usually accompanied by an increase in real estate listings and real estate sales.

   c. The recession and depression phases of the business cycle usually cause unemployment.

   d. A recession, depression, or unemployment may cause a borrower to go into default. The ensuing foreclosure may result in a loss to the lender.

3. **Inflation** - Inflation is a rise in prices which causes a decrease in the purchasing power of the dollar. It makes money worth less.

   a. The best hedge against inflation is the ownership of real property.

   b. An income producing property is one of the best real estate investments. This is because it usually maintains its value; therefore, it is a hedge against inflation.

   c. Assets increase in value during inflation. An individual would be wise to invest in equity assets as a hedge against inflation. An individual does not usually invest in savings accounts, trust deeds, or government bonds as hedges against inflation.

   d. A rise in the Consumer Price Index indicates to an investor that there is an inflationary economy.

   e. When real estate values decline, the value of the dollar increases.

   f. Inflation will cause a loss to a lender because the loan is being paid back with money which has less buying power.

g. Inflation is a benefit to the borrower because he is paying off the loan with money which has less buying power.

4. Changes in the real estate market are also created by land use regulations, consumerism, and judicial and legislative regulations of the real estate industry. Consumerism may be defined as how the consumer thinks.

B. REAL ESTATE ORGANIZATIONS - Most real estate licensees become members of trade and professional organizations to unite with others engaged in the real estate business, to promote good fellowship and fair business practice, and to maintain the reputation and dignity of the real estate industry. Membership in these organizations is voluntary. Membership is not limited to real estate licensees. Other professionals related to the real estate industry may become members of these organizations (Appraisers, Title Officers, Escrow Officers, Etc.).

1. Local Real Estate Board - The Local Real Estate Board will unite and serve the real estate professionals in a specific community.

2. California Association of Realtors (CAR) - The California Association of Realtors will unite and serve the real estate professionals in the State of California.

3. National Association of Realtors (NAR) - The National Association of Realtors will unite and serve the real estate professionals in the United States.

a. Realtor - The term "Realtor" may only be used by a real estate broker who is a member of the National Association of Realtors.
b. A real estate broker is in violation of the law if he used the term "Realtor" on his sign if he is not a member of NAR.
c. Membership in NAR does not authorize the California real estate broker to conduct real estate activities in another state. A California broker must have a license from another state to conduct real estate activities in that state.

4. National Association of Real Estate Brokers (NAREB) - The National Association of Real Estate Brokers was organized in 1947 to unite and serve the black brokers in the United States. The term **REALTIST** is used by the members of this organization.

5. Institute of Real Estate Management (IREM) - The Institute of Real Estate Management will unite and serve property managers in the United States.

a. Certified Property Manager (CPM) - Certified Property Manager is the professional designation for an individual who is a member of IREM.
b. Membership in this organization is limited to qualified individuals.

6. Appraisal Institute - The Appraisal Institute was created to unite and serve real estate appraisers in the United States. The initials **MAI** are used to designate its members.

C. OFFICE PROCEDURE

1. Company Dollar - "Company Dollar" refers to the income of an office after all commissions have been subtracted. Every real estate office should have a budget that reflects the company dollar.

2 . Desk Cost - The operation of a real estate office includes the cost of rent, telephone, utilities, advertising and other expenses. This total cost is added up and then divided by the number of desks in the office to calculate the cost for each desk.

3 . Policy Manual - Every real estate office should have an outline of the procedures under which the office operates. This is referred to as a policy manual.

4 . Worker's Compensation - Every real estate office must provide worker's compensation insurance for all licensed and unlicensed employees.

5 . Advertisement - Real estate advertisement is required to attract both buyers and sellers. The real estate broker should direct his advertisements toward a specific group of people and a specific geographical area. Real estate can be advertised by the use of newspaper display ads, classified ads, direct mail, open houses, display boards, signs, billboards, press releases, radio, television, etc.

    a . Real estate advertisement should include the elements of marketing. This is commonly referred to as "AIDA".

        1 . Attention - Get the potential attention of the prospect.
        2 . Interest - Create an interest in the product.
        3 . Desire - Arouse a desire for the product.
        4 . Action - The prospect purchases the product.

    b . Real estate advertisements are usually made by the real estate broker.

    c . A real estate salesperson may place a real estate advertisement. However, a salesperson must provide the name of the employing broker in an advertisement of a property. An individual salesperson's name may appear with the name of his employing broker.

    d . Blind Advertisement - A blind advertisement excludes the name of the licensee. A broker may be disciplined for a blind advertisement.

    e . Advance Fee for Advertisement - When a real estate broker takes any advance fee for advertisement, he must place the funds in his trust account, use the funds only for advertisement of the property, and provide the seller with a report which must itemize the disbursement of the funds.

    f . Deceptive or Misleading Advertisement - When attempting to sell a promissory note, any guaranteed yield or return which does not agree with the interest rate stated in an advertisement, is considered evidence of deceptive or misleading advertising. *Mega Buck Trust Deeds* is allowable if all terms are disclosed. *No Down Payment* is deceptive if the buyer is advised to borrow the down payment. *Move In Now* is deceptive if there is major structural damage. *Obtaining A Loan Over The Phone* is deceptive because facts have to be verified. *Advertising incentives* are legal if proper disclosure is made to all interested parties. *Prizes* are legal provided that the advertisement states that to receive the prize requires attendance at a sales presentation. Failure to disclose attendance requirement makes it deceptive. A *poorly drawn map* that makes a subdivision difficult to find is not considered to be deceptive or misleading advertising. A misspelled name or omission of price and terms is not considered to be deceptive or misleading advertising.

g . Advertisement Writing - When writing a real estate advertisement, a broker should appeal to the needs of the prospective client because every person has specific real estate goals.

  1 . When a real estate broker has a listing on a large spacious country home valued at $500,000, he should attempt to advertise for a buyer based on prestige.

  2 . When a real estate broker has a listing on an investment property which is an excellent investment, he should attempt to advertise for a buyer based on profit.

6. Commission - A real estate commission is not set by law. The maximum commission a broker may charge in a real estate transaction is completely negotiable between the broker and the owner (seller or landlord). The commission may be increased or decreased by agreement between both parties.

  a . A real estate commission is established by a written contract between the broker and the principal.

  b . The owner may agree to pay a larger commission when a broker has incurred additional expenses because a property was difficult to sell.

  c . The broker is considered to have earned his commission when the buyer and seller have signed the sales contract.

  d . The broker may file a civil suit against the seller for refusal to pay an earned commission to the broker.

  e . The broker may sue the seller for his full commission if the buyer and seller agree to rescind the contract. The broker cannot keep the deposit, he must return the entire deposit and then initiate civil action for his commission. A salesperson in a similar situation must also return the deposit, but may have grounds for legal action against his broker.

  f . Payment of Commission - Commission may be paid in any form that is acceptable to the broker. This includes, but is not limited to, the following:

    1 . Cash from the proceeds to the seller.
    2 . Personal note executed by the buyer or seller.
    3 . An assigned note secured by a trust deed.
    4 . Thirty acres of land valued at $200 per acre. If the broker received an offer to purchase for $500 per acre immediately after receiving the land, he could sell it for an immediate profit without being subject to fraud or receiving a secret profit.

  g . Dual Commission - A broker may receive a commission from both parties in the same transaction. The broker is required to both give knowledge and receive consent from both parties as to the dual commission. If the broker does not give knowledge and receive consent from both parties in reference to a dual commission, neither party is liable to pay a commission. A broker is likely to receive a commission from both parties in a tax free exchange.

h. Salesperson - A licensed real estate salesperson may only receive a commission from his own broker. This includes any bonus at the conclusion of a complicated or difficult transaction. The real estate broker and his salesperson divide the commission based on a written contract between the broker and his salesperson. Any advance commission pending the close of escrow may only be paid by the employing broker.

i. A California real estate broker may pay a commission to a licensed real estate broker in another state.

j. A real estate broker negotiating leases on commercial property usually bases his commission on a percentage of the rent received over the entire term of the lease.

k. A broker's right to a commission may be assigned.

l. A real estate broker is in violation of the Real Estate Law if he gives a commission to an unlicensed person for procuring listings.

m. Any agreement to split a commission with a cooperating broker does not have to be in writing to be enforceable.

n. A real estate broker may share a commission with an unlicensed buyer or seller with full disclosure to all parties.

7. Handling Money - When a real estate broker receives money in a real estate transaction, he must give the money to his principal, place it in his trust fund account, or place it into a neutral escrow depository on the next business day. If he does not do one of these three acts by the end of the next business day, he is guilty of commingling. A broker cannot deposit funds on a weekly basis. The funds received must be deposited on the next business day.

a. Commingling - Commingling is the mixing of personal funds with the funds of a customer or client. Commingling is the opposite of segregation.

b. Conversion - Conversion is the misappropriation and misuse of the client's funds.

c. Interpleader - Interpleader is the judicial proceedings which allows the court to decide the disposition of an interest in property or title to property. When a broker does not want to be involved with a conflict between the buyer and seller concerning a deposit of funds in his trust fund account, he would deposit the funds with the appropriate court for interpleader action.

d. Trust Fund Account (Trust Account) - A trust fund account is a bank account which is controlled by the real estate broker for the benefit of others. It is a special account that is separate from the broker's commercial account. The most important reason for a broker to maintain a trust account is to protect the client's funds in case legal action is taken against the broker. The courts may attach the broker's commercial accounts, but cannot attach his trust account.

e. Commissioner's Regulations - A real estate broker must retain a valid record of all funds received, even if the money was immediately deposited into escrow. There can never be an exception to this regulation.

1. A real estate broker is not required to have a trust account.

2. A trust account does not have to maintain a specific minimum balance.

3. A real estate broker may only have $100.00 of his own money in his trust account.

4. A real estate broker must be able to make withdrawals without any advance notice from his trust fund account.

5. A real estate broker must keep a record of all deposits and withdrawals in his trust fund account.

6. A real estate broker's trust fund account must be available for inspection by the Real Estate Commissioner or his deputies during business hours.

7. A real estate broker's trust fund account must have prenumbered checks. Immediate destruction of a prenumbered check that is "voided " is a violation of the Real Estate Law and Real Estate Commissioner's Regulations.

f. Trust funds cannot be used to pay either the broker's advertising and utility bills, or to pay for a fiduciary bond for an authorized agent. It is customary for the broker to pay plumbing repair bills, on a commercial property which the broker manages, from his trust fund account.

g. The handling of money in an out-of-state subdivision is the same as with an ordinary subdivision located in California.

h. An employee must be bonded to make withdrawals from a broker's trust fund account.

D. PROPERTY MANAGEMENT - Absentee ownership creates a need for a specialist in property management. An individual should be competent in bookkeeping and accounting procedures to specialize in the field of property management. Good property management should start prior to the acquisition of the investment property.

1. **Duties** - The duties of a property manager include:

    a. Rental of units. To secure desirable tenants and keep the units occupied.

    b. Collect rental fees.

    c. Order supplies.

    d. Maintenance of the property.

    e. Maintain records of his activities on behalf of the owner.

    f. Public relations (Hearing complaints of the tenants).

    g. Hiring services for maintenance, gardening, and repairs.

2. A real property manager does not establish the depreciation schedule.

3. A real property manager cannot retain discounts on supplies purchased for the property.

4. **Commission** - The property management commission is established by an agreement between the parties and may be in any form.

    a. A real property manager may collect a commission for negotiating leases.

b. A real property manager may collect a commission for alterations and remodeling.

c. A real property manager may accept a percentage of the gross rentals as commission. **EXAMPLE:** Broker Thompson negotiated a twenty-five year lease with a $15,000 annual rent and is to receive his commission annually based on the following schedule: 7% for the first year; 5% for each of the next four years; 4% for each of the next five years; 3% for each of the next ten years; and 1% for each year thereafter to the completion of the lease. **QUESTION:** How much commission has broker Thompson received at the end of the 19th year? **Answer: $11,100**

SOLUTION:

1st year	7% of	$15,000 =	$1,050	x	1	year	= $ 1,050
2 - 5 years	5% of	$15,000 =	$ 750	x	4	years	= $ 3,000
6 - 10 years	4% of	$15,000 =	$ 600	x	5	years	= $ 3,000
11 - 19 years	3% of	$15,000 =	$ 450	x	9	years	= $ 4,050

$11,100

5. The owner or manager of income property who establishes his rental schedule higher than the relative service opportunities will discover that this tends to force tenants to economize on space and results in vacancies.

6. It is considered illegal for a rental application to contain questions as to the marital status of a prospective tenant.

E. INVESTMENTS - Real estate is the basis for all wealth. There is not another investment that has the profit potential of real estate.

1. The return on real estate investments should be greater than the yield on trust deeds and bonds. This is because most real estate investments are made for a long period of time, require a large amount of money, are difficult to maintain, and usually have a slower turnover than most other types of investments.

2. An investor who purchases an apartment building might prefer his property to be located in an area populated by young married couples and where there are also nearby recreational, community, and cultural activities.

3. Leverage - Leverage is the use of other people's money to finance an investment in order to maximize the yield on the investment. An investor uses borrowed money to the maximum availability of funds to benefit from leverage. Leverage may be expressed as:

a. The ability to purchase property with a small down payment and maximum financing on the balance.

b. The ability to purchase property that appreciates in value with a small down payment, without increasing the investment.

c. Advantages of a small down payment are:

1. Borrower keeps most of his funds in a liquid or readily available state.

2. The borrower of a maximum loan will benefit when there is an increase in the value of the property.

3. Property is easily sold when there is a small difference between an assumable loan and the market price.

4. **Annuity** - An annuity is a series of payments to be made over a period of time or one lump sum payment that is to be paid in the future. A well secured long term ground lease is like having an annuity.

5. **Financial Manager** - A financial manager is sometimes employed by an investor to purchase, sell, and manage a portfolio of investment properties. A good financial manager should be concerned with liquidity, reserves, and diversification for his client.

   a. **Liquidity** - Liquidity means that assets can be quickly converted into cash.

   b. **Reserves** - Most investors have a reserve bank account. Funds are set aside to be prepared for future unexpected property expenses.

   c. **Diversification** - Diversification is the distribution of financial assets into various investments. Most prudent investors diversify their assets into different investments. Real estate investors diversify their assets into different properties.

F. **MOBILE HOME SALES** - A real estate licensee has the authority to sell a mobile home if it is permanently affixed to the foundation and properly certified and recorded. Once a mobile home has been transformed into real property (permanently affixed to the foundation), it is treated, for most purposes, as other residential real property offered either for sale, lease, or finance.

1. A real estate broker cannot take a listing on a new mobile home unless it has been registered with the Department of Motor Vehicles for at least one (1) year.

2. A real estate broker must withdraw all advertising of a mobile home for sale within 48 hours of the expiration of the listing.

G. **ESCROW** - An escrow is a neutral third party who is a dual agent for both the buyer and seller. Escrow will collect and disburse all the documents and monies in a real estate transaction and provide for the recordation of the proper documents to complete a transaction. Escrow begins when escrow instructions are executed by both the buyer and seller. Executed means that the escrow instructions are signed by both the buyer and seller. Escrow instructions are not usually recorded; therefore, it is not necessary to notarize them. When escrow instructions are executed by the escrow company, this means that all terms and conditions of the escrow instructions have been fulfilled. When all of the requirements of an escrow have been met, the escrow agency changes from a dual agency to a separate agency.

1. **Administration** - Escrow is under the jurisdiction of the Department of Corporations. An escrow company must be licensed as a corporation. An escrow company cannot be an individual or a partnership. When a real estate broker is concerned about an illegal escrow, he may receive assistance from the Corporation's Commissioner.

2. Exemptions

 a. A real estate broker may perform his own escrow without being licensed by the Corporation's Commissioner if he represents one or more parties in the transaction (with or without a fee). A real estate broker performing an escrow for another broker is illegal, unless he has formed a corporation and meets all of the requirements of the Corporation's Commissioner.

 b. An attorney may perform his own escrow without being licensed by the Corporation's Commissioner if he represents one or more parties in the transaction and the transaction is within the scope of his law practice.

3. Valid Escrow - The two essential elements of a valid real estate escrow are:

 a. A binding contract between buyer and seller.

 b. Conditional delivery of transfer instruments to the escrow.

4. Terms and Conditions

 a. Priority - The escrow instructions will take precedence when there is a conflict between the original sales contract and the escrow instructions.

 b. Modification - Any modification of the escrow instructions must be by mutual agreement between buyer and seller. Changes may be made on the escrow instructions or by amendment. Any changes which are made on the escrow instructions must be initialled by buyer and seller. An amendment must be signed by buyer and seller. One party cannot unilaterally alter the escrow instructions when the other party will not consent to the change.

 c. Length of Escrow - The length of escrow is usually determined by an agreement between buyer and seller. In the event the length of escrow is not stated in the escrow instructions, escrow will be for a reasonable time.

 d. Time of Possession - The time of possession of the property is usually determined by an agreement between buyer and seller. In the event the time of possession is not stated in the escrow instructions, the seller must surrender possession of the property to the buyer upon the close of escrow.

 e. Interpleader - When an escrow company cannot resolve a conflict between buyer and seller, the escrow can submit the transaction and the problem to the appropriate court for interpleader action.

5. Complete Escrow - A complete escrow contains all the necessary instructions which reflect an understanding between the buyer and seller, including which party will pay the documentary transfer tax, provisions for the existing fire insurance, termite report, etc.

 a. Documentary Transfer Tax - Documentary transfer tax is usually paid when the deed is recorded at the close of escrow.

  1. The tax applies when the new money exceeds $100. New money is any cash consideration or new loan placed on the property when title is transferred.

2. The tax does not apply to any existing loan which is transferred (assumed) by the buyer.

3. The tax is computed at a rate of:

   a. $1.10 per $1,000 of new money, or

   b. 55 cents for each $500 of new money or any fraction thereof.

4. **Examples**

   a. A property sold for $150,000 with $125,000 being subject to the transfer tax. The tax amounts to $137.50.

      SOLUTION: $125,000 is the same as 125 x $1,000;

      $1.10 x 125 = $137.50.

   b. The terms to purchase a $21,000 property include a $3,000 cash down payment, buyer to assume the existing $14,500 first trust deed, and buyer to execute a note in favor of the seller secured by a second trust deed for the balance. The documentary transfer tax to be paid in this transaction will be $7.15.

      SOLUTION: $21,000 Price - $14,500 existing 1st TD = $6,500. $6,500 is the new money ($3,000 cash plus new 2nd TD).

      $6,500 is the same as 6.5 x $1,000;

      $1.10 x 6.5 = $7.15.

b. **Fire Insurance** - A fire insurance policy is an indemnity agreement. This means that the insurance company agrees to repay the insured for any loss he may suffer. When a house is properly insured with fire insurance to indemnify the owner, this means that the insured owner may neither gain nor lose.

   1. A fire insurance policy transfers the risk of loss from the insured to the insurance company; it changes uncertainty to certainty, and guarantees the cost of replacement.

   2. A fire insurance policy may be **SHORT-RATED** in escrow. This means that a monetary portion of the insurance premium is returned to the insured individual when he cancels his policy.

   3. A fire insurance policy cannot be assigned without the consent of the insurance company.

   4. A fire insurance policy may be cancelled by the insurance company if the insurance company gives the insured written notification within a reasonable time period prior to cancellation of the policy.

c. **Termite Report** - A termite report is usually required during escrow; however, it is not required by law. A termite report is required on a home that is purchased using FHA or VA financing.

Termite reports are filed with the Structural Pest Control Board. Any individual may request a certified copy of a pest control report which was filed within the past two years. Termite reports should be ordered by the seller, prior to listing. If escrow receives two termite reports, both reports must be given to the buyer and seller. Buyer and seller will decide which one to use. If a termite report suggests preventative work, this is usually paid by the buyer. In a real estate transaction, if the buyer conditions the sale based upon the seller providing a certified inspection report from a licensed pest control operator, either the broker or seller will be required to deliver a copy of the report to the buyer as soon as is practical, prior to close of escrow.

6. **Disciplinary Action** - A real estate broker is subject to disciplinary action if he fails to deliver signed copies of the escrow instructions to the buyer and seller, delivers escrow instructions signed with a blank space to be filled in later, or fails to deliver copies of the closing (settlement) statement to all principals involved in the transaction.

7. **Closing Statement** (Settlement) - A closing statement is an accounting of where all the money is coming from and where the money is going to in escrow. The buyer and seller receive separate closing statements. The buyer's closing statement will balance itself to indicate how much money is required to close escrow. The seller's closing statement will balance itself to indicate how much cash the seller will receive at the close of escrow. The buyer's and seller's closing statements are not required to balance each other; however, they may balance each other.

   a. The closing statement is divided into two columns. The left column is for debits and the right column is for credits. Debit means minus and credit means plus.

   b. **Rules**

      1. **Price** - The price is always a credit for the seller and a debit for the buyer.

      2. **Cash** - Cash deposited into escrow is always a credit for the party who deposits it.

      3. **Loans** - All loans will appear opposite of the price. A loan on the buyer's closing statement will appear as a credit. Remember that the closing statement will show how much money is required by the buyer to close escrow. The lender will place loan funds into escrow; therefore, the loan will be credited to the buyer's account. A loan on the seller's closing statement will appear as a debit. When a loan is paid off or assumed by the buyer, it must be deducted to determine how much the seller will receive at the close of escrow.

      4. **Third Party Items** - The escrow is between the buyer and seller. Anyone else who is involved in the escrow is going to do a service in order to close escrow. Those individuals (brokers, appraisers, termite inspectors, title insurance companies, escrow companies, etc.) are referred to as third party items.

         a. Third party items always appear in the debit column.

         b. The same third party items never appear on the buyer's and seller's closing statement, except escrow charges. Escrow fees are usually paid by both parties; however, all escrow fees may be negotiable.

5 . Proration Items - Proration is the division of an item between the buyer and seller, proportionately, to the time of use or closing date. Proration items usually include prepaid rents and impound items (property taxes, fire insurance, assessment bond payments, and homeowner association fees).

a . Proration items will appear on both the buyer's and seller's closing statements.

b . Proration items always appear in opposite columns. This means that a debit for the seller will be a credit for the buyer, or a debit for the buyer will be a credit for the seller. In other words, if you can calculate a debit for one party, the other party will be credited the same amount.

c . Two dates are required to calculate prorations:

1 . Date of Item - The date in which the proration item is paid through. Draw a calendar and place this date on the calendar by using a curved arrow. The arrowhead must land on the date through which the proration item is paid.

2 . Closing Date of Escrow - Plot the closing date of escrow on the calendar.

d . Money Calculations - Find the difference in time between the two above dates and convert the time element to money. This is the amount of money to be prorated. NOTE: Always use a banker's year.

e . Debit Formula - Use the two dates to determine who will be debited for the proration item. Remember that proration items always appear in opposite columns. When you determine which party will be debited, the other party will be credited.

1 . BEYOND - DEBIT - BUYER - If the date of item is beyond the closing date, debit the buyer and do the opposite (credit) to the seller.

2 . SHORT - DEBIT - SELLER - If the date of item is short of the closing date, debit the seller and do the opposite (credit) to the buyer.

f . Helpful Hints

1 . Debits are items that are owed on a closing statement.

2 . Prepaid taxes appear as a credit to the seller on a closing statement.

3 . Prepaid rent received appears as a debit to the seller on a closing statement.

4 . Points charged on a VA loan transaction may be paid by either the buyer or seller; therefore, points may appear as a debit on the closing statement of either the buyer or seller.

5 . A closing statement that refers to "recurring costs" is describing impound items.

8. Escrow Mathematics

a. When purchasing a house, a buyer made a $1,200 cash deposit with his offer. The purchase price was $47,000 and closing costs were estimated at 3% of the price. Based on an appraisal of $45,000, the lender will loan 80% on a note secured by a first trust deed. What is the net amount of cash required by the buyer to close escrow? **Answer: $11,210**

SOLUTION:	DEBITS	CREDITS
Purchase Price	$47,000	
1st Trust Deed		$36,000
Closing Costs*	$ 1,410	
Total	$48,410	$36,000
Cash Required to Balance		$12,410
		$48,410

*Closing Costs $47,000		$12,410
x .03	Cash Deposit	-$ 1,200
$1,410		$11,210

b. The property taxes for the current tax fiscal year were paid and amounted to $1,380. The property was sold with the closing date of escrow on the first day of May. How much is the buyer required to pay in escrow?
Answer: $230.00

SOLUTION:

Given: Tax fiscal year for the calendar (July 1 to July 1). You should know the tax fiscal year. Property taxes are $1,380 per year. ($1,380 ÷ 12 = $115 per month).

Calculations: May 1 to July 1 is the difference between the closing date of escrow and the date of the proration item. This means there are two months to prorate.

The taxes are paid Beyond the closing date; therefore, you must debit the Buyer for two months (2 x $115 = $230).

c. The annual property taxes were $348 and the first half of the taxes were paid. The close of escrow was January 31, 1985. At the close of escrow, who was credited for a proration of the taxes, and how much was the proration?

Answer: A $29.00 credit to the buyer.

SOLUTION:

Given: Taxes are paid to January 1, 1985 (Half of the tax fiscal year). Property taxes are $348 per year ($348 ÷ 12 = $29 per month).

Calculations: January 1 to January 31 is the difference between the closing date of escrow and the proration item. This means there is one month to prorate.

315

The taxes are paid <u>S</u>hort of the closing date; therefore, you must debit the <u>S</u>eller for one month. If you debit the Seller you must do the opposite to the Buyer (Credit the Buyer for one month or Credit the Buyer $29.00).

d. A three year fire insurance policy was issued on March 1, 19XX and cost $316.80. The insured cancelled the policy effective the 16th day of November of the same year. What is the amount of the unused policy?

Answer: $242.00 Unused

SOLUTION: March 1st to November 16th is eight and one-half months used. Three years (36 months) minus 8.5 months = 27.5 months unused.

$316.80 ÷ 36 = $8.80 per month.

$8.80 x 27.5 months = $242.00

9. Executed Escrow - When all terms and conditions of the escrow instructions have been fulfilled, the escrow agent is responsible for reporting the sale to the Internal Revenue Service.

REVIEW QUIZ

SECTION I - **Matching** - Select the letter below which best describes, defines, or relates to the following numbered terms.

1. Realtor
2. Realtist
3. C. P. M.
4. M. A. I.
5. Conversion
6. Inflation
7. Interpleader
8. Commingling
9. Blind Advertisement
10. Gross National Product

a. A rise in prices which causes a decrease in the purchasing power of the dollar.
b. Used to designate a member of the American Institute of Real Estate Appraisers.
c. Designated name for a member of a group of predominantly black brokers.
d. Does not include the name of the licensee.
e. Mixing of personal funds with funds of a client.
f. The measure of total goods and services in the U. S. during one calendar year.
g. Judicial action which allows the court to decide the disposition of property.
h. A real estate broker who is a member of the National Association of Realtors.
i. Misappropriation and use of client's funds.
j. Professional designation for a member of the Institute of Real Estate Management.

SECTION II - **True/False** - Select either true or false in response to the following statements.

1. The prosperity phase of the business cycle is usually accompanied by an increase in real estate listings and real estate sales.
2. A real estate commission may only be paid in cash or by use of a cashier's check.
3. A California real estate broker may pay a commission to a licensed real estate broker in another state.
4. A real estate broker's right to a commission may be assigned.
5. Good property management should start at the close of escrow.
6. A real property manager will establish the depreciation schedules.
7. Real estate investments usually have a slightly slower turnover than most other types of investments.
8. A complete escrow contains all the necessary instructions which reflect an understanding between the buyer and seller.
9. A real estate broker may receive assistance from the Real Estate Commissioner in reference to an illegal escrow.
10. A real estate broker can make minor changes in the escrow instructions.

SECTION III - Multiple Choice - Select the letter which best completes the statement or answers the question.

1. The most important reason for a broker to maintain a trust account is:

   A. Because it is easier for accounting purposes.
   B. Consequences should legal action be taken against the broker.
   C. To control the distribution of funds to their ultimate destination.
   D. Because a bank would be responsible for the funds in the event of loss or embezzlement.

2. Which of the following is a proper disbursement of funds from a broker's trust account?

   A. To pay a bond for a fiduciary agent.
   B. To pay a gas bill for the broker's office.
   C. To pay advertising bills of the broker's office.
   D. To pay plumbing repair bills on a commercial property which the broker manages.

3. A policy manual is:

   A. An outline of the procedures under which an office operates.
   B. An outline of the code of ethics.
   C. A schedule of floor time for the salespeople.
   D. A book which describes insurance coverage and rates.

4. Termite reports are filed with the:

   A. Board of Realtors.
   B. City Termite Control Board.
   C. Structural Pest Control Board.
   D. None of the above.

5. Commingling is the opposite of:

   A. Neutral escrow depository.
   B. Mingle.
   C. Trust Fund.
   D. Segregation.

6. A property manager may do all of the following, except:

   A. Accept a percentage of the gross rental fees as commission.
   B. Collect a commission for the negotiation of leases.
   C. Collect a commission for alterations and remodeling.
   D. Retain discounts on supplies purchased.

7. If a real estate broker is sued for "conversion", the allegation is that he is:

   A. Misrepresenting.
   B. Commingling.
   C. Misappropriating his client's funds.
   D. Failing to disclose material facts.

8. Without being licensed by the Corporation's Commissioner as an escrow company, a real estate broker may :

   A. Handle only those escrows pertaining to property which he owns or in which he has an interest.
   B. Handle escrows for all brokers in the area where there are not any escrow companies.
   C. Handle escrows in connection with real estate transactions in which he acted as an agent.
   D. Never act as an escrow agent.

9. Which of the following is correct for an escrow to be complete?

   A. The recording of a document may or may not indicate passing of title.
   B. It contains all the necessary instructions which reflect an understanding of the parties.
   C. The total on the closing statements of the buyer and seller must be identical.
   D. A deed delivered to escrow transfers title.

10. An escrow closing statement that refers to "recurring costs" would be describing:

    A. Impound items.
    B. Escrow charges.
    C. Title insurance.
    D. Documentary Transfer Tax.

11. Which of the following is always a debit on the buyer's closing statement?

    A. Property taxes.
    B. Purchase price.
    C. Policy of title insurance.
    D. Interest accrued and unpaid on an assumed trust deed.

12. Which of the following appears on the debit side of the seller's closing statement?

    A. Sale of personal property.
    B. Prepaid rent received.
    C. Prepaid insurance premium.
    D. None of the above.

13. In the event there are not any provisions in the escrow instructions in reference to a termination date, the parties to the escrow have:

    A. 30 days.
    B. 3 months.
    C. A reasonable time.
    D. As long as either party desires.

14. In the absence of an agreement to the contrary, the seller, upon sale of the property, must surrender possession of the premises to the buyer:

   A. Within five days after close of escrow.
   B. Within 30 days after close of escrow.
   C. Within a reasonable time.
   D. Upon the close of escrow.

15. An escrow company may be licensed as:

   A. A partnership.
   B. A corporation.
   C. An individual.
   D. Any of the above.

Answers may be found in Appendix C (Back of text)

PROFESSIONAL CONDUCT

A. CODE OF ETHICS - NATIONAL ASSOCIATION OF REALTORS

Preamble... Under all is the land. Upon its wise utilization and widely allocated ownership depend the survival and growth of free institutions and of our civilization. The REALTOR should recognize that the interests of the nation and its citizens requires the highest and best use of the land and the widest distribution of land ownership. They require the creation of adequate housing, the building of functioning cities, the development of productive industries and farms, and the preservation of a healthful environment.

Such interests impose obligations beyond those of ordinary commerce. They impose grave social responsibility and a patriotic duty to which the REALTOR should dedicate himself, and for which he should be diligent in preparing himself. The REALTOR; therefore, is zealous to maintain and improve the standards of his calling and shares with his fellow REALTORS a common responsibility for its integrity and honor. The term REALTOR has come to connote competency, fairness, and high integrity resulting from adherence to a lofty ideal of moral conduct in business relations. No inducement of profit and no instruction from clients ever can justify departure from this ideal.

In the interpretation of his obligation, a REALTOR can take no safer guide than that which has been handed down through the centuries, embodied in the Golden Rule, "Whatsoever ye would that men should do to you, do you even so to them."

Accepting this standard as his own, every REALTOR pledges himself to observe its spirit in all of his activities and to conduct his business in accordance with the tenets set forth below.

Article 1 - The REALTOR should keep himself informed on matters affecting real estate in his community, the state, and nation so that he may be able to contribute responsibly to public thinking on such matters.

Article 2 - In justice to those who place their interests in his care, the REALTOR should endeavor always to be informed regarding laws, proposed legislation, governmental regulations, public policies, and current market conditions in order to be in a position to advise his clients properly.

Article 3 - It is the duty of the REALTOR to protect the public against fraud, misrepresentation, and unethical practices in real estate transactions. He should endeavor to eliminate in his community any practices which could be damaging to the public or bring discredit to the real estate profession. The REALTOR should assist the governmental agency charged with regulating the practices of brokers and salesmen in his state.

Article 4 - The REALTOR should seek no unfair advantage over other REALTORS and should conduct his business so as to avoid controversies with other REALTORS.

Article 5 - In the best interests of society, of his associates, and his own business, the REALTOR should willingly share with other REALTORS the lessons of his experience and study for the benefit of the public, and should be loyal to the Board of REALTORS of his community and active in its work.

Article 6 - To prevent dissension and misunderstanding and to assure better service to the owner, the REALTOR should urge the exclusive listing of property unless contrary to the best interest of the owner.

Article 7 - In accepting employment as an agent, the REALTOR pledges himself to protect and promote the interests of the client. This obligation of absolute fidelity to the client's interests is primary, but it does not relieve the REALTOR of the obligation to treat fairly all parties to the transaction.

Article 8 - The REALTOR shall not accept compensation from more than one party, even if permitted by law, without the full knowledge of all parties to the transaction.

Article 9 - The REALTOR shall avoid exaggeration, misrepresentation, or concealment of pertinent facts. He has an affirmative obligation to discover adverse factors that reasonable, competent and diligent investigation would disclose.

Article 10 - The REALTOR shall not deny equal professional services to any person for reasons of race, creed, sex, or country of national origin. The REALTOR shall not be a party to any plan or agreement to discriminate against a person or persons on the basis of race, creed, sex, or country of national origin.

Article 11 - A REALTOR is expected to provide a level of competent service in keeping with the Standards of Practice in those fields in which the REALTOR customarily engages.

The REALTOR shall not undertake to provide specialized professional services concerning a type of property or service that is outside his field of competence unless he engages the assistance of one who is competent on such types of property or service, or unless the facts are fully disclosed to the client. Any person engaged to provide such assistance shall be so identified to the client and his contribution to the assignment should be set forth.

The REALTOR shall refer to the Standards of Practice of the National Association as to the degree of competence that a client has a right to expect the REALTOR to possess, taking into consideration the complexity of the problem, the availability of expert assistance, and the opportunities for experience available to the REALTOR.

Article 12 - The REALTOR shall not undertake to provide professional services concerning a property or its value where he has a present or contemplated interest unless such interest is specifically disclosed to all affected parties.

Article 13 - The REALTOR shall not acquire an interest in or buy for himself, any member of his immediate family, his firm or any member thereof, or any entity in which he has a substantial ownership interest, property listed with him, without making the true position known to the listing owner. In selling property owned by himself, or in which he has any interest, the REALTOR shall reveal the facts of his ownership or interest to the purchaser.

Article 14 - In the event of a controversy between REALTORS associated with different firms, arising out of their relationship as REALTORS, the REALTORS shall submit the dispute to arbitration in accordance with the regulations of their board or boards rather than litigate the matter.

Article 15 - If a REALTOR is charged with unethical practice or is asked to present evidence in any disciplinary proceeding or investigation, he shall place all pertinent facts before the proper tribunal of the member board or affiliated institute, society, or council of which he is a member.

Article 16 - When acting as an agent, the REALTOR shall not accept any commission, rebate, or profit on expenditures made for his principal-owner, without the principal's knowledge and consent.

Article 17 - The REALTOR shall not engage in activities that constitute the unauthorized practice of law and shall recommend that legal counsel be obtained when the interest of any part to the transaction requires it.

Article 18 - The REALTOR shall keep in a special account in an appropriate financial institution, separated from his own funds, monies coming into his possession in trust for other persons, such as escrows, trust funds, clients' monies, and other like items.

Article 19 - The REALTOR shall be careful at all times to present a true picture in his advertising and representations to the public. He shall neither advertise without disclosing his name nor permit any person associated with him to use individual names or telephone numbers, unless such person's connection with the REALTOR is obvious in the advertisement.

Article 20 - The REALTOR, for the protection of all parties, shall see the financial obligations and commitments regarding real estate transactions are in writing, expressing the exact agreement of the parties. A copy of each agreement shall be furnished to each party upon his signing such agreement.

Article 21 - The REALTOR shall not engage in any practice or take any action inconsistent with the agency of another REALTOR.

Article 22 - In the sale of property which is exclusively listed with a REALTOR, the REALTOR shall utilize the services of other brokers upon mutually agreed upon terms when it is in the best interest of the client.

Negotiations concerning property which is listed exclusively shall be carried on with the listing broker, not with the owner, except with the consent of the listing broker.

Article 23 - The REALTOR shall not publicly disparage the business practice of a competitor nor volunteer an opinion of a competitor's transaction. If his opinion is sought and if the REALTOR deems it appropriate to respond, such opinion shall be rendered with strict professional integrity and courtesy.

B. EQUAL HOUSING OPPORTUNITY - In reference to equal housing opportunity, all prospective purchasers must be shown properties in all neighborhoods. It would be incorrect for a prospective purchaser not to be shown property in a racially transitional neighborhood. All prospective customers must be shown property based on what they can afford, regardless of the racial structure of the neighborhood. When a prospective purchaser requests to see a house in a specific neighborhood, a licensee may legally assume he is looking for a house with a particular architectural design. To specify a neighborhood does not imply that he is testing to see if a licensee will discriminate against him nor that he is interested in a house in a neighborhood composed of one ethnic group. To specify a neighborhood does not disqualify a prospective buyer from obtaining an FHA or VA loan.

1. Federal Legislation

a. Civil Rights Act of 1866 - The Civil Rights Act of 1866 provides that "All citizens of the United States shall have the same right in every state and territory, as is enjoyed by white citizens thereof, to inherit, purchase, lease, sell, hold and convey real and personal property."

b. Title VIII of the Civil Rights Act of 1968 (Federal Open Housing Law) - The Federal Open Housing Law was created to provide fair housing opportunities throughout the United States.

1. The Federal Housing Law applies equally to all of these real estate transactions.

    a. An owner of a single family residence who is selling through a real estate broker.

    b. The sale of three homes by three different individuals who also own three other homes in a subdivision.

    c. Sale of a six unit apartment house in which the owner resides in one of the units.

    d. The sale of recreational properties and second home transactions.

    Exemption: Owner occupied property of four units or less which is unencumbered. The Federal Open Housing Law has least effect on a single family residence which is owner occupied and unencumbered; however, this activity is considered to be unconstitutional based on *Jones vs. Mayer.*

2. Violations of the Federal Open Housing Law are enforced by the United States Attorney General. When a conspiracy exists to resist compliance with Federal Open Housing Laws, the United States Attorney General will investigate and prosecute the case.

3. An individual may seek legal action under the Fair Housing Laws if he is denied the privilege of having minority neighbors, evicted for having minority guests, or threatened because he sold to a minority buyer.

4. When an individual is discriminated against in the purchase of a home, he may go to court and the court can award specific performance, actual damages, and punitive damages to prevent reoccurrence, or to provide financial relief for humiliation and embarrassment. The court does not have the right to revoke or suspend a real estate license if the court concluded that the licensee discriminated. The Real Estate Commissioner has the authority to revoke or suspend the license.

5. Discrimination complaints have to be filed with HUD within one year of the violation.

6. An individual may seek legal action is state or federal court.

c. **Jones vs. Mayer** - Jones vs. Mayer is a United States Supreme Court case which ruled that housing discrimination laws were to be upheld throughout the United States.

d. **Shelley vs. Kraemer** - Shelley vs. Kraemer is a United States Supreme Court case which ruled that subdivision restrictions which limit the transfer of title to members of the Caucasian race were unenforceable.

1. Previously recorded restrictions which limit the conveyance or lease of property to the Caucasian race are unenforceable, even if there is an agreement by the owners. Such restrictions are a violation of the Fourteenth Amendment.

2. The conveyance of property in a subdivision is not affected by a clause which discriminates against a certain ethnic group. The discriminatory clause is unenforceable; however, the conveyance is valid.

e. **Equal Credit and Opportunity Act** - The purpose of the Equal Credit Opportunity Act is to prohibit discrimination among lenders.

1. All borrowers are entitled to complete information in reference to the availability of home financing.

2. A potential borrower may refuse to answer any questions on a loan application in reference to marital status, race, creed, religion, etc. Marital status and race are usually requested, but are optional.

2. California Legislation

a. **Rumford Act** (California Fair Employment and Housing Act) - The Government Code contains the California Fair Employment and Housing Act which is also known as the California Fair Housing Act or the Rumford Act.

1. The California Fair Housing Act applies equally to all real estate transactions. It prohibits discrimination in the listing, sale, lease, rental, or financing of real property due to race, religion, creed, sex, marital status, or physical handicap.

a. The seller cannot ask the listing broker the ethnic background of a prospective purchaser.

b. A broker cannot refuse to take a listing if the seller is a member of a minority race or if the property is in a minority neighborhood. The broker may only refuse to take a listing if the property is overpriced.

c. If an owner wants to list his property for sale with the broker, but does not wish to sell to minority buyers, the broker should not discuss listing the property with the owner. The broker cannot tell the owner to handle the sale himself and to not go through a broker, nor can he suggest pricing the property high so that minority buyers will not be attracted; nor can the broker take a listing and assure the owner that he will sell only to whites.

d. A landlord who refuses to lease to minority tenants is in violation of discrimination practices prohibited in the Government Code (Rumford Act).

e. A potential tenant may refuse to answer any questions on a rental application in reference to marital status, race, creed, religion, etc. The Attorney General for the State of California has ruled that this information is not a material fact and should not be disclosed when requested by the landlord.

f. A landlord cannot require a single tenant to have a co-signer.

g. To solicit tenants for an apartment house the owner is not allowed to discriminate on the basis of race, creed, religion, sex, marital status, etc. An advertisement cannot state, "no minorities" or "married couples only".

2. The California Fair Housing Act (Rumford Act) is enforced by the Fair Employment and Housing Commission. Complaints must be filed within 60 days.

3. Awarded damages include that the owner must complete the transaction or the complainant is entitled to the next available unit, or the owner must pay damages up to $1,000.

b. Unruh Civil Rights Act - The Unruh Civil Rights Act applies equally to all business establishments.

c. The Housing Financial Discrimination Act (Holden Act) - The purpose of the Holden Act is to prohibit discrimination in lending.

1. Redlining - Lenders draw a red circle on a map to designate certain areas as high risk areas, making it difficult for people (usually minorities) to obtain financing. Redlining is against the law.

2. Lenders cannot charge a translation fee for loan documents to be translated to non-English speaking individuals.

d. Commissioner's Policy - The Real Estate Commissioner's policy is to create a "color blind" real estate industry. Color blind means that a real estate licensee must conduct business according to the Golden Rule, without bias and discrimination. "Do unto others as you would have others do unto you."

1. Minority buyers must be treated like any non-minority customer. A real estate licensee must show property to all minority prospects as if he is showing property to any other prospect.

2. The color or ethnic background of the buyer is not a material fact. A real estate licensee will be in violation of the Fair Housing Law if he voluntarily discloses to the seller that the prospective purchaser is a minority buyer.

3. A real estate broker must refuse to be the agent of an owner when the owner tells the broker that he does not want to show or sell the property to a minority buyer.

4. A real estate licensee must refuse to be the agent of an owner when the owner wishes to sell his property to minority buyers at an inflated price. If a real estate licensee takes a listing under these terms, he can be held liable for damages if a lawsuit is initiated under the Fair Housing Law, and his license can be suspended or revoked by the Commissioner.

5. When a seller refuses an offer because the ready, willing, and able buyer is a minority, the real estate licensee should advise the seller that he is in violation of the Fair Housing Law. If the seller still refuses to sell to the minority buyer, the licensee can sue for his commission and should advise the minority buyer to file a complaint with HUD.

6. A real estate licensee would be in violation of the Fair Housing Law if he tried to discourage a minority or non-minority from purchasing or renting in a minority area, a non-minority area, or an area which is going through a transition from non-minority to minority.

3. Fair Housing Practice

a. **Advertisement** - Advertisements cannot be pointed toward a preference for a specific buying group (woman buyers, married buyers, etc.). A real estate broker cannot advertise that he will take a smaller commission from Caucasian sellers. A real estate broker cannot advertise that owners should sell now to save equity because a certain minority group is moving into the neighborhood.

b. **Blockbusting** (Panic Selling, Panic Peddling) - Blockbusting is an illegal procedure of trying to lower property values by spreading rumors among owners that certain ethnic groups are moving into the neighborhood.

1. Any real estate licensee who solicits or induces the sale, lease, or listing for sale or lease of residential property on the basis of loss of value, increase in the crime rate, or decline of the quality of the schools due to the present or prospective entry into a neighborhood of an individual or individuals of another race, color, religion, sex, marital status, ancestry, national origin, or physical handicap will be in violation of the California Fair Housing Act and subject to disciplinary action by the Real Estate Commissioner.

2. Blockbusting usually occurs in a real estate transaction between a broker and buyer when the buyer is also the seller. This means that the broker frightens the owner into selling at a price lower than market value. The buyer is usually an intimate business associate of the broker. After the

purchase, the co-conspirator buyer immediately sells the property at market value, or higher, to a minority buyer, resulting in a large profit. The broker also receives a second commission. Blockbusting must never occur. It is considered to be illegal conduct.

c. A subdivider or developer can never set quotas to sell a specific number of lots to certain ethnic groups. A subdivider or developer can never raise prices to discourage buying by certain ethnic groups.

d. A real estate licensee, seller, and individual neighbor will be in violation of the Civil Rights Law if they arrange a real estate transaction for a neighbor to purchase property to suppress the ownership of qualified minority buyers. Any qualified Caucasian buyer, whose offer was rejected by a seller in this situation, would not be in violation of the Civil Rights Law.

e. Discrimination does not occur when a real estate licensee complies with the instructions of his principal. When the owner states, "Do not show the property to anyone when I am not present", this means that a licensee may refuse to show property to a minority buyer when the owner is not at home. This is not discrimination. The broker is merely following the instructions of his client.

f. **Steering** - Individual buyers (usually minorities) are only shown property in a specific neighborhood. Steering is against the law. An agent cannot avoid showing minority buyers homes in a neighborhood where minorities currently do not live.

g. An agent must disclose if someone died on the property within the past three years; however, an agent cannot disclose that an occupant had AIDS or died of AIDS, unless he is asked.

h. Quoting high prices to minorities and low prices to others makes both the seller and his agent liable for damages.

i. When the seller and agent are guilty of discrimination, this usually does not affect an innocent buyer.

j. If an advertisement for a property in a minority neighborhood is placed in a newspaper that is directed toward minorities, it is not discrimination if the same property is advertised in a newspaper of general circulation.

C. DISCIPLINARY ACTION - Grounds for disciplinary action against a licensee, and the reasons for which a license may be denied include the following:

1. Misrepresentation - A false statement of the facts, or failure to disclose a material fact to the principals of a real estate transaction is misrepresentation.

a. A licensee may be disciplined for misrepresentation even though the misrepresentation did not result in a loss to the principal.

b. The seller may be sued by a broker for misrepresentation of a material fact under an oral listing. In this situation the oral listing is not the issue, so it cannot be used as a defense against misrepresentation.

c. A real estate broker can be disciplined for misrepresentation when he states that an apartment building will return a specific yield without taking into consideration the depreciation, vacancy factor, maintenance, or management expenses.

d. Fraudulent misrepresentation of a property by a real estate licensee can result in disciplinary action by the Real Estate Commissioner, civil court action, or criminal action. The broker is liable to the principal for any loss caused by fraudulent misrepresentation.

2. **False Promise** - A false promise is a statement used to influence or persuade. The promisor usually does not have control of any future event.

   a. A verbal promise to find the seller another suitable property prior to the close of escrow on his property may be construed as a false promise. A licensee may be subject to civil action by the injured party for any monetary damages caused by the licensee.

   b. When a licensee states, "it will be a goldmine and within a few years you will be able to sell the property for a substantial profit", he is making a false promise; especially when in a few years, the buyer tries to sell the property and similar properties are selling for less than his original price. Civil and disciplinary action can be taken against the licensee.

3. **Definite Termination Date** - A real estate licensee may be disciplined for failure to place an expiration date on an exclusive listing.

4. **Secret Profit** - A real estate licensee may be disciplined for failure to disclose a secret profit. Secret profit usually occurs when the broker has a high offer from a buyer and the licensee makes a lower offer through a "dummy buyer".

5. **Copy of Contract** - A real estate licensee may be disciplined for failure to furnish a copy of the contract to the individual who is signing it.

6. **Listing/Option** - A broker may take a listing and an option on a property at the same time. When the broker exercises his option prior to the expiration of the listing, he must disclose all material facts to include any outstanding offers to purchase the property, as well as his anticipated gain or profit. A broker who is selling property on which he holds an option must notify the buyer that he is a principal.

7. **Misuse of Trade Name** - Disciplinary action could be taken against a licensee for unauthorized use of the term "Realtor".

8. **Divided Agency** - A real estate licensee cannot be disciplined for acting for more than one party in a transaction with the knowledge and consent of all the parties. Disciplinary action can be taken against a licensee for receiving a commission from both the buyer and seller in a transaction without disclosure to both parties.

9. **Violating Government Trust** - Employment for a government agency may give the broker access to official records as well as to public records. Violation of the confidential nature of the government records will subject the broker to disciplinary action.

10. Miscellaneous Provisions

a. A real estate licensee may be disciplined for commingling and conversion.

b. A real estate licensee may be disciplined for telling a prospective buyer that his principal will sell for less than the listed price.

c. A real estate licensee may be disciplined if the seller discovers after the sale has been closed that the buyer is a relative of the broker.

d. A real estate licensee may be disciplined if he does not submit all offers when received, regardless of the terms and conditions of such offers.

e. A real estate licensee may be disciplined if he does not inform the buyer and seller in writing as to the exact amount of the selling price within one month after the close of escrow.

f. A real estate salesperson may be disciplined for receiving a commission from someone other than his employing broker. The broker who is aware of his salesperson receiving a commission from others (including finder's fees from lenders, escrows, title companies, etc.) will also be disciplined if he did not notify the Commissioner of the violation.

g. Puffing - Puffing is putting things in their best perspective. Examples of puffing are statements to a buyer, such as "Isn't this beautiful" or "This is the best house in the neighborhood". Puffing is not subject to disciplinary action.

h. A statement to the seller, "This is the highest offer the buyer will make", is not subject to disciplinary action. A statement to the buyer, "This is the lowest offer the seller will accept", is not subject to disciplinary action.

REVIEW QUIZ

SECTION I - Matching - Select the letter below which best describes, defines, or relates to the following numbered terms.

1. U. S. Attorney General
2. Jones vs. Mayer
3. Blockbusting
4. Unruh Civil Rights Act
5. False Promise
6. Shelley vs. Kraemer
7. Rumford Act
8. Puffing
9. Equal Credit & Opportunity Act
10. Fair Employment & Housing Commission

a. Supreme Court case which ruled that subdivision restrictions which limit the transfer of property to the Caucasian race are unenforceable.
b. Prohibits discrimination in California real estate transactions
c. Enforces the California Fair Housing Act.
d. An illegal procedure.
e. Supreme Court case which prohibits discrimination.
f. A legal procedure.
g. Prohibits discrimination among lenders.
h. A statement used to influence or persuade which relates to the future.
i. Enforces the Federal Open Housing Law.
j. Prohibits discrimination in business.

SECTION II - True/False - Select either true or false in response to the following statements.

1. The Realtor's Code of Ethics was created by the National Association of Realtors.
2. The California Fair Housing Act is enforced by the State Attorney General.
3. A real estate licensee may refuse to take a listing if the seller is a member of a minority race.
4. Asking a single tenant for a co-signer is a form of discrimination based on marital status.
5. All buyers, regardless of racial creed, are entitled to full disclosure in reference to home loans.
6. The Fair Housing Act does not apply to second homes and recreational homes.
7. A real estate licensee must show property to all minority prospects as if he was showing property to any other prospect.
8. Telling a prospective buyer that his principal will sell for less than the listed price is not a violation of the Real Estate Law.
9. Claiming a commission on a exclusive listing which does not have a definite termination date is a violation of the Real Estate Law.
10. A licensee may be disciplined for misrepresentation even though it did not result in a loss to the principal.

SECTION III - Multiple Choice - Select the letter which best completes the statement or answers the question.

1. Fraudulent misrepresentation of a property by a licensee may result in:

   A. Criminal action.
   B. Civil court action.
   C. Disciplinary action by the Real Estate Commissioner.
   D. All of the above.

2. A real estate licensee may be disciplined by the Real Estate Commissioner for all of the following, except:

   A. Failure to disclose a secret profit.
   B. Failure to place a final termination date on an exclusive listing.
   C. Failure to furnish a copy to the seller at the time the seller signs the acceptance.
   D. Failure to disclose to the buyer that the seller will accept a lower price than the listed price.

3. A real estate licensee may not be disciplined for which of the following?

   A. Any conduct which constitutes fraud.
   B. Acting for more than one party in a transaction with the knowledge and consent of all parties thereto.
   C. Making any substantial misrepresentation.
   D. Making any false promise of the character likely to influence or persuade.

4. A real estate licensee went into a neighborhood and attempted to solicit a listing by stating to the property owner that non-whites would be moving into the neighborhood and that this would make property values go down. This conduct is considered to be all of the following, except:

   A. Illegal conduct.
   B. Panic selling.
   C. Legitimate procedure.
   D. Blockbusting

5. Which of the following enforces the California Fair Housing Act?

   A. Local Planning Commission.
   B. Real Estate Commissioner.
   C. Division of Fair Housing.
   D. Fair Employment and Housing Commission.

6. If a minority customer asks to see all listings in a $75,000 price range, under Federal Law, what should the licensee do?

   A. Treat him like any other customer and show him property in the usual way.
   B. Show him an equal number of homes in both white and black neighborhoods.
   C. Ask the customer if he wanted to see any homes in a predominantly white neighborhood.
   D. Show him at least ten listings in the $75,000 price range.

7. Which of the following would be a violation of the Federal Fair Housing Law by a real estate licensee?

   A. Discouraging non-minorities from buying or renting in an area that is going through a transition from non-minority to minority.
   B. Discouraging non-minorities from buying or renting in non-minority areas.
   C. Discouraging non-minorities from buying or renting in a minority area.
   D. All of the above.

8. A salesperson brought in an offer from a qualified minority person. The salesperson's broker brought in an offer from a qualified white person. The seller will not accept either offer, however, he accepts an offer through the same salesperson from a neighbor in order to keep minorities out of the area. Who is not in violation of the Civil Rights Law?

   A. Salesperson.
   B. Seller.
   C. Neighbor.
   D. White prospect.

9. The Real Estate Commissioner's policy is to create a "color blind" real estate industry. The best definition of color blind is:

   A. "Do unto others as you would have others do unto you".
   B. Licensee will conduct business in a method to be without discrimination.
   C. Absolutely without bias.
   D. All of the above.

10. A seller requested you take a listing, but requested that you do not show the property to minority buyers. The licensee's response should be:

   A. The property has to be shown if a minority buyer asks to see it.
   B. Sorry, but you will have to sell the property without the service of a broker.
   C. A licensee must comply with the Fair Housing Law; therefore, I cannot take the listing.
   D. Do not worry, I will not show the property to any minority buyers.

11. The United States Attorney General will most likely act to enforce the Federal Open Housing Law whenever:

   A. State laws are not enforced by State Officials.
   B. A claim is filed with the Secretary of HUD.
   C. The subject of the claim filed by the aggrieved party is against the owner of more than four units.
   D. A conspiracy exists to resist compliance with the Federal Open Housing Law.

12. In 1918, restrictions were imposed on a subdivision that limited the conveyance or lease of property to persons of the Caucasian race. The restriction was to expire in 1995. These restrictions are presently:

   A. Invalid unless covered by title insurance.
   B. Unenforceable even though the owner's agree to the restriction.
   C. Valid because of the religious beliefs of the people in the subdivision.
   D. Valid if all of the neighbors agree to the restriction.

13. The Federal Open Housing Law was enacted for the purpose of:

    A. Eliminating prejudice throughout the United States.
    B. Providing fair housing for minority groups.
    C. Providing equal but separate housing within the States.
    D. Providing fair housing throughout the United States.

14. A real estate licensee may refuse to accept a listing under which of the following situations?

    A. A real estate licensee can never refuse to take a listing.
    B. When the property is in a minority neighborhood.
    C. When the seller is a member of a minority.
    D. When the property is overpriced.

15. What is the purpose of the Equal Credit Opportunity Act?

    A. To regulate the amount of credit extended by the lender.
    B. To minimize the cost of credit for the lender.
    C. To prohibit discrimination by lenders based on sex or marital status.
    D. To standardize the minimum requirement for obtaining credit from a lender.

Answers may be found in Appendix C (Back of text)

APPENDIX A - Glossary

Abstract - A brief summary.

Abstract of Judgment - An instrument given by the court which may be recorded in any county to create a judgment lien. A summary of court proceedings in probate.

Abstract of Title - A summary of all pertinent documents relating to conveyances and encumbrances affecting the property.

Abstraction - A method of valuing land. The indicated value of the improvement is deducted from the sales price.

Acceptance - The act of agreeing or consenting to the terms of an offer thereby establishing "the meeting of the minds" that is an essential element of a contract.

Accession - The right of an owner to add to his property by artificial or natural means.

Accretion - The gradual build-up of land as the result of the action of water.

Accrued Depreciation - Past depreciation. An appraiser's estimate of accumulated age depreciation with allowances for conditions based on the effective age of the property.

Acknowledgment - The formal declaration made before an authorized person by a person who has executed an instrument, stating that the execution was a free act.

Acre - A measurement of land equaling 43,560 square feet.

Actual Notice - An individual may be conscious of the circumstances in which the owner received title to the property and at the same time is aware that the owner has not recorded the deed nor is he in possession of the property. There is no constructive notice, only actual notice as to the owner of the property.

Administrator - An individual appointed by the court to handle the estate of a person who died intestate.

Ad Valorem - According to value.

Adverse Possession - The legal right to acquire title to property based on actual physical possession of the property. To take property from another person without paying for it.

Affidavit - A written statement testifying to the truth made by an individual who cannot conscientiously swear an oath.

Affirmation - A solemn declaration by an individual who is adverse to taking an oath.

Alienate - Conveys title to real property.

Alienation - To transfer property to another.

Alluvium - The deposits of dirt added to the land as a watercourse flows through the property.

Ambulatory - A will in which the terms and conditions may be changed.

Amenities - The attractive or beneficial features to be enjoyed from a home or neighborhood. They are not measured as monetary consideration; however, they are measurable on the market based on pride of ownership for well maintained property in a neighborhood and proximity to desirable elements.

Amortization - The liquidation of a financial obligation on an installment basis with level payments.

Annuity - A sum of money received at fixed intervals over a period of time.

Appropriation - The act of a non-riparian owner who diverts water from a nearby lake or river for his personal beneficial use.

Appurtenance - Anything that belongs to real property. Runs with the land. A benefit of the land.

Assemblage - The process of combining two or more contiguous parcels into one larger parcel which makes the one parcel more valuable than the separate parcels.

Assessment - The valuation of property for the purpose of levying a tax or the amount of the tax levied.

Assets - Anything of value owned by an individual or business.

Assignment - A transfer to another of any property in possession or in action, or of any estate or right therein. A transfer by a person of that person's rights under a contract.

Attachment - Seizure of a property for payment of money prior to a judgment.

Avulsion - The sudden or violent flow of water that may tear land away from the property.

Bailment - Personal property is transferred in trust for the accomplishment of a specific purpose. A possessory interest in personal property.

Balance Sheet - A statement of the financial condition of a business at a specific time.

Balloon Payment - An installment payment which is significantly larger than the other installment payments. Usually the final payment. An installment payment that is greater than twice the amount of the smallest installment under a promissory note.

Banker's Month - 30 days.

Banker's Year - 360 days. Most computations concerning interest in a real estate transaction are based on a banker's year.

Beneficiary - The lender in a trust deed.

Beneficiary Statement - A statement by the lender as to the status of a lien against the property. It provides information as to the amount of principal due on the loan.

Bequeath - To give by will.

Bequest - A gift of personal property by will.

Bill of Sale - An instrument used to transfer title to personal property.

Blighted Area - An area which is deteriorating because of extreme environmental changes or economic conditions.

Blind Advertisement - Advertisement that does not contain the name of the broker.

Blockbusting - The practice of inducing panic selling of homes at prices below market value by unscrupulous speculators or real estate agents.

Board Foot - A measurement of lumber equal to 144 cubic inches.

Bona Fide - In good faith. Without fraud or deceit.

Book of Abstracts - A key set of books maintained by a title insurance company.

Bracing - Framing lumber nailed at an angle in order to provide rigidity.

Bridging - Small pieces of lumber or metal used to brace floor joists.

B.T.U. - British Thermal Unit. A measurement used to rate the capacity of heating systems.

Bulk Sale - The sale by a business of a major portion of its stock-in-trade to someone other than customers.

Capitalization - The method of appraisal that bases present market value of the property on the anticipated future benefits of ownership in dollars and discounting them to a present worth at a rate which is attracting purchaser capital to similar investments.

Cash Flow - Monies left after deducting operating expenses and payments of principal and interest from the gross income.

Caveat Emptor - Let the buyer beware.

Chattel - A similar term for personal property.

Chattel Real - An estate related to real estate. An individual who holds a leasehold estate has a chattel real.

Chose in Action - A personal right to something not presently in the owner's possession, but recoverable by a legal action for possession.

Chose in Possession - Something in possession, rather than the right of possession.

Client - Refers to the principal of a real estate agent. This is usually the seller.

Cloud on Title - A claim, encumbrance or condition which impairs the title to real property.

Codicil - An addition, deletion, or supplement which changes a will.

Collateral - Anything of value a borrower pledges as security for a loan.

Collaterally - Refers to liens secured by other liens.

Collusion - An agreement between two or more persons to defraud another to obtain an object.

Color of Title - Title which appears to be good, but is not good title. A conveyance given when the owner did not have good title.

Commercial Acre - The remainder of an acre after the streets, sidewalks, and curbs have been deducted from an acre of land.

Condemnation - The act of taking property when using the power of eminent domain.

Condition - A qualification of ownership which can only be created by deed.

Condition Precedent - A qualification of ownership which must be met prior to the transfer of title.

Condition Subsequent - A condition attached to an already vested estate or to a contract whereby the estate is defeated or the contract is extinguished through the failure or nonperformance of the condition.

Consideration - Anything of value which causes an individual to enter into a contract.

Contiguous - Adjoining or touching upon, such as properties touching each other.

Contract Rent - The bargained rent between the landlord and the tenant that is actually paid by the tenant.

Corner Influence - The increase in value of a property because it is located on a corner lot.

Cost - The expenditure of monies necessary for the creation of improvements on a property.

Covenant - A promise. An agreement written into a deed or other instrument to do or not to do a certain activity.

Cul-de-sac - A dead end street.

Customer - A term used legally or commonly by a real estate broker to refer to the buyer.

Debt-Income Ratio - A ratio established between the income and long-term debt of a borrower to determine if a borrower is able to qualify for a loan.

Decedent - A deceased individual.

Deciduous - Trees which shed their leaves at seasonal intervals.

Defendant - An individual charged with committing an illegal act.

Deficiency Judgment - The amount of money for which the borrower is personally liable on a loan if the foreclosure sale does not bring enough money to cover the debt.

Demise - Transferring the right to or the right in an estate.

Depreciation - Loss of value due to any cause.

Depth Table - Used by appraisers to estimate the value of commercial property where lots vary in depth (4-3-2-1 Rule).

Deregulation - An easing and relaxing of rules and regulations for lenders.

Desk Cost - The total cost of rent, telephone, utilities, advertising and other expenses divided by the number of desks in a real estate office.

Devise - A gift of real estate by will.

Discounting - To sell the note for an amount less than the balance due at the time of the sale.

Discount Points - Used by lenders in FHA and VA loans to adjust their effective interest rate so that it is equal to the prevailing market rate.

Domicile - The permanent residence of an individual.

Duress - Unlawful constraint exercised upon a person whereby the person is forced to do something against his will.

Economic Life - Useful life of the improvement. The period for which an improvement is worth maintaining.

Economic Rent - The total net income that the property will bring on the open market at the time of the appraisal.

Effective Age - The age given by the appraiser based on the physical condition of the improvements.

Effective Gross Income - Gross income minus vacancy and collection losses.

Elevation Sheet - Drawings of the front and side views of the finished homes.

Emblements - The right of a tenant farmer to harvest his crops.

Encroachment - The extension of a building or other structure on one property onto an adjoining property.

Equitable Title - Use and possession of the property.

Equity - The value of real estate over and above the existing loans against the property.

Escheat - Property has reverted to the State.

Estoppel - A person is barred from asserting or denying a fact because of the person's previous acts or words.

Et al - And others.

Et ux - And wife.

Exception - **1.** Withholds part of the property from the grant in a deed. **2.** A builder may replace specific materials if the building inspector approves the new material which will not constitute a safety hazard.

Exculpatory Clause - Relieves the landlord of liability for personal injury to a tenant as well as property damage.

Executor - The individual named in a will to dispose of the decedent's estate.

Expropriation - To take by public authority through the power of eminent domain.

F.D.I.C. - The Federal Deposit Insurance Corporation insures the bank deposits.

Fiduciary - A person in a position of trust and confidence, as between principal and agent.

Fee - An estate of inheritance in real property.

Fee Simple Absolute - Ownership that does not have any limitations.

Fee Simple Defeasible Estate - The ownership is based on conditions or limitations as to the use of the property.

Fixture - Personal property is attached to a building or to the land so that it changes its character and becomes real property.

Flashing - Sheet metal or other material used to protect a building from seepage of water.

Footing - The base of the foundation.

Forecasting - Taking the past as a guide to the future, together with judgments from the projection of the future.

Freehold Estate - Any estate that is owned by an individual.

Fructus Industriales - Certain items produced by the annual labor (industry) of man. Planted crops.

Fructus Naturales - Certain items produced by nature.

Goodwill - Expectation of continued public patronage of a business.

Homestead - A statutory protection of real property used as a personal residence from the claims of unsecured creditors.

Hypothecate - To give an item as security for a loan without giving up possession of the item.

Impounds - A trust account established by lenders for the accumulation of borrower's property taxes and fire insurance.

Indemnify - To make payment for a loss.

Independent Contractor - An individual who is self-employed.

Injunction - A court order preventing a person from acting or restraining a person from doing a specific activity.

Interpleader - A court proceeding initiated by the holder of an interest in property which allows the court to decide which party is entitled to the property.

Intestate Succession - A legal method to provide for the disposition of a decedent's estate if a person dies without leaving a will.

Involuntary Alienation - Title to real property may be acquired or transferred by operation of law or court order.

Involuntary Conversion - The destruction, theft, seizure, requisition, or condemnation of property.

Joist - A parallel timber or beam that supports the floor and ceiling.

Judgment - The final court decision as to the rights of an individual in a lawsuit.

Junior Trust Deed - Any trust deed which is not a first trust deed. May be 2nd, 3rd, 4th, etc.

Key Lot - A lot which is located so that one side adjoins the rear of the other lots.

Kiosk - A small sales stall in a shopping mall.

Laches - Inexcusable delay in asserting a legal right.

Legatee - A person who receives personal property through a will.

Let - The temporary use of the property to be rented.

Level - Used in financing to express the payment where the monthly sum of principal and interest is always the same.

Leverage - The use of other people's money to finance an investment to maximize the yield on the investment.

Liability - The claim of creditors against a business.

License - The personal, revocable, and unassignable permission to do one or more acts on the land of another without possessing any interest therein.

Lien - A money encumbrance which is used to make property security for a voluntary debt or other involuntary financial obligations.

Life Estate - Ownership is limited to the life of the individual.

Lineal - 1. The line of ancestry. **2.** A straight line.

Liquidated Damages - An amount of money agreed upon by the parties to be full damages in the event of default by one of the parties to a contract.

Liquidity - The quickness with which assets can be converted into cash.

Lis Pendens - An instrument filed with the county recorder to give constructive notice to the public that the title or right to the possession of a specific property is in litigation.

Loan Origination Fee - A fee paid to the lender for the preparation of loan documents.

Material Fact - Any information which will influence the judgment or decision of the principal.

Megalopolis - A heavily populated urban area which includes many cities.

Mill - A taxation measurement equal to one tenth of a cent ($.001).

Misrepresentation - A false or misleading statement.

Monument - A fixed object and point established by surveyors to create land descriptions.

Mortgage Yield - The rate of return for the buyer of an existing loan that takes into consideration the interest rate, discount rate, loan servicing fees and the term of the loan.

Negotiability - Loan is capable of being sold on the secondary mortgage market.

Net Spendable Income - See Cash Flow.

Nominal Rate - The interest rate specified in the promissory note.

Novation - Existing contract is replaced by a new contract.

Nuisance - An interference or obstruction to the use and enjoyment of the property (overhanging trees, noise, pollution, odors, etc.).

Obligatory Advances - The terms of the original loan require the lender to release a set amount of additional money at a later date.

Obsolescence - Loss of value due to reduced desirability and usefulness of a structure because its design and construction becomes obsolete or it becomes old-fashioned and does not keep up with modern requirements.

Offset Statement - A statement by the owner of the property when the existing note secured by a trust deed is purchased or assigned to an investor. It provides information as to the status of a lien against the property.

Option - A contract to keep an offer open for a specified period of time.

Orientation - The placement of the structure on the lot in reference to the exposure of the sun, wind, privacy, and protection from noise.

Ostensible - An agency would be created when one individual intentionally or through negligence leads another individual to believe that he has the authority to perform activities for a third party, and the third party concurs with the first individual.

Outlaw - The Statute of Limitations has expired.

Parol Contract - A oral contract.

Patent - **1.** An ambiguous legal description. **2.** A sovereign grant.

Percolation - The ability of soil to absorb water.

Plaintiff - The individual initiating judicial action against the defendant.

Pledge - To use an item of personal property as security for a debt.

Plottage Value - Increase in value when several lots are combined to form a single unit.

Points - Means the same as percentages.

Potable - Drinking water.

Prima Facie - At first view.

Privity - Mutual relationship to the rights of property, such as ancestor to heirs and assignee to assignor.

Quantity Survey - A detailed estimate of all labor and materials is compiled for each component of the building when making an appraisal by the cost approach.

Recurring Costs - Any item that requires and impound account.

Redemption - The delinquent payments and the entire principal balance of a note are paid in full.

Redevelopment - Existing structures are demolished and new ones are immediately built.

Redlining - Lenders draw a red circle on a map to designate certain areas as high risk areas, making it difficult for people (usually minorities) to obtain financing. Redlining is against the law.

Rehabilitation - To restore an old property to its original condition without making any changes in the floor plan or architectural style.

Reinstatement - The delinquent payments on a note are made current.

Remodeling - To change the floor plan or architectural style of the improvements.

Rent - Consideration for the possession and use of the property for a certain length of time.

Rescission - To cancel a contract when each party restores the other party to his original position.

Reservation - Gives the grantor an implied warranty to enter and use the property for a specific purpose.

Reversion - The right of future possession or enjoyment of a property by an individual or his heirs, upon the termination of a life estate or a leasehold estate.

Rider - An amendment to a contract.

Salvage Value - The fair market value of the improvements at the end of its useful life.

Setback - Requires improvements on the property to be a specific distance from the property line.

Severalty - Sole ownership by a single person.

Severance Damages - When a portion of a lot is taken by eminent domain and the remaining portion of the lot loses its value because of the property division, the property owner may be able to sue for such losses.

Short Rate - The disproportionate amount of an insurance premium that is returned when an insured individual cancels his policy.

Simple Contract - Offer and acceptance.

Soil Pipe - Pipe used for sewers.

Specific Performance - Court action which compels an individual to perform pursuant to a valid contract.

Steering - Individual buyers (usually minorities) are only shown property in a specific neighborhood. Steering is against the law.

Subordination - To make a real estate loan junior or inferior to another loan.

Surrender - To cancel a lease by mutual consent of the parties prior to the expiration date.

Take Out Loan - Long term financing after construction is completed.

Tenancy - A mode of holding ownership.

Tender - An offer to perform all of one's obligations in a purchase contract. An offer to perform as promised.

Testate - To leave a will upon death.

Theft - As related to real estate, it includes entering and removing part of the realty, defrauding by misrepresentation, and taking away part of the security for a trust deed with the intent to defraud the beneficiary.

Trend - A series of related changes brought about by a chain of causes and effects.

Undivided Interest - A person cannot distinguish any specific portion of the property as his own.

Unearned Increment - An increase in real estate value without any effort on the part of the individual property owner.

Unilateral - Obligates only one party to a contract to perform.

Usury - Charging interest in excess of the provisions provided for under law.

Value - The relationship of the thing desired to a potential purchaser.

Variance - A petition for a one time minor change which will permit a property to be used for a purpose other than indicated by the present zoning.

Waiver - A voluntary relinquishment of a known legal right.

Walk-Up - An apartment building with two or more floors without an elevator.

Warehousing - The collection and packaging of many loans in order to sell to other lenders in the secondary mortgage market.

APPENDIX B - Abbreviations

A.B.C. - Alcoholic Beverage Control Act.
A.I.R.E.A. - American Institute of Real Estate Appraisers.
A.L.T.A. - American Land Title Association.
A.P.R. - Annual Percentage Rate.
B.T.U. - British Thermal Unit.
C.A.R. - California Association of Realtors.
C.C.&R's. - Covenants, Conditions, and Restrictions.
C.L.T.A. - California Land Title Association.
C.O.E. - Close of Escrow.
C.P.M. - Certified Property Manager.
C.R.V. - Certificate of Reasonable Value.
D.B.A. - Doing Business As.
D.V.A. - Department of Veterans Affairs.
F.D.I.C. - Federal Deposit Insurance Corporation.
F.H.A. - Federal Housing Administration.
F.E.D. - Federal Reserve Board.
F.H.L.B. - Federal Home Loan Bank.
F.H.L.M.C. - Federal Home Loan Mortgage Corporation (Freddie Mac).
F.N.M.A. - Federal National Mortgage Association (Fannie Mae).
G.N.M.A. - Government National Mortgage Association (Ginnie Mae).
G.N.P. - Gross National Product.
H.U.D. - Housing and Urban Development.
I.R.E.M. - Institute of Real Estate Management.
L.T.V. - Loan to Value Ratio.
M.A.I. - Member of American Institute of Real Estate Appraisers.
M.L.S. - Multiple Listing Service.
M.O.G. - Mineral, Oil, and Gas.
M.P.R. - Minimum Property Requirements.
N.A.R. - National Association of Realtors.
N.A.R.E.B. - National Association of Real Estate Brokers.
N.A.R.E.L.L.O. - National Association of Real Estate License Law Officials.
N.I.R.E.B. - National Institute of Real Estate Brokers.
P.I.T.I. - Principal, Interest, Taxes and Insurance.
P.M.I. - Private Mortgage Guaranteed Insurance.
P.U.D. - Planned Unit Development
R.E.I.T. - Real Estate Investment Trust.
R.E.S.P.A. - Real Estate Settlement Procedure Act.
S.A.I.F. - Savings Association Insurance Fund.
U.C.C. - Uniform Commercial Code.
V.A. - Veterans Administration.
V.I.R. - Variable Interest Rate.
V.R.M. - Variable Rate Mortgage.

APPENDIX C - Review Quiz Answers

CHAPTER 1   Matching: 1-f; 2-e; 3-a; 4-i; 5-h; 6-j; 7-d; 8-g; 9-b; 10-c.
True/False: 1-T; 2-F; 3-F; 4-F; 5-T; 6-F; 7-T; 8-T; 9-F; 10-F.
Multiple Choice: 1-b; 2-a; 3-b; 4-c; 5-d; 6-d; 7-c; 8-d; 9-d;
10-d; 11-c; 12-d; 13-c; 14-b; 15-c.

CHAPTER 2   Matching: 1-h; 2-g; 3-i; 4-f; 5-j; 6-c; 7-b; 8-d; 9-a; 10-e.
True/False: 1-F; 2-T; 3-T; 4-T; 5-T; 6-F; 7-F; 8-F; 9-T; 10-F.
Multiple Choice: 1-b; 2-c; 3-a; 4-b; 5-d; 6-c; 7-a; 8-c; 9-a;
10-b; 11-d; 12-c; 13-d; 14-b; 15-b.

CHAPTER 3   Matching: 1-f; 2-h; 3-j; 4-g; 5-d; 6-i; 7-b; 8-c; 9-a; 10-e.
True/False: 1-T; 2-F; 3-T; 4-F; 5-T; 6-T; 7-T; 8-T; 9-F; 10-T.
Multiple Choice: 1-b; 2-c; 3-d; 4-a; 5-c; 6-d; 7-b; 8-b; 9-b;
10-c; 11-d; 12-a; 13-c; 14-b; 15-a.

CHAPTER 4   Matching: 1-h; 2-e; 3-j; 4-i; 5-a; 6-g; 7-f; 8-b; 9-d; 10-c.
True/False: 1-F; 2-T; 3-F; 4-T; 5-F; 6-T; 7-T; 8-F; 9-F; 10-F.
Multiple Choice: 1-a; 2-c; 3-c; 4-b; 5-d; 6-a; 7-b; 8-d; 9-b;
10-d; 11-c; 12-b; 13-a; 14-d; 15-a.

CHAPTER 5   Matching: 1-f; 2-j; 3-a; 4-h; 5-c; 6-b; 7-e; 8-d; 9-i; 10-g.
True/False: 1-T; 2-F; 3-T; 4-T; 5-F; 6-T; 7-F; 8-F; 9-T; 10-T.
Multiple Choice: 1-b; 2-c; 3-d; 4-d; 5-a; 6-d; 7-b; 8-b; 9-d;
10-d; 11-d; 12-b; 13-a; 14-c; 15-d.

CHAPTER 6   Matching: 1-j; 2-d; 3-i; 4-b; 5-a; 6-g; 7-h; 8-c; 9-f; 10-e.
True/False: 1-F; 2-T; 3-T; 4-T; 5-F; 6-F; 7-T; 8-F; 9-F; 10-F.
Multiple Choice: 1-c; 2-a; 3-d; 4-c; 5-b; 6-b; 7-a; 8-a; 9-a;
10-b; 11-b; 12-a; 13-d; 14-c; 15-c.

CHAPTER 7   Matching: 1-j; 2-e; 3-i; 4-a; 5-c; 6-b; 7-f; 8-d; 9-g; 10-h.
True/False: 1-F; 2-T; 3-F; 4-T; 5-F; 6-T; 7-T; 8-T; 9-F; 10-T.
Multiple Choice: 1-d; 2-b; 3-a; 4-c; 5-c; 6-a; 7-c; 8-d; 9-c;
10-c; 11-c; 12-b; 13-d; 14-a; 15-d.

CHAPTER 8   Matching: 1-f; 2-j; 3-g; 4-i; 5-a; 6-b; 7-h; 8-e; 9-d; 10-c.
True/False: 1-T; 2-T; 3-F; 4-F; 5-F; 6-F; 7-T; 8-T; 9-T; 10-F.
Multiple Choice: 1-b; 2-c; 3-b; 4-d; 5-a; 6-b; 7-c; 8-c; 9-a;
10-c; 11-c; 12-d; 13-a; 14-d; 15-a.

CHAPTER 9   Matching: 1-i; 2-h; 3-g; 4-j; 5-c; 6-b; 7-a; 8-d; 9-f; 10-e.
True/False: 1-F; 2-T; 3-F; 4-T; 5-T; 6-F; 7-F; 8-T; 9-F; 10-F.
Multiple Choice: 1-c; 2-d; 3-d; 4-b; 5-a; 6-b; 7-c; 8-c; 9-c;
10-c; 11-d; 12-d; 13-b; 14-a; 15-a.

CHAPTER 10 Matching: 1-h; 2-e; 3-j; 4-g; 5-a; 6-b; 7-i; 8-f; 9-d; 10-c.
True/False: 1-T; 2-F; 3-T; 4-T; 5-F; 6-T; 7-F; 8-T; 9-F; 10-T.
Multiple Choice: 1-c; 2-d; 3-b; 4-d; 5-a; 6-d; 7-b; 8-a; 9-d;
10-d; 11-c; 12-d; 13-b; 14-b; 15-d.

CHAPTER 11 Matching: 1-f; 2-j; 3-g; 4-d; 5-i; 6-b; 7-e; 8-h; 9-c; 10-a.
True/False: 1-F; 2-T; 3-T; 4-T; 5-F; 6-T; 7-T; 8-T; 9-F; 10-F.
Multiple Choice: 1-d; 2-a; 3-b; 4-a; 5-b; 6-d; 7-a; 8-d; 9-c;
10-a; 11-c; 12-d; 13-b; 14-b; 15-a.

CHAPTER 12 Matching: 1-f; 2-d; 3-h; 4-j; 5-g; 6-c; 7-a; 8-e; 9-b; 10-i.
True/False: 1-T; 2-T; 3-F; 4-F; 5-F; 6-T; 7-F; 8-F; 9-F; 10-F.
Multiple Choice: 1-c; 2-b; 3-d; 4-a; 5-c; 6-c; 7-c; 8-b; 9-d;
10-a; 11-d; 12-c; 13-d; 14-b; 15-d.

CHAPTER 13 Matching: 1-g; 2-i; 3-e; 4-j; 5-b; 6-a; 7-h; 8-c; 9-f; 10-d.
True/False: 1-F; 2-F; 3-T; 4-F; 5-T; 6-T; 7-T; 8-T; 9-F; 10-F.
Multiple Choice: 1-c; 2-d; 3-b; 4-a; 5-d; 6-c; 7-b; 8-d; 9-c;
10-d; 11-a; 12-a; 13-d; 14-d; 15-d.

CHAPTER 14 Matching: 1-i; 2-j; 3-f; 4-b; 5-h; 6-c; 7-d; 8-g; 9-a; 10-e.
True/False: 1-T; 2-T; 3-F; 4-F; 5-T; 6-F; 7-F; 8-T; 9-T; 10-F.
Multiple Choice: 1-b; 2-c; 3-a; 4-d; 5-a; 6-b; 7-c; 8-a; 9-b;
10-b; 11-a; 12-c; 13-d; 14-b; 15-a.

CHAPTER 15 Matching: 1-f; 2-j; 3-e; 4-h; 5-c; 6-d; 7-i; 8-a; 9-g; 10-b.
True/False: 1-T; 2-F; 3-T; 4-F; 5-F; 6-T; 7-F; 8-F; 9-T; 10-F.
Multiple Choice: 1-b; 2-d; 3-b; 4-c; 5-a; 6-b; 7-b; 8-c; 9-b;
10-d; 11-d; 12-d; 13-a; 14-a; 15-c.

CHAPTER 16 Matching: 1-f; 2-h; 3-b; 4-e; 5-a; 6-c; 7-j; 8-i; 9-g; 10-d.
True/False: 1-F; 2-T; 3-T; 4-T; 5-F; 6-T; 7-F; 8-F; 9-T; 10-T.
Multiple Choice: 1-b; 2-d; 3-a; 4-c; 5-d; 6-b; 7-d; 8-a; 9-a;
10-b; 11-d; 12-d; 13-c; 14-c; 15-a.

CHAPTER 17 Matching: 1-i; 2-a; 3-c; 4-j; 5-h; 6-e; 7-g; 8-f; 9-b; 10-d.
True/False: 1-F; 2-T; 3-T; 4-F; 5-T; 6-F; 7-F; 8-F; 9-T; 10-F.
Multiple Choice: 1-c; 2-b; 3-d; 4-a; 5-b; 6-d; 7-c; 8-c; 9-b;
10-d; 11-b; 12-c; 13-b; 14-b; 15-a.

CHAPTER 18 Matching: 1-i; 2-g; 3-j; 4-h; 5-b; 6-d; 7-e; 8-c; 9-a; 10-f.
True/False: 1-F; 2-F; 3-T; 4-T; 5-F; 6-T; 7-F; 8-T; 9-F; 10-T.
Multiple Choice: 1-c; 2-d; 3-b; 4-a; 5-b; 6-b; 7-c; 8-d; 9-a;
10-d; 11-a; 12-c; 13-a; 14-c; 15-c.

CHAPTER 19 Matching: 1-i; 2-e; 3-h; 4-d; 5-f; 6-j; 7-c; 8-g; 9-b; 10-a.
True/False: 1-F; 2-T; 3-T; 4-F; 5-F; 6-T; 7-T; 8-T; 9-F; 10-F.
Multiple Choice: 1-b; 2-d; 3-d; 4-a; 5-b; 6-b; 7-c; 8-a; 9-c;
10-c; 11-c; 12-d; 13-d; 14-c; 15-c.

CHAPTER 20 Matching: 1-i; 2-g; 3-e; 4-j; 5-a; 6-d; 7-c; 8-h; 9-f; 10-b.
True/False: 1-T; 2-F; 3-T; 4-T; 5-T; 6-F; 7-T; 8-F; 9-T; 10-F.
Multiple Choice: 1-a; 2-b; 3-c; 4-d; 5-c; 6-b; 7-c; 8-c; 9-b; 10-d; 11-c; 12-a; 13-d; 14-a; 15-b.

CHAPTER 21 Matching: 1-h; 2-c; 3-j; 4-b; 5-i; 6-a; 7-g; 8-e; 9-d; 10-f.
True/False: 1-T; 2-F; 3-T; 4-T; 5-F; 6-F; 7-T; 8-T; 9-F; 10-F.
Multiple Choice: 1-b; 2-d; 3-a; 4-c; 5-d; 6-d; 7-c; 8-c; 9-b; 10-a; 11-b; 12-b; 13-c; 14-d; 15-b.

CHAPTER 22 Matching: 1-i; 2-e; 3-d; 4-j; 5-h; 6-a; 7-b; 8-f; 9-g; 10-c.
True/False: 1-T; 2-F; 3-F; 4-T; 5-T; 6-F; 7-T; 8-F; 9-T; 10-T.
Multiple Choice: 1-d; 2-d; 3-b; 4-c; 5-d; 6-a; 7-d; 8-d; 9-d; 10-c; 11-d; 12-b; 13-d; 14-d; 15-c.

APPENDIX D
Index

A

Abstract of Judgment, 34, 69
Abstract of Title, 36
Acceleration Clause, 57
Accession, 27
Accretion, 27
Accrual For
    Depreciation, 194
Accrued Depreciation, 190, 195
Acknowledgment, 39, 335
Acre, 262
Actual Agent, 113
Actual Fraud, 132
Actual Notice, 40
Add-On Clause, 57
Adjusted Cost Basis, 241
Adjusted Sales Price, 241
Administrator, 35
Adult, 129
Ad Valorem, 233
Advance Fee, 293, 305
Adverse Possession, 31
Advertisement, 305
Affidavit, 335
Affirmation, 335
Age Life, 195
Agency, 113
Agency Disclosure, 114
Agent, 113
Alcoholic Beverage
    Control Act, 297
Alienation, 29, 335
Alienation Clause, 57
Aliens, 130
All-Inclusive Trust
    Deed, 53
Allowable Expenses, 181
Alquist Priolo Act, 273
A.L.T.A. Policy of Title
    Insurance, 37
Alluvium, 27
Ambulatory, 34
Amenities, 170
American Land Title
    Association, 37
Amortization, 218
Amortization Table, 219
Anchor Bolt, 273
Anchor Tenant, 170
Annual Audit, 119

Annual Percentage Rate, 226
Annuity, 310
Anticipation, 169
Application for License, 105
Appraisal, 177
Appraisal Institute, 304
Appraisal Process, 178
Appraisal Report, 178
Appraiser, 102, 177
Appropriation, 28
Appurtenances, 1
Appurtenant Easement, 79
APR, 226
Area, 285
Arithmetic, 281
Assemblage, 169
Assessed Value, 166
Assessment Appeals Board, 235
Assessment Liens, 235
Assets, 294
Assignment, 13, 134
Assignment of Lease, 13
Assignment of Rents
    Clause, 57
Assumption Fee Clause, 59
Assumption of Loan, 58
Attachment, 69
Attorney-in-Fact, 102
Authorization to Sell, 143
Avulsion, 27

B

Backfill, 273
Bailment, 336
Balance Sheet, 294
Balloon Payment, 122
Band of Investment, 182
Banker's Year, 221
Base Line, 253
Base Line and Meridian
    Intersections, 253
Bearing Wall, 273
Benchmark, 273
Beneficiary, 47
Beneficiary Statement, 56
Bequeath, 35
Bequest, 35
Bilateral Contract, 136
Bill of Sale, 293
Blanket Encumbrance, 52
Blighted Area, 171
Blind Advertisement, 305, 336
Blind Exemption, 235
Blockbusting, 327
Board Foot, 273

Board of Realtors, 304
Bona Fide, 136
Book of Abstracts, 38
Book Value, 166
Boot, 244, 245
Bracing, 273
Breach of Contract, 134
Breakdown, 195
Bridging, 273
British Thermal Unit, 273
Broker License, 104
Broker's Loan Statement, 121
B.T.U., 273
Building Codes, 83
Building Paper, 273
Building Permit, 83, 273
Building Residual, 186
Bulk Sales Law, 294
Bundle of Rights, 27
Business and Professions
    Code, 91,
Business Cycle, 303
Business License, 108
Business Opportunity, 293
Buyer's Market, 167

C

California Association of
    Realtors, 304
California Fair Employment
    and Housing Act, 325
California Farm and Home
    Purchase Act, 206
California Land Title
    Association, 37
California Sales and Use
    Tax Provisions, 296
Cal-Vet Loan, 206
Cancelled License, 106
Capable Parties, 129
Capital Gains, 236, 240
Capital Gains Formula, 241
Capital Improvement, 248
Capitalization
    Approach, 180
    Taxation, 236
Capitalization Rate, 181
Capitalized Income, 195
Capital Loss, 240, 243
Cash Flow, 184
Caveat Emptor, 336
C. C. & R's., 84
Certificate of Clearance, 296
Certificate of Discharge, 46
Certificate of Eligibility, 205
Certificate of Occupancy, 85

347